Studien zum Datenschutz

Edited by
Prof. Dr. Dr. h.c. Spiros Simitis †
Prof. Dr. Indra Spiecker genannt Döhmann, LL.M.

Volume 80

Indra Spiecker gen. Döhmann | Christoph Burchard (Eds.)

Algorithmic Transformation and Diffusion of Power: Trust, Conflict, Uncertainty and Control

Nomos

The Deutsche Nationalbibliothek lists this publication in the Deutsche Nationalbibliografie; detailed bibliographic data are available on the Internet at http://dnb.d-nb.de

1st Edition 2025

Published by
Nomos Verlagsgesellschaft mbH & Co. KG
Waldseestraße 3–5 | 76530 Baden-Baden
www.nomos.de

Production of the printed version:
Nomos Verlagsgesellschaft mbH & Co. KG
Waldseestraße 3–5 | 76530 Baden-Baden

ISBN 978-3-8487-8548-3 (Print)
ISBN 978-3-7489-2909-3 (ePDF)
DOI https://doi.org/10.5771/9783748929093

Online Version
Nomos eLibrary

Preface

In our rapidly evolving digital landscape, algorithms – or rather: algorithmic systems – have become an integral and pervasive element of our daily lives, exerting a profound and often unconscious influence on our behaviour and actions. The reliance on tools, services and support through digital means is increasing accordingly, and ubiquitous computing is synonymous with this development. Artificial intelligence (AI), algorithms and technologies for processing and analysing and analysis of large volumes of data (big data) are at the heart of the digital revolution. In today's global world, they affect not only production and the working environment, but almost all areas of social life. Examples range from social networks and search engines to Industry 4.0, predictive policing, medical research and the insurance and financial market sector (FinTech). Shared structures, the common good, social cohesion and the foundations for understanding are changing, as are business models. Closely interwoven with this and similar impacts are questions of the (re)distribution of power because the increasing emphasis on decisions based on correlations and statistical probabilities not only harbours risks of distortion and discrimination but also fosters a concentration of social and economic power.

Algorithms – and the actors behind them – are measuring and influencing more and more dimensions of our modern lives and are increasingly taking over decisions. They recommend which movies to watch, they calculate risk appropriate credit scores, and they play a role in imposing "just" punishments, to name just a few areas. At the same time, they claim to correct imperfect human decisions and add new dimensions of information to previously impossible decisions. Algorithmic systems are thus a major driving force behind the transformation of well-established normative orders in a new predictive society. This challenges at least two core concepts of legal governance, i.e. trust and control. Especially as the inherent often unrecognized algorithmic normativity, which is referred to as "black box" in artificial intelligence, is (not) produced in forums of justification and legitimation, it is unclear where trust can develop and through which social conflicts. This also affects the standards for judgments: It is unclear what trust we can place in algorithmic systems, but it is also unclear how much – if any – trust algorithms can and should place in citizens. Conversely, it is just as much a challenge to determine how much control human decision-makers can and should retain over algorithmic decision-making and information gathering as it is to determine the extent to which algorithms can and should exercise control over humans. Answering the long-standing question of machine-human-interaction is becoming urgent in a new guise in order to secure autonomy, freedom of choice and individuality.

This also reaches out into specific areas of the social: Algorithms are becoming increasingly political. In our democracies in particular, they are changing the shape of political power and order. For better or worse, they are able to influence, stabilize, transform and even disrupt our political systems. For this reason alone, their use requires democratic (co-)shaping. Hopes for more democratization, flexibility and cross-border sociality are thus countered by fears of economic surveillance, discriminatory classification, digital disenfranchisement and data illiteracy.

This book brings together authors from various disciplinary backgrounds. All are experts in the interdisciplinary analysis of digitization who are concerned with the potential changes algorithmic systems bring to trust and control, how they affect democracy and increase uncertainty and diffusion of power. Almost all of them have been part of a lecture and discussion series at Goethe University Frankfurt a. M. that began in the fall of 2020 and continued until 2023. Starting with lectures on "Power Shifts through Algorithms" (2020/2021), lectures on "Algorithms between Trust and Control" (2021) were the next focus. The series "Algorithms and the Transformation of Democracy" (2021/2022) concentrated on one specific area of digital effects, while the lectures on "Algorithms, Uncertainty and Risk" (2022) looked at developments through a particular analytical lens. Also, the workshop "Autonomy in times of diffusion of responsibility through algorithms" (2022) provided highly valued additional input. The final lecture series (2022/2023) looked at future developments: "Algorithms: a brave new world?"

The lectures in the series were held, for the most part, virtually under the umbrella of the ConTrust research network, the Normative Orders research network and in cooperation with the Frankfurt Talks on Information Law at Goethe University Frankfurt a. M. as well as the Institute of Information Security and Dependability (KASTEL) at Karlsruhe Institute of Technology (KIT). The Center for Responsible Digitalization in Hesse (zevedi) also provided partial funding, in particular for the workshop and – in part – to this publication. We are very grateful to all the institutions involved for giving us the opportunity to conduct this conference series and to subsequently publish the results.

As always, however, it is the people behind who form and are decisive for the success of this endeavour: We are very grateful to all our speakers but in particular those who were willing to contribute and expand their analyses – also for their patience during the publication process. Our audiences during the lecture series and workshops were extremely attentive, responsive and encouragingly interested despite the partly new virtual/hybrid format in which we started and then continued our lecture series. We thank the student researchers and research assistants at our chairs for their wonderful assistance, our colleague Roland Broemel for hosting the first lecture series with us, and in particular Anke Harms and Rebecca Schmidt at the Normative Orders/ConTrust research network for their never-ending enthusiasm and practical help. Christina Gräfin von Wintzingerode and Paul Dieler were indispensable in the publication process.

In the more than twenty contributions of this anthology the international group of authors of multidisciplinary research fields such as, but not limited to, law, computer science, sociology, ethics, IT-security and political science provide their individual analysis and their particular approach to using of their respective backgrounds to discuss the notions of uncertainty, risk, trust, control, power and more. All provide an innovative compass through the new digital world by exploring the complex interplay between trust, control, and uncertainty in the face of diffusion of power in a democratic environment. This includes the perspective of both private and state actors. All links referenced in the individual articles were last updated in October 2024.

Opening the first part of the book on the tension "between trust and control", *Burkhard Schäfer* deals with the topic of apologies by algorithmic systems and whether these are suitable for restoring trust after a previous violation of justified expectations of human interactors. Using different methods, he proposes distinct requirements for automatically generated apologies as a specific human action turned into a digital service to be meaningful and possibly fitting for an AI.

Jonathan Simon portrays the situation of using algorithms for criminal prosecution in the US by outlining the current state of crime risk scoring and other algorithmic systems used by law enforcement entities. He sheds light on their history and the discriminatory threats that came with them. He shows in particular how a deep-rooted racism from the late 19th century and beyond continues to influence the justice system and, by extension, the algorithms developed and used in that environment.

Turning to the use of algorithms in credit scoring, *Katja Langenbucher* examines the different methods used, in the light of the new EU directive on discriminatory credit underwriting. The paper covers the relationship between anti-discrimination laws in Europe and the US and the challenges that algorithms pose accordingly in the credit scoring process.

Stephan Brink and *Clarissa Henning* explore the different angles of the – potentially outdated – idea of trust and control we have adopted as a consequence of the analogue era and why we as a society are still attached to it in the age of digitalization. This is most evident in the conflict between the citizens' often blind trust in digitality due to and at the same time despite of the complexity of data processing and the little control possible – be it the control over citizens by the processor or instead the control of the individual or of authorities over the algorithm.

Lucia Zedner considers the trust in algorithmic systems on predictive policing that may allow officials to intervene before crimes have been committed. Her paper approaches the topic from an ethical viewpoint focusing on the multiple issues of risk prediction through algorithmic systems beyond discrimination, transparency or accountability. It looks more closely at how historical factors or group membership affect individuals as defendants and analyses the ability of criminal justice officials to address flaws in algorithmic decision-making.

Frank Pasquale and *Mathieu Kiriakos* focus on applications of algorithmic systems in the private area when they examine the pros and cons of a narrative-based credit scoring as a "second chance" for credit applicants who were first rejected. They propose a possibility for customers to present their narrative and their perspective as an alternative to being a passive partitioner in an anonymous algorithmic procedure.

Hadar Dancig-Rosenberg introduces the desired goal and the effect of algorithms used in the criminal legal system and rounds off the first part hereby. She discusses a desirable change towards a more objective law enforcement on the one hand and on the other hand the problem of perpetuated bias of judges, prosecutors, and police officers therein, in addition to the concepts of legitimacy and accountability.

In the second part on "The Transformation of Democracy and Diffusion of Power", the scope broadens and looks more towards societal factors and state theory. *Sabine Müller-Mall* and *Johannes Haaf* make a first impact by pointing out the parallels between the internal structure of algorithms and the constitutional order of our society. The authors argue that algorithms could possibly become a competitor of the political-legal order embodied in the democratic constitution. They detect a shift from the legality of the law to a "legality of the normal", that could also detach the constitution from law and politics and public considerations.

Expanding the societal focus to different kinds of algorithm use, *Sofia Ranchordas* addresses the role and significance of gender, especially regarding the expression "human-centric" in automation of administrative decision-making. She argues that the differences between gender do matter, when the often-experienced invisibility of certain gender-specific patterns lead to casual or incident discrimination, that could be perpetuated by AI.

Beatrice Brunhöber and *Bernhard Jakl* analyse the legislator's approach, also in the recently adopted AI Act, that trust in normative orders can be fostered through the imposition of bans. In contrast, the authors argue for an institutional-argumentative reassessment of this approach, with recourse to legal philosophy and the comparison between the reception of trust and prohibition in criminal and civil law.

Martin Belov discusses the changes that have occurred in our postmodern society because of the technological advancements of recent years, with particular attention to different forms of government, authority, and constitutional orders. He touches on the impact on democratic systems, populism, truth and technocracy.

Michael Bäuerle warns against the diffusion of responsibility through algorithms, especially when used by police and other security authorities. For this, he uses a constitutional law approach, which he bases, among other things, on an analysis of recent decisions by the German Supreme Court. He shows that its comprehensive case law on the security authorities' informational powers provides a suitable framework for the reallocation of responsibility.

This leads directly to the third part of the volume about "Uncertainty, Risk and Responsibility". *Tobias Singelnstein* takes a closer look on the use of algorithmic systems by the state in the area of predictive policing. This anticipatory concept comes with severe issues regarding uncertainty, exculpation and the variety of crimes to name a few, and above all, regarding the rule of law. By analysing these and other challenges that this new way of dealing with unlawful behaviour can bring about, he establishes a link between how deviance is dealt with, seen, understood and conceptualized particularly in law.

Kiel Brennan-Marquez' contribution to the volume centres around the concept of mercy, its relation to law and justice and how the increasing use of algorithms could change this perception. He argues that caution should be exercised when using algorithms in the field of justice, as they lack a sense of morality in their actions.

The important, but often not acknowledged topic of IT-Security within algorithmic systems is raised by *Jürgen Beyerer* and *Tim Zander*. They discuss the risk of cyber-attacks on the backbone of the digital society from the perspective of computer science. They suggest a graph structure for the illustration of risk to provide a common basis for experts of different disciplines that must work together to ensure safety and security. Further, they discuss the challenges and opportunities associated with implementing this framework.

Anna Beckers and *Gunther Teubner* look at failures and flaws of algorithmic systems. They justify why the legal provisions of the AI Act's risk-based approach, which focuses on the severity of the technology or the overall risk of the algorithmic system, may not be sufficient to adequately allocate responsibility. The authors argue for a regulatory shift towards a responsibility for risks deriving from the integration of algorithms within the respective social context in which it is used. In this way, the essence of the problem posed by the delegation of decisions to algorithms could be better captured.

Will we really enter "A brave new world" through algorithmic systems? The following chapters in the fourth part deal in many ways with what such a world looks like in the present and future and what this could actually mean for coexistence and human-machine interaction. *Jörn Lamla* argues from the perspective of sociology for a new understanding of the interplay between AI and its user. He concentrates on the relation of humans and algorithms as hybrid and analyses their relationship in the light of different sociological and anthropological theories.

Klaus Günther examines the use of algorithms to prevent deviant behaviour. He points out the significance of being able to choose whether to conform or to deviate and explores the effects of self-binding to certain norms within a particular normative order. Light is shed on the impact AI could have on these institutional settings, particularly if the certainty of algorithms gradually abolishes the opportunity to opt out or deviate.

Ingo Sarlet and *Andressa de Bittencourt Siqueira* provide a detailed international overview of the development of information- or digitalization law from a Brazilian perspective. The authors analyse the advantages and disadvantages of regulatory approaches such as regulated self-regulation or oversight boards of private companies citing their leading examples and examine whether their assumptions are fulfilled.

Approaching the fundamental question whether AI can actually help, *Gerd Doeben-Henisch* characterizes the relationship of humans and algorithms as becoming a new form or even a supplement for human intelligence. He gives an inventory about the state of human and societal advances, develops the concept of a "collective human intelligence" and shows how AI could fit into it.

Bernard Harcourt rounds off the volume with a reflective view on the algorithmic age and how we live in an "expository society". In this, our subjectivity as a core element of being is challenged and algorithms increasingly shape who we are. He draws on several different philosophies to develop a further understanding of the being in algorithmic times.

We wish all our readers similar groundbreaking insights that we have gained during this lecture series, the workshops and the many interactions with our authors and the audience.

Frankfurt am Main / Cologne, July 2025
Prof. Dr. Indra Spiecker gen. Döhmann, LL.M. (Georgetown)
and
Prof. Dr. Christoph Burchard, LL.M. (NYU)

Table of Contents

Between Trust and Control

The Transformation of Democracy and Diffusion of Power

Uncertainty, Risk and Responsibility

A Brave New World?

Between Trust and Control

AIpology: when saying sorry is the hardest string to compute

Burkhard Schäfer

Apologies play an important role in trust recovery in post-conflict scenarios. As we increasingly interact with autonomous systems, HCI researchers too have discovered the power of apologies for situations where AIs or robots violated justified expectations of the humans they interact with. But are AIs the type of entity that can meaningfully apologise? Drawing on conceptions of apologies across a range of legal field, the chapter identifies requirements for robot-generated apologies that ensure not only their ethically sound deployment, but also, potentially, their recognition in law.

A. Introduction: The author wants to apologise for any inconvenience caused

This chapter explores how apologies generated by AIs – AIpologies – can generate, restore or sometimes undermine rational trust in autonomous devices, their ethical and legal implications, and what they can teach us more broadly about the intersection between trust, law and conflict.

At this point, I should apologise for the terrible AIpology pun – but also warn you that there are more to come. There are some other apologies I would like to make: I should apologise for some of the more challenging aspects of this chapter. It is located in the intersection of several disciplines: robotics, human-computer-interaction, psychology, business studies, linguistics, law, ethics and philosophy. As I can only claim expertise in a small sub-section of these, if any, my accounts may sometimes be wrong or misleading. If you don't understand any of the arguments, well then you'll have only your insufficient preparation to blame, and I recommend that you come back after doing some further reading. I tried initially to avoid this problem, and also save myself a lot of work, by simply having ChatGTP summarise the respective research fields and claim its insights as my own, unfortunately its output was spotted by the editors as machine generated, and I had to promise to write my own text.

If after reading the last paragraph, you now feel a mix of confusion, irritation, or even anger - then the rest of the chapter will hopefully be for you (and I apologise for leading you, for pedagogical purposes, briefly down this garden path). Apologies *can* be a powerful tool to restore trust after a norm violation occurred, and they also play an important role in several of the legal fields that ConTrust explored, from media regulation to criminal law to international law and post-conflict resolution between communities, societies and countries. As we will see, their potency has also been recognised increasingly in the field of robotics and human-computer interaction.

However, just in the same way in which we must distinguish trust from rational *trustworthiness*, we also have to distinguish the mere apology *rituals* from "rationally successful apologies". To fulfil their positive function, apologies have to be done the right way, and the above paragraph contained several violations of the felicity conditions for apologies as a specific kind of speech act. We will see how the difference between trust and justified trust, a distinction that was also central for ConTrust,[1] maps onto different types of AIpologies. While all of them potentially increase the feeling of trust in the recipients of the apology, only some of them can improve trustworthiness. A key question that we will have to explore is if AIs are at least in principle capable to generate not just sentences that contain the word "sorry" at the syntactically right place – a trivial task – but meet all the success conditions for valid apologising.

A second element that we can note in my attempted apologies is the close link between apologies and explanations. All but one of the "apologies" above contained also an "explanation" of sorts, though they differed in the explanans. One referred to my lack of skills and knowledge, the other to my lack of character, and we will delve a bit deeper into the linguistic and psychological research on apologies to explore the difference between these two below.

Explanations and explainable AI (XAI) have in recent years become a pivotal design requirement for law compliant autonomous software systems. One of the "apologies" offered above in particular shares some features with an influential approach to explainable AI, the counterfactual model proposed by Wachter, Mittelstadt and Russel (Henceforth WMR) in the context of the (contested) right to explanation for automated decision

1 Rainer Forst, *The Justification of Trust in Conflict. Conceptual and Normative Groundwork*, (ConTrust Working Paper, No. 2, ConTrust 2022) 7 https://publikationen.ub.uni-frankfurt.de/frontdoor/index/index/docId/70591 <last accessed 1.5.2024>.

making in the GDPR.[2] This connection between apologies and explanations will allow us to ask if for legal purposes, where the law requires explanations or explainability, sometimes what it should be asking for are instead apologies, or conversely, whether an AI that can create valid apologies for its actions also complies with legal explainability requirements.

We will also see how WMR-type explanations *can* enhance trust, but work best in a collaborative environment where from the outset, both sides share a common goal. This too makes them the mirror image of apologies, whose explanatory force presumes, and is shaped by, conflict. This not only allows us to contrast explanations with excuses and apologies, it also creates a second conceptual link with ConTrust. ConTrust is premised on the insight that while traditionally, trust has been seen as juxtaposed to conflict, this overlooked the importance, but also fragility, of trust in conflict and post-conflict situations. Similarly, I will argue that some approaches to make AI trustworthy through explainability are premised on the same understanding of the relation between justification, transparency and trust, and not sufficiently responsive to the dynamical dimension where conflict and trust evolve in creative tension.

We can now introduce the three interrelated issues that this chapter hopes to address.

- Are autonomous machines the type of agent that can, in principle, make a trustworthiness- enhancing apology?
- If machines can apologise, what does this mean for AI regulation. Can they be treated also as a form of explanation where the law requires these? Should they get privileges for litigation purposes?

The next section will introduce and briefly discuss WMR's counterfactual model of explanation. It will conclude that while appropriate in many contexts, it can deliver inappropriate results in situations where apologies rather than explanations would be the expected response from a human interlocutor. We will then look at examples from HCI research that tries to give robots the ability to apologise to the humans they interact with. I will introduce briefly an experiment carried out by Institute for Network Science at Yale University, in which a mixed human-robot teams participated in a collaborative game. When the team lost, the robot would either stay

2 Sandra Wachter, Brendt Mittelstadt, Chris Russell, 'Counterfactual explanations without opening the black box: Automated decisions and the GDPR' (2017) 31 Harv. Journal of Law & Technology 841.

silent, make a factual statement about the scores, or make a self-deprecating apology. The research showed the beneficial impact this last strategy had on group cohesion and trust repair, but for me also created a profound sense of unease. I will then try to account for this unease by discussing the way in which the law thinks about apologies, looking at examples across the case studies that were also at the centre of ConTrust: criminal law, media law, and political conflicts.

From this discussion, I will try to extrapolate those features that any legally relevant AI-generated apology should have. I will argue that to the extent that AIs are capable of meeting these requirements, their utterances should get appropriate legal recognition, too.

B. Better luck next time: the counterfactual approach to AI explanations

One important aspect of the current regulatory debate regarding AI is the demand for explainability. While at the beginning of the 21th century, George Orwell's *1984* encapsulated for many the fear of technology-enabled data *collection*, their increased *use* by powerful AI systems found another literary classic reference point. Kafka's *The Castle* anticipated the fear of the "Black Box Society",[3] where judgements are handed out by an impersonal machine whose inner workings are forever hidden from those affected, became a golden threat that tied together several regulatory initiatives.

The EU High Level expert group on AI for instance writes:

> "Explicability is crucial for building and maintaining users' trust in AI systems. This means that processes need to be transparent, the capabilities and purpose of AI systems openly communicated, and decisions – to the extent possible – explainable to those directly and indirectly affected. Without such information, a decision cannot be duly contested."[4]

Transparency is seen here as precondition for trustworthiness: we trust those who are open with us.[5] It is also a precondition for agency: we can

---

3 Frank Pasquale, *The black box society: The secret algorithms that control money and information* (Harvard University Press, 2015).

4 EU High Level Expert Group on AI, '*Ethics Guidelines For Trustworthy AI*', (2019) https://digital-strategy.ec.europa.eu/en/library/ethics-guidelines-trustworthy-ai 13 <last accessed 1.5.2024>.

5 Steven Norman, Bruce J Avolio, Fred Luthans, 'The Impact of Positivity and Transparency on Trust in Leaders and their Perceived Effectiveness' (2010) 3 The Leadership

often only decide how best respond to a decision when we understand the reasons on which it is based. Explainability then leads to transparency – once we know the reasons why a decision-maker decided against us, we can either agree with the reasoning and adjust our behaviour, or if we disagree with the reasoning, contest the decision.

One particularly influential proposal to turn legal requirements – at the time the (contested) explainability requirements of the GDPR – into actionable design decisions by software developers, is the above mentioned "counterfactual" approach by Wachter, Mittelstadt and Russel.

Consider an software agent that decides on credit card applications. After answering several set questions about the applicant, the system creates a risk model for them that combines data of past applicants and decisions about them with characteristics they share with the current applicant. Their risk score is then compared against a pre-defined value, and if the applicant is deemed too risky, the application is rejected.

A helpful explanation then could be of the form of a counterfactual: "Your application was rejected. But *if* your monthly income had been £50 higher, *then* application would have been granted."

WMR write about their approach:

> "In the existing literature, "explanation" typically refers to an attempt to convey the internal state or logic of an algorithm that leads to a decision. In contrast, counterfactuals describe a dependency on the external facts that led to that decision. This is a crucial distinction. In modem machine learning, the internal state of the algorithm can consist of millions of variables intricately connected in a large web of dependent behaviours"[6]

This sees explanations, not as a mechanistic report of the inner workings of the decision maker, but as a chain of reasons from external facts to an utterance (the credit decision). We will follow this characterisation also in this paper.

One reason for this is that WMR's approach is much closer to the understanding of "explanation" that we find in law. When the law requires judges to "explain" their decisions, we are not normally looking for an autobiographical account ("I first got interested in justice when as a child...")

Quarterly 350. Applied to AI, see Warren J von Eschenbach, 'Transparency and the Black Box Problem: Why we do not Trust AI' (2021) 34 Philosophy & Technology 1607.

6 Wachter and others (2) 845; in a similar vein, but with a more philosophically grounded analysis, John Zerilli. 'Explaining Machine Learning Decisions' (2022) 89 Philosophy of Science 1.

or as an account of the neurological basis of the movement of their mouth that uttered the decision ("the information presented by the prosecution triggered a c-fibre in my brain that led to a movement of my..."), even though these can be valid explanations for some purpose in some contexts.

Second, this understanding of the nature of an explanation also means we can speak of an AI explaining itself, without having to commit ourselves to talk about inner mental states, something that will become important when we distinguish different ways to conceptualise apologies.

WMR has been highly influential in the discussion on machine generated explanation. Counterfactual explanations have a number of desirable formal characteristics that make it possible for the AI to generate not only a number of them for any given decision, but also to rank them, recommending for instance the course of actions that is the least complicated for the applicant. A good explanation tells them to increase their savings by £50 every month for a year, rather than to go back to university, get a degree, and on that basis get a much higher paid job. While both can be strategies that achieve the desired result, the more outlandish they are, the more likely the applicant will not perceive them as guidance for action, but will feel mocked.

While technological feasibility will have undoubtedly contributed to the popularity of this approach, we can also speculate that it resonates in many ways with academics: a WMR explanation shares many aspects with good student feedback – not (merely) justifying a mark, but pointing to the ways in which it can be improved the next time round.

While this is an advantage in many contexts, in others it is either not applicable, or even harmful and counterproductive. The benefits are obviously greatest when there is recurrent engagement, less so for one-off interactions, just as students benefit most from feedback in their first essays, least in their final dissertation.

A somewhat different question is if the recommendation must be "actionable", that is if the addressee of the explanation must have it in their power to bring about the suggested change. Telling a credit card applicant "if you had been born to very rich parents, your application would have been successful" is not very helpful, true as it may be. Sometimes though, non-actionable explanations can be both appropriate and helpful – they tell the decision subject that there is nothing they can do, which can prevent self-blame or futile resource allocation, for instance if an application for a high-risk profession such as pilot is rejected due to a congenital illness that makes them prone of suffering brain embolisms at high altitudes.

The main benefit of a counterfactual explanation approach is that it assists the persons affected by an AI decision to react constructively, and through their actions change the outcome in the future. In cases where the AI decision was correct, this is extremely helpful. It is even more helpful when the interest of the AI provider and the subject of the decision ultimately converge. In the credit card example, while a rejection will feel painful, ultimately it is also in the interest of the applicant not to be burdened with a loan that they have no chance of repaying. Failing students who lack the required competency levels not only protects, in the case of law students and medics at least, the general public, but also them, from the stress that comes from being an "imposter" in high-stake environments to possible litigation against them for malpractice.

This discussion allows us to connect our discussion more directly with ConTrust. Counterfactual explanations work best in cooperative environments where there is a high level of background trusts between the parties and also the possibility of ongoing, mutually beneficial interactions between them. The responsible lender, the good teacher, or even the judge who does not want to see the accused before them again will give explanations of this type and their credibility also depends to a degree that the subject of the decision ultimately trusts in the benevolence of the decision maker. Just as ConTrust asked the question of the role of trust and trustworthiness in conflict situations, we can now also explore the limits of counterfactual explanations in conflict situations.

In some conflict situations, back-engineering the explanation could lead to undesirable actions. If for instance a money-laundering detection system refuses a transaction, it should not generate as an explanation: "The law requires that transactions above £10000 must not be anonymous. If the transaction had been split into two transactions of £5000 send a few hours apart, these transactions would have been approved". This problem has also been recognised in the EU AI Act, which exempts in Art 61 police users of AI from disclosing certain sensitive operational information even if it is needed by the developers of the system to assess if it is working correctly.

But even in less obviously adversarial scenarios, one objective that legislators pursue through a legally mandated use of explainable AI is to also to create contestability of results. Contestability is a corner stone of the rule of law and is irreconcilable with a black box society where "the computer says no" ends the discussion.[7] XAI therefore also need to cover situations where the AI comes to the wrong result, or where the situation between the parties is shaped by conflict rather than convergence of interest. Here counterfactual explanations can be highly inappropriate. We saw this already in the first paragraph, when I admitted to difficulties in explaining my ideas clearly, but then counterfactually explained that if *you* were to read up on the material, you would get more out of this chapter. But obviously, shifting the "duty to rectify" to you when the fault was all mine rendered this ineffectual as an apology, and indeed offensive.

Counterfactual explanations can assist contestability, but only indirectly. There are two ways how this can happen:

If the generated explanation refers to a false statement about the world as explanans, contestation is the most straightforward:

> AI: "If you earned more than £30000 annually, you would get the credit card"
> Customer: "But I do earn more than £30000 already, and said that much on section 8 of the form"

This, strictly speaking is not an explanation at all, merely an attempt at one. More difficult is a situation where an illegitimate criterion as opposed to a false fact is given as part of the explanation:

> AI: "If you had been male, you would have been given a credit card"
> Customer: "Hang on, that can't be right…"

This may well be a "correct" explanation, in the sense that it faithfully describes how the AI reached its decision, and we may even grant for the sake of the argument that there is a relevant causal connection between gender and ability to repay credit. The explanation fails for legal reasons (and that means, fails in some, but not necessarily all, jurisdictions), because it uses an illegitimate explanans. In either case though, the applicant has to deduce that something went wrong – the AI is good at judging the applicant and telling them how to do it right, less good and helpful at judging itself. This can create significant burdens on the individual, especially in the second scenario that requires from the applicant knowledge and understanding of

7 Margot E Kaminski, Jennifer M. Urban, 'The Right to Contest AI' (2021) 121 Columbia Law Review 1957; Marco Almada, 'Human Intervention in Automated Decision-making: Toward the Construction of Contestable Systems' In Floris Bex (ed), *Proceedings of the Seventeenth International Conference on Artificial Intelligence and Law,* (ACM 2019).

discrimination law, and the resources (in time, money etc) to take appropriate action.

This also highlights another way in which the counterfactual approach to explanation maps onto the "conflict-antagonistic" understanding of trust, trustworthiness and transparency that ConTrust challenged. It reflects an underlying trust in technology, which in turn shapes the understanding of the role of law regarding its governance. This leads to the paradox that even though the aim is to reign in technologies that are perceived as dangerous or even out of control, the method of control is rooted in the same optimism regarding our ability to predict, and with that control, our environment that gave rise to these technologies in the first place.

In the case of machine generated explanations, the paradox becomes particularly visible: If I require an explanation to trust the AI, why should I trust the AI to have generated a correct explanation? Maybe we need explainable AI, to be able to trust *that* module too. This is not facetious. Some of the more technically oriented criticism of WMR and other post-hoc explanations showed their vulnerability to both intentional and unintentional manipulation.[8] This means a user of an XAI system needs to understand its limitations and risks to make informed decisions how much they can trust the explanation that was given. Here too we find the tension between transparency and conflict – adversarial settings lend themselves particularly to the manipulation of the explanation module.[9] To assure the subject of a decision could therefore also require explaining the way the explanation was generated, and equally, the requirements of Art 14 of the EU AI Act that deal with the knowledge of training of the human in the loop may require an understanding of XAI in addition of understanding the logic that lead to the primary decision.

The counterfactual explanation model works best when the AI is right, and it is then up to the individual to adjust their actions to achieve a

8 Dylan Slack and others, 'Counterfactual Explanations can be Manipulated' in Marc'Aurelio Ranzato and others (eds), *Advances in Neural Information Processing Systems 34* (NeurIPS 2001); Ahmad-Reza Ehyaei, and others, 'Robustness Implies Fairness in Causal Algorithmic Recourse' In Sara Fox and others (eds), *Proceedings of the 2023 ACM Conference on Fairness, Accountability, and Transparency,* (ACM 2023).

9 Dylan Slack and others, 'Fooling Lime and Shap: Adversarial Attacks on Post Hoc Explanation Methods', in Anette Markham and others, *Proceedings of the AAAI/ACM Conference on Artificial Intelligence, Ethics, and Society,* (ACM 2020); Sebastian Bordt and others, 'Post-hoc Explanations Fail to Achieve their Purpose in Adversarial Contexts' In Charles Isbell and others (eds), *Proceedings of the 2022 ACM Conference on Fairness, Accountability, and Transparency,* (ACM 2022).

desired goal. Contestability in case the AI got it wrong is at best a side result, assumes knowledge by the affected individual to interpret the answer correctly, and requires that they use their resources to complain and contest the decision.

We can now ask how an approach to explainability would look like that takes the scenario where the AI did *not* decide correctly as a starting point. Rather than focussing on *creating* trust, how can we restore trust once it was broken?

Let us reconsider the two mini-dialogues from above:

> AI: "If you earned more than £30000 annually, you would get the credit card"
> Customer: "But I do earn more than £30000 already, and said that much on section 8 of the form"
> AI: "If you had been male, you would have been given a credit card"
> Customer: "Hang on, that can't be right..."

In this situation, the decision maker committed a mistake, trust in them is now broken and needs to be repaired. How would a human act in this situation? One obvious and very natural trust repair strategy would be to apologise: "I am so sorry, I misremembered what you told me", or "You are quite right, I apologise, this can't be right, of course you get a credit card, and the first two months are on us". Structurally, apologies are the mirror image of WMR's counterfactual explanation. At a bare minimum, WMR's:

> "If *YOU* had done/are going to do X, you would/will avoid Y"

Now becomes:

> "*WE* should have done X to avoid Y, and [....]"

[...] stands for now as a placeholder that completes the apology. We will discuss some candidates for this below.

In the next section we will look at a real-world example of a robot apologising, to tease out some of the intuitions that will influence the answer to these questions.

C. *"Everything is my fault, I'll take the blame"*

That apologies can be highly effective in restoring trust when issued by humans is a well-supported fact, with a wealth of empirical studies from psychology showing the beneficial effects for trust repair.[10] Business psychology and management studies in particular have embraced for a long time the benefits of apologies for efficient leadership internally, and repair of trust with customers and the wider public externally.[11]

Their effectiveness has more recently been recognised also by HCI researchers and roboticists, and it seems indeed that apologies issues by a robot or chatbot can have the same positive effect on trust repair as those done by human interlocutors.[12] Industrial robots apologising for sudden unexpected movements improved post-incident trust in the human co-workers.[13] Two robots apologising for the same mistake increased customer trust in a service robot environment.[14] Even in high stake environments such as simulated emergency evacuation, a timely apology by the guide-robot helped repair trust in its abilities.[15]

However, *why* apologies are trust-enhancing, and furthermore, if they also enhance trustworthiness, is much more debatable. Some apologies are obviously superfluous, for instance apologising for bad weather, yet they still increase trust in the apologiser, human or machine.[16] Conversely,

---

10 See e.g. Fengling Ma and others, 'Apologies Repair Trust via Perceived Trustworthiness and Negative Emotions, (2019) 10 Frontiers in Psychology 758; Aaron Lazare, *On Apology*. (Oxford University Press 2005); Chris Reinders Folmer, and others, 'Repairing Trust Between Individuals and Groups: The Effectiveness of Apologies in Interpersonal and Intergroup Contexts', (2021) 34 International Review of Social Psychology 14.

11 See e.g. Eric Schniter, Roman M. Sheremeta, Daniel Sznycer, 'Building and Rebuilding Trust with Promises and Apologies', (2013) 94 Journal of Economic Behavior & Organization 242; Marie Racine, Craig Wilson, and Michael Wynes, 'The Value of Apology: How do Corporate Apologies Moderate the Stock Market Reaction to Non-financial Corporate Crises?', (2018) 163 Journal of Business Ethics 485; Wei Shao and others, 'Toward a theory of corporate apology: mechanisms, contingencies, and strategies', (2022) 56 European Journal of Marketing 3418.

12 See e.g. Gyounghwa Na, Junho Choi, Hyunmin Kang, 'It's not my Fault, But I'm to Blame', (2023) International Journal of Human–Computer Interaction [2023] 1.

13 Piotr Fratczak, and others, 'Robot Apology as a Post-accident Trust-recovery Control Strategy in Industrial Human-robot Interaction', (2021) 2 International Journal of Industrial Ergonomics 103078.

14 Yuka Okada, and others, 'Two is Better than One: Apologies from two Robots are Preferred', 18 (2023) *PLOS one* https://doi.org/10.1371/journal.pone.0281604.

15 Xinyi Zhang and others, 'Sorry, it was my Fault": Repairing Trust in Human-Robot Interactions' (2023) 175 International Journal of Human-Computer Studies 1.

16 Alison Wood Brooks, Hengchen Dai, Maurice E. Schweitzer, ''I'm Sorry About the rain! Superfluous Apologies Demonstrate Empathic Concern and Increase Trust', (2014) 5 Psychological and Personality Science, 467.

not all apologies are equally efficient. For both humans and robots, apologies that reference competence deficits are more effective than those that reference character deficits.[17] If you re-read the introductory section, ask yourself if my apology for (almost) plagiarising with ChatGPT was as trust-restoring as my apology for straying into fields for which I lack training. And even more puzzling, apologies increase trust even in situations where people distrust the sincerity of the apology.[18] This points us to an important distinction that will concern us for the rest of this chapter:

a) Which, if any, type of apology by humans is rationally restoring violated trust?
b) Are robots capable in principle to produce the type of apology which, had it been given by a human, would rationally restore violated trust?

To unpack these questions, we will now look in more detail at one particularly interesting study into robot apologies. In 2018, researchers at Yale conducted an experiment in which a vaguely humanoid, child-sized robot played together with several humans in a group activity.[19] In order to win, all group members had to work together. What was tested was the effect that apologies by the robot after a lost game would have on the group. To engineer this, the robot would randomly fail at its task. In some groups, the robot would say nothing when its action caused the team to fail, in others it would make a mere factual statement (announcing the score), and in the third group it would apologise to the other players and display vulnerability:

> "Sorry guys, I made the mistake this round. I know it may be hard to believe, but robots make mistakes too."

Or

> "Sorry, I sometimes run out of memory and can't process things fast enough".

17 Zhang, X., Lee, S.K., Maeng, H. and Hahn, S., 2023. Effects of Failure Types on Trust Repairs in Human–Robot Interactions. International Journal of Social Robotics, 15(9), pp.1619-1635.

18 Alice MacLachlan, 'Trust me, I'm Sorry": The Paradox of Public Apology' 98 (2015) The Monist, 441.

19 Sarah Strohkorb Sebo and others, 'The Ripple Effects of Vulnerability: The Effects of a Robot's Vulnerable Behavior on Trust in Human-robot Teams' In Takayuki Kanda, Selma Ŝabanović (eds), *Proceedings of the 2018 ACM/IEEE International Conference on Human-Robot Interaction*, (ACM 2018).

These interventions positively influenced the trust group members placed in the robot. They interacted more with the machine, showed greater willingness to listen to it, and also used more non-verbal cues of trust such as gaze that are typical for human-to-human communication.[20] According to the researchers, the robot accepted responsibility, and through self-disclosure made itself vulnerable. As vulnerability and trust are closely aligned concepts, if this is indeed what the robot is doing, the effect on the trust relations should not be surprising. We might wonder however what it means for a robot to "make itself vulnerable", and if this is a correct description of its actions. The Yale experiment is not the only one that frames robot apologies in the terminology of "vulnerability", and its findings align with other studies that tested human reactions to robot apologies.[21] But they also point to an obvious problem with this approach. John Wayne in *She Wore a Yellow Ribbon* famously said, "Never apologise Mister, it's a sign of weakness", and undoubtedly, for many humans apologising, or admitting mistakes, does come with a strong feeling of dread. But does the same apply in a meaningful way to a machine, or are robots that apologise merely deceiving their human collaborators, making these, rather than themselves, vulnerable? It has indeed been argued that there is something profoundly unethical and deceptive about robot apologies.[22] But is this a problem with robot apologies, specifically, or do they merely inherit the problematic and highly ambivalent features that all apologies as trust-recovery strategy exhibit? To answer this question, I suggest to analyse the way in which the law thinks about and uses apologies as a comparator.

20 Margaret Traeger and others, 'Vulnerable Robots Positively Shape Human Conversational Dynamics in a human–robot team." (2020) 217 PNAS 6370.

21 See e.g Nikolas Martelaro and others. 'Tell me More. Designing hri to Encourage more Trust, Disclosure, and Companionship." In Christoph Bartneck and others (eds), *11th ACM/IEEE International Conference on Human-Robot Interaction*, (IEEE 2016); for mutual vulnerability Zachary Daus, 'Designing Mutually Vulnerable Human-Robot Interaction: Challenges and Possibilities' (2021) 2 Giornale di Filosofia 127.

22 Makoto Kureha, 'On the Moral Permissibility of Robot Apologies' (2023) 38 AI & Society, 1.

D. Those salty robot tears

The most obvious objection against the Yale robot is that its statements are, in essence, lies. Apologies in this view are also, or even mainly, reports of an inner state. In Searle's terminology, they are expressives.[23] To be sincere, they require a feeling of remorse or regret. "Whatever else is said or conveyed, an apology must express sorrow".[24] Robots lack internal emotional states, so they cannot possibly truthfully apologise. The robot *says* sorry, but it *is* not sorry.

Other studies in machine apologies went in this respect much further than the Yale experiment. A particularly problematic example is the experiment by Pompe et al, that showed that explicit expressions of remorse are particularly effective in restoring trust.[25] To achieve what they call "genuine apology", they combine the verbal expression of remorse with appropriate body language, using the same type of vaguely anthropomorphic machine. *If* a feeling of remorse however is a defining element of true apologies, then this is merely an even more devious form of manipulation.

In legal contexts, displays of remorse are particularly important during sentencing in criminal trials.[26] Displays of sincere remorse is seen as a redeeming quality that merits consideration, while lack of remorse is seen as an indication of dangerousness.[27] Remorse and apology become here an indicator if not of "good character", then at least of "character capable of redemption". This requires more than an abstract, "learned" recognition of one's wrongdoing, rather, what sways judges and juries is evidence of

23 John R Searle, 'A Classification of Illocutionary Acts.', 5 (1976) *Language in society* 1, 4 and 12-17.

24 Nicholas Tavuchis, *Mea Culpa: A Sociology of Apology and Reconciliation*, (Stanford University Press 1993) 36.

25 Babiche L. Pompe, Ella Velner, Khiet P. Truong 'The Robot that Showed Remorse: Repairing Trust with a Genuine Apology.' In Silvia Rossi & Antonio Sgorbissa (eds) 31st *IEEE International Conference on Robot and Human Interactive Communication RO-MAN)*, (IEEE 2022).

26 So in particular Cristopher Bennet, *The Apology Ritual. A Philosophical Theory of Punishment*, (Cambridge University Press 2008).

27 A list of examples, with an ultimately sceptical assessment, is In Jeffrie G. Murphy, 'Remorse, Apology, and Mercy' (2006) 4 Ohio St. J. Crim. L. 423; see also Stephanos Bibas, Richard A. Bierschbach, 'Integrating Remorse and Apology into Criminal Procedure.' (2004) 114 Yale lJ 85.

almost physical pain, expressed e.g. by tears.[28] As the Court put it in State v Thornton: "[the trial justice apparently detected no salt in the offender's tears; nor do we".[29] While robots that shed tears have been built too,[30] for anyone who considers apologies as expressives that report an emotional state, machine apologies are impossible.

But while this is one way of thinking about apologies, it is not the only one. As noted above, apologies are used extensively as a managerial tool, and a considerable amount of the literature on the trust-repairing effect of apologies issued by, or on behalf of, companies. Apologies also play an important role in post-conflict societies, and have been instrumental in quasi-judicial procedures such as the South Africa Truth and Reconciliation commission. When Tony Blair apologised for Britain's role in the slave trade, he will not have felt personal remorse.

It is true that the lack of remorse, or personal responsibility, is often seen as cheapening the currency of apologies and potentially manipulative.[31] But if these apologies are manipulative, then it is a manipulation where we are all willing and informed participants – nobody thinks that really, a spokesperson for a government or a company "feels remorseful" when saying what their job requires them to say, and despite this knowledge, the "healing effect" is real and measurable.[32] Furthermore, not only are these "public apologies" intelligible to us, we still distinguish successful from unsuccessful apologies, legitimate from illegitimate ones.

This allows us to identify criteria that are needed so that the apology restores trust, criteria that can be different from those we use when humans apologise for their own actions.[33] For this reason, we will for the rest of this chapter talk of and contrast two types of apologies. One is the "remorse

---

28 See e.g. Kate Rossmanith, 'Affect and the Judicial Assessment of Offenders: Feeling and Judging Remorse.' (2015) 21 Body & Society 67; Margreet Luth-Morgan, 'Sincere Apologies: The Importance of the Offender's Guilt Feelings' (2017) 46 Neth. J. Legal. Phil. 121.

29 STATE v. THORNTON (2002) Nos.99-376-C.A., 98-263-C.A.

30 Akiko Yasuhara, Takuma Takehara, 'Robots with Tears can Convey Enhanced Sadness and Elicit Support Intentions. (2023) 10 Frontiers in Robotics and AI 1121624.

31 So e.g. Lee Taft, 'Apology Subverted: The Commodification of Apology.' (1999) 109 *Yale LJ* 1135.

32 See e.g. Michael R Marrus, 'Official Apologies and the Quest for Historical Justice' (2007) 6 Journal of Human Rights 75.

33 Taenyun Kim, Hayeon Song, 'How should Intelligent Agents Apologize to Restore Trust? Interaction Effects between Anthropomorphism and Apology Attribution on Trust Repair' (2021) 61 Telematics and Informatics 101595.

expression" (RE) apology that we use for personal wrongdoings between people. The other is the "public apology" (PA). While the way these are expressed in language is in parts similar, and in particular shares expressions such as "sorry" or "I apologise", they do have their own distinctive logic.

A related objection is that a sincere apology requires that it is given voluntarily. Blair may not have felt personal remorse, but the decision to apologise on behalf of the UK came with political risk that he was willing to take. By contrast, the Australian Prime Minister Howard refused to apologise on behalf of the Australian government.[34] In each case, the ethical salience, and the effect on trust in their leadership, might reside in the fact that they could have done otherwise. The Yale robot did not have this choice, and maybe this lack of freedom undermines, or should undermine, any assessment of its sincerity. And indeed, we find that the more schematic and "enforced" a robot apology is (think as an extreme example of 404 error messages), the more its sincerity is doubted.[35] But in law, apologies can also be ordered by a court as a civil remedy.[36] The historical precursor of John Wayne's bon mot dates back to 1869 when the *New York Tribune* criticised *The Times* for reversing an editorial position without openly admitting the change:

> "It never apologizes, never retracts, never allows its readers to remember that it is eating its own words"[37]

Depending on jurisdiction, today *The Times* may find itself ordered by a court to print an apology[38], or at least face more severe sanctions by its regulator for violations of the Editors' Code if no apology is forthcoming.[39]

34 Mary R. Power, 'Reconciliation, Restoration and Guilt: The Politics of Apologies', (2000) 95 Media International Australia 191.

35 Xingyu Wang, Yoo Hee Hwang, Priyanko Guchait, 'When Robot (vs. Human) Employees Say "Sorry" Following Service Failure.', 24 (2023) International Journal of Hospitality & Tourism Administration, 540.

36 Brent T. White, 'Say you're Sorry: Court-Ordered Apologies as a Civil Rights Remedy' (2005) 91 Cornell L. Rev 1261.

37 1869 March 9, New-York Tribune, Foreign News: The Rejection of the Alabama Convention, Quote Page 1, Column 4, New York, New York. From https://quoteinvestigator.com/2023/01/20/howl/#320b2489-64e7-486e-afb0-e18cd36f7eba.

38 Wannes Vandenbussche, 'Rethinking Non-Pecuniary Remedies for Defamation: The Case for Court-Ordered Apologies', (2020) 9 J. Int'l Media & Ent. L. 109.

39 http://www.editorscode.org.uk/downloads/codebook/codebook-clause-1.pdf.

While it is true that the wisdom of court-ordered apologies is controversial[40], they are no doubt intelligible as apologies.

How do (forced or freely given) public apologies function without an internal feeling of remorse? To answer this question, we have to ask why apologies can restore trust in the first place.

One way to account for RE apologies as *rational* trust repair is that they give us good reasons to believe that the same harm won't occur in the future. 'Moral emotions" such as remorse matter for both ethics and psychology because the express our ability to self-reflect[41]. With the ability for self-reflection comes the ability to understand where we went wrong – and with that also the ability to correct our behaviour next time round. Apologies externalise this internal mode of reflection. As Tavuchis puts it, an apology is a performative utterance that in the case of RE converts the remorse of the offender from "a private condition into public communion".[42] Remorse, especially remorse that reaches the level of pain, is then the motivating factor that allows us to conclude that the apologiser will act on their insight. The first apology I gave at the beginning of this paper failed because it was immediately followed by a pragmatic retraction, my announcement that I would keep sinning For Tavuchis, the promise of change is so inextricable intertwined with the expression of remorse that it does not even need saying, it is always implied.[43]

PA and RE share this external form of "public communion". What is missing in many forms of PA is the internal, motivating factor for change. How can it be replaced? If the role of remorse is as warrant for a future change in behaviour, then an externally enforceable promise of change can take its place for the purpose of trust repair. Here the law can come into play. Change when making a RA is an implied consequence that "may" not need stating explicitly, because our folk psychology tells us that the pain of remorse will lead to change in behaviour[44]. In a PA, this commitment to change becomes part of the felicity conditions of a successful apology

40 Nick Smith, 'Against Court-Ordered Apologies', (2013) 16 New Criminal Law Review 49.

41 Jerome Kroll, and Elizabeth Egan, 'Psychiatry, Moral Worry, and the Moral Emotions' (2004) 10 Journal of Psychiatric Practice 352. For a philosophical discussion see Benjamin Vilhauer, 'Kantian Remorse with and without Self-Retribution' (2022) 27 Kantian Review 421.

42 Tavuchis, (23) 64.

43 Ibid. 23.

44 Many theorists of apologies suggest that also an effective RE will normally require an offer of reparation and/or promise of change. See e.g. Aviva Orenstein, 'Apology

that need to be communicated and stated explicitly. Apologies then do not so much report an internal state of regret, rather they report a line of reasoning where the offender

1. takes responsibility, which includes a causal account of the actions and conditions that led to the harm
2. states the steps that will be taken to prevent the same mistake happening again
3. possibly makes an offer of "making good" – compensation that is commensurate to the harm inflicted and the degree of responsibility

1) turns the apology into the exact mirror image of the account of "explanation" that we discussed above. Just as an explanation is not an account of the inner processes that led someone to reach the right result, but a publicly verifiable account of a valid chain of reasoning, so is an apology often not an account of the inner processes that led to a mistake (that would be "making excuses") but a publicly auditable account of what caused the harm. Because of this symmetry, I argue that for regulatory purposes, we should consider this form of apology as an appropriate way to meet explainability requirements, even if it does not disclose the inner working of the AI.

We can now also express more clearly the objections against the Yale robot. The problem is not that it deceives its audience by claiming to have an internal state that machines do not possess – its machine nature is too obvious for this. Rather, by using the verbal form, or logic, of an RA apology, it deceives us in inferring also conditions 1-3, that is we falsely infer that:

1) the reason the robot states for its failure is the causally relevant reason (in the example: processor not fast enough)
2) that the same issue will not happen again, that there will be change.

In the experiment the robot's "failure" was externally enforced, not the result of an unsuitable processor being used for the task, it was a "placebo explanation" that unfortunately can be as efficient in restoring trust as real explanations.[45] Because the causal explanation is already false, there is no pathway from a recognition of responsibility to an effective change in future

Excepted: Incorporating a Feminist Analysis into Evidence Policy Where You Would Least Expect It' (1999) 239 Southwestern U. Law. *Rev* 221.

45 Malin Eiband and others 'The Impact of Placebic Explanations on Trust in Intelligent Systems.' In *Extended abstracts of the 2019 CHI conference on human factors in computing systems*, (ACM 2019) 1 https://dl.acm.org/doi/10.1145/3290607.3312787.

behaviour. Furthermore, the robot does not have the capacity to effect the change that its own words indicate. It cannot for instance upgrade itself, or refuse to play next time it encounters a scenario that requires speedy responses.

A PA apology that does not just restore trust, but trustworthiness, therefore requires at the bare minimum a correct causal account of the contribution that an action or omission had for the harm, and an enforceable or auditable promise of future change. Not

> "Sorry, I sometimes run out of memory and can't process things fast enough".
> But
> "I'm sorry, I was not fast enough in move 3, I'm going to download an upgrade before the next game, and I'll also pay the participation fee for the next round of gaming".

This structure of an apology also mirrors definitions found in some legal systems. The Apology Scotland Act (2000) for instance defines as valid apology for the purpose of the act

> "any statement made by or on behalf of a person which indicates that the person is sorry about, or regrets, an act, omission or outcome and includes any part of the statement which contains an undertaking to look at the circumstances giving rise to the act, omission or outcome with a view to preventing a recurrence."

If we read the expression of regret as acceptance of (causal) responsibility, then the "undertaking to look into the circumstances [...]" equates to a causal explanation of why the harm occurred, while the prevention element is forward looking and gives reason to restore trust.

The purpose of this Act is to encourage apologies, which are often what the victim prefers over other remedies, but which are often actively discouraged by an institution's or corporation's lawyers.[46] Apologies, so their reasoning, can be constructed as admissions of legal liability, even though the legal requirements may be much more exacting than a personal feeling of responsibility. [47] Apologies that conform with the structure prescribed

46 Elizabeth Latif, 'Apologetic Justice: Evaluating Apologies Tailored Towards Legal Solutions', (2001) 81 Boston University Law Review 28.

47 See Jennifer K Robbennolt, 'Apologies and Legal Settlement: An Empirical Examination' (2003) 102 Michigan Law Review 460.

by the Act are privileged for the purpose of litigation, that is they can't be adduced as evidence by a complainer if they decide to sue for damages.[48] This does not mean that receiving an apology bars them from brining an action for damages, only that they need to find evidence other than the apology itself.

This type of liability shield should be attractive to anyone who contemplates allowing robots to apologise on their behalf, as it mitigates the risk of apologies that turn out to have been premature, or in some other way not merited. At the same time, because apologies that are valid for the purpose of the Apology Act are also the mirror image of explanations, they help complying with transparency requirements under instruments such as the EU AI Act.

E. Robot-Love means never having to print 1001001001010

The second ConTrust working paper stated:

"Normatively justified trust relations in situations of conflict come about and persist when the right to justification (in a broad sense) is in place despite and in light of conflict."[49]

In this chapter, I tried to argue that if XAI were to take this insight at heart (as it should), we need in addition to "cooperative AI explanations" of the type WMR developed also "conflict-centric" XAI that operates after norms or reasonable expectations were violated by an AI.

Having identified apologies as the type of speech act that meets the requirements for a trust-restoring, conflict-centric "explanation", the question became whether AIs are in principle capable of apologising, arguing that most if not all currently developed "apologetic" robots are undermining rather than enhancing justified trust. Drawing from ideas across a range of legal disciplines, I argued that we must distinguish two different types of apologies. One relies on internal mental states as a guarantor for change, the other on making actionable promises in a public forum. The former can only be performed successfully by humans, the latter also by companies, states or other abstract entities and the people who speak on their behalf. The reason that the Yale robot (and others like it) are ethically dubious is

48 Prue Vines, 'Apologies and Civil Liability in the UK: a view from elsewhere. (2008) 12 Edinburgh Law Review 200.

49 Forst (1) 8.

that they are not the right type of agent to make the first type of apology, and on the other hand they are not using the correct format for participating in the second type of apology game.

For the normative issues, we concluded that to the extent that robots apologise, they should always only use type 2 (PA) apologies. If they use PA apologies, then this is a valid way to establish the type of explainability that legal instruments such as the AI Act mandates. To encourage building the capacity of type 2 apologies into AIs, we should consider for those jurisdictions that give litigation privileges to human-authored apologies to extend them to robot-issued apologies.

From eugenics to big data:
Towards a Genealogy of Criminal Risk Assessment in the United States

Jonathan Simon

Criminal Risk Assessment (CRA) has been a critical part of the United States criminal legal system since the early 20th century when eugenic beliefs about the heritability and racially concentrated sources of criminality crystallized into a belief that crime was mostly the product of a dangerous minority among law breakers. The emergence of explicitly risk oriented judgments in criminal law, the focus on groups rather than individuals, and the increasing reliance on formal model based instruments of CRA, what this chapter calls algorithmic justice, is only the latest variation on this powerful myth that crime can be efficiently contained by identifying and incapacitating the dangerous minority, if only the right formula is at hand.

A. Introduction

Having co-authored an article that helped draw attention to a major shift in the logics of criminal risk assessment (CRA) in American criminal law, I want to revisit this history and reflect more deliberately on the complexities we can observe as we consider the longer arc of risk and justice in the United States in a less synthetic and simplifying approach than we took thirty years ago.[1] This historical reflection is shaped by a number of broader issues and developments of the present moment. One is the role that algorithms (as reflected in the title of this volume) that are coming to operate in American justice more generally and especially in the criminal legal system. This pressure is one being felt globally. As the age of big data pushes us toward an embrace of artificial intelligence based decision systems generally, pressure to conform criminal justice authority to it will build as well. A second source of social and legal change, one which perhaps has more

1 Malcolm Feeley and Jonathan Simon. "The New Penology: Notes on the Emerging Strategy of Corrections and its Implications' (1992)." Criminology 30: 449.

salience in the United States than more globally is a reckoning with the long history of racism in the US criminal legal system. Indeed, so tightly is CRA in the US bound with processes of racialization that an alternative title for this chapter might be "from eugenics to big data: criminal risk assessment as a genealogy of anti-Black racism in the United States." The shocking murder of George Floyd, an unarmed Black man accused of a minor crime by Minneapolis police, seen by millions in June of 2020 due to videos and social media saturation, brought public disquiet with police violence against Black citizens to a new peak with calls to dramatically transform or even defund the police and other criminal legal institutions. That was followed very rapidly, as it often is in the US, with a backlash in which racial justice reforms were presumptively linked to increasing crime in the pandemic years of 2020 and 2021.

The sudden popularity of the algorithm in criminal justice reform and the need to answer deep questions about racial bias are two sides of a legitimacy crisis facing criminal justice, a deeper one than any in generations. Several examples will provide a sense of the significance of the change now underway especially in contrast to the one Malcolm Feeley and I predicted thirty years ago in "the new penology." After decades of making prison sentences longer for almost everyone convicted of certain crimes, nearly half the US states introduced algorithm risk assessment tools into their sentencing process with the authority to allocate shorter sentences to low risk defendants.[2] A second example is from pretrial detention, where after decades of money bail conditions being set by police charges and the criminal record (both viewed by experts as highly vulnerable to racial bias), new CRA instruments using formal algorithms developed on big data sets to predict risk are being promoted in a number of states.[3] My final example is policing where after decades of giving police more discretion to use their authority to seize and question people deemed by them to be suspicious, major police departments like Los Angeles Police Department

2 To be sure, almost nowhere are judges required to rely on it, and it is not clear empirically how often it controls the sentence but it is a change from an era when mandatory sentences were generally based on the crime which the prosecutor chose to bring and the criminal record, both highly suspected of being infected with racial bias.

3 An important driver has been the Arnold Foundation, a philanthropy funded by tech fortunes, that has developed and promoted sophisticated risk instruments for use in pretrial detention and related decisions. https://www.arnoldventures.org/stories/public-safety-assessment-risk-tool-promotes-safety-equity-justice.

have adopted algorithm based systems to determine the deployment of police around areas of predicted high crime.[4]

It is possible to argue that this recent spread of algorithmic justice is just a delayed arrival of what we called "the new penology". The logic of risk we called "actuarial justice"[5] is perhaps not so different from the algorithmic justice that is emerging today in social science being a few decades off with your predictions, might not be a bad record. However, for purposes of understanding the deeper genealogy of CRA in the US criminal legal system I want to explore the discontinuities between the two moments of potential change in the methodology and approach to CRA. In "the new penology" we argued based on our independent empirical work on different aspects of criminal justice, that dramatic changes were coming, driven by the pervasiveness of the risk logic we claimed to describe. These changes were not just in one aspect of criminal justice but in, one might say, the entire paradigm. This included a shift in the objectives of justice, - from reform, deterrence and rehabilitation, to risk management through levels of penal control; a shift in the target of justice— from the individual criminal offender to the statistically defined social group; and in the logics and methods of expertise from a clinical gaze on the individual penal subject as a holistic entity to a statistical analysis of crime prevalence in a statistically analysed population or sample. Against a fuller genealogy of CRA our claims seem overly dramatic and simplistic (as plenty of critics suggested at the time).

In the remainder of this chapter, I will situate both the present moment and the false dawn of the new penology three decades ago alongside two other moments that together fill out a twentieth century genealogy of CRA in American justice. We are going to start with the present, which I have already characterized as one of emerging algorithmic based technologies of CRA at many crucial nodes of decision making in the modern criminal legal system. Is this the moment we predicted, just late? We next revisit the 1980s and 1990s to understand in retrospect for the failure of actuarial justice to take off in that time. Next we are going to leap over the mid-twentieth century so called golden era of rehabilitation in American corrections and clinical and psychological forms of expertise within the juridical and

4 Sarah Brayne, Predict and Surveil: Data, discretion, and the future of policing. Oxford University Press, USA, 2020.

5 Malcolm Feeley and Jonathan Simon. "Actuarial justice: The emerging new criminal law." The futures of criminology 173 (1994): 174.

carceral institutions of justice to the deepest, earliest, and consequential layer of our genealogy, the early 20th century when fuelled by a larger embrace of eugenics as governmental rationality CRA really took root in the American justice system. Then we will briefly return to the mid-20th century which we implicitly took to be the baseline against which we defined a "new penology".

To contextualize these shifts, we'll look first at the legitimacy problems facing the justice system to which different logics of CRA have been offered as technocratic and policy rational solutions. Second, we will identify the epistemic conditions of possibility that have allowed different forms of CRA to take root in the justice system. These include intellectual production (new ideas, ideologies or governmentalities) as well as advances in technology that spur knowledge production. Of particular importance in this regard are three advances in the long computer revolution that has swept the US (and the world) since the mid-20th century. Finally, we will examine some exemplary expressions of CRA.

B. Algorithmic Justice 2007

Examples of algorithmic justice abound today as they really did not in the early 1990s. A good example of algorithmic justice in action is PredPol, a privately developed and licensed set technology for police to use their own data to predict times and places where crimes are more likely and adopted by a large number of police departments including the LAPD, one of the nation's largest and best funded.

What has made algorithmic justice more successful now than its superficially similar actuarial cousin in the 1990s? Taking what we can call following Foucault a problematization approach, today the US justice system faces more promising problems than it did in the 1990s when the only real question was how fast it could grow its punitive capacity. In particular, two enduring challenges to the legitimacy of justice in its extended late 20th century form of "mass incarceration.": cost and racism. Actuarial justice is by nature a fiscal logic (as befits its origins in insurance) and it can only thrive if institutions are compelled to prove their efficiency in some transparent way. Thus, it was only as the real cost of our distended prison sentences became visible and politically undeniable, that the parsimonious logic of algorithmic justice could become a virtue rather than a compromise with public safety (as it was for much of the late twentieth century). The fiscal crisis of 2008 which sent many state budgets (which is where most of American justice is bought and paid for) into steep revenue declines.[6] More than a decade after the end of the Great Recession, austerity concerns seem to have become a permanent condition in criminal justice policy.

But if overspending is a problem for the legitimacy of the criminal legal system, it is a problem that brings it into line with the larger challenges facing the taxing and spending powers of the government in times of enduring hostility to high taxes. It is racism and particularly the justice systems disproportionate harm through surveillance, incarceration and violence, that drives its most acute crises of legitimacy today. The history through which public safety was built in twentieth century America, largely to exclude and punish Black Americans, is one that was never fully covered up (certainly not for Black communities) and has recently been subjected to a wave of studies by historians.[7]

In our moment of at least partial criminal legal system reform since the mid 2000s, two legitimacy problems have emerged that were not consistently viewed as problems in before the turn of the century: austerity and racism. If algorithmic CRA is more popular than it was before, our hypothesis is that it is, or appears to be (which is the same thing for games of legitimacy) it is in large part because it appears to provide reasons to be optimistic that through better CRA the criminal legal system can become cheaper, more efficient, and less racist. Our goal in this chapter will not be to assess those substantive claims as to note their role as a condition of possibility for the recent take off of algorithmic justice.

The most promising problems of legitimacy will lead to significant reforms unless the epistemic conditions are such as to make some new forms of expertise available to address them. The big data moment we are experiencing is associated with a range of new technologies and methodologies to exploit them that are only the most recent revolution in computational power to shape the justice system. The sudden appearance and now seeming inevitability of artificial intelligence has been made possible by the proliferation beyond military fields of super powerful processors, as well as the emergence of tools to make different sets of data in a common

6 Hadar Aviram, Cheap on crime: Recession-era politics and the transformation of American punishment. University of California Press, 2015.

7 See for example, Kelly Lytle Hernandez, City of Inmates: Conquest, rebellion, and the rise of human caging in Los Angeles, 1771–1965 (2017); John K. Bardes, The Carceral City: Slavery and the Making of Mass Incarceration in New Orleans, 1803-1930 (2024).

framework of analysis through scraping and other techniques that take advantage of the increasing proliferation of data accessible digitally. This revolution is taking place across the economy and society and the criminal legal system is hardly the most advanced sector.

These new computational methods offer the promise of being able to boost the efficiency of the justice system but often at the cost of making its potential racial biases invisible. Leaving it to presumption that the systems are less biased than the human decision makers they replace. Some of the most successful algorithmic CRA approaches like PredPol are those that promise rather visibly to target criminal legal system resources more precisely these legitimacy crises and questions about the expertise claimed by the criminal legal system about crime. As American Studies scholar Jackie Wang puts it: "PredPol draws on many of the tenets of the 'police science' paradigm to solve two contemporary crises: the crisis of legitimacy suffered by the police and the broader epistemological crisis that could be called the crisis of uncertainty."[8] Again, whether it works is not the focus of this chapter, nor easily discernible. PredPol may direct police where to go but it does not control their discretionary decision making once they get there. Once police saturate an area it is likely they will find some crimes whether or not they are the robberies, assaults or burglaries that people fear.

Actuarial Justice: 1982-1994

The article, "the new penology", published in 1992, offered a dramatic account of big changes in the nature of expertise and methods of CRA in the justice system. While our conclusions turned out to be inaccurate about the direction of criminal justice in the late decade of the twentieth century, we were right that something was stirring. In the US generally, and in California particularly, prison populations were in a period of unprecedented and sustained growth. Mass imprisonment was becoming visible and controversial. It was this growth that formed the potential legitimacy problem that actuarial justice was intended to solve.

The other major push toward actuarial justice came from the implosion of confidence in clinical methods of CRA. Popular since the turn of the

8 Jackie Wang, Carceral Capitalism (SemioTexte 2018), 230.

20th century, clinical justice was the implicit if not explicit template for some of the most important decisions made by the justice system including prison sentence length, opportunity for probation supervision rather than some or all of a prison or jail sentence, and the possibility of early release from prison. Long associated with the objectivity and the expertise of medical and psychiatric professionals, clinical assessment in the 1970s went through a full legitimacy crisis of its own.[9] America in the 1950s and 1960s had a very large psychiatric custodial population and in the 1960s and 1970s this was coming under scrutiny as being abusive and even totalitarian in the ease with which adults could be confined against their will without being convicted or a crime. It was the closing of several large hospitals under pressure from courts that created the empirical backlash against clinical prediction as scores of patients who had been deemed too dangerous to release under those methods returned to the community largely without adverse reaction. Some claimed that a psychologist evaluating dangerousness based on a holistic examination was no better than chance at predicting accurately who would go one to behave violently. In the justice system, clinical justice in functions like parole release were widely accused of being biased against the increasingly large population of Black people imprisoned.

If prison population growth and unreliability and perhaps racism of clinical CRA were motivating problems, the emergence of actuarial justice as a plausible solution also required changes in the epistemic capacities of the criminal legal system. A significant development for a logic that required data analysis of large data sets (not yet big data but large) was the computing revolution that emerged with the desktop computer in the very late 1970s and early 1980s. Prior to the early 1980s virtually no state or local criminal legal system in the US had a computer system of their own of the kind that would be necessary to turn produce actuarial predictions reliably and cheaply. Access to large "mainframe" computers was expensive and largely at the disposal of hard scientists, the military, and state governments.

An additional epistemic condition was the overall rise in the prestige of numbers in public policy, a long running trend but one that was accelerated in adjacent and related legal field by the rise of economics and especially

9 Jonathan Simon "Reversal of fortune: The resurgence of individual risk assessment in criminal justice." Annu. Rev. Law Soc. Sci. 1, no. 1 (2005): 397-421.

economic analysis of law. While the first generation of law and economics was more theoretical than empirical, it raised the prestige of numbers (even made up numbers) in the fields of law and public policy. The rising faith in numbers to legitimize even the most problematic facets of the US criminal legal system. In 1976 the Supreme Court would cite although it claimed not to rely on simplistic regression analyses showing a deterrent effect of the death penalty in affirming the constitutionality of a suite of new capital sentencing laws.[10]

Another offshoot of economic analysis with even more quantitative uptake was cost-benefit analysis, the systematic data based analysis of whether proposed laws or regulations would produce more social benefits than costs. The Reagan administration (1981-1989) institutionalized cost-benefit analysis as a requirement for all proposed regulations as a way of shrinking the regulatory burden on the economy, but successive more social-democratic administrations have maintained it. In this respect, as we argued in the "new penology," the quantification of criminal legal operations required by the logic of actuarial CRA was a late transfer of quantitative methods of prediction being absorbed across government and with deep roots in the financial sector of the private economy.

In retrospect the new penology article had relatively few examples that really exemplified actuarial CRA as we described it. The widely known U.S. Sentencing Guidelines, adopted in 1984, had a very quantitative looking grid that governed the range of months in prison that a judge could impose (it was originally mandatory) but in fact the scheme eschewed consideration of the kinds of social facts about defendants that would emerge in actuarial CRA and instead relied completely on a combination of crime seriousness and criminal record. Criminal record was at best a crude measure of risk and certainly not driven by data. Likewise, the 1980s.

Perhaps the most convincing example we identified was one that was never actually adopted. The RAND Corporation's 1982 study "Selective Incapacitation," authored by criminologist Peter Greenwood, and published just as tougher sentencing policies and laws was beginning to produce severe overcrowding in California prisons (and before the big boom in new prisons) offered what actuarially driven CRA as an alternative to mass imprisonment. The RAND study used self reported surveys of prisoners to derive relative criminal activity scales and multivariate analysis to estimate the

10 Gregg v. Georgia, 438 United States Reports 153, 186.

effect on criminal activity of individuals of a wide variety of demographic and behavioural variables to determine the most efficient predictors of levels of criminal activity. The original study identified eight factors that could predict membership in the high risk group with an accuracy level above 90 percent. The promise being that using such indicators to shape length of sentence could allow California to reduce crime significantly without the cost of a general incapacitation strategy in which everyone convicted of the same crime received the same sentence (thus the concept of selective incapacitation). Good social scientists, the RAND investigators ultimately dismantled their own claims by more closely examining their data and assumptions.[11] But the dream of more accurate and valid instruments has remained.

Thus, while the new penology we predicted was at best in embryonic form at this point, it's plausibility[12] to us reflected very real problems we saw facing the legitimacy of the criminal legal system. The United States was in the midst of what we now know would be a historically epic growth in its prison population. Overcrowding was indeed growing to levels that combined with flawed mental and medical health care delivery systems in prisons would create constitutional violations and ultimately court interventions. Indeed, the people who wrote the selective study were very much trying to catch the attention of California correctional managers and convince them that mass imprisonment might not be necessary— if they could pick the right people to imprison. The second problem was the collapse of confidence in psychologically oriented clinical CRA. While much of the problem with clinical prediction was its perceived lack of measurable reliability, the strongest normative concerns go back to the problem of systemic racism, especially anti-Black racism, in CRA. The early 1970s was a period when many people who were pursuing racial justice and civil rights began to suspect that clinical risk prediction by judges and parole boards could be influenced by preexisting even unconscious assumptions that Black people are more criminally inclined. As we will see in the next section what may have been unconscious in the 1970s was a very conscious process of linkage fifty years earlier. Actuarial CRA rose in its prospects (and in our estimation) because it was poised to leverage greater statistical

11 Peter Greenwood and Susan Turner. "Selective incapacitation revisited." Why High-Rate Offenders Are Hard to Predict. Santa Monica (1987).

12 Jonathan Simon, Mass Incarceration on Trial: A Remarkable Court Decision and the Future of American Prisons (New Press, 2014).

research conducted on accessible desktop computers and the general rise in the prestige of quantitative calculation in law and policy.

Eugenic Justice: 1905-1945

Much of the debate over different modes of CRA has turned on their consequences for racial bias and the resulting overconcentration of punishments and surveillance on communities already marginalized by long histories of racial discrimination in society much of it effectuated through the justice system. This laudatory concern (which is only active in some phases of our history) also provides its own evidence that such bias is real and systemic. Indeed, it is the main argument of this chapter that the shifting views of high crime levels in racialized communities is the driving force behind the assessment of future dangerousness in all CRA modalities. And this is no accident but has a clear history and a beginning in which this racial vision was not disguised in the least but taught as respectable foundations for criminology and sociology in the new and to some miraculous science of eugenics.

We begin our genealogy with the first decades of the twentieth century, what historians may learn to call the eugenic era (instead of the more commonly used "progressive era"). This high water moment of scientific racism and the construction in particular of Black people as the chief threat to urban civilization and safety is also the birth era in important respects of American criminal risk assessment and when the idea that criminal dangerousness could be located in a type of individual (a group therefore), like the criminal persistent criminal or habitual criminal, or natural criminal. As the modern institutional structure of the American justice system was completed in this era with the addition of new penal authority and institutions such as parole, probation, and juvenile courts, the system and its leaders embraced CRA as the crucial to its vision of how to stay on top of a wave of urban crime perceived as out of control in this era (blamed on immigration for the most part and the racial inferiority of those immigrating at the turn of the century.

The number one legitimacy problem facing the American justice system was its perceived failure to counter mounting crime, especially in large cities. This failure could be said to have two faces, one at the individual level and one at the population. Individually (although in aggregate as well) was perceived in the growing problem of recidivism (the supposed return to crime or at least arrest) of a person formerly incarcerated in a state penitentiary. The repeat offender (or "habitual offender" in one common formulation for extended prison sentences), recidivist, or persistent or habitual criminal was new face of criminal danger. While their existence suggested the prison was a failure as a reformatory for many, the statistical analysis of recidivism emerged as the basis for an optimistic search for criteria with which to predict who these recidivists are in advance of releasing them (the power given by new mechanisms like parole and probation).

Second, the criminal problem was to be identified more and more in American cities with immigrants flowing to the United States from southern eastern Europe following the Civil War in the 1870s and 1880s. Criminal law experts blamed the racial and cultural defects of immigrants for what was taken to be a rise in violent and organized crime as well as labour radicalism and anarchism. Facing this overlapping threats (immigrants were surely more likely to be recidivists in the reasoning of the time) penal reformers embraced CRA as a crucial upgrade to common law legal system of the 19th century with its emphasis on retributive or deterrent justice efforts to a capacity to exclude the dangerous multitudes and select out the dangerous individuals. The former project would fall mostly to immigration law (which virtually excluded immigrants from outside of northern Europe after 1924 and until 1965). It also reflected the power implied by modes of CRA to address the faces of the new crime threat.

The eugenic approach to government favoured aggressive use of coercive legal authority, whether in immigration enforcement or criminal justice to remove and exclude those with undesirable characteristics and above all the lower mental capacity that eugenics associated with crime and host of other bad personal and social outcomes. The method used to determine a person's eugenic threat could be appallingly shambolic even for that day.[13] Such was the confidence that criminal difference existed, explained most of crime and was foreshadowed by racial differences, that the actual method of assessment was unimportant. The methods of risk assessment in this era embraced both clinical and statistical analysis reflecting the variety of disciplines and professions that claimed some expertise about the aetiology

13 For example, the conclusion that a woman was an "imbecile" and likely to give birth to further imbeciles if not segregated in an asylum and ultimately sterilized. These were medical doctors who were presumed to have confident diagnostic skills but who in fact operated mostly on their class based judgment of working class women. See Andrew Cohen (2017). Imbeciles: The supreme court, American eugenics, and the sterilization of Carrie Buck. Penguin.

of crime but also the fact that both were consistent with the eugenic belief system that bad traits existed in the genetic inheritance of the individual and could be observed both at the population level through statistics or at the individual through close social analysis (which of course would include racial history).

What made CRA seem a plausible solution was indeed the primacy of eugenic thinking in this period across American public policy, government, and academia. No other democracy embraced eugenics at the scale and level of the United States and the criminal legal system found a way to revitalize its legitimacy in this title wave of optimism that an assertive state could engineer problems like crime and poverty and illness by controlling reproduction as well as immigration while the degenerate already here could be removed surgically through sterilization and for men through long sentences in the criminal justice system (extended by juvenile courts, probation officers, and parole).

While remarkably uniform in its acceptance of the eugenic logic of CRA, reformers were quite varied in the methodology they employed. Probation officers exemplified the new clinical approach. Trained in the same methods of the contemporary social work movement, probation combined a holistic analysis of family (race), education, and work history, with criminal record, to provide the juvenile or adult court judge an expert view on the criminality and reformability of the individual.[14] At virtually the same time (and in the same city, Chicago) a kind of actuarial justice was being generated by University of Chicago sociologists which cooperated with the corrections department of Illinois to keep statistical records of prisoners and recidivism and subject those to a close analysis of correlation (multivariate methods were still lacking). The Chicago method drew on social types, like the alcoholic and the ne'er do well (the latter basically suggesting non-work) identify the differences in recidivism levels. The result was a simple additive scale based on the types and demographic characteristics with the greatest correlations to recidivism (including race and nationality).[15]

While European immigrants were the main focus of the urban crime panic at the turn of the century, the huge wave of migration of Black

14 Michael Willrich. City of courts: Socializing justice in progressive era Chicago. Cambridge University Press, 2003.

15 Bernard Harcourt, Against Prediction. Chicago: University of Chicago Press. Harlow, Caroline Wolf, 2000.

Americans from the rural south to the urban north and south, which began even before but accelerated during World War I, quickly brought Black Americans, and particularly unemployed Black men who were an inevitable part of the ups and downs of a racially segmented and exploitative capitalist labour market with few protections to the forefront of concern of a now enlarged and eugenically oriented criminal legal system.

Clinical justice: 1945-1980

By the 1950s, eugenics as a racial governance project had largely collapsed among policy and academic experts tainted by its association with Nazi regime in Germany which had followed America in embracing aggressive racial legislation and followed up with murder[16] and by the advance genetic science which undermined most of the simplifying claims about the heritability of complex social outcomes like crime and undermined the belief that a problem free society could be engineered by removing those with bad traits from reproductive opportunity. Biological theories of crime, and their explicitly racist implications fell out of favour with crime experts who preferred to rely on sociological and cultural explanations for crime patterns that were now well embedded in the very structure of law enforcement and segregation in the mid-century metropolitan landscape. The eugenic assumptions about race, immigrant status, and mental disability as associated with repeated and serious crime and that the criminal justice system could remove a dangerous minority of largely unredeemable criminals remained deeply influential, having been taught as scientific truth to a generation of law enforcement and legal professionals who were only coming into their own peak of leadership responsibilities in the 1960s.

It was this hangover of eugenics and its shadow in well established patterns of race discrimination in the provision of what small amounts of resources for betterment and reform the system had to provide, that formed the predominant legitimacy problem for which a shift to seemingly more humanistic psychological approaches would be perceived as a solution. The bad association of the criminal legal system (and the asylum system) with eugenics led to campaigns for reform led by journalists and lawyers in many states. Asylums in many states are closed down as they are associated with

16 James Q. Whitman, Hitler's American model: The United States and the making of Nazi race law. Princeton University Press, 2017.

pointless warehousing of people defined as defective. Prisons came in for similar critique as cruel and inhumane with little effectiveness. The new efforts to push clinical CRA offered a way to address this legitimacy crisis head on by giving the individual the dignity and careful scrutiny that they were accused of denying.

The CRA methods of assessment of this period continued to include both clinical and actuarial modes of prediction but clinical received the greatest attention. This was the high cultural tide of psychiatry as a science of stable societies much of its influenced in the United States by Freudian psychoanalysis which became the dominant teaching methodology for psychiatrists in the 1950s and 1960s. Prisons in progressive states like California offered group therapy and sought to link psychological dynamics linked to crime with strategies for rehabilitative programming factors in the penal subject to the kinds of outcomes on parole that had been studied since the early 20th century (a kind of hybrid of clinical and actuarial). Prison sentences in many systems had come to rely in theory completely on the supposed clinical expertise of parole boards generally made up of retired law enforcement officers with no particular training in psychology or criminology. Although the validity of clinical assessment would soon come into major questioning (as discussed above in the section on actuarial justice), its appeal had less to do with its proven effectiveness and more with the appearance of humanizing and caring close examination of the person within a system premised on the possibility of their rehabilitation. This could stand in stark contrast to the determinism and racism now associated with the eugenic justice model.

The first large scale actuarial risk prediction system was developed for the federal probation system as a tool for determining low risk candidates for earlier release from prison sentences a process that was perceived as both unscientific and racist. The so-called "salient factors scores" gave federal parole decision makers an objective test.

C. Race, Risk and Anti-Black: A Philadelphia Story

It would not be until WWI and the full flow of the Great Migration of Black people from the American rural south to the cities of the Northeast and Midwest that Black communities would become the central focus of the criminal legal system. But the grounds for their arrival were already laid by the criminology of the late 19th century discussed above which depicted Black people as the primary threat to urban order and security. Much of this battle would play out in the city of Philadelphia which was the only major northern city with a large population dating back to the American revolution. According to historian Kahlil G. Muhammad "Philadelphia was one of the most important black-criminality research sites in the nation".[17] Although many other cities would experience the same processes of migration, segregation, discrimination, Philadelphia stands out as a kind of implicit background to the focus of 20th century CRA on anti-Blackness. This arc which runs through the full length of our genealogy may be the most significant through line in the twisting path. Remarkably some of the foundational studies in modern criminology around which contemporary urban crime and its racial patterning have been normalized were drawn from work done in Philadelphia by social scientists associated with the city's leading research university, the University of Pennsylvania.

We begin at the very end of the 19th century when Frederick Hoffman made Philadelphia one of the cities he studied for his influential 1896 book, *Race Traits And Tendencies Of The American Negro.* As detailed by Muhmmad, Hoffman used census data to support his eugenics derived conclusion that as an inferior race Black workers could not compete in the supposed free economy of the North and therefore must turn to crime for survival. It was to combat this already emerging consensus among academic and policy experts that some years before Hoffman's book was published W. E. B. Du Bois, now seen as one of the inventors of empirical sociology in America went to Philadelphia on a fellowship from the University of Pennsylvania to write a dissertation on Black people in Philadelphia in all their social and economic complexity to earn his PhD from Harvard University (the first Black American to do so). The resulting study became his first book and perhaps the first piece of American sociology, *The Philadelphia Negro: A Social Study* (1899).

Du Bois undoubtedly chose Philadelphia because its long standing Black community was by far the largest outside the South, making it the only large northern city in America with a distinct and identifiable urban Black community. Du Bois was interested in more than crime. He understood sociology to be the study of modern urban people and wanted a place where he could document to full measure of how Black people navigated

17 Khalil Gibran. The condemnation of Blackness: Race, crime, and the making of modern urban America, with a new preface. Harvard University Press, 2019.

city life. His broad conclusions were that Black people faced the same problems and prospects, including criminalization, as other urban dwellers, but exacerbated by prejudice and discrimination which relegated them to the more precarious and least rewarding jobs. Du Bois clearly understood the priority of the crime issue for his White audience of academics and policy experts and did not shy away from highlighting the high level of crime in the segregated Black neighbourhood in which he and his young family resided during his fellowship (being no less subject to segregation despite his high academic prestige). Paradoxically the price of that attention was to spotlight the risk of Black crime as a central concern for the emerging science of sociology. Like other Black elites, he hoped more attention to Black crime might mean more resources put into preventive measures and who had been generally ignored by the criminal system as long as their crimes stayed within the Black community. These early Black law and order advocates were trying to get the attention of prosecutors and judges and police commanders much more concerned about crime among immigrants and radical labour organizers. Thus, debate that continues about whether Black neighbourhoods suffer more from over or under policing begins in this era as side effect of the rendering criminal risk an increasingly "black" problem rather than a broader social problem (the opposite of what Du Bois was attempting).

No city has a longer-term pattern of anti-black criminal justice than Philadelphia and even though by mid century it had been surpassed in the size of its Black population by New York and Chicago, its legal system remained one of the most racist criminal legal systems in the country. The heart of this anti-Black racism as urban politics and policy was Philadelphia's notorious police department. They play a central in unacknowledged role in the next important piece of empirical sociology to cast Black Philadelphians as the heart of the city's crime problem. We do not know if the importance of Philadelphia in the origin story of urban sociology was a causal factor, perhaps it's a coincidence that another sociologist with an interest in crime, Marvin Wolfgang, would locate one of the most influential 20th-century pieces of empirical sociology in that city. Wolfgang and his colleagues researched the pattern of juvenile arrests among every boy born in the city in 1945 who had ever been arrested. (importantly the first year of the "baby boom" cohort whose huge size is often seen as a factor in the crime wave of the 1960s through 1980s). The results, published at the height of the crime panic of the period, suggested that a small minority of arrested youth (about 5 percent), disproportionately accounted for most of the serious crime arrests among the cohort as a whole. While the study did not attempt to derive predictive factors, one variable was overwhelmingly indicated, the high arrest minority were almost all Black juveniles. In short, Blackness was a predictor of crime risk in Philadelphia. Wolfgang and colleagues did not consider how the long history of Philadelphia police concentrating on Black youth may have shaped this result.

The birth cohort study, considered one of the most methodologically rigorous of its times, had a huge influence on thinking about crime prevention at a time of rising demand to address crime. Incarcerating Black youth was a plausible way to reduce the overall burden of urban crime on this reasoning. Wolfgang, unlike Frederick Hoffman, was no reflexive White supremacist; indeed, his research was mobilized in support of efforts to persuade the Supreme Court to strike down the American death penalty disproportionate application to Black defendants. Yet his research would cement the image of urban crime as Black crime and the notion that things were getting worse. In a follow up study of the 1958 birth cohort (toward the end of the baby boom) concluded that the younger brothers of the original cohort were even more violent and dangerous.

Through the end of the century Philadelphia remained one of the most racist and violent criminal legal systems in the country, with a district attorney infamous for seeking the most severe sentences possible and sending the largest number of Black people to prison and to capital punishment of any city outside of the deep south. The obsession of Philadelphia's police department with controlling its Black community remained high throughout the 20th century. In 1972 its notoriously anti-Black long time police chief Frank Rizzo became mayor and led an ongoing and explicitly racist campaign of violent policing against the Black community in the name of protecting its remaining white "ethnic" communities.[18] In 1985, under a Black Mayor, in support of a raid on a house where a radical Black power community resided in the heart of the city's historic Black neighbourhood resulting in a fire that killed everyone in the commune and destroyed much of the surrounding neighbourhood.

---

18 Donovan Schaefer, The City's Salvation: Frank Rizzo and White Christian Nationalism in Philadelphia, University of Virgina, Religion, Race, and Democracy Lab, https://religionlab.virginia.edu/projects/the-citys-salvation-frank-rizzo-and-white-christian-nationalism-in-philadelphia/.

From the Actuarial to the Algorithmic

If anti-Black racism has been the continuity in the role of CRA in the American criminal legal system, the pendulum swings between different methodologies and logics of risk justice has been the major source of variation. Today's advent of algorithmic instruments driven with the tools of big data is the latest and arguably most significant variation yet. Significant in part because this most recent computerization revolution can make algorithmic CRA operational at the micro-level of practice at a far more affordable cost than has ever been true. That does not mean frontline criminal justice decision makers will accept its authority over their discretion, but that the capacity to bring sophisticated modern data techniques to the capillary level of probation offices and courts is now in place or rapidly becoming so.

Rightly perceiving the importance of the two issues (anti-Blackness and big data), much of the current debate is not between clinical and actuarial style but whether this latest extension of actuarial into the algorithmic will make the racial bias of CRA better or worse.

The best aspect of the new data techniques from the perspective of the longer genealogy of CRA is its ability to break out of the traditional institutional silo of criminal records kept by courts, police, or prisons. It becomes possible, through data hacking to bring other data sets that reflect health, education, and welfare systems into the analysis. As modelling methodology becomes stronger it also becomes possible to reverse the system and attempt to correct statistically for the bias that is acknowledged in the system. However, the history of places like Philadelphia suggests that the social construction of crime risk and race ran in parallel since the early 20th century in ways that will make any effort at analytical separation or debiasing limited at best.[19]

D. Conclusion

The recent emergence of big data based algorithms at the core of critical decision making junctures in the American criminal legal system reflects the increasing problem of legitimacy facing that system in an era of permanent fiscal austerity and enduring concern about racial inequality. At the heart of this unresolvable knot is the linkage, drawn at the dawn of the modern

19 Sandray Mayson, "Bias In, Bias Out," 128 Yale Law Journal 2218 (2019).

era by the eugenics fuelled reshaping of local government in the early 20th century, between race (mostly anti-Black racism) and urban crime. The ongoing war on crime that has been directed against Black communities since that period, guarantees that all methods of CRA will reproduce over concentration on Black people as criminal risk and minimize their vulnerability to systems of surveillance and punishment.

The surprising Impotence of Anti-Discrimination Law in the Age of AI
... and a comment on Art. 6 Directive 2023/2225 on Credit Agreements for Consumers

Katja Langenbucher

This paper takes up the EU's new rule on discriminatory credit underwriting. I build on earlier work, exploring how anti-discrimination law fares when fitting algorithmic credit scoring and creditworthiness evaluation into the regime of EU direct/indirect discrimination and US disparate treatment/disparate impact doctrine.[1] *I suggest that anti-discrimination law, when faced with redundant encoding, runs into doctrinal and practical problems. These manifest in proving but-for causation, in scenarios resembling algorithmic redlining, and in a more fundamental misfit between anti-discrimination law and big data analytics. The paper summarizes these challenges, addresses recent changes in US law, and submits that the new EU Directive has missed the chance to provide for a modern rule, fit to cope with algorithmic credit underwriting.*

A. Introduction

Credit scoring and creditworthiness evaluation provide excellent examples for both, the inclusive power of algorithms and the risk of algorithmic discrimination. Any decision to hand out a loan and price interest rates includes an assessment of the borrower's credit risk. Naturally, this involves a distinction among applicants to make an informed choice. Advanced

1 Parts of the following text are based on Katja Langenbucher, 'Consumer Credit in the Age of AI – Beyond Anti-Discrimination law' (2022) ecgi working paper 663/2022. In that (much longer) paper, written prior to new EU rule, I explore some of the arguments put forward here in more depth. In the following text, I occasionally use sentences and whole paragraphs with identical wording to my earlier paper.

statistics has been a classic tool for that task.[2] Today, big data and machine learning algorithms promise a disruption in how creditworthiness is evaluated.[3] The popular remark "All data is credit data. We just don't know how to use it yet"[4] suggests that leveraging a loan applicant's digital footprint has considerable potential to produce more accurate credit risk assessments. Online payment history, performance on lending platforms, age or sex, job or college education, ZIP code, income or ethnic background can all have predictive force. Additionally, consider preferred shopping places, social media friends, political party affiliations, taste in music, number of typos in text messages, brand of smartphone, speed in clicking through a captcha exercise, daily work-out time, or performance in a psychometric assessment. All these "input variables" include information about the applicant that is potentially relevant for computing his creditworthiness. Many of these are *redundantly encoded* in several data points: The fact that the applicant is female might be encoded in her preferred shopping places, her social media friends, her first name or her college. This paper submits that redundant encoding of this type causes a fundamental problem to received anti-discrimination law.

At first glance, the availability of big, so-called "alternative data", coupled with AI-based scoring promises to enhance access to credit markets. Mostly, this is due to lower search costs for lenders.[5] It is important to remember that lenders have long been aware that a low credit score is not necessarily an accurate reflection of an applicant's creditworthiness. However, in consumer credit markets it has not been cost-efficient for the lender to invest in locating "invisible prime"[6] applicants: While many applicants will be good

---

2 Josh Lauer, *Creditworthy, A History of Consumer Surveillance and Financial Identity in America* (CUP 2017) 200.

3 J Burrell and M Fourcade, 'The Society of Algorithms' (2021) Annual Review of Sociology Vol. 47 213, 222; D Citron and F Pasquale, 'The Scored Society": Due Process for Automated Predictions' (2014) Washington Law Review, Vol. 89 1, 4.

4 Quentin Hardy, 'Just the Facts. Yes, All of Them.' New York Times (New York, 25 March 2012) discussion at Emily Rosamond, '"All Data is Credit Data": Reputation, Regulation and Character in the Entrepreneurial Imaginary' (2016) Paragrana, Vol. 25, No. 2 112.

5 Katja Langenbucher, 'AI credit scoring and evaluation of creditworthiness – a test case for the EU proposal for an AI Act, in ECB, Continuity and change – how the challenges of today prepare the ground for tomorrow' (2022) ECB Legal Conference 2021 362.

6 Term proposed by M Di Maggio and D Ratnadiwakara, 'Invisible Primes: Fintech Lending with Alternative Data' (2021) 1 (2) <https://papers.ssrn.com/sol3/papers.cfm?abstract_id=3937438> accessed 24 June 2025.

credit risk and present an attractive business case, search costs to identify them may far outweigh the expected return.[7] Algorithmic scoring models have changed that equation and, in that sense, promise inclusion.

At the same time, the quality of an AI's prediction is only as good as the match between the world according to the training data and the world as it is today.[8] If the training data reflect past inequality, an applicant who shares features with a historically underserved group will be flagged as a higher credit risk than a comparable applicant who does not share the relevant feature (*historic bias*).The fact that training data are, in this way, shaped by history has direct implications for how the AI builds its model.[9] Variables that the AI finds for most candidates who were successful in the past will be accorded most weight, for instance a specific job, sex or race. Candidates whose profile does not include the relevant positive variable will face a risk premium (*majority bias*).[10] The same logic applies to variables that send a negative signal. The AI learns from historical data and singles out variables that have in the past been a predictor for high credit default risk. Applicants whose profile includes the risk-variable see their credit score sink. This happens even if a particular risk-variable does not reflect relevant details of the default situation across all applicants. The same is

7 Lauer (n 2) 210.

8 Deborah Hellman, 'Measuring Algorithmic Fairness' (2020) Virginia Law Review Vol. 106 811, 841; Langenbucher, 'AI credit scoring and evaluation of creditworthiness – a test case for the EU proposal for an AI Act, in ECB, Continuity and change – how the challenges of today prepare the ground for tomorrow' (n 5) 372 et seq.; Sandra Mayson, 'Bias In, Bias Out' (2019) The Yale Law Journal Vol. 128 2218, 2251: "The premise of prediction is that, absent intervention, history will repeat itself".

9 L Blattner and S Nelson, 'How Costly is Noise? Data and Disparities in Consumer Credit' (2021) 1 (12), "model bias" <https://www.researchgate.net/publication/351656623_How_Costly_is_Noise_Data_and_Disparities_in_Consumer_Credit> accessed 24 June 2025.

10 S Barocas and A Selbst, 'Big Data's Disparate Impact' (2016), California Law Review, Vol. 104 671, 689; Talia Gillis, 'The Input Fallacy' (2022), Minnesota Law Review, Vol. 106 1175; Jennifer Graham, Risk of discrimination in AI systems, Evaluating the effectiveness of current legal safeguards in tackling algorithmic discrimination in Alison Lui, Nicholas Ryder (eds), *FinTech, Artificial Intelligence and the Law* (2021), 211, 211; Katja Langenbucher, 'Responsible A.I. credit scoring – a legal framework' (2020), European Business Law Review, Vol. 31 527; Dan L Burk,: Algorithmic Legal Metrics (2021), Notre Dame Law Review, Vol. 96 1147, 1163; Antje von Ungern-Sternberg, 'Diskriminierungsschutz bei algorithmenbasierten Entscheidungen' in Anna Katharina Mangold and Mehrdad Payandeh, *Handbuch Antidiskriminierungsrecht* (Mohr Siebeck 2022) § 28, note 15 et seq.

true if the observed risk-variable is less informative for some applicants if compared with others.[11]

Algorithmic biases of that type matter even more when combined with concerns about data quality, incorrect labelling,[12] or omitted variables. Data can vary in its reliability across a population, for example if there is less data available for specific groups such as recent immigrants.[13] Additionally, the use of certain alternative data, for instance stemming from social networks, increases the risk of inaccuracies. This concerns individual loan applicants if the data used to evaluate them is inaccurate. It also impacts the entire AI model that learns from (partially) inaccurate training data. The more inaccuracies are hidden in big datasets, the more the AI model is shaped by a world that does not even adequately reflect yesterday's world, much less today's.

In what follows, I briefly summarize the US and EU legal framework for anti-discrimination (below II). I move on to highlight core challenges this framework faces when dealing with redundant encoding (below III.). The paper closes with a comment on Article 6 of the new EU Directive on Credit agreements for Consumers (below IV).

B. The Legal Framework

The observation that credit scoring sometimes produces unfair results is neither a novel concern nor a worry that is specific to AI-based underwriting. Traditional scoring models with their limited number of input variables necessarily provide a crude picture of an individual applicant.[14] Many are shaped by path-dependent historical choices of what is deemed relevant for a score. Lenders enjoy discretion to strike a balance between predictive accuracy, costs for model and data, and market expansion.[15] Furthermore, financial stability concerns provide a reason to err on the side

11 European Data Protection Board/European Data Protection Supervisor (EDPB/EDPS) (2021): Joint Opinion 5/2021; Gillis (n 11) 1178; Burk (n 11) 1164.

12 Von Ungern-Sternberg (n 11) § 28 note 16 (sampling bias), note 17 (labelling bias), note 18 (feature selection bias).

13 Mayson (n 9).

14 In the EU, not all Member States have credit reporting and credit scoring agencies similar to the US. While Germany and the UK do, France does not and has lenders score applicants in-house.

15 Burrell and Fourcade (n 3) 217 et seq.

of caution, rather than hand out a loan to an applicant with a high credit default risk.

I. The US legal framework

In the US, anti-discrimination law has been navigating this space since the late 1960s. Discriminatory lending is addressed by the Equal Credit Opportunity Act (ECOA) and the Fair Housing Act (FHA). Both, the ECOA and the FHA prohibit decisions that are – loosely speaking – caused or motivated by a protected characteristic such as race, gender, age, or similar protected attributes. The FHA prohibits discrimination in the context of mortgages, the ECOA concerns access to credit more generally. The Trump Administration's Executive Order on "Restoring Equality of Opportunity and Meritocracy" of April 23, 205 has stipulated that agencies roll back disparate impact doctrine for both scenarios.[16]

1. Disparate Treatment

Disparate treatment involves a lender who denies credit "because of" an applicant's protected characteristic. Key questions have to do with discriminatory intent, with (conscious or subconscious) motives, and with burden of proof. In the US, many of the finer doctrinal details of anti-discrimination law have not been developed for credit underwriting, but in Title VII cases, addressing employment discrimination.

In the context of this paper, it is of particular interest to understand how courts have established discriminatory motives, which often rest on circumstantial evidence. In *McDonnell Douglas*, a Title VII case[17] that was partly overruled by *Ames v. Ohio Dept. of Youth Services*,[18] the US Supreme Court established a three-step strategy for individual inferential proof.

First, a plaintiff bears the initial burden of establishing a *prima facie* case by producing enough evidence to support an inference of discriminatory motive.[19] He might, for instance, show that he is a member of a protected group, was qualified for a position, was rejected by the potential employer,

16 See below B.I.2.

17 *McDonnell Douglas Corp. v. Green*, 411 U.S. 792 (1973).

18 *Ames v. Ohio Dept. Of Youth Services*, 605 U.S. ___ (2025).

19 *McDonnell Douglas Corp. v. Green*, 411 U.S. 792 (1973) 802.

and the position remained open, suggesting discriminatory motives. In *Ames*, the Court clarified that members of a majority group cannot be asked to satisfy a heightened evidentiary standard than members of a minority group.[20] Additionally, Justice Thomas, concurring, invited the Court to, in the future, consider "whether the *McDonnell Douglas* framework is an appropriate tool to evaluate Titel VII claims at summary judgment".[21]

Second, if the plaintiff succeeds, the burden shifts to the defendant to articulate a legitimate, nondiscriminatory reason.[22] She does not have to prove that the reason she advances did in fact drive her decision. Instead, it is only a burden of production.

Third, the plaintiff must have a fair opportunity to show that the reasons the defendant has proffered are pretextual.[23] In *Ames*, Justice Thomas, concurring, more generally criticized the criteria set forth in *McDonnell Douglas*, submitting that they demand more from the plaintiff than the text of Title VII.[24] *McDonnell Douglas* requires a plaintiff to prove that the justificatory reasons the defendant offered were but a pretext. By contrast under Title VII it suffices to prove that a protected characteristic as a motivating factor, even though other factors also motivated the practice.[25]

Another core aspect of how US law approaches burden of proof concerns situations where it is not in doubt that a discriminatory element contributed to the decision, but the defendant disputes causation. In *Manhart*, the Supreme Court held that an employer's policy of requiring women to make larger pension fund contributions than men violated Title VII. There was no doubt that an unlawful factor was at play, given that the policy

---

20 *Ames v. Ohio Dept. Of Youth Services*, 605 U.S.___ (2025) 9.

21 *McDonnell Douglas Corp. v. Green*, 411 U.S. 792 (1973), Justice Thomas, concurring 7.

22 *McDonnell Douglas Corp. v. Green*, 411 U.S. 792 (1973) 802; For a similar strategy in Germany see Ute Sacksofsky, 'Was heißt: Ungleichbehandlung „wegen"?' (Mohr Siebeck 2017) Simon Kempny and Philipp Reimer (eds), Gleichheitssatzdogmatik heute 63, 73.

23 *McDonnell Douglas Corp. v. Green*, 411 U.S. 792 (1973) 804.

24 *Ames v. Ohio Dept. Of Youth Services*, 605 U.S.___ (2025), Justice Thomas 11.

25 If the plaintiff fails to show individual inferential proof, the Court has in Title VII cases accepted a showing of intentional discrimination through circumstantial evidence (group or systemic inferential proof). Plaintiffs use statistics to prove a "pattern and practice" revealing that their group is underrepresented. "Such imbalance", the Court held in *International Brotherhood of Teamsters v. United States*, 431 U.S. 324, 339 (1977), "is often a telltale sign of purposeful discrimination". Defendants may bring in different statistics or put forward a legitimate non-discriminatory explanation for the underrepresentation of the plaintiff's group.

specifically targeted women. Still, the employer had argued that he had no *discriminatory* intent and did not treat women differently *because of* their sex. Rather, he suggested, actuarial logic dictated a "life-expectancy adjustment".[26] It is a claim any economist would have embraced, pointing to the logic of statistical discrimination. Arguably, in a credit underwriting context, a similar logic applies. In the same way as sex influences life expectancy, hence, is relevant for pension contributions, sex will often influence creditworthiness. Still, in *Manhart*, the US Supreme Court did not follow the defendant's statistical defense. Instead, it stressed that the impermissible attribute (sex) was a but-for factor for the employer's decision. Removing the attribute "female", so the Court held, would have led to a different, non-discriminatory outcome. In a similar case, the European Court of Justice also rejected the claim of insurance companies that had argued statistics and actuarial logic required higher fees for women.[27]

2. Disparate Impact

The important challenges that a disparate treatment plaintiff faces when providing discriminatory evidence have encouraged the development of a second line of anti-discrimination doctrine. This doctrine focuses on facially neutral variables or practices. If a neutral attribute or practice consistently triggers less favorable treatment of protected communities, this makes it "suspicious", as it were. Possibly, one line of argument goes, a decision-maker has found an (only seemingly) neutral attribute or practice to hide his true discriminatory motivations. In the words of the US Supreme Court, disparate impact doctrine works as "an evidentiary tool used to identify genuine, intentional discrimination - to 'smoke out,' as it were, disparate treatment".[28]

---

26 *City of Los Angeles v. Manhart*, 435 U.S. 702 (1978); the ECJ followed the same logic Case C-54/07 *Feryn* [2008] ECJ; Sacksofsky (n 23) 73.

27 Case C- 236/09 *Association Belge des Consommateurs Test-Achats and others* [2011] ECJ.

28 *Ricci v. DeStefano*, 557 U.S. 557 (2009); discussed at Gillis (n 11) 1200; overview at Langenbucher, 'Responsible A.I. credit scoring – a legal framework' (n 11) 554; on EU law's trajectory from a formal to a more substantive approach of indirect discrimination doctrine see R Rebhahn and C Kietaibl, 'Mittelbare Diskriminierung und Kausalität, Recht der Internationalen Wirtschaft' (2010) Rechtswissenschaft: Zeitschrift für rechtswissenschaftliche Forschung 373, 384 et seq.; further Ute Sacksofsky, 'Unmittelbare und mittelbare Diskriminierung' in Anna Katharina Mangold

Disparate impact doctrine has not stopped there. In many cases, the doctrine has been understood as going beyond a mechanism that only serves to uncover hidden disparate treatment. Especially when faced with the government discriminating against a private citizen, most courts and scholars have so far followed some version of a "substantive" approach.

Those who follow a substantive approach understand disparate impact doctrine not as a tool to unearth covert motives, hidden behind a facially neutral attribute. Instead, they investigate whether available legislation – such as the FHA – prohibits discriminatory consequences, irrespective of motives.[29] If this is the case, the fact that the net result of a defendant's decisions consistently plays out worse for a minority group if compared to the majority *prima facie* can trigger a prohibition, even if the defendant had no discriminatory intent or motive. A defendant must then put forward a business defense and show that there was no less discriminatory strategy available.

The Executive Order of April 23, 2025 represents a move away from disparate impact doctrine. Its section 1 stresses that equality under the US Constitution refers to "equality of opportunity, not equal outcomes". Section 4 requests agencies to deprioritize enforcement based on disparate impact liability. Section 6 requests the Attorney General, the Secretary of Housing and Urban Development, the Director of the Consumer Financial Protection Bureau, the Chair of the Federal Trade Commission and other relevant agency heads to "evaluate all pending proceedings that rely on theories of disparate impact liability" as far as the Equal Credit Opportunity Act and the Fair Housing Act are concerned.

---

and Mehrdad Payandeh (eds), *Handbuch Antidiskriminierungsrecht* (Mohr Siebeck 2022), § 14 note 105; von Ungern-Sternberg (n 10) § 28 note 91; for EU law see A Mangold and M Payandeh, 'Antidiskriminierungsrecht – Konturen eines Rechtsgebiets' in Anna Katharina Mangold and Mehrdad Payandeh (eds.), *Handbuch Antidiskriminierungsrecht* (Mohr Siebeck 2022), § 1 note 109, listing the prohibition to circumvent anti-discrimination law as well as shifting the burden of proof.

29 *Griggs v. Duke Power Co.*, 401 US 424 (1971) 432; *Smith v. City of Jackson*, 544 U.S. 228 (2005) 236; *Texas Department of Housing and Community Affairs v. Inclusive Communities Project Inc.* 135 S. Ct. 2507 (2015) 2522; discussed at Gillis (n 10); see further Mayson (n 9); Cass R Sunstein,: Algorithms, Correcting Biases (2019) Social Research: An International Quarterly, Vol. 86 499; Rebhahn and Kietaibl (n 28) 389.

3. Discriminatory credit underwriting

While there is US Supreme Court guidance as to disparate impact doctrine under the FHA, [30] it has been unclear whether disparate impact doctrine extends to access to retail credit. In *Inclusive Communities* the Court held that "disparate impact claims are cognizable under the Fair Housing Act (...)", the reasoning stressing that its "text refers to the consequences of the actions". The ECOA, by contrast, lacks a results-oriented language of this type. While the FDIC and the Fed have in the past seemed generally open to considering disparate impact in their supervisory activities, both agencies have stressed that "the fact that a policy or practice creates a disparity on a prohibited basis is not alone a proof of a violation." They require an agency that finds a lender's practice to have a disparate impact to determine whether it is justified by a manifest business necessity and whether there was an alternative practice serving the same purpose with less discriminatory results. [31] It is an open question whether the Fed and the FDIC will change course after the Executive Order of April 23, 2025. The same goes for courts.[32]

For the plaintiff, disparate impact cases often turn on the relevant standard of proof. A disparate impact case has so far required a *prima facie* showing of an outcome that is disproportionate for a protected group. The Executive Order of April 23, 2025 is critical of this practice, understanding it as an "insurmountable presumption of unlawful discrimination".

For an outcome to be disparate, a relevant set of persons must be identified and the outcome for these persons must be compared to the rest of the relevant sample.[33] Defendants can, among other defenses, deny that there was a disproportionate outcome by questioning group membership.

---

30 *Texas Department of Housing and Community Affairs v. Inclusive Communities Project, Inc.*, 135 S. Ct. 2507 (2015) 2519.

31 FDIC(Federal Deposit Insurance Corporation), 'Consumer Compliance Examination Manual' – December 2024 <https://www.fdic.gov/resources/supervision-and-examinations/consumer-compliance-examination-manual/documents/4/iv-1-1.pdf> accessed 24 June 2025; Federal Fair Lending Regulations and Statutes Overview <https://www.federalreserve.gov/boarddocs/supmanual/cch/fair_lend_over.pdf> accessed 24 June 2025.

32 *Ramirez v. Greenpoint Mortgage Funding, Inc.*, 633 E. Supp. 2d 922 (2008) 926 et seq.; Gillis (n 11) 1198.

33 See Pauline Kim, 'AI and Inequality' (2021) Washington University in St. Louis Legal Studies Research Paper No. 21-09-03 on difficulties in practice to collect data about outcomes across the applicant pool.

Assume, for example, that a lender's practice results in denying loans to 70% of female and 20% of male applicants. Given that (roughly) 50 % of the population are female, this looks like a disproportionate outcome across the sexes. However, the lender might claim that in the credit underwriting context, group membership cannot be limited to sex alone. Instead, he might suggest that only similarly situated sets of applicants ought to be compared.[34] To decide which set is similarly situated to another set, he could propose to look at variables such as net worth, income, or credit history, all of which influence credit default risk. The effect might not be disproportionate if, for similarly situated sets of loan applicants, no sex discrimination shows. It is obvious that many cases will turn on building and comparing such sets of loan applicants. The narrower the group that serves as benchmark for a disparate impact comparison, the more difficult for a plaintiff to establish a case.

If private parties are litigating, the move towards substantive anti-discrimination theories is considerably less pronounced than if the government is involved. Most start from the ground rule that private parties enjoy free contracting choices. Against this background, disparate impact on protected groups comes across as an unwelcome, but usually legal, side effect. Various business necessity defenses are available to justify the practice despite the disproportionate output.[35] The most natural defense for a lender is that he is required to carefully assess credit default risk. Statistical evaluation and scoring procedures have developed as a sensible and legitimate tool over the last century. AI-based scoring will provide another tool. The burden then shifts back to the plaintiff to show that there was a less discriminatory way to achieve that same goal.

II. The EU framework

EU law has largely followed similar doctrinal patterns as the US. However, courts have interpreted anti-discrimination rules more broadly in two ways. Firstly, a rule that prohibits direct discrimination has so far been read as prohibiting indirect discrimination as well. Secondly, the courts have

34 Langenbucher, 'Consumer Credit in the Age of AI – Beyond Anti Discrimination law' (n 1) 28.

35 Noting that there is little guidance on this question under US law: Gillis (n 11) 1249; critical on the vagueness of the (English) concept Sacksofsky (n 30) § 14 note 45, 129 et seq.

often been open to applying anti-discrimination rules not only between government and citizen, but also between private citizens.

Art. 51 para. 1 s. 1, 21 of the Charter of Fundamental Rights protect against discriminatory treatment based on 15 enumerated attributes or characteristics. While the text of the Charter is silent as to bringing it to bear on private law relations between citizens, the ECJ has in many situations interpreted it along those lines.[36] In the area of employment, Art. 157 TFEU's guarantee of equal pay between the sexes has since the 1970s been understood to prohibit discrimination between private parties.[37]

Various EU directives address specific relationships between private citizens. Some focus on employment,[38] two directives concern access to publicly available goods or services.[39] All of these explicitly cover both, direct and indirect discrimination. In these directives, indirect discrimination is understood as a situation "where an apparently neutral provision, criterion or practice would put persons "who share a protected characteristic" at a particular disadvantage compared with other persons, unless that provision, criterion or practice is objectively justified by a legitimate aim and the means of achieving that aim are appropriate and necessary".[40]

These directives leave details of private enforcement and litigation to Member States' national law, as long as Member State law respects *effet*

---

36 Overview at Andrea Edenharter, 'Wie argumentieren EuGH und BVerfG in Grundrechtsfragen?' (2022), EuR 2022 302; Oliver Mörsdorf, 'Europäisierung des Privatrechts durch die Hintertür? Einige Gedanken zum Einfluss der Grundrechte-Charta auf das nationale Privatrecht in der jüngeren Rechtsprechung des EuGH' (2019) JZ Juristenzeitung Vol. 74 Issue 22 1066.

37 Case C - 149/77 *Defrenne / Sabena* [1978] 130 ECJ; Case C-13/94 - *P / S and Cornwall County Council* [1996] 170 ECJ; Case C-144/04 - *Mangold* [2005] 709 ECJ; Case C-555/07 - *Kücükdeveci* [2010] 21 ECJ; Case C-414/16 - *Egenberger* [2018] 257 ECJ; Case C-684/16 - *Max-Planck-Gesellschaft zur Förderung der Wissenschaften* [2018] 874 ECJ; Case C-193/17 - *Cresco Investigation* [2019] 43 ECJ; Brief overview at P Donath and D Schrader, 'Arbeitsrecht' in Katja Langenbucher (ed), *Europäisches Privat- und Wirtschaftsrecht* (Nomos 2022), § 7 note 35.

38 Directive 2000/78/EC establishing a general framework for equal treatment and occupation; Directive 2006/54/EC on the implementation of the principle of equal opportunities and equal treatment of men and women in matters of employment and occupation (recast).

39 Directive 2000/43/EC implementing the principle of equal treatment between persons irrespective of racial or ethnic origin; Directive 2004/113/EC implementing the principle of equal treatment between men and women in the access to and supply of goods and services.

40 See for instance Art. 2 para. 2 lit. b Directive 2000/43/EC implementing the principle of equal treatment between persons irrespective of racial or ethnic origin.

utile. One example of *effet utile* reigning in on Member State's discretion concerns burden of proof. The European Court of Justice (ECJ) has, in the context of employment discrimination, required Member States to adjust their rules on burden of proof to guarantee a minimum standard of enforceability.[41] Similarly to US law, the plaintiff must make a *prima facie* showing of facts, "from which it may be presumed that there has been direct or indirect discrimination". If he succeeds, burden of proof shifts to the defendant "to prove that there has been no breach of the principle of equal treatment".[42] A classic argument for the defense, like under US law, concerns group membership. The defendant may show that the plaintiff is not similarly situated to the set of persons that are treated more favorably.[43]

Prior to October 2023, there was no explicit directive addressing discriminatory credit underwriting under EU law, leaving the issue to Member State law. While several directives have dealt with instances of discrimination between private citizens, credit underwriting fell outside of their scope. Two directives had to do with access to publicly available goods or services.[44] However, the relevance of personal attributes in a credit underwriting context excluded an understanding of loan contracts as a publicly available good.[45]

Art. 6 of Directive 2023/2225 on Credit Agreements for Consumers changes this.[46] The rule protects consumers who are legally resident in

41 See Case C-109/88 - *Handels- og Kontorfunktionærernes Forbund i Danmark / Dansk Arbejdsgiverforening, agissant pour Danfoss* [1989] 383.

42 Art. 8 EU Directive 2000/43; similar: Art. 9 EU Directive 2004/113. In the context of employment and occupation, Art. 10 EU Directive 2000/78/EC of 27 November 2000 establishing a general framework for equal treatment in employment and occupation provides a similar rule. Following up (but only in this context), Art. 19 EU Directive 2006/54 of 5 July 2006 on the implementation of the principle of equal opportunities and equal treatment of men and women in matters of employment and occupation lays down more granular rules to be transposed by the Member States.

43 Case T-473/12 - Aer Lingus v Commission [2015] 473 ECJ; Case C-356/09 - Kleist [2010] 703; Case C-366/99 - Griesmar [2001] 648 ECJ discussing "comparable situations".

44 Directive 2000/43/EC implementing the principle of equal treatment between persons irrespective of racial or ethnic origin; Directive 2004/113/EC implementing the principle of equal treatment between men and women in the access to and supply of goods and services.

45 For examples see F Rödl and A Leidinger, 'Diskriminierungsschutz im Zivilrechtsverkehr' in Anna Katharina Mangold and Mehrdad Payandeh (eds.), *Handbuch Antidiskriminierungsrecht* (Mohr Siebeck 2022), § 22 note 42 et seq.

46 Available at <https://eur-lex.europa.eu/legal-content/EN/TXT/PDF/?uri=OJ:L_202302225> accessed 24 June 2025.

the EU against discrimination "on ground of their nationality or place of residence or any other ground as referred to in Article 21 of the Charter of Fundamental Rights of the European Union". The drafting of the new Directive, if compared to other anti-discrimination directives, includes a surprising feature. All EU anti-discrimination directives have so far explicitly defined and prohibited both, direct and indirect discrimination. By contrast, Directive 2023/2225 follows a strategy that is more common in human rights texts such as Art. 21 of the Charter. It mentions protected attributes and prohibits discrimination "on grounds of" these.[47] Departing from earlier directives, Directive 2023/2225 neither defines direct and indirect discrimination, nor explicitly proscribes the latter.[48]

C. The Shortcomings of Received Doctrine

I. The Metaphor of Building Blocks

So far, we have seen that anti-discrimination law is triggered by input to a decision-making process, namely attributes or characteristics of a person. [49] I refer to these as "building blocks" of a decision. There are outright prohibited building blocks, and facially neutral ones. Direct discrimination/disparate treatment prohibits the use of certain building blocks, for instance race or sex, even if they are of direct empirical relevance. By contrast, facially neutral building blocks can be lawfully used unless they trigger indirect discrimination/disparate impact. A paradigm case is the 1970s US Supreme Court decision in *Griggs*. It illustrates how a specific practice caused disparate impact across racial groups. An employer had used the score in an intelligence test as decisive for the position as a manual laborer. This practice statistically discriminated against minority

47 See Sacksofsky (n 28) § 14 note 5 distinguishing this EU secondary law strategy (explicit mentioning of indirect discrimination) from human rights texts which list protected categories and proscribe discrimination "on grounds of" these categories. The US ECOA (albeit statutory law, not a human rights text) falls in that second category.

48 See below D.I.

49 On input see M Berman and G Krishnamurthi, 'Bostock was Bogus: Textualism, Pluralism, and Title VII' (2021) Notre Dame Law Review Vol. 97 67, 98; Andrew Koppelman,: 'Bostock and Textualism: A Response to Berman and Krishnamurthi' (2022) Notre Dame Law Review Reflection Vol. 98 89, 98 (the latter criticizing the former, but in agreement about this basic point).

employees, however there was no evidence of discriminatory intent on the side of the defendant.[50] In *Griggs*, Justice Burger stressed that "the Act does not command that any person be hired simply because he was formerly the subject of discrimination, or because he is a member of a minority group". Hence, bringing in statistics to show a significant underrepresentation of Black employees, without identifying the intelligence test used, would not have been a successful strategy. However, the Justice continued, "the Act proscribes not only overt discrimination, but also practices that are fair in form, but discriminatory in operation."[51] To establish this, the plaintiff successfully made two showings: the disparate outcome across black and non-black job applicants and the identification of the intelligence test as one necessary building block of the employer's decision.

II. Building blocks and redundant encoding

This paper puts a spotlight on the role of "building blocks" such as the IQ test in *Griggs*. Metaphorically speaking, traditional doctrine requires one building block with discriminatory potential to be involved in the decision. The law's role is, first, to carefully examine such building blocks and to determine whether the decision would have looked differently if the unlawful building block was removed: Would the same employees have been hired if the IQ test was not run? A second legal requirement, the availability of justificatory defenses for using the relevant building block, is beyond the scope of this paper.

With improving technology, the core notion of anti-discrimination law to require a specific building block faces a novel challenge.[52] Big data furnishes a universe of different data points. Machine learning algorithms unearth innumerable correlations between those data points. Depending on the AI model used, the lender may be unable to identify salient data points, their weight, or core correlations. For the law this translates into a tricky problem: In many cases, the building block, such as the IQ test, will influence the outcome, but be unknown to the decision-maker. The same

50 Today, following a Title VII amendment of 1991, the law explicitly prohibits employment tests that are not a reasonable measure of job performance.

51 *Griggs v. Duke Power Co.*, 401 US 424 (1971), p. 430 et seq.

52 A Fuster et al., 'Predictably Unequal? The Effects of Machine Learning on Credit Markets' (2022) Journal of Finance Vol. 77 5, 8; along similar lines: Gillis (n 11).

goes for the plaintiff. He can show a statistically disparate outcome, but not the individual building blocks that might have triggered it.

Sometimes, work-arounds for the problem exist. The first is using an explainable AI (or simple regression models)[53] in combination with a limited number of input data points to train the model. However, limiting input data for training purposes seriously compromises on predictive accuracy, foregoing the added predictive force that alternative data offers.[54]

A second work-around might be offered by rules such as Art. 18 para. 3 EU Consumer Credit Directive. The rule requires lenders to use "relevant" information which is "necessary and proportionate to the nature, duration, value and risks of the credit for the consumer" and excluding protected categories of data. The Directive lists evidence on income, financial assets and liabilities, or information on other financial commitments as examples.[55] In that way, the Directive excludes traditionally offensive building blocks like the IQ test in *Griggs*. However, it is unclear whether this also provides a satisfying solution if the applicant delivers "relevant", small data only, but the AI is trained on big, alternative data. Due to redundant encoding, sophisticated models will sort applicants based on learned patterns, even if individual applicants only deliver limited data points.

A third work-around are explainable AI methods that work with counterfactuals such as DiCE.[56] The lender might run the model multiple times, and at each step change one data point, for instance sex, or race, or religious belief of the applicant. If changing one data point triggers a different outcome, the lender will assume that the removed building block has a meaningful impact on the decision. Note, however, that this strategy only

53 The German credit scoring company SCHUFA has decided to use such regression models, not more sophisticated AI models.

54 Additionally, the explanation the AI delivers will not necessarily help. Especially if prohibited characteristics, such as race or sex, are not included in the AI's training data, its explanation will, at best, produce a first step towards evaluating individual loan decisions. Take, for instance, an explainable AI that tells us core data points were first name and height. This explanation might raise the suspicion that (indirect) sex discrimination is going on. However, to confidently say so, we would need to establish a necessary correlation between sex and those variables.

55 For more detail see Annex 2 of EBA Guidelines on loan origination and monitoring, p. 71 et seq.

56 On DiCE and other methods of explainable AI see: Katja Langenbucher, 'Explainable AI as a Component of Building Trust The Case of Regulating Creditscoring' in S Bücker et al. (eds), *Digital Governance* (2025) (forthcoming).

works smoothly if the data points do not correlate, hence, that there is no redundant encoding involved.

Against this background, redundant encoding poses a fundamental challenge to received anti-discrimination doctrine. The model often learns the information that is embodied either in the protected characteristic or in the facially neutral attribute from other data points. Traditionally, a plaintiff litigates to have the discriminator remove the building block from his decision-making practice. In *Griggs*, this meant: not running the IQ test. In the case of algorithmic scoring and creditworthiness evaluation, removing one such building block is mostly unhelpful. If the plaintiff succeeds with his case, the lender deletes one building block from the training data (or from the applicant's digital profile). This could be, for instance, the building block "first name". The outcome will remain unchanged if a pattern, which the AI has detected, still emerges, now on the basis of other data points.

III. Two hypothetical Lenders to Illustrate the Challenges

To illustrate the challenge that anti-discrimination doctrine faces, I introduce two hypothetical lenders.[57] The first hypothetical lender reasons as follows: "The training data for my AI model includes data points of all kinds, including protected attributes. I include these data points because, statistically, sex is an important indicator when calculating credit risk. Women have a higher default risk. However, this is just one of the many observable variables I use. Of course, I do not want to discriminate against anyone, and it is not the only data point I use!"

The second hypothetical lender claims: "I understand that denying credit because of a protected characteristic is impermissible. I use a data filtering method that makes sure that the AI is not trained with data on sex, race, religion, or any other protected characteristic. The model still works fine."[58]

57 See Langenbucher, 'AI credit scoring and evaluation of creditworthiness – a test case for the EU proposal for an AI Act, in ECB, Continuity and change – how the challenges of today prepare the ground for tomorrow' (n 5) 16 et seq.

58 See for this strategy in Fintech lending: Di Maggio and Ratnadiwakara (n 6) 4; see further: On this argument K Langenbucher and P Corcoran, 'Responsible AI Credit Scoring – A Lesson from Upstart.com' in Emilios Avgouleas and Heikki Marjosola (eds), *Digital Finance in Europe: Law, Regulation, and Governance* (DeGruyter 2022) 143.

1. Causation, But-For Standard, and Proof

The first hypothetical lender submits that sex was but one of the many data points his model was trained on. His underwriting decision on female applicants, so he suggests, includes their sex, but only as one among various other factors. At first glance, this is not a valid defense. Neither US nor EU law require the protected characteristic to be the *sole* building block towards the decision.

As explained above, under US law relevant doctrine has revolved around employment discrimination under Title VII. In *Price Waterhouse v. Hopkins*, the court rejected the argument that a discrimination case requires the contested decision to be triggered *only* by a protected characteristic such as sex. It pointed to the text of the statute that did not read "solely because of".[59] Instead, established practice requires plaintiffs to prove that the protected attribute was one out of various but-for factors that caused the decision.[60] Events can have multiple but-for causes of this type. To win their case, plaintiffs must show that removing the protected attribute would have changed the outcome.[61]

If US courts adopted that standard for the ECOA and the FHA, a lender could not escape liability if a plaintiff can show that a protected attribute was one but-for cause. Arguably, the wording of the ECOA and the FHA support this line of reasoning. Section 2000e-2(a)(1) of Title VII stipulates that it is unlawful to discriminate "because of" a protected attribute. In *Bostock*, the Court has invoked this terminology to apply what it understands as the but-for standard of causation. Similarly, the FHA speaks of discrimination "because of" protected characteristics. The ECOA makes it unlawful to discriminate "on the basis of" certain protected attributes. [62] None of these statutes require that the outcome was reached "solely" because of the protected attribute, [63] suggesting that both statutes can be read along the

59 *Price Waterhouse v. Hopkins*, 490 U.S. 228 (1989).

60 Berman and Krishnamurthi (n 51) 100 et seq.; Benjamin Eidelson, 'Dimensional Disparate Treatment' (2022) Southern California Law Review Vol. 95 785, 797 et seq.; on a narrower reading of the term "because of" as "by reason of"; see R Dembroff and I Kohler-Hausmann, 'Supreme Confusion About Causality at the Supreme Court, City University of New York' (2022) Law Review Vol. 25, 74.

61 *Bostock v. Clayton County*, 590 U.S. (2020) 6; Dembroff and Kohler-Hausmann (n 62) 58.

62 EU law's close analogue reads: "on grounds of".

63 15 USC Chapter 41 § 1691; 42 USC § 3604.

same lines as Title VII. EU law reaches the same result via its *conditio sine qua non* test:[64] Under Art. 6 of the 2023 Directive, discrimination is prohibited "on ground of" a protected attribute, not "solely on grounds of".[65]

2. The challenge of producing a counterfactual

Following these standards, a hypothetical female plaintiff must show that the first hypothetical lender would have reached a different outcome if the AI had not had access to her sex. In practice, this will be a *probatia diabolica*.[66] The plaintiff would have to run the lender's model (to which he rarely has access) twice: First, she needs to repeat the procedure that the lender followed. Second, she needs to come up with a suitable counterfactual. Maybe there is a way to omit her sex in her application for credit. She could, for instance, change it to male but leave everything else intact. For her case to succeed, the counterfactual would need to look different. However, the more data points the AI model has been trained on, the less likely this is. Omitting her sex entirely or changing it to male, leaves all other data points of her digital footprint untouched. The plaintiff still has a female first name, her height, taste in music or preferred shopping place, the college she attended, or her medical bills might "give her away" to the AI.

The Fintech lender Upstart provides an illustration. To decide on a loan application, it uses bundles of data points, such as education, employment history and more. Upstart only processes variables in concert, not in isolation.[67] Working with the services offered by Upstart, a NGO ran a form of mystery shopping exercise. Applicants were construed as identical except for the college they had attended. Holding all other inputs constant, the authors of the study found a discriminatory result. A hypothetical applicant who attended Howard University, a historically black college, paid higher origination fees and higher interest rates over the life of their loans than

64 Rebhahn and Kietaibl (n 30) 378.
65 Rödl and Leidinger (n 47) § 22 note 52; Sacksofsky (n 30), § 14 note 43 et seq.
66 von Ungern-Sternberg (n 11) § 28 note 27.
67 Consumer Financial Protection Bureau (CFPB), Consumer Response Annual Report (2017), 4.

an applicant who was construed as having attended New York University.[68] Similar results were observed for New Mexico State University, a Hispanic Serving Institution.[69] There is a variety of hypotheses to explain these empirical results. We might be looking at taste-based discrimination of the lender, persistent despite its economic inefficiency. Alternatively, lenders might engage in strategic pricing, charging higher interest rates for protected communities because of their higher willingness to sign above-market.[70] Yet alternatively, historic data might have trained the model to discount applicants from certain colleges.

Either way, the problem with the mystery shopping exercise's methodology is that Upstart uses a bundle of data points that redundantly encode the same information. Giving a comprehensive answer that a plaintiff could have used to make a court case would have required the NGO to run another counterfactual. It would have had to eliminate the variable "college attended" entirely and retrain the model. If Upstart uses a small set of training data only, this might have been the core variable that determined the result. By contrast, the broader Upstart's trainingdata base, the higher the probability that the model would have arrived at the same conclusion without including the college the applicant attended. The AI would have redundantly encoded the same information in other data points – for instance first name, geographical location during term time, friends on social media or taste in music.

3. The challenge of gaining access to the AI

The example has so far assumed that the plaintiff can get access to the lender's AI. In practice, this is not necessarily the case. US, but not EU law allows for pretrial discovery. Even if EU courts are open to changing this, lenders will claim a business defense to keep their AI secret. [71]

68 Student Borrower Protection Center, 'Educational Redlining' (2020), methodology described at 16.

69 Student Borrower Protection Center (n 68), findings described at 17 et seq.

70 Along those lines, R Bartlett et al., 'Consumer-Lending Discrimination in the FinTech Era' (2022) Journal of Financial Economics Vol. 143 30; Gills (n 11), 1188, 1252 et seq.; Hurlin et al., 'The Fairness of Credit Scoring Models' (2021)., HEC Paris Research Paper No. FIN-2021-1411.

71 Note, however, that in a different context, the ECJ did not accept that argument. An employer had used a non-transparent bonus payment system that yielded disparate outcome across men and women. The ECJ required the employer to show that the

Even if courts adjust the plaintiff's burden of proof, a further problem emerges. The lender himself might not have all the relevant data. A recent ECJ case has highlighted the somewhat paradoxical situation of the loan applicant, if a scoring agency is involved.[72] A German loan applicant was denied a loan by a lender, due to a low credit score. Turning to the scoring company to explain the score was not an option: Prior to that ECJ decision, courts and scholars had read the EU GDPR as excluding a private right to be informed on details of a scoring model against the scoring agency. For the applicant, it would not have been helpful to ask the lender to furnish this information either: The lender did not have access to the scoring agency's model. The ECJ remedied the situation, allowing for a private right of action against the scoring agency, at least if the score is of "paramount importance" for a decision on credit. However, even if courts adjusted the burden of proof and are ready to support plaintiffs in access to information regarding lender, credit reporting and scoring agency, redundant encoding still poses a problem. If plaintiffs must show that removing one protected attribute, for instance "sex", triggers a different outcome, they will fail if various data points encode sex.

4. Hard Cases

The second hypothetical lender mentioned above[73] claims to escape liability because the training data for his model does not include any data points that qualify as protected characteristics. It is impossible, so he submits, that he discriminated "on the basis of sex", because he filtered the data his model is trained on. No protected characteristics are used as training data

system was not discriminating against women, rejecting the employer's argument that this would make the bonus system overly transparent. Case C-109/88 - *Handels- og Kontorfunktionærernes Forbund i Danmark / Dansk Arbejdsgiverforening, agissant pour Danfoss* [1989] 383 ECJ, note 15; similar decisions concern Art. 157 AEUV: Case C-170/84 - *Bilka / Weber von Hartz* [1986] 204 ECJ, note 31; Case C-228/89 - *Farfalla Flemming v Hauptzollamt München-West* [1990] 265 ECJ, note 16; Case C-184/89 - *Nimz / Freie und Hansestadt Hamburg* [1991] 50 ECJ, note 15; see Olaf Muthorst, 'Beweisrecht' in Anna Katharina Mangold and Mehrdad Payandeh (eds.), *Handbuch Antidiskriminierungsrecht* (Mohr Siebeck 2022), § 19, notes 30 et seq.

72 Case C-634/21 - *SCHUFA Holding (Scoring)* [2023] 957 ECJ; Katja Langenbucher, 'Die Schufa vor dem EuGH' (2024) BKR-Zeitschrift für Banken-und Kapitalmarktrecht 66; Katja Langenbucher, 'Wirschaft – Medien – Digitalisierung' in E Mand et al. (eds), *Festschrift für Georgios Gounalakis* (Nomos 2025), 715.

73 See C.III.

– like Art. 18 of the 2023 EU Consumer Credit Directive suggests. Faced with cases such as these, courts and scholars in the EU and in the US have so far followed the same ground rules. Either, a protected variable, such as sex, appears as one building block of the decision or else the plaintiff must show a case of disparate impact/indirect discrimination. However, in both jurisdictions there have been hard cases, blurring this bright-line distinction. A common characteristic of these hard cases is that they start from a facially neutral attribute. While this would – in theory – call for the disparate impact/indirect discrimination standard, some attributes stand out as especially "suspicious", distinguishing them from "truly neutral" attributes. As such, they suggest that a decisionmaker might hide his true discriminatory intent behind an attribute that is neutral in form only.[74]

Both jurisdictions have paradigm examples for hard cases like these. In the US, redlining is a classic illustration of a practice that differs in name only from racial discrimination.[75] It refers to the practice of denying an applicant a mortgage in a predominantly minority-owned neighborhood, even though the applicant may generally be eligible for a loan. This form of redlining has been held by courts and regulatory agencies to be an illegal practice[76] entailing disparate treatment (not disparate impact) liability.[77] In this context, it does not matter that the lender does not explicitly refer to "race". Redlining is understood to correlate closely good with race to serve as a proxy. Courts will treat the lender as if he had used the protected attribute itself.

In the EU, there is no comparable history of redlining,[78] but Europe has its own hard cases. An example is provided by a UK court case concerning sex and age discrimination. The defendant was a town that lowered

74 "Covert discrimination", Sacksofsky (n 30) § 14 note 54.

75 Kim (n 33) 15.

76 See <https://www.federalreserve.gov/boarddocs/supmanual/cch/fair_lend_fhact.pdf> accessed 24 June 2025 with exceptions for redlining to identify an area on a fault line or a flood plain.

77 See <https://www.ffiec.gov/PDF/fairlend.pdf> accessed 24 June 2025, iv for the OCC, the FDIC, the Fed Board, the Office of Thrift Supervision and the National Credit Union Administration; similarly A Prince and D Schwarcz, 'Proxy Discrimination in the Age of Artificial Intelligence and Big Data' (2020) Iowa Law Review Vol. 105 1257, 1257; C Campbell and D Smith, 'Distinguishing Between Direct and Indirect Discrimination' (2023) The Modern Law Review, Vol. 86, 307, 315.

78 See for redlining as indirect discrimination B Dzida and N Groh, 'Diskriminierung nach dem AGG beim Einsatz von Algorithmen im Bewerbungsverfahren' (2018) NJW-Neue Juristische Wochenschrift Vol. 71 Issue 27 1917.

prices for a public swimming pool based on "pensionable age". The term "pensionable age", so the court held, had become a shorthand expression referring to the age of 60 in a woman and to the age of 65 in a man. Hence, for access to the swimming pool, there was sex and age discrimination against men involved.[79] Where ZIP codes stood in for race in US cases, "pensionable age" worked as a proxy for sex and age and allowed to consider it a proxy for a protected characteristic.[80]

Similar hard cases revolve around attributes that not only correlate with a protected trait but are understood to be somehow implied by it.[81] Pregnancy is a classic example.[82] Neither US nor EU law had originally listed the term "pregnancy" as a protected characteristic. A textualist reading would expect courts to address the issue as one facially neutral variable that correlates with a protected characteristic. This is indeed what US courts did in the 1970s. In *Gilbert*, the US Supreme Court held that exclusion of pregnancy from a disability benefits payments plan was not based on sex.[83] Congress had to amend Title VII to extend its protection to pregnancy, closing an apparent gap. By contrast, the European Court of Justice, following more purposive principles of interpretation, found that pregnancy is "inextricably linked" to the female sex. A refusal to employ an applicant due to pregnancy, so the Court reasoned, can only concern women.[84] Rather than have plaintiffs wait for a legislative amendment, the Court proceeded with a broad reading of the term sex. Pregnancy was addressed as an attribute "inextricably linked" to sex.

---

79 *James v Eastleigh Borough Council* (1990) 2 AC 751.

80 I read this as a hard case which blurs the bright-line distinction, not as supporting the broader view of J Adams-Prassl et al., 'Directly Discriminatory Algorithms' (2023) The Modern Law Review Vol. 86 144 that EU law's scope of direct discrimination is broader than US law's disparate treatment.

81 See Adams-Prassl (n 82) 157: "inherently discriminatory"; G Krishnamurthi and P Salib, 'Bostock and Conceptual Causation' (2020) Yale Journal of Regulation Notice and Comment Blog <https://www.yalejreg.com/nc/bostock-and-conceptual-causation-by-guha-krishnamurthi-peter-salib/> accessed 24 June 2025: "Conceptual Causation"; referring to the latter:Berman and Krishnamurthi (n 51) 88 et seq.; discussing "being a mother" as a "true subset of one sex" on p. 105; Sacksofsky (n 30) § 14 note 58 et seq.

82 For the sake of this example, I do not address the situation of transitioning persons where a man might become pregnant, see Sacksofsky (n 23).

83 *General Electric Co. v. Gilbert*, 429 U.S.125 (1976), para 149.

84 Case C-177/88 *Dekker / Stichting Vormingscentrum voor Jong Volwassenen* [1990] ECJ I-3941, para 12.

Hard cases that sit in between doctrinal categories, such as the ones explained in the preceding section, are neither a novel phenomenon nor necessarily a reason to revisit the starting point of doctrinal distinctions. So far, these cases have in anti-discrimination law been quite sparse, and the debate has profited from the implicit understanding that there is a very limited number of attributes that are *de facto* identical to (or implied in) the protected trait. Additionally, most examples seem to concern deciders who deliberately seek out attributes that are generally understood to be identical to the protected characteristic – such as redlining and race or pregnancy and sex. Imposing disparate treatment liability made sense to close a gap for circumventing the rule.

With the advent of big data and AI models, these implicit assumptions seem less compelling. When discussing the first hypothetical lender, it has become apparent how difficult it was for the plaintiff to prove that omitting the building block "sex" would change the outcome. The reason for this was redundant encoding. Even if the lender omitted sex in the training data or if the plaintiff changed her sex on the credit application, many other attributes "gave her away".

What was a problem of proof in the case of the first hypothetical lender morphs into a question of distinguishing "suspicious" from "truly" neutral variables for the second hypothetical lender. Traditionally, courts had been looking at one suspicious building block ("ZIP code", "pregnancy") that stood in for a protected attribute ("race", "sex"). Now, an AI model unearths correlations between innumerable data points. What used to be an outlier case of an only seemingly neutral attribute (such as ZIP codes) to stand in as a proxy for a protected characteristic (such as race) becomes the new standard. If the correlations the AI will find are as good as the predictive power of pregnancy for sex, can we say that using an AI "implies" a protected attribute? How useful is litigation that targets individual building blocks, if big data will immediately replace one attribute with another? One of the cornerstones of anti-discrimination law, the distinction between protected and neutral attributes, is blurred, due to data analytics redundant encoding. Plaintiffs will find it increasingly impossible to identify distinct building blocks that have caused a discriminatory decision.

D. Art. 6 Directive 2023/2225 on Credit Agreements for Consumers

The EU has stood out for active rulemaking where AI is concerned. Its AI Act[85] stipulates a risk-based approach based on the legislator's perception of especially risky AI use cases. AI-based credit scoring and creditworthiness evaluation count among these, Art. 6 para. 2 AI Act, Annex III Nr. 5b. Recital (58) AI Act explains why this is the case: These AI systems determine "access to financial resources or essential services", they "may lead to discrimination (…) and may perpetuate historical patterns of discrimination (…) or may create new forms of discriminatory impacts". The AI Act's answer are product-specific compliance requirements for developers and users of these systems. By contrast, the Act does not explicitly deal with the relationship between loan applicant and lender or credit scoring company. It is the 2023 Consumer Credit Directive that zooms in on loan applicant and lender.

I. Art. 6's unhelpful text/part 1: "do not discriminate (…) on ground of"

Art. 6 of Directive 2023/2225, for the first time, includes a prohibition of discriminatory lending practices. Its unhelpful drafting style has been mentioned above.[86] Departing from what has been established practice for all EU directives that prohibit discrimination, the new Directive neither defines nor proscribes indirect discrimination. Instead, it prohibits discrimination "on ground of" various protected characteristics. In this way, the rule introduces legal uncertainty into lending practices. Additionally, it misses the chance for a modern rule that gives guidance for the challenge of redundant encoding.

Arguably, the EU legislator did not intend to prohibit only direct discrimination, despite foregoing the established explicit reference to indirect discrimination in its statutory text. It has been explained above that EU courts have read both, Art. 157 TFEU and Art. 21 of the Charter broadly, covering direct and indirect discrimination. Had the EU legislator wanted to change direction, one would have expected a clear sign. Instead, the

85 Regulation (EU) 2024/1689 of the European Parliament and of the Council of 13 June 2024 laying down harmonised rules on artificial intelligence and amending Regulations (EC) No 300/2008, (EU) No 167/2013, (EU) No 168/2013, (EU) 2018/858, (EU) 2018/1139 and (EU) 2019/2144 and Directives 2014/90/EU, (EU) 2016/797 and (EU) 2020/1828 (Artificial Intelligence Act) [2024] OJ L 2024/1689.

86 See above B.II.

Directive's recitals (29) and (31), along with the wording of Art. 6 reference the Charter without a qualifier.

Following those same lines, the unusual wording should not be understood as restricting its scope to the relationship between government and private citizens. While the Charter explicitly addresses only the institutions of the Union and its Member States when they are implementing Union law,[87] courts have extended anti-discrimination provisions to cover contracting choices of private parties.[88] The credit underwriting context will mostly concern these, and the Directive's Art. 3 para. (2) is well aware, defining "creditor" as "a natural or legal person who grants or promises to grant credit in the course of that person's trade, business or profession". Against this background, there is no reason to assume that the Directive's prohibition of discriminatory lending practices is to be read narrowly. Still, its text obscures, rather than clarifies the rule's scope.

II. Art. 6's unhelpful text/part 2: "without prejudice to the possibility of offering different conditions (...) where (...) duly justified by objective criteria"

Discrimination presupposes that like cases have not been treated alike and that there is no justificatory reason available. In a credit discrimination case, this makes for two defenses: *Either*, the plaintiff is not like the members of the group he claims he belongs to, hence, not "similarly situated", *or* there was a good reason to treat him differently. Both, EU, and US law subscribe to the admissibility of some form of business defense in disparate impact/indirect discrimination cases. However, neither US nor EU law spell out in detail what an acceptable business defense looks like. While *Manhart* and a similar decision by the ECJ, concerning an earlier anti-discrimination Directive, [89] had ruled out a defense of statistical discrimination, neither

87 Charter of Fundamental Rights of the European Union, Art. 51 para. 1 s. 1, see Klaus Ferdinand Gärditz in Anna Katharina Mangold and Mehrdad Payandeh (eds), *Handbuch Antidiskriminierungsrecht* (Mohr Siebeck 2022), § 4 note 66.

88 See above B.II.

89 Case C- 236/09 *Association Belge des Consommateurs Test-Achats and others* [2011] ECJ.

court has extended this jurisprudence to discrimination on grounds of other protected characteristics.[90]

The wording of the new rule, instead of providing a clear guideline, veers on the side of caution. Art. 6 para. 2 stresses that the non-discrimination rule "shall be without prejudice to the possibility of offering different conditions". Recital (31) adds that "this should not be understood as creating an obligation for creditors or credit intermediaries to provide services in areas in which they do not conduct business". Denying credit altogether or asking for higher interest is acceptable if "those different conditions are duly justified by objective criteria". What these criteria could entail remains open. That they must be "objective" seems evident and rules out a procedure that allows for a subjective assessment of creditworthiness.

Much will depend on national law, regulating the burden of proof for plaintiffs. If the applicant bears the burden, he will need access to the lender's AI model, data and business strategy. A recent ECJ decision seemed open towards an approach suggested by the referencing Austrian court: The lender was not required to deliver this information to the loan applicant but, instead, to the court.[91] However, even if the lender produced all information and even if the courts – relying on experts – was able to meaningfully assess these, the applicant would need to produce some form of counterfactual data to show that he should have been offered the loan. This might be impossible, given that the AI learns which loans it should *not* have offered because borrowers did worse than predicted (false positives). But it does not usually learn which loans would have been attractive (false negatives). Because the denial of a loan (or a certain interest rate) implies that the loan (or the interest rate) was not offered to the applicant, the AI has no chance to learn whether the applicant would have paid back.[92]

The EU legislator has not explained what counts as "duly justified objective criteria" to justify disparate impact, leaving the issue for regulators and judges to settle. The EU AI Act is more helpful than the Directive. Its recital (58) starts from the premise that "AI systems used to evaluate the credit score or creditworthiness of natural persons should be classified as high-risk". The recital moves on to clarify that the high-risk category does not apply to AI systems used "for prudential purposes to calculate credit

90 See Antje von Ungern-Sternberg in Anna Katharina Mangold and Mehrdad Payandeh (eds), *Handbuch Antidiskriminierungsrecht* (Mohr Siebeck 2022) § 28 note 57.

91 Case C-203/22 *Dun & Bradstreet Austria* [2025] ECJ.

92 Kim (n 33) 5.

institutions' and insurances undertakings' capital requirements". It stands to reason that, in the scope of the Directive, (statistical) discrimination based on prudential purposes provides a "duly justified objective criterion". Beyond that, recitals (31) and (46) suggest leeway for the lender to structure his business model as he sees fit. It remains to be seen, how this liberal approach fits together with EU courts prohibiting discriminatory underwriting between private parties in its directly or indirectly discriminatory form.

III. The Consumer Credit Directive in the age of AI: Algorithms for inclusion?[93]

The Consumer Credit Directive regulates consumer lending more generally, remarks on AI-based creditworthiness evaluation are sparse. As is evident from recital (56), legislators are aware of (some) risks that algorithmic scoring and underwriting entail but decided to refrain from going into details. The problem of redundant encoding is not addressed nor are problems of proof. There is a right to obtain human oversight where creditworthiness assessments involve automated processing of personal data, Art. 18 para. 8, recital (56). Additionally, Art. 18 para. 3 s. 5 rules out "social networks" as a source of information for assessing creditworthiness of the consumer.

The Directive does not specify what a "social network" is, nor does it allow to use social network data if it helps the consumer or if he consents. The US Consumer Financial Protection Bureau (CFPB) offers an illustration of how this could work.[94] Early on, it had issued a no-action letter for the Fintech Upstart mentioned above, drawing a comparison of traditional and novel credit scoring methods.[95] It first simulated outcomes under Upstart's proprietary model. Then, the Bureau compared them with outcomes

93 Orly Lobel, *The Equality Machine, Harnessing digital technology for a brighter, more inclusive future* (Public Affairs New York 2022).

94 Discussion at Langenbucher, 'AI credit scoring and evaluation of creditworthiness – a test case for the EU proposal for an AI Act, in ECB, Continuity and change – how the challenges of today prepare the ground for tomorrow' (n 5) 34.

95 P Ficklin and P Watkins, 'An update on credit access and the Bureau's first No-Action Letter' (Consumer Financial Protection Bureau Blog, 6 August 2019) <https://www.consumerfinance.gov/about-us/blog/update-credit-access-and-no-action-letter/> accessed 24 June 2025.

under a hypothetical model using FICO scores (a common US scoring agency).[96] The simulation had Upstart approve 27 % more borrowers than traditional lending models. Personal loan interest rates were 16 % lower on average.[97] The CFPB found no disparities for minorities, females, or applicants who are 62 years or older. Put differently: Minority borrowers had better chances to be eligible for a loan under Upstart's model than under the (hypothetical) traditional model.[98]

One concern the Bureau did not address is that the distribution remained skewed. Black and black-Hispanic minority borrowers, who were eligible under Upstart's model, were still facing disadvantages. These emerged when comparing their group with the group of white and white-Hispanic persons eligible under Upstart's model. The disadvantage showed as to relative numbers of access to credit, origination fees, and interest rates. The Bureau's thinking might have been: If in absolute numbers more protected-group-borrowers have access to loans than under a hypothetical FICO score, this provides for more inclusion. Against that background, the Bureau might have claimed: it does not matter if the surplus is unequally distributed. Everyone is better off than before and, in that sense, we are looking at something like pareto-optimality.[99]

Comparing a hypothetical simulation with a standard credit score as the counterfactual is not entirely unreasonable where access to loans follows a standardized routine. It rewards lenders who offer an advantage, at least for some groups and at least if compared with the current situation. To be sure, this form of "pareto-optimality" test along the CFPB's lines is incompatible with received disparate impact doctrine. Anti-discrimination law tries to remedy relative disadvantages of one group when compared with another group. The Bureau focused instead on the surplus produced by Upstart's model, irrespective of the relative composition of the group of borrowers. While this makes the strategy unhelpful for private claimants, it could offer some guidance for public enforcement or supervisory oversight.

96 Critical as to this method: Student Borrower Protection Center (n 68) 21 (fn. III) but see above C.III.2 for a critique of the mystery shopping exercise.
97 Ficklin and Watkins (n 95).
98 Ficklin and Watkins (n 95).
99 On this argument see Langenbucher and Corcoran, (n 60) 156.

E. Take-aways

This paper has explored shortcomings of received anti-discrimination doctrine when faced with redundant encoding. Many concern the burden of proof where big data encodes the protected attribute via various not-protected attributes. Additionally, plaintiffs would need access to data and model, potentially from various actors, including the lender, scoring agencies, and credit reporting bureaus, to make their case. Should courts be ready to adjust the burden of proof, redundant encoding will still in many situations rule out proof.

For disparate impact doctrine, it has under US law been unclear whether its scope covers credit underwriting. The Executive Order of April 23, 2025 requests agencies to stop proceeding under this doctrine.

The EU Consumer Credit Directive has not been explicit on this point. Received court practice would suggest that the doctrine is applicable. Still, it suffers from the problems mentioned above: Anti-discrimination doctrine requires the plaintiff to establish a specific "building block" – an attribute, a characteristic, a criterion or a certain practice – that has triggered the disparate output across groups. If the lender uses big data, redundant encoding makes this approach toothless. As soon as one building block is removed, for instance a protected characteristic or a facially neutral attribute deleted from the data, various correlating data points take its place.

Unhelpfully, the EU Directive 2023/2225 on Consumer Credit Agreements has put the ball in the field of regulatory agencies and courts. This raises various challenges for consumers, for credit scoring agencies and for financial institutions that wish to lawfully employ AI. Among these are legal risks as to discriminatory conduct, the admissibility of business defenses, the tools supervisory agencies may employ, and burden of proof issues for plaintiffs.[100] Mostly, the Directive's anti-discrimination regime in Art. 6 seems geared towards traditional, limited-data credit scoring and underwriting. If consumer lending increasingly moves towards big data analytics EU regulators and courts will have to decide how to deal with redundant encoding.

100 An exploration in detail is beyond this current paper's scope, see Katja Langenbucher, 'Financial Profiling' in: Langenbucher (ed) *The Regulation of Credit Scoring in Europe* (forthcoming in Edward Elgar 2025) for further details.

The AI Act offers the chance to reorient the discussion, replacing the intricacies of algorithmic discrimination with internal validation, regulatory supervision, product quality checks and testing of both, AI model and data.[101] Arguably, this product-regulation approach provides a better fit with the challenges raised by AI-based credit underwriting than traditional anti-discrimination doctrine.

101 Katja Langenbucher, 'AI credit scoring and evaluation of creditworthiness – a test case for the EU proposal for an AI Act, in ECB, Continuity and change – how the challenges of today prepare the ground for tomorrow' (n 5) 370 et seq.

The functionality of data protection in a digitizing society – a systemic view of control and trust

Stefan Brink, Clarissa Henning

> *Billions have no idea how a computer works, let alone algorithms. How they can be manipulated, what is manipulated, they stare at pixels and trust, which is actually touching. It makes you so angry, so angry that you get the feeling on the net that everything depends on your own stupid opinion.*
> Marc Bauer: The Blow-Up Regime

Our society now functions digitally, yet we still cling to ideas of system trust and control that date back to analogue times and are increasingly proving to be an illusion. Why do we cling to a trust that has become a relic, in the hope that digitality, controlled by algorithm-based decisions, can be made controllable?

Trust. A value that is a decisive stabilizing factor in a liberal democratic society. People trust that others will adhere to unspoken but culturally anchored norms and thus enable regulated social interaction. We trust that institutions, companies and politicians will abide by the law. If not, then we trust that we can demand it. Trust reduces the complexity of the world, as we do not know everything, cannot (and do not want to) control everything, but trust and can trust that things are as they appear to us, that they function as we expect them to, that they are aligned with the norms we have learned. Trust makes the world controllable and calculable for the individual and creates security. However, the question arises as to whether trust in a society that now functions digitally is not rather the clinging to the illusion of a system that now follows completely different laws that we no longer know or can even comprehend. If we follow Marc Bauer's description of the situation, we have to ask ourselves the question: Are we holding on to a trust that has become a relic, in the hope that digitality, controlled by algorithm-based decisions, can already be made just as controllable?

In order to approach the value of trust in the digitalized society, it should first be noted that the question raised cannot be answered with a clear "yes" or "no". Even at the micro level of the European social system, it is clear that self-determination, privacy and co-determination are still of great importance for the individual sense of freedom of digital citizens. However, as the much-cited and persistent privacy paradox[1] attests, the behaviour of users in the digital society deviates massively from this sense of values. While at the time of the planned census in 1983, the disclosure and permanent storage of personal data such as "information on family and civil partnership, living situation, school and studies, employment, profession and training, childcare"[2] led to storms of protest among the population, citizens today apparently voluntarily disclose a much larger amount of private information to a much larger audience - the world of the Internet. Despite the (more or less existing) knowledge that data is used for countless purposes, most of which remain opaque, and that one paves the way for the manipulation of oneself, trust in the democratic system (macro level of society) seems to contain and silence possible concerns about a society- and culture-dominating process such as digitization. If there was a threat to citizens, the prevailing belief seems to be that political and legislative institutions (meso level) would intervene and regulate digital freedom with a view to the ideal - the macro level - of society. But they would! Freedom is taken, must be taken, in order to maintain freedom. We will return to this supposed contradiction later on.

First, we will look at how trust in the system is responded to within the system, so that the system changes brought about by digitalization do not negatively affect the norms and values at the macro level - or rather: even support them. A new subsystem is created that is to be understood as a reaction to the changes in the environment and is itself an expression of the new challenges or needs that have arisen. According to Niklas Luhmann, "*each* subsystem reconstructs the comprehensive system to which it belongs and which it participates in, through its own (subsystem-specific) *difference between system and environment.* Through system differentiation, the sys-

1 To cite one of the most recent study reports on the topic, see for example Sabine Trepte, Philipp K. Masur, 'Privacy Attitudes, Perceptions, and Behaviors of the German Population.' Research Report (2017) Online: https://www.forum-privatheit.de/wp-content/uploads/Trepte_Masur_2017_Research_Report_Hohenheim.pdf.

2 'Census ruling of 1983 and its significance.' (2023) Online: https://www.juraforum.de/lexikon/volkszaehlungsurteil.

tem multiplies itself in itself, so to speak, through ever new distinctions between systems and environments within the system."[3] What does this mean for the outlined system influence through digitalization? The trust vacuum created by digitalization requires an answer at the meso level. In order to concretize this and build a bridge between the theoretical consideration of system-immanent changes and data protection, it is necessary at this point to trace this systemic change in concrete terms:

It may seem surprising at first that Europe's first law on data protection was passed in the state of Hesse in 1970 - before the development that today bears the name "digitization" was foreseeable. This is because it was only as a result of the aforementioned census that the so-called census ruling of the Federal Constitutional Court in 1983 established in black and white what had long been an inherent systemic need: "Under the modern conditions of data processing, the free development of personality presupposes the protection of individuals against the unlimited collection, storage, use and disclosure of their personal data. This protection is therefore covered by the fundamental right of Art. 2 para. 1 in conjunction with Art. 1 para. 1 GG. In this respect, the fundamental right guarantees the right of the individual to determine the disclosure and use of his or her personal data."[4]

This led to the development of the right to informational self-determination as a good protected by the Basic Law, which in turn led to a series of "causal chains". As Luhmann shows, the differentiation within a subsystem leads to further operations, for example the emergence of another subsystem, which at the same time always has an effect on the overall system and results in new changes or differentiations. A subsystem can never exist independently of the others (for Luhmann, the environment). This also explains why the manifestation of a change or a need always emerges from the system itself and was therefore already present in the system long beforehand. The entry into force of the GDPR in 2016, which has been in force throughout the EU since 25.05.2018, represents a further differentiation, which in turn was only possible in an exceptional historical situation, namely the social and political reality caused by Edward Snowden's revelations.

3 Niklas Luhmann, *Die Gesellschaft der Gesellschaft* (11th edn. Suhrkamp 2021) 598 (italics in orig.).

4 BVerfGE 65, 1; Online: https://www.bundesverfassungsgericht.de/SharedDocs/Entscheidungen/DE/1983/12/rs19831215_1bvr020983.html.

The GDPR assigned new functions to the state data protection authorities and the Federal Commissioner for Data Protection, which have now become tangible for all other subsystems of society for the first time: Advice - control - sanction. The state data protection authorities and the Federal Commissioner joined forces to form the Data Protection Conference (DSK) in order to exchange information, but the data protection authorities are still organized on a federal level - there is therefore no single opinion on the correct handling of the right to informational self-determination in its many different application contexts, and of course no uniform interpretation of the regulation throughout Europe. As a result, the "data protection" system is in a constant exchange with itself and is becoming increasingly differentiated. As algorithm-driven technologies permeate all areas of society, changing and shaping them and thus posing a direct threat to the individual, data protection in its manifestation through the data protection authorities also influences all areas of society in order to protect the fundamental right to informational self-determination, which is syntagmatically linked to digitalization. Data protection is the system's reaction to the vacuum of trust described above in order to fill this vacuum and thus redeem the individual's trust in the social system.

However, Luhmann also states: "Society has no address. Nor is it an organization with which one could communicate."[5] Rather, society communicates with itself and about itself in the self-referential form of its subsystems - data protection is one of them. Data protection is making its presence felt with its new function of sanction, making it impossible for political and economic forces to ignore it. The possibility of sanctioning responsible data processors with up to four percent of their worldwide annual turnover (cf. Art. 83 GDPR) expresses in figures the importance that the European GDPR attaches to safeguarding informational self-determination in terms of system standards. However, the data protection authorities are not only focusing on data controllers. A new, legally stipulated task is to inform and advise citizens so that they do not just stare at pixels and trust that they will not be exploited and manipulated (if they are aware of this danger at all), but can literally take their informational self-determination into their own hands and thus preserve their autonomy. However, it is also a fact that the causal series described by Luhmann, which an event, a change, triggers, leads to the fact that not only the triggering (sub-)system

5 Niklas Luhmann, *Die Gesellschaft der Gesellschaft* (11th edn. Suhrkamp 2021) 866.

becomes increasingly differentiated, but also the systems interacting with it, which "[...] trigger completely different causal series due to a change in the *environment* of these systems. And this even though it is the *same* event for all systems! This results in an enormous dynamization, an almost explosive reaction pressure, against which the individual subsystems can only protect themselves by building up thresholds of indifference. Differentiation therefore inevitably results in: an increase in dependency and independence at the same time under specification and systemic control of the aspects in which one is dependent or independent."[6]

Data protection is a reaction to a system in which the increasing collection and processing of data by algorithmic applications in turn creates more and more intransparency of the digitized system for the individual and the trust of users is rewarded with control. As a result of the increasing collection and processing of data, which data protection is supposed to protect against, each individual is actually becoming the regrettably powerless user that Marc Bauer is so angry about in the opening quote. Users are becoming more and more transparent, while the system of digitalization and its computing operations is becoming less and less transparent. This also reduces the complexity of the world, but precisely the opposite of what is being sought: Control (of citizens) instead of trust (in digitalization).

Algorithmic calculations and the benefits derived from the calculations influence the overall system at the macro level. The fundamental values to which all system-inherent processes and subsystems are aligned are thus undermined. However, the system also reacts to this by countering control with control. This is the driving force behind the GDPR and its guiding principle. As a consequence, one of the core functions of the data protection authorities is therefore to monitor data controllers. However, this control works differently to the control of digitality. The control of data protection authorities is based on the fundamental values of its environment. And thus on trust.

To illustrate this, let's take a concrete example from everyday official practice: digital contact tracing during the pandemic. A health crisis situation affects the entire system and has a serious impact on its functions. Here too, the subsystems react in very different ways to deal with the crisis. And especially through such a serious event as a pandemic, in the light of the systemic reaction to it, the nature of this system and its laws are reflected and checked for correctness. This was also reflected in the fact

6 Ibid, 599 (italics in orig.).

that digital applications were seen as the saviour for restoring the normal state of the overall system or at least paving the way for it. One building block in this emergency plan should be smartphone applications. This digital approach should enable contacts to be documented and the risk of a possible infection to be tracked by means of a subsequent comparison so that protective and preventive measures can be initiated and spread if necessary. The Corona Warning App (CWA) was an initial digital tool in this regard, giving individuals the responsibility to respond to the new challenges posed by the pandemic situation with the support of a digital solution. The CWA dispenses with the centralized collection and storage of user data, but it is up to the user to compare the data stored locally in the app with infection reports, which must also be made voluntarily and in a self-determined manner via the app, and to derive appropriate actions from them if necessary. When the impression arose in the political arena that this was not providing the hoped-for benefits, criticism of the CWA's data protection friendliness was voiced - which, however, ran counter to securing the systemic "normal state". A step was to be taken away from trust in and responsibility for the individual towards more control by the state and transparency for the individual. Data protection responded to this once again, and the Luca app for contact tracing began its triumphal march. The Luca app is not an anonymized contact tracing service. It allows contact information to be saved in the app so that it can be used to "log in" to events. However, the contact details are stored in encrypted form with the app provider and the health authorities can access the data if an infection is reported. The personal data is encrypted for all other accessing parties (e.g. for the event organizer). The health authorities can only read the data if the organizer provides it and it is decrypted. This small example illustrates how data protection was able to fulfil its system-stabilizing function as well as temporarily changing system requirements without losing sight of the normal state of the system.

Nevertheless, there were opposing calls from the online community asking whether the data protection authority had not checked the source code as part of its control function. And it is precisely at this point that the difference in the concept of control, according to which the various subsystems function, can be illustrated: The criticism demands that the data protection authorities must understand the source code - i.e. the algorithmic instructions for action in machine-readable form - in order to prevent any potential danger to users. This would correspond to the control concept of digitality, which reads citizens' thoughts in order to be able to influence the social system. The control concept of data protection is different and therefore also the task of the data protection authorities. It is not the algorithms that are being monitored here, but those responsible for the algorithms, because it is not the algorithms that dictate further actions resulting from the calculations, but those responsible for data collection and evaluation. The data processors must account for the legal basis on which they base the data processing, they must submit a data protection impact assessment, demonstrate suitable technical and organizational measures to ensure data security and submit a privacy policy. De facto, this means that it is the statements made by the controller and not the source code itself that are monitored. This may seem problematic, as the user often does not even know what calculations the algorithm used performs. Nevertheless, the GDPR stipulates that the controller must be accountable (see Art. 5 para. 2 GDPR), even if they may not be able to bear the responsibility. This shifts the risk from the manufacturer, provider or programmer of the algorithmic application to the controller as the person who uses the digital application.

The concept of control, which is reflected here, closes the circle to the importance of trust: data protection is based on the citizens' ability to handle digital applications and use them responsibly (in the sense of the GDPR). In addition, the technologies used are not checked directly in the first step, but rather the statements and presentation of the controller are relied upon.

This approach to control and responsibility will not change by law in the near future. With the emergence of the data protection subsystem, the overall system has reacted to the changes brought about by digitalization and developed it from within - with the aim of preserving freedom at the micro level by controlling freedoms at the meso level. Nevertheless, a system managed by algorithms follows completely different system-constituting laws than the original system.

From the considerations outlined here, it follows that the system-immanent dangers that imperceptibly emanate from algorithm-based influences in all system areas must not be thought of at the micro or meso level of society - just like data protection in interaction with this: "The realization of functional differentiation as the primary form of social differentiation profoundly changes the environmental conditions of the systems, both of the overall system of society and its subsystems."[7] The direction in which this profound change will take is to be expected.

7 Ibid, 789.

Trust in the Machine: Algorithmic Justice and the Challenges of Prediction

Lucia Zedner[*]

Risk assessment in criminal justice has been partially automated using algorithmic risk instruments that promise greater accuracy and effectiveness in predicting offending and protecting the public. Yet legal academics and practitioners are increasingly troubled by the ethical implications of algorithmic prediction. Common concerns include their predictive reliability, discriminatory inputs and outcomes, and implications for transparency, accountability, and due process. Even if these issues could be resolved, an enduring problem remains. The criminal process is predicated on the idea that the individual is a responsible agent who can justly be held to account for their wrongful conduct. Yet algorithmic risk assessment instruments (RAIs) tend to disregard the offender's agency and capacity for change. RAIs also intrude upon the decision-making role of criminal justice professionals and limit their ability to exercise discretion in the interests of justice. In the rush to automate risk assessment, do we place too much trust in the algorithm and lose sight of the core commitment of the criminal process to hold the responsible individual to account? And does reliance on risk instruments undermine trust in the professional capacity, experience and expertise of criminal justice officials?

A. Introduction

Algorithmic tools now have a prominent place in policing and criminal justice, promoted as an effective means of assessing risk and preventing offending to reduce the harms inflicted by crime and the pains of punishment. Risk assessment is driven by the demands of public protection, by increasingly sophisticated technologies of actuarial calculation, and their profitability as commercial products. Recourse to automated risk technolo-

* I am grateful to participants at seminars at the Oxford Uehiro Centre for Practical Ethics; the Centre for Criminology, University of Oxford; University of Pennsylvania Law School; the Queensland Supreme Court Annual Judges Seminar, Kyriakos N. Kotsoglou, and Nicola Lacey, for their comments on earlier drafts.

gies is also prompted by declining faith in the expertise of criminal justice professionals, psychiatrists, and judges to assess risk accurately. Algorithmic Risk Assessment Instruments (hereafter RAIs) purport to employ robust statistical methods that align with legal values of impartiality and accuracy and thereby minimise conflict and uncertainty. Terms like 'actuarial justice' and 'algorithmic justice' draw much-needed attention to RAIs but raise the issue of whether these tools promote justice or impair it. This chapter examines the claims made for algorithmic justice and the challenges of using RAIs in practice. In particular, it considers their impact on individual actors, whether as suspects, defendants, and offenders they are the objects of criminal justice, or as police, lawyers, judges, and criminal justice officials they are its agents.

Algorithmic risk assessment instruments are high-value products sold as effective, reliable predictive tools that increase the efficiency of policing and criminal justice by replacing fallible human judgement with scientifically rigorous risk assessment. RAIs are widely used to assess individual risk and predict future offending. They mine data to enable automated risk assessment and thereby inform decision-making by police and criminal justice officials.[1] These new technologies also promise to identify 'risky' populations, which are then targeted by the police and subject to preventive measures or detention by the courts. Across all these domains, RAIs classify individual citizens by level of risk and serve as tools of social sorting for predictive purposes.[2] More recently, the revolution in artificial intelligence (AI) and machine learning has transformed the practice of risk assessment, reconfiguring policing, criminal justice practice, and the trial in ways unforeseeable when these tools were first introduced. Although they have been widely incorporated in facial recognition technologies, predictive policing, and individual risk assessment particularly at sentencing and in the prison system, RAIs remain problematic.[3]

Despite the growing sophistication of RAIs and the claims made for their scientific objectivity, academic research raises doubts about their im-

1 House of Lords Justice & Home Affairs Committee, *Technology Rules? The Advent of New Technologies in the Justice System* HL Paper 180 (2022) 14-15, https://publications.parliament.uk/pa/ld5802/ldselect/ldjusthom/180/180.pdf (last visited 18 April 2024).

2 See Jan W Keiser, Julian Roberts, and Jesper Ryberg (eds), *Predictive Sentencing: Normative and Empirical Perspectives* (Hart Publishing 2019).

3 The Law Society, *Algorithms in the Criminal Justice System* (The Law Society of England and Wales 2019), https://www.lawsociety.org.uk/support-services/research-trends/algorithm-use-in-the-criminal-justice-system-report/ (last visited 18 April 2024).

partiality, predictive power, and validity. One leading systematic review of validation studies found, 'Overall, the predictive performance of the included risk assessment tools was mixed, and ranged from poor to moderate.'[4] Academics like Mayson raise concerns about the propensity of algorithmic tools to bake in bias and demand a 'fundamental rethinking of the role of risk in the criminal justice system.'[5] The legal profession has also voiced concerns about the use of algorithms in criminal justice.[6] Lawyers object that, in their reliance on historical data generated by discriminatory human decision-making, RAIs reproduce and compound existing prejudices, generating higher risk scores for the 'usual suspects', often from ethnic minorities and marginalised communities,[7] in contravention of requirements of fairness and non-discrimination.

The proliferation of predictive algorithms in policing and punishment has prompted disquiet about their implications for justice. Lawyers object that using predictive technologies in criminal justice risks undermining the presumption of innocence, the right to a fair trial, and even the rule of law.[8] Even if it were possible to resolve problems of predictive reliability and eliminate discriminatory outcomes, the adverse impact of RAIs on individuals caught up in the criminal process remains an abiding concern. Academics and professional lawyers worry that by claiming to predict the future, RAIs pay insufficient regard to individual capacity for reform.[9]

---

4 Seena Fazel et al, 'The Predictive Performance of Criminal Risk Assessment Tools Used at Sentencing: Systematic Review of Validation Studies' (2022) 81 Journal of Criminal Justice 1, 1.

5 Sandra G Mayson, 'Bias in, Bias Out' (2019) 128(8) The Yale Law Journal 2122–2473, 2225.

6 In the UK see The Law Society, *Algorithms in the Criminal Justice System* (The Law Society of England and Wales 2019), https://www.lawsociety.org.uk/support-services/research-trends/algorithm-use-in-the-criminal-justice-system-report/ (last visited 18 April 2024).

7 Ibid. 18.

8 Karen Yeung and Adam Harkens, 'How Do "Technical" Design-Choices Made When Building Algorithmic Decision-Making Tools for Criminal Justice Authorities Create Constitutional Dangers? (Part 1) (Public Law forthcoming, SSRN December 7, 2022), 14 at https://ssrn.com/abstract=4319307 (last visited 18 April 2024).

9 Renée Jorgensen, 'Algorithms and the Individual in Criminal Law' (2021) 52(1) Canadian Journal of Philosophy 1-17; The Law Society, *Algorithms in the Criminal Justice System* (The Law Society of England and Wales 2019) 17; Andrew Ashworth and Lucia Zedner, 'Some Dilemmas of Indeterminate Sentences: Risk and Uncertainty, Dignity and Hope' in Jan W Keiser, Julian V Roberts and Jesper Ryberg (eds) *Predictive Sentencing: Normative and Empirical Perspectives* (Hart Publishing 2019) 127-148.

This chapter explores the claim that the use of RAIs poses challenges to ideas of agency and responsibility that are central to criminal justice. If a defendant can justly be held to account for his past conduct, he must surely be presumed capable of exercising agency in future to change. Yet, instead of regarding suspects and defendants as responsible persons with agency and, therefore, the potential to reform, RAIs largely reduce individuals to a set of risk indicators, traits, or characteristics that they share with a larger population identified as risky. Reliance on risk assessment thus shifts attention from what a particular individual decided to do and how they might change in future, and to focus instead on their resemblance to a statistical class of known offenders. This disregard for individual agency is troubling, and as the UN Special Rapporteur on Human Rights recently acknowledged, '[t]he use of AI has direct consequences for the individual as regards personal interface with the power of the State, including its coercive capacity.'[10]

RAIs tend to discount the agency of suspects and offenders, and limit the capacity of criminal justice officials and expert witnesses in court to exercise their professional and clinical judgement. RAIs are technical tools for use by criminal justice actors, but, in practice, ensuring meaningful human oversight of their use has proved challenging. The UK rights organisation Liberty has cast doubt on 'the flawed notion of a "human in the loop"', noting the 'lack of evidence as to our ability as humans to provide meaningful intervention over algorithms and decisions made by machines'.[11] Moreover, the powerful impact of RAIs on these two very different populations of criminal justice professionals and their subjects is interlinked in that official reliance on RAIs constrains the capacity of criminal justice actors to assess and exercise judgement over the individual defendant. If automated justice is not to erode the defendant's right to be recognised as a responsible subject, we need to consider what happens when RAIs rule.

Our primary focus is, therefore, on the impact of algorithmic risk assessment tools on individual agency in the criminal justice system. The chapter begins by considering the development and widespread deployment of

10 Fionnuala Ní Aoláin, *Report of the UN Special Rapporteur on Human rights implications of the development, use and transfer of new technologies in the context of counterterrorism and countering and preventing violent extremism*, 13 at https://www.statewatch.org/media/3755/un-sr-ct-human-rights-new-tech-counter-terrorism-2-23.pdf (last visited 18 April 2024).

11 Liberty response to The Law Society, *Algorithms in the Criminal Justice System* (The Law Society of England and Wales 2019) 28.

RAIs and the challenges their use poses to criminal justice values and principles. It asks what is lost and by whom when 'trust in the machine' prevails. The first section considers the deployment of algorithmic tools at different stages of policing and the criminal process. The second section examines in what ways the use of RAIs challenges the core precept that the individual is a responsible subject. It asks, even if it were possible to redesign and apply RAIs more fairly and consistent with criminal justice values, whether RAIs nevertheless would still discount individual agency. The third section explores how risk assessment tends to fix the future by claiming to assess remote eventualities. In section four, the chapter turns from the subjects of criminal justice (suspects, defendants, and convicted offenders) to examine the impact of RAIs on the role of criminal justice professionals and officials. The final section asks whether RAIs could be rendered consistent with regard for the individual as a responsible and responsive recipient of state censure and sanction, and how they might better respect the expertise, experience, and judgement of those who exert that power. It concludes by suggesting some refinements and reforms to the use of RAIs that might restore trust and bring their use closer to core criminal justice values.[12]

B. The place of algorithmic tools in the criminal justice system

Algorithmic risk assessment instruments are widely used tools of criminal justice. Police and criminal justice professionals deploy RAIs to target risky individuals, identify suspects, and inform sentencing and release decisions. In the early 1990s, Feeley and Simon coined the terms 'new penology' and 'actuarial justice' to draw academic attention to the emerging role of RAIs.[13] These terms identify a shift in policing and criminal justice from their focus on individual criminal liability to making risk assessments of aggregate populations for preventive purposes. Feeley and Simon famously observed that whereas 'Old Penology is rooted in a concern for individuals, and preoccupied with such concepts as guilt, responsibility and obligation',

12 Gabrielle Watson, *Respect and Criminal Justice:* (Oxford University Press 2018) ch 6.

13 Malcolm Feeley and Jonathan Simon, 'The New Penology: Notes on the Emerging Strategy of Corrections and Its Implications', (1992) 30(4) Criminology, 449-74; Malcolm Feeley and Jonathan Simon, 'Actuarial Justice: The Emerging New Criminal Law', in David Nelken (ed), *The Futures of Criminology* (Sage 1994) 173-201.

by contrast, New Penology 'is actuarial. It is concerned with techniques for identifying, classifying, and managing groups assorted by levels of dangerousness.'[14] While there is much truth in this claim, the judge at sentencing remains focused on the risk posed by the lone individual in the dock. Moreover, while Feeley & Simon's critical account of 'actuarial justice' is deservedly influential,[15] the term might be read to suggest that actuarial tools deliver justice. Some scholars suggest there are good reasons to think the opposite is true.[16]

Traditional methods of policing and punishment rely primarily on professional experience and expertise to recognise suspects, identify defendants, inform assessments of individual culpability and determine individual capacity for dangerousness. By contrast, RAIs are structured automated tools that calculate individual risk based on aggregate data drawn from 'risky' populations with similar characteristics. Actuarial tools are mostly used to determine future risk by making predictions about one individual that rely primarily on observations made of *other* people.[17] Scholars disagree about the statistical validity of drawing inferences about individual character, qualities and future riskiness based on observations of aggregate populations.[18] Yet algorithms are widely used, for example in live facial recognition technologies in CCTV surveillance cameras that scan and check facial features against photos of people already on police 'watch lists'.[19] Reliance on these technologies limits police exercise of discretion,

14 Ibid Feeley and Simon, 'Actuarial Justice: The Emerging New Criminal Law' 173.

15 Ibid; Malcolm Feeley, 'Actuarial Justice and the Modern State' in Gerben Bruinsma et al (eds), *Punishment, Places, and Perpetrators: Developments in Criminology and Criminal Justice Research* (Willan Publishing 2004) 62-77.

16 See eg Bernard Harcourt, *Against Prediction: Profiling, Policing, and Punishing in an Actuarial Age* (University of Chicago Press 2007).

17 Renée Jorgensen, 'Algorithms and the Individual in Criminal Law' (2021) 52(1) Canadian Journal of Philosophy 1-17; Rasmus Wandall, ''Actuarial Risk Assessment: The Loss of Recognition of the Individual Offender' (2006) 5 Law, Probability and Risk 175–200.

18 See eg SD Hart et al, 'Precision of Actuarial Risk Assessment Instruments: Evaluating the "Margins of Error" of Group V. Individual Predictions of Violence' (2007) 190 Journal of Psychiatry 60-65; John Monahan and Jennifer L Skeem, 'Risk Assessment in Criminal Sentencing' (2016) 12 Annual Review of Clinical Psychology 489-513; Christopher Slobogin, 'A Defence of Modern Risk-Based Sentencing' in Jan W Keiser, Julian V Roberts and Jesper Ryberg (eds), *Predictive Sentencing: Normative and Empirical Perspectives* (Hart Publishing 2019) 107-125, 115.

19 London Policing Ethics Panel *Final Report on Live Facial Recognition* (May 2019) 6. http://www.policingethicspanel.london/uploads/4/4/0/7/44076193/live_facial_recog

resulting in discrimination and over-policing, and cases of mistaken identity that erode public trust in the police.[20] Digital 'matches' made by algorithms trained on white faces are less reliable when identifying people of colour, which further erodes trust among ethnic minority groups.[21] Coglianese and Lai counterclaim that even supposedly individualised, non-statistical assessments are probabilistic and that human judgement also relies on generalisation.[22] However, their comparison is problematic because human judgments are probabilistic in a different way to algorithms. Claims of objectivity also overlook the fact that algorithmic risk assessments often rely on aggregate data generated by human decision-making that may be discriminatory or biased.[23] To the extent that RAIs are human constructs and thus fallible is problematic in a criminal justice system which depends on certainty and trust.

The criminal process and trial are legal institutions tasked to establish individual responsibility for wrongful conduct, uphold the rule of law, and protect human rights.[24] Before conviction, the defendant enjoys the right to a fair trial,[25] important elements of which include the requirements of capacity and 'fitness to plead',[26] the presumption of innocence, the right to legal representation, and the requirement that the prosecution prove the individual defendant's guilt beyond all reasonable doubt.[27] Yet, the intervention of risk assessment undermines the core commitment of the

---

nition_final_report_may_2019.pdf (last visited 18 April 2024); House of Lords Justice & Home Affairs Committee, *Technology Rules? The Advent of New Technologies in the Justice System* HL Paper 180 (2022) 15.

20 See Liberty *Policing by Machine* (2019) https://www.libertyhumanrights.org.uk/issue/policing-by-machine/ (last visited 18 April 2024).

21 Clare Garvie and Jonathan Frankle 'Facial-Recognition Software Might Have a Racial Bias Problem' The Atlantic (2019) https://apexart.org/images/breiner/articles/FacialRecognitionSoftwareMight.pdf (last visited 18 April 2024).

22 They argue that the human brain itself operates algorithmically, see Cary Coglianese and Alicia Lai, 'Algorithm vs Algorithm' (2022) 72 *Duke Law Journal* 1281-1340.

23 Sandra G. Mayson, 'Bias in, Bias Out' (2019) 128(8) The Yale Law Journal 2122–2473.

24 The Law Society, *Algorithms in the Criminal Justice System* (The Law Society of England and Wales 2019) 19-20.

25 Protected under Article 6 ECHR.

26 See eg UK Criminal Procedure (Insanity and Unfitness to Plead) Act 1991.

27 Liz Campbell, Andrew Ashworth, and Mike Redmayne, *The Criminal Process* (Oxford University Press 2nd ed 2019); Victor Tadros and Stephen Tierney, 'The Presumption of Innocence and the Human Rights Act' (2004) 67 MLR 402-34; Andrew Ashworth, 'Four Threats to the Presumption of Innocence' (2006) 123 South African Law Journal 62-96.

criminal process to hold the individual to account justly and fairly. Risk assessment at the pre-trial stage dilutes the presumption of innocence by seeking to establish how risky the individual is even before proof of guilt in a criminal court. In more serious cases, those assessed as high risk at bail hearings can be committed on remand to pre-trial detention,[28] the effect of which is to cast doubt on the remanded prisoner's innocence, restrict their freedom, and adversely impact their ability to prepare the case for their defence or engage in plea negotiations.[29] The knowledge that a defendant was preventively detained pre-trial may adversely influence jury deliberation, and make judges unwilling to impose terms of imprisonment shorter than the time already spent in prison on remand, which may result in longer sentences.[30]

At trial, the key issue before the court is whether the individual is responsible for the criminal conduct of which he or she is accused. A finding of guilt follows only if the prosecution can establish beyond all reasonable doubt that the defendant is a free agent with the capacity for moral choice, who has committed all the elements of the offence without justification or excuse. The very purpose of the criminal trial is to recognise and respond appropriately to individual agency and hold the individual responsible for their choice to engage in criminal conduct recklessly or intentionally. To find that an individual chose to do wrong is simultaneously to acknowledge their capacity for choice, and thus that they also have the capacity to change.[31]

In court, it is the responsible individual who is held to account and who faces the punitive consequences of adverse risk assessments made at sentencing. It sits ill with the role of the criminal court in determining individual responsibility to calculate their future risk and detain them on

---

28 Megan Stevenson and Sandra G Mayson, 'Pretrial Detention and the Value of Liberty' *Faculty Scholarship at Penn Law* (2022) 2429 https://scholarship.law.upenn.edu/faculty_scholarship/2429 (last visited 18 April 2024).

29 Antony Duff, 'Pre-Trial Detention and the Presumption of Innocence' in Andrew Ashworth, Lucia Zedner and Patrick Tomlin (eds), *Prevention and the Limits of the Criminal Law* (Oxford University Press 2013).

30 Thomas Douglas, 'Is Preventive Detention Morally Worse Than Quarantine?' in Jan W Keiser, Julian V Roberts and Jesper Ryberg (eds), *Predictive Sentencing: Normative and Empirical Perspectives* (Hart Publishing 2019) 69-88, 73.

31 Andrew Ashworth and Lucia Zedner, 'Some Dilemmas of Indeterminate Sentences: Risk and Uncertainty, Dignity and Hope' in Jan W Keiser, Julian V Roberts and Jesper Ryberg (eds), *Predictive Sentencing: Normative and Empirical Perspectives* (Hart Publishing 2019) 127-148, 129.

preventive grounds where such calculations are based primarily on their similarity to a larger population of offenders.[32] As Colvin and colleagues pointedly ask, 'Is it a crime to belong to a reference class?'[33] Setting aside questions about the validity of statistical inference, there remain grave doubts about the appropriateness of using aggregate data to calculate risk scores for individuals based on characteristics they share with an aggregate 'risky' population,[34] particularly where these factors include place of birth, race, or sex, over which the individual has no control. Small wonder then that a House of Lords investigation in 2022 concluded, 'We see serious risks that an individual's right to a fair trial could be undermined by algorithmically manipulated evidence.'[35] These risks demand close attention to the impact of RAIs and the challenges they pose to individual agency, rights, and interests.

C. Algorithmic challenges to the responsible subject

This section considers some of the serious challenges that arise when criminal justice decisions rely on applying aggregate actuarial data to individual defendants. A primary challenge is that reliance on algorithmic tools seems inconsistent with the commitment of the legal system to treat suspects and hold defendants accountable as individuals not just as members of suspect communities. In the leading US case of *Loomis*,[36] the defendant's claim that the use of an algorithmic tool infringed his right to an individualised sentence failed on the grounds that whilst algorithmic assessment relies on aggregate data, in this case, it was not the sole basis for decision-making by the court. Yet, as Kehl et al observe, *Loomis* 'does not, of course, foreclose this line of argument in the future. It remains to be seen whether the

32 Andrew Ashworth and Lucia Zedner, *Preventive Justice* (Oxford University Press 2014) 260. See 'principle O'.

33 Mark Colyvan, Helen M. Regan and Scott Frison, 'Is It a Crime to Belong to a Reference Class?' (2001) 9(2) The Journal of Political Philosophy 168-181; see also Kyriakos N Kotsoglou, 'The Specific Evidence Rule: Reference Classes – Individuals – Personal Autonomy' (2023) 4 Quaestio facti 11-37.

34 Although for a counterview, see Kasper Lippert-Rasmussen, '"We Are All Different": Statistical Discrimination and the Right to Be Treated as an Individual' (2011) 15 The Journal of Ethics 47-59, 50.

35 House of Lords Justice & Home Affairs Committee, *Technology Rules? The Advent of New Technologies in the Justice System* HL Paper 180, 76.

36 *State v Loomis* 881 N.W.2d 749 (Wisk. 2016).

limitations described by the court are sufficient to protect a defendant's right to an individual sentence'.[37]

Interestingly, Jorgensen contests the claim that the right to be treated as an individual forbids the use of algorithmic tools because, she suggests, 'it isn't immediately obvious what the right to be treated as an individual forbids, because it isn't clear what it is a right *to*, exactly.'[38] Rather than seeking to resolve this conundrum, Jorgensen focuses on the interests that the right protects, in particular the individual's rightful claim 'to a fair distribution of the burdens and benefits of the rule of law', which, she argues, rules out, 'treating wrongdoing by some as justification for imposing extra costs on others.'[39] To ensure that the legal system does not regard suspects and defendants merely as statistical entities, composed only of measurable traits, and whose risk level is determinable by reference to a larger population, requires that the law recognise each one as a whole, separate, and responsible person. This requires us to recognise that '[m]embership of a group or similarity to other cases in a dataset do not cause criminality.'[40] To resist the reductive tendency to see the defendant as no more than a bundle of statistically significant risk factors requires that criminal justice actors avoid making risk assessments based on historic factors and traits beyond their control. It follows that RAIs should only include risk factors that are responsive to individual agency. This, in turn, requires that the workings of risk assessment instruments and the input factors upon which they rely must be publicly accessible, transparent, and open to challenge by the defence.

A second challenge is that police and court decisions informed by predictive assessments rarely give priority to the individual subject to them. More often, such decisions are made in the interests of wider public safety, security of persons and property, and public order. High risk scores typically prompt policing and penal interventions that are intrusive, infringe rights

37 Danielle Kehl et al, 'Algorithms in the Criminal Justice System: Assessing the Use of Risk Assessments in Sentencing' *DASH.HARVARD.EDU* (2017) 22 https://dash.harvard.edu/bitstream/handle/1/33746041/2017-07_responsivecommunities_2.pdf (last visited 18 April 2024).

38 Renée Jorgensen, 'Algorithms and the Individual in Criminal Law' (2021) 52(1) Canadian Journal of Philosophy 1-17, 4.

39 Renée Jorgensen, 'Algorithms and the Individual in Criminal Law' (2021) 52(1) Canadian Journal of Philosophy 1-17, 4.

40 The Law Society, *Algorithms in the Criminal Justice System* (The Law Society of England and Wales 2019) 19.

or inflict hard treatment on those to whom they are applied. Algorithmic tools may result in increased police suspicion, interference, and repeated stop and search on the street.[41] Adverse risk assessments in court may result in the denial of bail and lead to pre-trial remand in custody. Post-conviction, risk assessment may result in the court imposing extended determinate, indefinite or whole life sentences that infringe on liberty far into the future. To justify the infliction of long prison terms, it cannot suffice that the individual merely shares the characteristics of other wrongdoers. Rather, the police interventions and punishments to which individuals are subject should be a direct, proportionate response to their exercise of agency, whether in the past or, for preventive measures, in a future that is presently unknowable.

While risk assessments often aggravate sentences, lower risk scores ought to (but rarely do) result in less severe penal outcomes.[42] Better matched responses to lower risk scores might include using police cautions or diversion in place of prosecution, award of bail instead of pre-trial remand, imposition of non-custodial sentences instead of prison, and, for more serious offenders, fixed-term over indeterminate sentences. For those imprisoned, reduction of risk scores over their time in custody, often resulting from therapeutic intervention or rehabilitative programmes, should be considered grounds for early release from custody. To work effectively and fairly, this requires that all prisoners have access to risk-reductive interventions and a right to regular review of their case, both of which may be lacking or difficult to guarantee in a poorly resourced penal system.[43] Absent a commitment to ensuring that risk assessment results in policing practices and penalties proportionate to the risk posed, and to the funding of risk-reductive treatment, individual interests are always likely to be overridden in the interests of public safety.

Thirdly, the tendency of RAIs to downplay individual capacity for choice and thus for change remains an enduring problem. Early risk assessment tools were particularly problematic in that they conceived risk as a prod-

41 Alpa Parmar, 'Stop and Search in London: Counter-Terrorist or Counter-Productive?' (2011) 21(4) Policing and Society 369-382.

42 Kelly Hannah-Moffat, 'Actuarial Sentencing: An "Unsettled" Proposition' (2013) 30(2) Justice Quarterly 270-296, 288-289.

43 Andrew Ashworth and Lucia Zedner, 'Some Dilemmas of Indeterminate Sentences: Risk and Uncertainty, Dignity and Hope', in Jan W Keiser, Julian Roberts, and Jesper Ryberg (eds), *Predictive Sentencing: Normative and Empirical Perspectives* (Hart Publishing, 2019) 127-148.

uct of the individual's personal history, social environment, and criminal record, often relying on static risk factors over which the individual had no control such as sex, race, and place of birth.[44] By assessing risk based on irreversible factors, using RAIs is prone to ignore the possibility that the individual might in future choose to alter their views, lifestyle, or conduct in ways that reduce their risk of offending. Securing permanent employment, buying a home, and getting married are also acknowledged 'protective factors' against re-offending. Moreover, reliance on static factors resulted in predictions that purported to pre-determine the individual's risk based on fixed characteristics or past criminal record, ignoring the risk that this record might be partly a product of racial or other discriminatory bias.[45] As critics like Hannah-Moffat were quick to point out,[46] historic reliance on static factors to assess risk at sentencing ignored the defendant's present and future agency, ironically, often only moments after the court had held them criminally liable as autonomous agents responsible for their decisions and wrongful actions.

As algorithmic risk assessment became more sophisticated, new RAIs were developed to incorporate dynamic risk factors. Growing recognition that individuals are not prisoners of their past and that they may choose to do otherwise permitted all but the most dangerous individuals to be regarded as amenable to rehabilitative interventions designed to lower their risk score.[47] This shift allowed factors that had previously been identified as risks to be reconceived as 'criminogenic needs' that are still correlated to the likelihood of recidivism, but which evidence a need for risk-reductive intervention and support.[48] Subsequent generations of RAIs, developed to

44 Paula Maurutto and Kelly Hannah-Moffat, 'Assembling Risk and the Restructuring of Penal Control' (2006) 46 British Journal of Criminology 438-454, 441-442; Julian V Roberts and Richard S Frase, 'The Problematic Role of Prior Record Enhancements in Predictive Sentencing' in Jan W Keiser, Julian V Roberts and Jesper Ryberg (eds), *Predictive Sentencing: Normative and Empirical Perspectives* (Hart Publishing 2019) 149-173.

45 Sandra G Mayson, 'Bias in, Bias Out' (2019) 128(8) The Yale Law Journal 2122–2473, 6.

46 Kelly Hannah-Moffat, 'Actuarial Sentencing: An "Unsettled" Proposition' (2013) 30(2) Justice Quarterly 270-296, 274-275.

47 Kelly Hannah Moffat, 'Actuarial Sentencing: An "Unsettled" Proposition' (2013) 30(2) Justice Quarterly 270-296, 274-275.

48 Paula Maurutto and Kelly Hannah-Moffat, 'Assembling Risk and the Restructuring of Penal Control' (2006) 46 British Journal of Criminology 438-454, 442; UK Ministry of Justice *Guidance: Offender behaviour programmes and interventions* (2022) https:/

identify dynamic risk factors susceptible to intervention, better recognised the inherent fluidity of risk.

The inclusion of dynamic risk factors in more recent iterations of risk assessment instruments partially resolves the problem that static risk factors do not sufficiently recognise offender agency and capacity for change, but only partially. Although recognising that a factor is dynamic may reduce the chances of fixing an individual's risk score, as we shall explore further below, the exact point in time at which the offender's risk is to be predicted remains contentious. A risk assessment conducted at a single point in time has limited capacity to take into account the impact of dynamic risk factors, changing personal circumstances, and life choices that may alter an individual's risk over time. And, as we have seen, it cannot anticipate how penal sanctions, rehabilitative interventions, and major life changes may alter the risk an individual poses. This realisation led Barabas and colleagues to suggest that RAIs might better be reconceived and deployed as

> a broader diagnostic tool, one used to help practitioners address risk as a dynamic, intervenable phenomenon. When risk assessments are recast in this light, we can ask whether or not regression and machine learning methods can help in diagnosis and intervention, rather than prediction.[49]

Fourthly, the right to a fair trial is a fundamental precept of the criminal justice system.[50] Yet algorithmic tools are sophisticated, highly technical instruments, which make them difficult to interpret and apply, and even harder for the defence to challenge. Empirical research by Hannah-Moffat and others 'has consistently shown that judges and practitioners routinely misapply and misinterpret risk scores.'[51] To protect against such eventualities, due process requires that criminal process practices be transparent[52]

/www.gov.uk/guidance/offending-behaviour-programmes-and-interventions (last visited 18 April 2024).

49 Chelsea Barabas, et al, 'Interventions over Predictions: Reframing the Ethical Debate for Actuarial Risk Assessment', *Proceedings of Machine Learning Research,* 81(1) (2018) 1-15, 2.

50 https://www.echr.coe.int/documents/guide_art_6_criminal_eng.pdf (last visited 18 April 2024).

51 Kelly Hannah-Moffat, 'The Uncertainties of Risk Assessment: Partiality, Transparency, and Just Decisions', *Federal Sentencing Reporter,* 27(4) (2015) 244–247, 246.

52 Carolyn McKay, 'Predicting Risk in Criminal Procedure: Actuarial Tools, Algorithms, AI and Judicial Decision-Making' (2020) 32(1) Current Issues in Criminal Justice 22-39, 27, 33-34.

and allow the defence access to evidence and information used against them.[53] It follows that the lack of openness regarding the input data, design, and methodology of algorithmic tools routinely used in the criminal court, and their inaccessibility to the agents and subjects of criminal justice are a serious hindrance to justice.

The inscrutability of RAIs is exacerbated by the fact that most are proprietary products. RAIs input data, analytics, and architecture are guarded as commercial secrets, inaccessible to the public and even defence counsel, despite the fact that their operations adversely affect defendants' lives and sentencing outcomes. Commercial secrecy renders the workings of RAIs largely unknowable other than to their creators, operators, clients, and those few researchers privileged to have access. The data on which RAIs rely and the assumptions underpinning their operation remain largely hidden from effective academic and legal scrutiny.[54] This secrecy breeds distrust about their operation, particularly among those whose fate is subject to their calculations and the lawyers who struggle to represent clients' interests against the verdict of the algorithm. Poor transparency limits accountability, undermines justice throughout the criminal process and damages the principle of equality of arms between defendants and the state at trial.[55] Commercial secrecy may also impede the ability of suspects to contest police profiling and of defendants to challenge their sentence for disproportionality, particularly when risk assessments result in onerous punishments like extended or indefinite sentences, or other forms of preventive detention. This leads McKay to conclude, 'the proprietorial nature of algorithms created by private organisations challenges the fundamental principles of procedural justice, particularly, open justice and individualised justice.'[56]

The development of AI and machine learning makes RAIs even more opaque and inaccessible. Machine learning enables RAIs to 'learn' from

53 See TRS Allan, *Constitutional Justice: A Liberal Theory of the Rule of Law* (Oxford University Press 2003) 81; Lucia Zedner and Carl-Friedrich Stuckenberg, 'Due Process', in Kai Ambos and Antony Duff (eds) *Core Issues in Criminal Law and Justice* volume one (Cambridge University Press 2019) 313-316.

54 Alyssa M Carlson, 'The Need for Transparency in the Age of Predictive Sentencing Algorithms' (2017) 103 Iowa Law Review 303-329.

55 House of Lords Justice & Home Affairs Committee, *Technology Rules? The Advent of New Technologies in the Justice System* HL Paper 180, Ch3 'Transparency' 39-46.

56 Carolyn McKay, 'Predicting Risk in Criminal Procedure: Actuarial Tools, Algorithms, AI and Judicial Decision-Making' (2020) 32(1) Current Issues in Criminal Justice 22-39, 32.

existing databases to develop more effective means to identify risk factors, which claim to produce more reliable predictions.[57] However, by promising greater predictive accuracy, machine learning runs 'the risk of swinging the trend of assessment back towards prediction, rather than intervention'.[58] Machine learning also makes it more difficult to see how RAIs make calculations and arrive at results that may be driven more by the availability of quantifiable data and technological possibility than by clear, legitimate criteria or objectives. These trends are exacerbated because machine learning conceals the factors on which RAIs rely, obscuring whether these factors are valid or are covert proxies for race or other problematic characteristics, which may be legally prohibited from inclusion.[59] Machine learning is also liable to conceal the weight given to these factors in arriving at risk scores. Such opacity conceals how far RAIs rely on such proxies and makes it difficult for individuals to alter their appearance or conduct to avoid fitting a 'risky' profile. As a result, it is even harder for individuals to avoid attracting suspicion or unwanted police attention, to escape being categorised as high risk, and harder still to contest resulting risk classifications. All this contravenes the fundamental rule of law requirements of transparency and certainty, which make it possible for citizens to choose to act lawfully,understand and contest the prosecution case if they are charged with contravening the law.

D. Fixing the future self

Using RAIs at sentencing to calculate the defendant's future risk does not adequately acknowledge human capacity for change.[60] Although RAIs increasingly incorporate dynamic risk factors, these are still used to justify

57 Though see Sandra G Mayson, 'Bias in, Bias Out' (2019) 128(8) The Yale Law Journal 2122–2473, Part III 'No Easy Fixes'.

58 Chelsea Barabas, et al, 'Interventions over Predictions: Reframing the Ethical Debate for Actuarial Risk Assessment', *Proceedings of Machine Learning Research,* 81(1) (2018) 1-15, 6.

59 Bernard Harcourt, 'Risk as a Proxy for Race: The Dangers of Risk Assessment' (2015) 27(3) Federal Sentencing Reporter 237-243; Pamela Ugwudike, 'Digital Prediction Technologies in the Justice System: The Implications of a 'Race-Neutral' Agenda' (2020) 24(3) Theoretical Criminology 482-501.

60 Andrew Ashworth and Lucia Zedner, *Preventive Justice* (Oxford University Press 2014) ch 6; Danielle Kehl, et al, 'Algorithms in the Criminal Justice System: Assessing the Use of Risk Assessments in Sentencing' *DASH.HARVARD.EDU* (2017) https://das

extended and indefinite prison sentences. The problem would be less concerning if RAIs were used only to assess an individual's risk at the time of sentencing. Indeed, Duff has defended the claim that an assessment of dangerousness is less a prediction of future outcomes than a statement of the individual's present condition -

> an unexploded bomb is dangerous even if it does not explode; to call it dangerous is not just to offer the possibly mistaken prediction that it will explode. So too, a person could be in the relevant sense 'dangerous', even if he will not actually commit a serious crime in the future[61]

Historically, the UK Supreme Court (UKSC) defended this 'presentist' position. Indeed, in *R v Smith* (2011), the Supreme Court held that to require the court to try to see so far into the future, possibly several decades hence, 'places an unrealistic burden on the sentencing judge',[62] contending,

> imagine, as in this case, that the defendant's conduct calls for a determinate sentence of 12 years. It is asking a lot of a judge to expect him to form a view as to whether the defendant will pose a significant risk to the public when he has served six years ... It is at the moment that he imposes the sentence that the judge must decide whether, on that premise, the defendant poses a significant risk of causing serious harm to members of the public.[63]

R v Smith thus set down a clear direction that the court should assess the risk the defendant posed at the time of sentencing. It held that attempting to anticipate the possible risk the defendant might pose at the time of release was not reasonable or realistic.

Surprisingly, however, UK courts have since taken a different approach. After struggling to decide whether the court should assess risk at the point of sentencing, or, if the offender were sentenced to prison, at the time of

---

h.harvard.edu/bitstream/handle/1/33746041/2017-07_responsivecommunities_2.pdf (last visited 18 April 2024).

61 Antony Duff, 'Dangerousness and Citizenship' in Andrew Ashworth and Martin Wasik (eds), *Fundamentals of Sentencing Theory* (Clarendon 1998) 152.

62 *R v Smith* [2011] UKSC 37 [15].

63 Ibid. Note that in the UK a prisoner sentenced to 12 years is eligible for release on parole at the halfway point.

their eventual release,[64] the UK Supreme Court held in *Turnham v The Parole Board* (2013) that

> there is nothing unrealistic about asking a sentencing judge to assess whether an offender presents a risk for a period which cannot reliably be estimated and may well continue after the tariff period.[65]

In *R v Bryant* (2017), the Court of Appeal confirmed this position, holding that 'the consistent practice of this court has been to consider the dangers that the offender *will present on eventual release*'.[66] Whilst the Court suggested that 'to do otherwise would be to ignore entirely the progress which an offender may make following conviction and during the course of his sentence', the obvious difficulty is that at the time of sentencing, the court cannot readily anticipate what the rate or effect of the prisoner's progress will be. Moreover, in all cases where the prisoner is eligible for early release on licence or subject to an indeterminate sentence, the release date is set only after the halfway point when the Parole Board concludes that confinement is no longer necessary 'for the protection of the public'.[67] So the court is doubly burdened: it is asked to anticipate risk in the distant future and at a date impossible to anticipate at the time of sentencing. To insist the court must assess risk on release, when that date may be decades into the future, makes it almost impossible for the judge passing sentence to consider the offender's capacity for change or potential for reform.[68]

The stipulation that the relevant risk to be assessed is that which will be posed at the time of eventual release has the effect of fixing the individual's future in two significant ways.[69] First, it is liable to result in the imposition

64 Andrew Ashworth and Lucia Zedner, 'Some Dilemmas of Indeterminate Sentences: Risk and Uncertainty, Dignity and Hope' in Jan W Keiser, Julian V Roberts and Jesper Ryberg (eds), *Predictive Sentencing: Normative and Empirical Perspectives* (Hart Publishing 2019) 127-148.

65 *R (on the Application of Turnham) (Appellant) v The Parole Board of England and Wales and Another (Respondents) (No 2)* [2013] UKSC 47 [36].

66 *R v Bryant* [2017] EWCA Crim 1662 [8].

67 See https://www.gov.uk/guidance/how-we-make-our-decisions (last visited 18 April 2024); Roger Hood and Stephen Shute, *Parole Decision-Making: Weighing the Risk to the Public* (Home Office 2000).

68 *R (on the Application of Turnham) (Appellant) v The Parole Board of England and Wales and*
Another (Respondents) (No 2) [2013] UKSC 47 [36]; *R v Bryant* [2017] EWCA Crim 1662 [8].

69 Lucia Zedner, 'Fixing the Future? The Pre-Emptive Turn in Criminal Justice' in Bernadette McSherry, Alan Norrie and Simon Bronitt, (eds), *Regulating Deviance:*

of an extended or indeterminate sentence of imprisonment, with all the attendant restrictions on liberty that follow. Secondly, the attempt to assess risk at the time of release requires the sentencing court to anticipate factors presently unknown and unknowable. What, for example, will be the offender's future ability or willingness to change? What will be the impact of incarceration and the company of other offenders? Will rehabilitative or other interventions be available, and will they reduce risk?[70] Given that the court cannot know the answers to any of these questions, the prudent judge will surely be tempted to err on the side of safety, typically by imposing a longer sentence.[71]

How do these issues impact the individual? Mayson has argued that '[p]redictive restraint ... does not deny agency per se' because '[t]he restraining authority might believe that she has full capacity to obey and still prefer to eliminate the risk of her choosing not to.'[72] Mayson's argument that the sentencing court does not so much deny the defendant's agency, but rather seeks to override it, is persuasive. Nonetheless, the imperative to minimise risk leads judges to impose significantly longer sentences that may be disproportionate and severely limit individual liberty and freedom of choice long into the future.

Leading UK cases like *Turnham* and *Bryant* have prompted Andrew Ashworth and me to ask

> whether a prediction of risk at the point of release is capable of allowing for the possibility that an individual might in the future reform to such a degree as to bear little resemblance to the risky person in the dock. If it does not, is this not a denial of the offender's capacity for moral

The Redirection of Criminalisation and the Futures of Criminal Law (Hart Publishing 2009) 35-58.

70 Andrew Ashworth and Lucia Zedner, 'Some Dilemmas of Indeterminate Sentences: Risk and Uncertainty, Dignity and Hope' in Jan W Keiser, Julian V Roberts and Jesper Ryberg (eds), *Predictive Sentencing: Normative and Empirical Perspectives* (Hart Publishing 2019) 127-148.

71 Lucia Zedner, 'Erring on the Side of Safety: Risk Assessment, Expert Knowledge, and the Criminal Court' in Ian Dennis and GR Sullivan (eds), *Seeking Security: Pre-Empting the Commission of Criminal Harms* (Hart Publishing 2012) 221-241.

72 Sandra G Mayson, 'Collateral Consequences and the Preventive State' (2015) 91(1) Notre Dame Law Review 301-361, 322.

choice, which is difficult to reconcile with ideas of individual autonomy and respect for human dignity?[73]

The vital link between individual agency and respect for human dignity figures prominently in the leading judgment of the European Court of Human Rights in *Vinter v UK* (2013) in which Judge Power-Forde insisted that even,

> [t]hose who commit the most abhorrent and egregious of acts and who inflict untold suffering upon others, nevertheless, retain their fundamental humanity and carry within themselves the capacity to change. Long and deserved though their prison sentences may be, they retain the right to hope that, someday, they may have atoned for the wrongs which they have committed. They ought not to be deprived entirely of such hope. To deny them the experience of hope would be to deny a fundamental aspect of their humanity and, to do that, would be degrading.[74]

Requiring the criminal court to assess risk at the point of release is surely at odds with Power-Forde's insistence that respect for human dignity requires recognition of human capacity for change.[75] The person who is ultimately released may, as a result of her experiences and changing attitudes, have made life choices that result in her posing a much lower level of risk than that reasonably foreseeable by the court at the point of sentencing. A sentencing exercise required to estimate the defendant's risk at the time of eventual release, a date possibly decades hence, cannot reasonably be expected to predict the individual's capacity to respond to treatment or rehabilitative intervention, to repent their wrongdoing, or renounce formerly anti-social or violent ways. It follows that a sentence based on algorithmic

---

73 Andrew Ashworth and Lucia Zedner, 'Some Dilemmas of Indeterminate Sentences: Risk and Uncertainty, Dignity and Hope' in Jan W Keiser, Julian V Roberts and Jesper Ryberg (eds), *Predictive Sentencing: Normative and Empirical Perspectives* (Hart Publishing 2019) 127-148, 130.

74 *Vinter and Others v United Kingdom* (ECHR Grand Chamber, 2013: Application Nos 66069/09, 130/10 and 3896/10) 54. Although the Strasbourg Court (ECtHR) subsequently retreated somewhat from this position, see Natasha Simonsen 'Too Soon for the Right to Hope? Whole Life Sentences and the Strasbourg Court's Decision in Hutchinson v UK', European Journal of International Law Blog (2015) https://www.ejiltalk.org/too-soon-for-the-right-to-hopewhole-life-sentences-and-the-strasbourg-courts-decision-in-hutchinson-v-uk (last visited 18 April 2024).

75 Though note that in *Hutchinson v the United Kingdom* (2015) 239, while the Grand Chamber reiterated the Vinter principles, it held that English law does comply with Article 3 (freedom against torture, inhuman or degrading treatment).

predictions that cannot anticipate the future exercise of individual autonomy constitutes a serious disregard for human dignity.

This fundamental concern for human dignity led The Law Society (the professional body for solicitors in England and Wales) to establish a Technology and the Law Policy Commission on the use of algorithms within criminal justice. In its landmark 2019 report, *Algorithms in the Criminal Justice System,*[76] The Law Society distinguished instrumental goals and 'justificatory concerns, which surround the legitimacy or illegitimacy of a decision system using algorithms' from vital 'dignitary concerns which relate to the threat to individual human beings being respected as whole, free persons'.[77] This analytical separation is important because it addresses the concern that a criminal justice system that presumes the effectiveness of algorithmic tools and prioritises instrumental goals like efficiency is liable to fail to treat individuals as human beings, and in so doing to 'place dignity at risk'.[78]

E. Limits on the agency of criminal justice professionals

The impact of algorithms on those subject to criminal justice interventions has attracted considerable critical attention. Far less attention has been paid to how and in what ways predictive tools inform and direct decisions by criminal justice actors, like policymakers, police, lawyers, judges, and experts in court or on parole boards. Yet RAIs may also erode or even override the agency of criminal justice professionals, limiting their capacity to exercise discretion, expertise, and good judgement. Quite how this silent actuarial takeover of professional expertise has occurred without attracting major controversy and political debate is puzzling. In his book *Against Prediction,* Harcourt argues '[t]hat the use of predictive methods has begun ... to mould our notions of justice, without our full acquiescence'.[79] He decries 'the influence of technical knowledge on our sense of justice', and

76 The Law Society, *Algorithms in the Criminal Justice System* (The Law Society of England and Wales 2019).

77 The Law Society, *Algorithms in the Criminal Justice System* (The Law Society of England and Wales 2019) 17.

78 The Law Society, *Algorithms in the Criminal Justice System* (The Law Society of England and Wales 2019) 20.

79 Bernard Harcourt, *Against Prediction: Profiling, Policing, and Punishing in an Actuarial Age* (University of Chicago Press 2007) 31.

concludes '[w]e have become slaves of our technical advances.'[80] Harcourt may overstate the claim by suggesting that predictive technologies have overridden the agency of criminal justice actors. Nonetheless, he rightly draws attention to challenges now faced by lawyers, judges and other professionals in defending their sphere of authority to exercise discretion and good judgement in decision-making.

The ascendency of RAIs is better understood not as a technological takeover, but as the consequence of political pressures and policy choices. These include populist demands for public protection and the rise of precautionary approaches to crime prevention.[81] Resort to RAIs has also been fuelled by a wider loss of faith in professional education, experience, and expertise.[82] Forensic psychiatrists and other penal experts have voiced doubts about the reliability of clinical risk assessments and concerns about the ethical issues that arise when doctors and psychiatrists undertake risk assessments on behalf of the court.[83] Lum and Koper note the common accusation that criminal justice decision-making is based on 'hunches and best guesses; traditions and habits; anecdotes and stories; emotions, feelings, whims, and stereotypes; political pressures or moral panics; opinions about best practices; or just the fad of the day'.[84] Algorithmic tools promise to guard against these hazards and 'counteract the behavioural biases of individual decision makers'.[85] In place of a criminal justice process influenced by the culture of the police canteen or local courthouse, or by populist or political pressures, algorithmic instruments have been promoted as tools

80 Bernard Harcourt, *Against Prediction: Profiling, Policing, and Punishing in an Actuarial Age* (University of Chicago Press 2007) 32.

81 Jude McCulloch and Dean Wilson, *Pre-Crime: Pre-Emption, Precaution and the Future* (Routledge 2016); Lucia Zedner and Andrew Ashworth, 'The Rise and Restraint of the Preventive State' (2019) 2 Annual Review of Criminology 429-450.

82 Ian Loader, 'Fall of the Platonic Guardians: Liberalism, Criminology and Political Responses in England and Wales' (2006) 46(4) British Journal of Criminology 561-586.

83 Nigel Eastman, 'The Psychiatrist, Courts and Sentencing: The Impact of Extended Sentencing on the Ethical Framework of Forensic Psychiatry' (2005) 29 The Psychiatrist 73-77; Paul S Appelbaum, 'Ethics and Forensic Psychiatry: Translating Principles into Practice' (2008) 36 Journal of the American Academy of Psychiatry and the Law 195-200.

84 Cynthia Lum and Christopher S Koper, 'Evidence-Based Policing' in Gerben Bruinsma and David Weisburd (eds), *Encyclopedia of Criminology and Criminal Justice* (Springer 2014) 1429.

85 The Law Society, *Algorithms in the Criminal Justice System* (The Law Society of England and Wales 2019) 16.

of systematic, evidence-based decision-making that centralise control and increase consistency, effectiveness, and efficiency. But at what cost?

In practice, the adoption of algorithmic tools does not merely limit the exercise of discretion by criminal justice professionals, it directs decision-making and curtails judicial independence. Where legislation mandates using risk assessment, judges are obliged to assume dangerousness in specified circumstances.[86] Resort to predictive tools thus also impacts the authority of officials and experts, denies the value of their experience and professional expertise, and curtails their ability to inform appropriate criminal justice outcomes.[87] The limits placed upon the freedom and role of criminal justice professionals matter, especially insofar as RAIs restrict officials' ability to treat suspects and defendants with decency and compassion, to explain their decisions, and to be held accountable. Although the widespread adoption of actuarial risk assessment tools results from deliberate choices made by politicians and policymakers, their promotion as the 'appliance of science' has had an enduring impact on the agency and authority of criminal justice professionals.

The dominance of algorithmic systems thus risks creating a substantially automated criminal justice system in which the exercise of human judgement, expertise, and moral compass is overborne by an increasingly 'dehumanised justice'.[88] The capacity of algorithmic technologies to override human judgement is well-documented,[89] and risks licensing the exercise of state coercive power in ways that human actors, even criminal justice officials at the highest levels, find difficult to contest.[90] In its report on *Algorithms in the Criminal Justice System*, the UK Law Society notes the concerns of the Chief Constable of Durham that 'human decision makers

86 In England and Wales, s.229(3) Criminal Justice Act 2003 obliged judges to assume the defendant was dangerous under specified conditions and to impose a sentence of Imprisonment for Public Protection. This statutory presumption of risk was controversial because it ousted judicial discretion and it was repealed three years later (s.17 Criminal Justice and Immigration Act 2008); no 69 above, 224.

87 Kevin R Reitz, 'Risk Discretion at Sentencing' (2017) 30(1) Federal Sentencing Reporter 68-73, 68.

88 The Law Society, *Algorithms in the Criminal Justice System* (The Law Society of England and Wales 2019) 20.

89 Karen Yeung, '"Hypernudge": Big Data as a Mode of Regulation by Design' (2017) 20 Information, Communication & Society 118-136.

90 Carolyn McKay, 'Predicting Risk in Criminal Procedure: Actuarial Tools, Algorithms, AI and Judicial Decision-Making' (2020) 32(1) Current Issues in Criminal Justice 22-39, 34-35.

may lack the confidence and knowledge to question or override an algorithmic recommendation.'[91] Even experienced criminal justice actors, from police officers through lawyers and judges to parole board members, appear to feel constrained to 'follow the algorithm' because they lack 'the authority and competence to change the decision'.[92] This inability to challenge RAIs may lead them to accept output, overemphasise quantifiable factors and pay insufficient regard to countervailing qualitative considerations, such as adherence to criminal justice values, human rights, and the exercise of moral judgement necessary to treat suspects, defendants, and offenders with decency, compassion, and mercy.

Reliance on RAIs risks generating automated forms of decision-making that sideline and hinder human capacity for moral reflection. The use of proprietary predictive software limits transparency and restricts officials' ability to reflect critically on the validity of risk assessments, the decisions they inform, and their accountability.[93] Automation, especially machine learning, undermines the capacity of criminal justice actors to challenge the imposition of disproportionate or inappropriate punishments and to prevent or rectify miscarriages of justice, especially in policing and at sentencing.[94] Criminal justice actors need to retain sufficient agency, the authority, means, and the power to question decisions made and exercise moral judgement to uphold due process and ensure that justice is done.[95]

---

91 The Law Society, *Algorithms in the Criminal Justice System* (The Law Society of England and Wales 2019) 20.

92 The Law Society, *Algorithms in the Criminal Justice System* (The Law Society of England and Wales 2019) 28.

93 Lyria Bennett Moses and Janet Chan, 'Algorithmic Prediction in Policing: Assumptions, Evaluation, and Accountability' (2018) 28(7) Policing and Society 806-822, 818.

94 Kent Roach, 'Wrongful Convictions: Adversarial and Inquisitorial Themes' (2010) 35 North Carolina Journal of International Law and Commercial Regulation 388-446; Carolyn Hoyle, 'Victims of the State: Recognising the Harms Caused by Wrongful Convictions' in Mary Bosworth, Carolyn Hoyle, and Lucia Zedner (eds), *Changing Contours of Criminal Justice: Research, Politics and Policy* (Oxford University Press 2016) 270-283.

95 Lucia Zedner and Carl-Friedrich Stuckenberg, 'Due Process', in Kai Ambos and Antony Duff (eds) *Core Issues in Criminal Law and Justice* volume one (Cambridge University Press 2019) 313-316, 321-323.

F. RAIs and Regard for Individual Agency

Respect for the individual is a core value of criminal justice that trumps instrumental goals of efficiency and effectiveness.[96] Yet, as Duff has argued, '[a]ny liberal society which takes seriously the values of autonomy and freedom must tolerate a significant level of crime' and this may require it to 'foreswear certain methods of efficient crime prevention ... because they would infringe the autonomy of those subject to them.[97] Duff's caution that efficiency should not be permitted to infringe individual autonomy is particularly germane when considering the future use of algorithms and how they might be better used.

Regard for individual agency and responsibility requires adherence to the following precepts. RAIs should not be constructed in ways that treat individuals unfairly by assessing the level of risk they pose based primarily on static characteristics or factors they cannot alter. Their use should abide by the values and principles of due process and give sufficient access to the workings of the algorithms to allow the defence to contest the case for the prosecution. This requirement is difficult to fulfil for complex algorithmic systems subject to commercial secrecy or reliant on machine learning that obscures the methodology by which scores are calculated. Even with legal assistance, most defendants will struggle to access, understand, or contest these calculations or have recourse against faulty risk assessments.[98] For these reasons, Jorgensen argues for greater regard for due process and proportionality,

> what fair distribution of burdens and benefits demands depends on context: pre-conviction, all individuals must have fair opportunity to avoid hostile encounters with law enforcement; at trial, they must not face disproportionate likelihood of false conviction; postconviction, they must not be subject to disproportionate punishment.[99]

96 Gabrielle Watson, *Respect and Criminal Justice:* (Oxford University Press 2018).

97 Antony Duff, 'Dangerousness and Citizenship' in Andrew Ashworth and Martin Wasik (eds) *Fundamentals of Sentencing Theory* (Oxford: Clarendon, 1998) 151.

98 Chelsea Barabas et al, 'Interventions over Predictions: Reframing the Ethical Debate for Actuarial Risk Assessment', Proceedings of Machine Learning Research 81(1) (2018) 1-15, 2.

99 Renée Jorgensen, 'Algorithms and the Individual in Criminal Law' (2021) 52(1) Canadian Journal of Philosophy 1-17, 8.

These ambitious precepts require more robust limits than those currently applied in the UK. Taken together, respect for individual agency, regard for due process and proportionality suggest a more limited role for algorithmic risk assessment tools in criminal justice than is presently the case.

In 2019, The Law Society voiced its concern for the 'new ethical, legal and social issues' posed by algorithmic technologies, based on an extensive review of their operation in the criminal justice system.[100] To improve oversight of their use, it recommended that the UK Centre for Data Ethics and Innovation[101] should be 'given a statutory footing as an independent, parliamentary body, with a statutory responsibility for examining and reporting on the capacity for public bodies, including those in criminal justice'.[102] Further Law Society recommendations aimed to ensure adequate data protection, enhance equality and respect for rights, improve transparency and accountability, ensure the lawfulness of algorithmic systems, and enable criminal justice actors and institutions to use algorithms appropriately and responsibly in policing and the criminal process.[103] More recently, the UK Ministry of Justice has promoted 'risk, needs and responsivity principles' which promote targeted programmes to address areas of need 'adapted to respond to people's individual circumstances, abilities and strengths', 'motivate, engage and retain participants', and produce evidence that 'the techniques used will help offenders to change' to reduce risk factors and enable them to desist from offending.[104]

This chapter has also observed how RAIs tend to sideline the experience and expertise of criminal justice professionals, limiting their freedom to exercise discretion in the interests of justice. For these reasons, the UK Law Society report stresses the need for 'meaningful human intervention' in decision-making to ensure that decisions and disposals within the criminal justice process are not 'based solely on automated processing' – a recom-

100 The Law Society, *Algorithms in the Criminal Justice System* (The Law Society of England and Wales 2019) 9.

101 https://www.gov.uk/government/organisations/centre-for-data-ethics-and-innovation (last visited 18 April 2024).

102 The Law Society, *Algorithms in the Criminal Justice System* (The Law Society of England and Wales 2019) 63.

103 The Law Society, *Algorithms in the Criminal Justice System* (The Law Society of England and Wales 2019) 5-8.

104 Ministry of Justice *Guidance: Offender behaviour programmes and interventions* (2022) https://www.gov.uk/guidance/offending-behaviour-programmes-and-interventions (last visited 18 April 2024).

mendation that speaks directly to concerns about limits on the agency of criminal justice officials.[105] To ensure greater transparency and accountability, The Law Society recommends the creation of a National Register of Algorithmic Systems, new statutory transparency rights, and greater powers for the UK Information Commissioner to examine algorithmic systems proactively. It further proposes that algorithms be liable to 'automatic, full qualitative review' and subject to a statutory Code of Practice.[106] Together, these recommendations would create a more robust framework for regulating the use of algorithms in criminal justice to improve their respect for human agency and adherence to fundamental rule of law values.

Independent ethical evaluation of algorithmic technologies to ensure their use in the criminal justice system respects individual agency and human dignity and accords with criminal law principles and due process values remains essential. The publication in 2021 of a UK national *Algorithmic Transparency Standard* for public sector departments and bodies is a welcome development.[107] It introduces regular publication of 'Algorithmic Transparency Reports',[108] which encourage best practice when using algorithmic tools, increase public trust, and enhance legitimacy.[109] Nonetheless, problems remain. The *Algorithmic Transparency Standard* is not on a statutory footing and does not impose transparency obligations on public officials.[110] Legal challenges to algorithmic technologies persist,[111] and a recent

105 The Law Society, *Algorithms in the Criminal Justice System* (The Law Society of England and Wales 2019) 6.

106 On the role of the Information Commissioner see https://ico.org.uk/ (last visited 18 April 2024).

107 CDEI Blog 'Developing the Algorithmic Transparency Standard in the open' https://cdei.blog.gov.uk/2022/10/10/developing-the-algorithmic-transparency-standard-in-the-open/ (last visited 18 April 2024).

108 See https://www.gov.uk/government/collections/algorithmic-transparency-reports (last visited 18 April 2024).

109 Marion Oswald et al, *The UK Algorithmic Transparency Standard: A Qualitative Analysis of Police Perspectives* (SSRN, 2022) https://papers.ssrn.com/sol3/papers.cfm?abstract_id=4155549 13 (last visited 18 April 2024).

110 Public Law Project 'Algorithmic Transparency Standard Pilot', https://publiclawproject.org.uk/content/uploads/2022/04/The-Algorithmic-Transparency-Standard-PLPs-feedback_.pdf (last visited 18 April 2024).

111 See Liberty 'Met to overall 'racist' Gangs Matrix after landmark legal challenge' (11 November 2022) - a legal challenge that led to the removal of c.1,000 names of young black men from the Matrix. See https://www.libertyhumanrights.org.uk/issue/met-to-overhaul-racist-gangs-matrix-after-landmark-legal-challenge/ (last visited 18 April 2024).

parliamentary investigation has reinvigorated calls for reform.[112] The House of Lords Report *Technology Rules?* (2022) concluded that, without adequate oversight or statutory regulation, the proliferation of algorithmic and other technologies risks creating a 'new Wild West' in the justice system.[113] To avert this prospect, RAIs urgently need to be brought closer in conformity with rule of law values and respect for individual agency, human dignity and rights.

G. Conclusion

The growing recognition that the advance of algorithmic tools poses serious risks to respect for individual agency and rights in policing and criminal justice has led to calls for radical reforms. These include a national oversight body, a task force, and a mandatory register of algorithms used by public officials.[114] Whether regulatory oversight alone is sufficient is doubtful, however. Arguably a more profound cultural change is needed.

To bring the use of algorithmic tools in closer conformity with the fundamental precept that the defendant is an autonomous agent, who can justly be called to account for her criminal conduct, requires closer attention to human dignity and capacity for choice. Throughout the criminal process, officials should treat individuals as responsible agents, capable of change. Rather than regarding risk factors primarily as evidence of prospective threats, a more positive approach is to see them as indicating needs that require intervention to tackle patterns of offending behaviour, substance abuse, or violent tendencies through programmes which encourage self-management and support desistance from further offending.[115] To ensure that the persuasive power of technology does not override the expertise and experience of criminal justice professionals, RAIs should be used in a more

112 House of Lords Justice & Home Affairs Committee, *Technology Rules? The Advent of New Technologies in the Justice System* HL Paper 180. For a list of recent similar inquiries see Box 2 'Previous work' 12. For a list of recent similar inquiries see Box 2 'Previous work' 12.

113 House of Lords Justice & Home Affairs Committee, *Technology Rules? The Advent of New Technologies in the Justice System* HL Paper 180, 3.

114 House of Lords Justice & Home Affairs Committee, *Technology Rules? The Advent of New Technologies in the Justice System* HL Paper 180, 42-46.

115 Ministry of Justice *Guidance: Offender behaviour programmes and interventions* (2022) https://www.gov.uk/guidance/offending-behaviour-programmes-and-interventions (last visited 18 April 2024).

limited way to guide, but not displace, structured professional judgement.[116] In these ways, we can seek to ensure that trust in the machine does not trump trust in individual responsibility and the agency, expertise, and authority of criminal justice professionals.

In conclusion, the central task of officials in the criminal process and at trial is to hold the responsible individual to account for their past choices and impose liability for their decision to engage in wrongful conduct. This chapter has shown how the widespread use of algorithmic risk assessment tools has the potential to discount the agency and responsibility of defendants and downplay the expertise of criminal justice professionals. It has tracked how, at each stage of the criminal process, resorting to algorithmic prediction risks disregarding fundamental legal values and individualised justice. The claim of risk assessment instruments to predict the future and the UK Supreme Court decision that the criminal court must assess the risk posed by the offender at the time of release limit freedoms and individual agency far into the future. Against these challenges, the European Court of Human Rights has rightly ruled that even those offenders sentenced to the longest terms should not be denied human dignity and the right to hope. In so doing, the Strasbourg Court offered welcome recognition of every individual's capacity for moral choice and potential for change.[117] In the face of rapid technological change, we need to ensure that algorithmic risk assessment instruments accord with the rule of law, respect human dignity, and to restore trust in the legal system. In this way, we may be able to mitigate the many hazards of our misplaced trust in the machine.

116 Mike Redmayne, *Character in the Criminal Trial* (Oxford University Press 2015) 264.

117 Andrew Ashworth and Lucia Zedner, 'Some Dilemmas of Indeterminate Sentences: Risk and Uncertainty, Dignity and Hope' in Jan W Keiser, Julian V Roberts and Jesper Ryberg (eds), *Predictive Sentencing: Normative and Empirical Perspectives* (Hart Publishing 2019) 127-148, 138; see also Kimberley Brownlee, 'Punishment and Precious Emotions: A Hope Standard for Punishment' (2021) 41(3) Oxford Journal of Legal Studies 589–611.

Contesting the Inevitability of Scoring: The Value(s) of Narrative in Consumer Credit Allocation

Frank Pasquale, Mathieu Kiriakos

When firms allocate credit to consumers, credit scoring often seems both inevitable (how else could the decision be made?) and desirable (how else could the decision be objective and fair?). This article challenges both of those assumptions, after exploring the power asymmetries generated by scoring. Evaluation of narrative accounts of creditworthiness is plausible in at least some scenarios, despite the volume of credit applications. Moreover, these alternative paths to credit reflect normative values (such as intelligibility and fair consideration) that are just as compelling as the objectivity and fairness attributed to scoring.

One of these values is trust. While quantitative assessments of reliability based on third-party data are designed to enable "trustless" transactions, qualitative accounts of creditworthiness depend on evaluators' trusting the accounts of creditworthiness offered by those applying for credit for themselves. What this shift potentially loses in efficiency it has the potential to gain in mutual understanding, the alleviation of alienation, and opportunities for redemption. It also represents a democratization of power in financial relationships, requiring those with funds to lend to do a bit more to understand at least some of those applying for credit on their own terms, rather than forcing applicants into Procrustean beds of data analytics.

A. Introduction

The usual rationale for scoring is to replace the alleged imprecision and subjectivity of human judgment with the objectivity of machine calculation. However, there is human judgment in any evaluative system; the judgment is simply at a remove in most cases of machine scoring, reflected in decisions about what data to include and how to analyse it. The real target of scoring appears to be natural language. The words of credit histories are replaced with numerical data, as the allegedly subjective thought and writing of loan officers are displaced by the exacting and automatic logic of code and mathematics.

Both industry analysts and finance academics have celebrated this shift as a step toward more fair and inclusive banking. However, critics have documented problems of inaccurate, biased, or inappropriate data used in scoring systems old and new.[1] This has in turn led to numerous efforts to reform scoring via law, aimed at improving the accuracy, representativeness, and propriety of data used. This chapter suggests a complementary direction for the fields of algorithmic accountability and fairness in machine learning: the exploration, explication, and prescription of narrative approaches as alternatives to scoring systems for some subset of applicants rejected by automated decision-making. Rather than only trying to critique (and by implication improve) credit scoring, scholars might also articulate language-driven evaluative practices to be used in alternative paths to credit.[2] Articulation of scoring's "other" (here generalized as narrative) will also assist researchers seeking to better understand scoring—and may even reveal patterns that allow quantitative analysts to improve scoring itself. Such narrative paths to credit may also vindicate dignitary interests of applicants long noted by scholars of procedural justice in the context of adjudications.[3]

The modesty of our claims should be noted at the outset. We are not introducing narrative accounts of creditworthiness as a panacea for the shortcomings of scoring. The sheer volume of applications for credit would make it impossible to replace scoring with narrative. Nor are we arguing that narrative would outperform scoring on any particular metric. Rather, we introduce it below as a way of illuminating shortcomings in scoring, and potentially addressing critical concerns of some of those marginalized by scoring systems if they wish to make their case via an explanation of their creditworthiness. We examine and recommend alternatives to scoring in a spirit of consumer empowerment and social experimentalism, demonstrating that well-designed narrative-driven application processes may well lead to the discovery of data and patterns that improve scoring itself.

---

1 Pamela Foohey and Sara Greene, 'Credit Scoring Duality' [2021] 85 Law and Contemporary Problems 101.

2 Frank Pasquale, 'Power and Knowledge in Policy Evaluation: From Managing Budgets to Analyzing Scenarios' [2023] 86(3) Law and Contemporary Problems.

3 Pamela Foohey, 'A New Deal for Debtors: Providing Procedural Justice in Consumer Bankruptcy' [2019] 60(8) Boston College Law Review.

Part B below motivates the chapter by documenting the prevalence of problematic data and decisions in financial scoring systems. Part C characterizes the dominance of scoring in consumer credit as a cognitive monoculture and explores the practical advantages of a limited re-introduction of narrative accounts of creditworthiness provided by applicants themselves. Part D addresses objections to such narrative evidence of creditworthiness, while Part E makes the case for valuing them not only on instrumental, but also on intrinsic grounds. Part F concludes with reflections on how the articulation of practical alternatives to algorithmic evaluation processes may promote a more refined critical theory of automated decision making.

B. Normative and Practical Shortcomings of Scoring

In the rapidly evolving landscape of credit scoring, where algorithms powerfully influence financial opportunities, a critical concern has emerged: while credit scoring systems are touted as objective and fair, their users operate within legal frameworks riddled with ambiguities and limitations.[4] For example, while "alternative credit scoring is often presented to applicants as a 'second chance' after they have been denied credit based on a traditional credit score," the reality for many is "coerced surveillance and predatory inclusion".[5] Regulators and consumers may also find it difficult to apply existing laws to many alternative forms of credit assessment because of new data sources and technologies that these alternative tools use.[6] As law professor and sociologist Ifeoma Ajunwa has demonstrated, "in some instances, automated decision-making has served to replicate and amplify bias".[7]

The lack of transparency in proprietary algorithms raises significant concerns about privacy and accuracy. Even when borrowers can understand key aspects of the data and algorithms used to deny them credit (or offer it on substandard terms), there are further shortcomings of algorithmic

4 Janine Hiller and Lindsay Jones, 'Who's Keeping Score? Oversight of Changing Consumer Credit Infrastructure' [2022] 59 Am Bus Law J. 61.

5 Lindsay Sain Jones and Goldburn Maynard Jr., 'Unfulfilled Promises of the Fintech Revolution' [2023] 111 California Law Review 801.

6 Mikella Hurley and Julius Adebayo, 'Credit Scoring in the Era of Big Data' [2016] 18 Yale Journal of Law and Technology 148.

7 Ifeoma Ajunwa, 'The Paradox of Automation as Anti-Bias Intervention' [2020] 41(5) Cardozo Law Review 1671.

scoring unlikely to be addressed under current law. Many laws were created before the digital age and do not address the complexities of modern credit scoring, especially concerning the use of big data and AI algorithms, leaving consumers vulnerable to unfair practices.[8] As law professor Nikita Aggarwal has observed, "The growing reliance on consumers' personal data by lenders, coupled with the ineffectiveness of existing data protection remedies, has created a data protection gap in consumer credit markets that presents a significant threat to consumer privacy and autonomy".[9]

Several reforms internal to algorithmic processes have been proposed to address these issues, ranging from mandates for more representative data to new algorithmic methods. However, these reforms are still premised on computational thinking: understanding human behaviour and solving social problems by drawing on "concepts fundamental to computer science".[10] Evaluating abilities and proclivities through performance-based metrics is a nearly-universal assumption of the reformist literature on credit scoring in both the legal field, and emerging academic communities like the Association for Computing Machinery's Conference on Fairness, Accountability, and Transparency (ACM FAccT).

Credit scoring systems exemplify computational thinking by integrating abstraction, reduction, and decomposition to treat applicants like "algorithmic selves".[11] It reduces the applicant to a series of data points and comparisons, rather than the type of "enstoried" self the applicant herself might narrate.[12] Credit scoring is premised on a narrow definition of problem-solving and system design, leveraging vast amounts of data (often secret) and statistical models (often proprietary) to make lending decisions, embodying the analytical strategies that Jeannette Wing has described as essential to computational thinking.[13] Thus algorithmic scoring will require applicants for credit to remain dependent on certain aspects of a digital persona that is difficult to control, or even access. By contrast, a narrative

8 Frank Pasquale, *The Black Box Society* (Harvard University Press 2015).
9 Nikita Aggarwal, 'The norms of algorithmic credit scoring' [2021] 80(1) Cambridge Law Journal 42.
10 Jeannette Wing, 'Computational thinking' [2006] 49(3) Communications of the ACM 33.
11 Frank Pasquale, 'The Algorithmic Self' [2015] 17(1) The Hedgehog Review.
12 Christian Smith, *Moral, Believing Animals: Human Personhood and Culture* (Oxford University Press 2003).
13 Jeannette Wing, 'Computational thinking' [2006] 49(3) Communications of the ACM 33.

account of creditworthiness allows its author to apprehend and reason about aspects of her own life and experience that are close-to-hand. It is in this sense a form of lifeworld-based resistance against systemic colonization.[14]

To be sure, the importance of offering consumers access to their credit data cannot be overstated; such access signifies a shift from opacity to transparency, and when successfully used for advocacy, from helplessness to empowerment. Consumers, armed with the ability to scrutinize their credit data, can identify, and rectify errors based on their statutory rights. This proactive involvement not only ensures the accuracy of individual credit reports, but also holds credit reporting agencies and financial institutions accountable for the data they collect and utilize. However, even if credit applicants were able to access all of the data used to judge them, and could assure it is accurate, appropriate, and non-discriminatory, those adversely impacted by computational evaluation systems may have good grounds for believing that the system has not taken into account all potential positive or crediting information about them.[15] A vast amount of our actions, words, proclivities, and other characteristics are never captured in data that is available to those deploying credit scoring systems. Nor could they be; to argue otherwise is to entertain the possibility of truly invasive surveillance, an "omni-opticon" that does not seem worth building in a society giving even a scintilla of value to privacy.

Finally, even if we can imagine a hypothetical realm where a critical mass of concerns about inaccurate and inappropriate data are resolved, the subjective experience of an entirely computationally administered realm of credit may be very corrosive. Legal scholars have discussed the grounding of a right to a human decision in human rights law.[16] But one need not believe in an inalienable right to a human decision in order to recognize that there are certain situations that simply demand some level of personalized

14 Jürgen Habermas, The Theory of Communicative Action II: Lifeworld and System: A Critique of Functionalist Reason (Thomas McCarthy trans., Beacon Press 1987).

15 Katrina Geddes, 'The Death of the Legal Subject: How Predictive Algorithms Are (Re)constructing Legal Subjectivity' [2023] 35 Vanderbilt Journal of Entertainment & Technology Law 25.

16 Yuval Shany, 'The Case for a New Right to a Human Decision Under International Human Rights Law' [2023] Working Draft (SSRN: https://ssrn.com/abstract=4592244).

response.[17] Critiques of alienation have been developed in critical theory and sociology for over a century, and they have a renewed relevance when machines judge humans.[18]

The foundation of such concerns about alienation lies in the subjective experience of meaninglessness and powerlessness.[19] Meaninglessness can in turn be analytically decomposed into at least two other dimensions. First, when computational evaluative methods are strictly protected via trade secrecy, or are too complex to be meaningfully explained, they cannot be reliably interpreted. Whereas an explicable evaluation provides some level of guidance as to how one can behave in the future in order to obtain a better outcome, inexplicable ones can leave their subjects unable to understand how they fell short in the past, and how they can do better in the future. Second, even if all factors are explained, there is often a sense of injustice sparked by a realization of how arbitrary the connection between states of affairs in the world and numbers meant to represent them can be.

The site "How Normal am I" offers some jarring examples of this flattening reductionism (HowNormalAmI.eu, 2022). It will, for example, generate an attractiveness score for any user between one and ten. No rationale is offered for the score. Of course, there is a burgeoning literature of academic and quasi-academic accounts of facial symmetry, and similar rationales for such evaluation. But in common experience, the diversity of such evaluations is well understood: beauty is in the eye of the beholder. Flattening all such evaluations into a single number on an ordinal scale introduces what might be called a curse of two-dimensionality: a dangerous compression of complex qualitative judgment into a since metricized scale. More dangerously, it can lead to a homogenization of evaluations once those whose apprehension of a given quality are now outliers, learn about a generalized score, and start to adjust their own opinions accordingly.

Aside from these concerns about meaninglessness, powerlessness is also a separate, but intertwined, aspect of the problem of alienation. Although decisions with respect to hiring, job performance evaluation, credit determination, and educational admissions, should not be as hedged in by due process protections as, say, a criminal trial, they nevertheless have some

17 Kiel Brennan Marquez, Karen Levy, and Daniel Susser, 'Strange Loops' [2019] 34(3) Berkeley Technology Law Journal 745.

18 Frank Pasquale, New Laws of Robotics (Harvard University Press 2020).

19 Melvin Seeman, 'On the Meaning of Alienation' [1959] 24(6) American Sociological Review 783.

juridical character. The power of the litigant in a courtroom consists in the ability to challenge the case against himself, and to advance his own account of the application of legal standards to facts. A subject of credit scoring who has been given no such ability, thanks to computational decision-making, senses a loss of power relative to older forms of evaluation, which at least offered some forms of intelligibility. It is a particularly total and technical form of "private governance," in philosopher Elizabeth Anderson's memorable formulation.[20]

C. Normative and Practical Advantages of Narrative Accounts of Creditworthiness

None of the above arguments should be taken as a blanket condemnation of the use of credit scoring in evaluations of persons. There are, of course, many ways in which it has improved on older forms of evaluation. Nor is a "right to a human decision" normatively desirable in all of the contexts mentioned above.[21] Some decisions are simple enough to be automated in so many instances that the cost of avoiding errors or inappropriate actions is so small, relative to the cost of human intervention, that it makes little sense to provide human review in every decision scenario.

Nevertheless, the decision here is not between *always* automating decisions, or *always* putting a human reviewer in the loop. Rather, it is possible to imagine varied middle grounds.[22] For example, there may be a lottery or sortition to decide who, among those rejected by an automated system, is able to press their case to a human decisionmaker with the right to override the automated decision. Such a lottery might be imposed at the beginning of a decision-making process, too, giving some percentage of applicants the opportunity to make their case narratively, or in person, bypassing the algorithmic evaluation entirely. For example, bank regulators could require mortgage lenders to permit, say, 1% to 10% of applicants to have the option to bypass algorithmic assessment, and to have their application judged holistically by a loan officer. Applicants previously rejected by an algorithmic assessment would be most likely to take advantage of

20 Elizabeth Anderson, Private Government: How Employers Rule Our Lives (and Why We Don't Talk About It) (Princeton University Press 2017).

21 Aziz Huq, 'The Right to a Human Decision' [2020] 106 Virginia Law Review 611.

22 Rebecca Croot of, Margot Kaminski, and Nicholson Price, 'Humans in the Loop' [2022] 76 Vanderbilt Law Review 429.

such an opportunity. Alternatively, 1% to 10% of rejected applicants might automatically be given this opportunity to draft a narrative appeal of the decision against them.

Varied rationales may emerge from narrativization. For example, a consumer applying for a car loan to gain access to a more profitable or specialized job opportunity might benefit from the opportunity to explain this situation in a written statement. A family seeking credit for a particular housing situation could gain from submitting a detailed account of their ability and willingness to pay. Lenders might develop processes that guide applicants toward useful narratives by prompting them with specific questions, requesting relevant documents, and asking for written personal statements. Video testimony may also allow individuals to convey their circumstances in a more personal manner. Allowing multiple formats would allow a wider array of applicants to effectively communicate their story.

The great advantage of narrative explanations from borrowers themselves is that they can reflect the kaleidoscopic complexity of contemporary life. Indeed, the openness of narrative may be the only way to fairly implement what Cen and Raghavan call the "right to be an exception to a data-driven rule".[23] Designers of an algorithmic system can only try to anticipate relevant factors; an invitation to self-explanation invites in the wisdom of crowds, as well as their apprehensions of meanings of events rarely if ever captured in automated data gathering. Consider the Consumer Financial Protection Bureau's call for narrative complaints about financial institutions, which created a very useful source of information for regulators.[24] It represents useful advocacy on behalf of consumers to give them an opportunity to be heard. Financial institutions could be required to give such opportunities to some portion of applicants as well, re-inscribing juridical conceptions of fairness in scenarios from which they have long been unduly evacuated.

Given past work categorizing and analysing narratives of creditworthiness on niche peer-to-peer lending sites like Prosper, many modes of

23 Sarah Cen and Manish Raghavan, 'The Right to be an Exception to a Data-Driven Rule' [2022] ArXiv <https://arxiv.org/abs/2212.13995>.

24 Matthew Bruckner and CJ Ryan, 'The Magic of Fintech? Insights for a Regulatory Agenda from Analyzing Student Loan Complaints Filed with the CFPB' [2022] 127 Dickinson Law Review 49; Matthew Bruckner, and CJ Ryan 'Student Loans and Financial Distress: A Qualitative Analysis of the Most Common Student Loan Complaints' [2023] 35 Loyola Consumer Law Review 203.

self-presentation have been documented.[25] Given narrative's range and scope, any particular sketch of a compelling narrative can only suggest the contours of insight available. Nevertheless, four concrete examples might be useful in demonstrating the value of such first-person accounts of credit-worthiness.

First, consider the plight of a large, multigenerational family of low-income persons applying to buy an eight-bedroom home. Existing credit scoring systems may only assess the creditworthiness of one person, or a couple, when credit is sought. While the whole family unit together may have more than enough income to pay the mortgage, any particular person or couple within it may be considered far from qualified considered alone. This may in turn be exacerbated by their suffering a relatively thin credit file with respect to large purchases. An alternative system, allowing an applicant to explain the entire family's situation, could easily lead to a loan decision that would be welfare-enhancing all around.

Second, consider the challenges faced by immigrants in accessing credit, despite potentially having a strong credit history in their country of origin, thanks to the difficulty of transferring such crediting information to credit bureaus in their new home. Traditional credit scoring systems might categorize them as high-risk due to the lack of a domestic credit file. A narrative approach would enable immigrants to share their financial history, including credit status and repayment behavior in their home country, as well as their reasons for immigration, professional skills, and employment prospects.

Third, student loan debt may create a misleading impression when unaccompanied by more granular data about the value of an applicant's degree and training. Traditional credit scoring can easily penalize recent college graduates who have invested in their education and have high earning potential, but are burdened early in their career with student loan repayment. Adopting a narrative approach could allow these individuals to explain their career trajectory, their field of study, and the expected increase in their income as they gain experience. This perspective could provide a more

25 Michal Herzenstein, Scott Sonenshein, and Uptal M. Dholakia, 'Tell Me a Good Story and I May Lend You Money: The Role of Narratives in Peer-to-Peer Lending Decisions' [2011] 48 Journal of Marketing Research S138; Laura Larrimore, Li Jiang, Jeff Larrimore, David Markowitz, and Scott Gorski, 'Peer to Peer Lending: The Relationship Between Language Features, Trustworthiness, and Persuasion Success' (2011) 39(1) Journal of Applied Communication Research 19.

nuanced understanding of their financial situation and future ability to manage and repay debt.

A final narrative example revolves around the kind of debt or delinquencies a person may have accumulated. For many years, credit bureaus in the U.S. have reported medical debt like any other debt, despite its often unpredictable occurrence and occasionally devastating (but temporary) impact on the debtor's ability to work and pay off debt. A narrative accounting of the *reasons* for a delinquency may stimulate sympathy from a loan officer, or even self-interest—the realization that the applicant is far less likely to default again than someone who wilfully refused to pay back a debt. In this way, narrative has the potential to make credit determinations a more morally intelligible process, rather than a realm of abstract, mathematicised prediction.

Mandates for consideration of such alternative, narrative evaluations are helpful in a further way. Considering algorithmic systems as socio-technical assemblages that evolve over time, new and unexpected types of data derived from alternative, narrative systems of evaluation may help improve the performance of the algorithmic system. It is simply impossible for such a system to "know" all there is to be ascertained about any set of persons. Data from alternative systems will thus help alleviate the familiar problem of cognitive monoculture: the fragility that can result when a given firm or set of firms relies too heavily on one particular way of apprehending the world which may become outdated over time. As Amar Bhide has observed, the rapid, imitative adoption of similar algorithms by financial institutions for the assessment of mortgage applicants contributed to the financial crisis of 2008.[26] Alternative modes of evaluation could have suggested more robust classifiers, or helped uncover the wishful thinking that lay behind many "no income, no job or assets" borrowers who ultimately defaulted on their loans. Empirical research has already demonstrated the complementarity of quantitative data and narratives, concluding that supplementing the former with the latter enables more accurate prediction of defaults.[27] Mandatory consideration of narratives could further enhance this effect.

26 Amar Bhidé, A Call for Judgment: Sensible Finance for a Dynamic Economy (Oxford University Press 2010).

27 Yufei Xia, Lingyun He, Yinguo Li, Nana Liu, and Yanlin Ding, 'Predicting Loan Default in Peer-to-Peer Lending Using Narrative Data' [2020] 39 Journal of Forecasting 260.

D. Addressing Objections

Admittedly, at least four objections may be lodged against even a limited re-introduction of narrative accounts of creditworthiness. First, allowing some applicants to put their case narratively, while denying that chance to others, may seem unfair to those who are not given a narrative "second chance." Second, from a very different perspective, those who take a more positivistic orientation toward credit scoring may argue that the grant of credit is optimally a value-free process, free of value-laden narratives. Third, there is a concern that narrative evaluation is more susceptible to discrimination than that constrained by "hard" data and algorithmic processes. Fourth, there is a fear that narrative writers will game the system, using rhetorical strategies unconnected to either creditworthiness or normative values in order to tilt the evaluative playing field in their favour. We address each concern below.

First, on a "horizontal" level, sortition to determine which applicants are able to present their case narratively may seem unfair. Some percentage of applicants would receive a privilege that the rest do not enjoy. One way to mollify this effect would be to preferentially open the narrative option to those who have already been rejected by an automated credit scoring system. In this way, the narrative, non-algorithmic option is reserved first for those who have already been disadvantaged by dominant, algorithmic systems. True, their disadvantage may have been "deserved" in some sense; for example, someone who has wilfully refused to pay back loans may find future credit options restricted or non-existent. However, it is difficult to see how we could truly determine "desert" even in those scenarios without some opportunity for the person affected to make the case that they had committed to a different behavioural path in the future. Non-algorithmic, narrative accounts of oneself are one way to offer such a second chance. They are especially necessary as the weight of data about past conduct exerts more influence on individuals as surveillance and data recordation become more persistent, encompassing, and accessible.[28]

The mention of "merit" above may give rise to a second objection: That we have mistaken an empirical process of assigning capital to its most profitable use, for a normative evaluation of the worth of persons. The rationale for alternative modes of evaluation is strongest if we think of a

28 Arvind Narayanan, 'The urgent need for accountability in predictive AI' [2023] <https://www.cs.princeton.edu/~arvindn/talks/insight_forum_statement.pdf>.

given credit opportunity as something that an applicant deserves. But even persons with perfect scores on their exams do not always obtain entrance to the university they consider the best. Nor is it easy to articulate a rationale for why some subset of, say, one thousand applicants for ten loans, are clearly more deserving than those who were ultimately chosen. Viewed from a value-free perspective, the choice of applicants is simply a pattern matching problem. From an even more positivistic perspective, the market will ultimately punish those entities which are using inappropriate systems, as the only test of the validity of the system is its ability to advance the commercial interests of the firm using it.

There are at least two responses to such a tough-minded perspective on credit scoring based on big data and AI. First, there is always a plurality of values at stake in any automated decision-making system. As sociologist and law professor Ari Ezra Waldman has argued, "We need a robust, substantive approach to ensure that algorithmic systems meet fundamental social values other than efficiency".[29] These systems do not exist simply in order to advance the key performance indicators of the entity imposing them. It is legitimate for authorities to ensure that credit scoring is in some way responsive to social concerns, even if this results in a system that does not maximize profits. Profit maximization is often narrow and distortive in its own right, and has never been the exclusive object of well-functioning financial systems.

Furthermore, even if it is assumed that the maximands and key performance indicators now driving big data and AI driven credit scoring systems capture all relevant social values, there still is a case for implementing alternative mechanisms for choosing applicants, to better advance such values. No such system will be able to encompass all potentially relevant data as it determines who will be most likely to maximize its key performance indicators. Alternative evaluation systems permit applicants to nominate their own categories of potentially relevant data. For example, consider the possible rationales that may be given by applicants offering narrative accounts of why they deserve to be given a loan. They may focus on aspects of their own reliability that are now overlooked by algorithmic ranking and rating systems. For example, a person may note that they always send cards to their friends two weeks before their birthdays. If a pattern emerges, whereby some critical mass of alternative applicants brings up this self-nominated

29 Ari Ezra Waldman, 'Power, Process, and Automated Decision-Making' [2019] 88 Fordham Law Review 613.

indicator of reliability, and it turns out that it is indeed correlated with reliable repayment of a loan, then developers of the algorithmic system may in turn try to incorporate such data in future versions of their algorithms. In this way, alternative evaluation systems assist mainstream credit scoring to move from local to global maxima, continually highlighting the type of data that may be useful, but at present left out of, existing databases.

A third objection arises out of the history of narrative in consumer credit, focusing on the original public service rationales for moving toward "hard" data. While rapid numerical evaluations of credit history could be reductive, they also tended to be less privacy-invasive than credit bureaus' narratives, and more resistant to discriminatory construction or interpretation. As Professor Kenneth Lipartito helpfully recounts, "For all the dangers posed by databanks in a free society, their potential to eliminate traditional forms of discrimination through hard data, combined with the efficiency they offered to credit granters, made them appear more equalitarian and less liable to abuse than traditional methods that emphasized character and the narrative of lifestyle".[30] Empirical research on recent uses of narrative in consumer credit offers some confirmation of this concern. For example, one study of a peer-to-peer lending site that permitted would-be borrowers to include their picture with their profile found "evidence of significant racial disparities," as "listings with blacks in the attached picture [were] 25 to 35 percent less likely to receive funding than those of whites with similar credit profiles".[31] Direct or indirect references by applicants to their gender, race, religion, sexual orientation, or other protected class characteristics may lead to discriminatory decision-making by those who evaluate narratives.

It is important to address this risk. Finance regulators should require credit-granting entities to release aggregate reports on the relative percentages of denials with respect to each protected class. If the narrative portion of credit determination was resulting in disparately negative impacts with respect to minorities, penalties could be imposed. Auditors may also require decisionmakers to give an account of how they decided on particular narrative applications, to ensure that non-discriminatory reasons were decisive.

30 Kenneth Lipartito, 'The narrative and the algorithm: Genres of credit reporting from the nineteenth century to today' [2010] 2010 Harvard Business School History Seminar.

31 Devin Pope and Justin R. Sydnor, 'What's in a Picture?: Evidence of Discrimination from Prosper.com' [2011] 46(1) Journal of Human Resources 53.

Though narrative determinations may seem more amenable to discrimination than quantitative ones, it is important not to overstate this case. Many of the data points critical to quantitative determinations may themselves have been shaped by discrimination. Moreover, narratives' construction and interpretation are far less susceptible to the "black box" and trade secrecy problems that so often confound regulation of algorithms. On this ground alone they offer a more egalitarian mode of evaluation. As Jenna Burrell thoughtfully explains, with respect to "second chance" narrative appeals similar to the ones we propose:

A citizen can appeal to a clerk at the Department of Motor Vehicles, try to explain a misunderstanding to a social worker, or describe exceptional circumstances to a judge or a jury and, in these very human ways, challenge bureaucracies or leverage human judgment and discretion within systems of rules. Skills of human communication and persuasion vary by individual. However, there are far fewer of us who are capable of communicating with or understanding automated decision-making tools. With wider use of automation, important human skills and ways of acting and doing in the world are at risk of being displaced.[32]

The explainability of narratives and their evaluation offers a path to contestation (with respect to discrimination, or on other grounds) that is all too often lacking in the case of trade secret protected, black boxed algorithms. On this ground alone, those concerned about problems of discrimination should welcome what we propose: the limited re-introduction of narrative on the initiative of consumers denied credit algorithmically.

The fourth objection, focused on gaming, is familiar from the realm of algorithmic credit scoring. One of the main reasons that scoring entities refuse to reveal their methods is a professed fear that some applicants will strategically alter their behavior to gain advantage over others, by changing their behavior in ways that conform to the record of optimal applicants, but which are not actually signs of increased creditworthiness in their case. As empirical studies of narrative-driven credit evaluation develop, the same may happen in the case of qualitative accounts of creditworthiness. For example, one study of European peer-to-peer lending found that successful narratives often featured orthography (proper spelling) and positive

---

32 Jenna Burrell, 'Automated Decision-Making as Domination' [2024] 29(4) First Monday.

emotional terms.[33] A study of narratives offered on Chinese peer-to-peer lending site Renrendai concluded that negative sentiment reduced the likelihood of credit offers.[34] If such studies became widely known, they could encourage inauthentic self-presentation, or corrode the signifying power of characteristics like orthography.

Our response to this objection is necessarily ambivalent. Modulating self-expression to please the powerful is a real harm to autonomy. However, strategic self-presentation is also a mainstay of modern life).[35] If applicants are incentivized to become better spellers strategically, there is probably little to complain about: this skill will help in other situations (such as employment applications) as well. Similarly, the authenticity (and thus normative value) of expressions of negative affect can be fruitfully questioned. Sometimes the construction of a more positive self-presentation may be useful to the credit applicant, a route to hope via reflection. Nevertheless, we do acknowledge that further study of the self-shaping effects of narration is warranted.

E. The Intrinsic Case for Narrative Accounts of Creditworthiness

We have so far made the case for narrative accounts of creditworthiness in largely instrumental terms, emphasizing how they could assist rejected applicants, and advance the key performance indicators and other goals of the implementers and regulators of algorithmic systems. We now turn to an intrinsic case for narrative accounts of creditworthiness. This intrinsic case is built on the merit and value of narrative in human reasoning in general. It also rests on the normative value of an "opportunity to be heard" familiar from literature on due process.[36]

---

33 Gregor Dorfleitner, Christopher Priberny, Stephanie Schuster, Johannes Stoiber, Martina Weber, Ivan de Castro, and Julia Kammler, 'Description-Text Related Soft Information in Peer-To-Peer Lending–Evidence from Two Leading European Platforms' [2016] 64 Journal of Banking & Finance 169.

34 Jing-Ti Han, Qun Chen, Jian Guo Liu, Xiao-Lan Luo, and Weiguo Fan, 'The Persuasion of Borrowers' Voluntary Information in Peer to Peer Lending: An Empirical Study Based on Elaboration Likelihood Model' [2018] 78 Computers in Human Behavior 200.

35 Erving Goffman, *The Presentation of Self in Everyday Life* (University of Edinburgh Social Sciences Research Centre 1956).

36 Sara B. Tosdal, 'Preserving Dignity in Due Process' [2011] 62(4) Hastings Law Journal 1005.

Narrative offers a way to reduce the burden of alienation that black box models can impose on those judged by them. As noted above, alienation has at least two subjective dimensions: a sense of powerlessness and meaninglessness.[37] Algorithmic decisions can create a sense of powerlessness when the data subject affected by them feels that they have failed to take into account an important aspect of the situation, and nevertheless the subject is unable to obtain some recognition of that aspect. The finality of a black boxed score is rankling, portending an expertocratic, technocratic decision-making process impervious to challenge.[38] This is one reason why the legitimacy of public administration has always hinged on some combination of expertise, legal regularity, and democratic accountability.[39] Knowledge of *why* a decision was made is just as important as the legitimacy of the decision-making process itself. The problem of meaninglessness entails epistemic frustration: a sense that the decision made was not based on recognizable categories of distinction, but may well have been fundamentally arbitrary or, worse, based on grounds that should be forbidden (such as race or gender).

Narrative channels for evaluation can help address both meaninglessness and powerlessness.[40] First, an invitation to give a narrative account of one's desert—with the concomitant assurance that at least some percentage of submitters will be granted the benefit or status they seek—is a way to connect one's own sense of value with that of powerful institutions. Researchers examining extant narratives in peer to peer lending, a niche areas of consumer finance that does often permit them, have found that extended narratives are often persuasive to lenders.[41] Such lenders realize that there are many worthy and deserving individuals who fall through the cracks of algorithmic sorting systems. However well-designed a complex, automated decision-making system may be, it will still create some number

37 Melvin Seeman, 'On the Meaning of Alienation' [1959] 24(6) American Sociological Review 783.

38 Frank Pasquale, & Danielle Keats Citron, 'Response and Rejoinder: Promoting Innovation While Preventing Discrimination: Policy Goals for the Scored Society' [2014] 89(4) Washington Law Review 1413.

39 Peter Schuck, 'Multi-Culturalism Redux: Science, Law, and Politics' [1990] 11(1) Yale Law & Policy Review 1.

40 Byung-Chul Han, *The Crisis of Narration* (John Wiley & Sons 2024).

41 Laura Larrimore, Li Jiang, Jeff Larrimore, David Markowitz, and Scott Gorski, 'Peer to Peer Lending: The Relationship Between Language Features, Trustworthiness, and Persuasion Success' [2011] 39(1) Journal of Applied Communication Research 19.

of "losers" who consider their classification not only unfair, but meaningless. Permitting at least some of them a chance to present their merits on their own terms helps alleviate this aspect of alienation.[42]

Of course, narrative accounts of creditworthiness are no cure-all. Regulators are unlikely to require firms to develop alternative evaluation pathways for more than, say, 10% of those rejected by an algorithmic system, and likewise may not be willing to require acceptance of more than 10% of those alternative applicants. Critics may complain that, in such a minimalist implementation, alternative evaluation pathways may only help 1% of those applicants disfavoured by an opaque algorithmic system. However, over the course of a lifetime, a person may be adversely affected by many algorithmic systems. Chances to make one's case may come up many times. Moreover, the very act of making a case for oneself enacts a sense of self-esteem and a sense of self-worth, via articulation of a creditable reputation).[43] It also offers an opportunity for critical self-reflection, since a convincing narrative account will need to take into account rationales that can be accepted by one's audience.

This process of self-assertion is also important for alleviating sensations of powerlessness. The mere knowledge that some authority has recognized the potential unfairness of algorithmic systems—and has given those affected by them an unusual kind of appeal—signals to those excluded by algorithms that some power in society has taken their problems into account. Indeed, narration itself can be a form of power and empowerment.[44] As "story-telling animals", persons will frequently find themselves inclined to relate events causally, in order to find meaning in the past.[45]

Narrative accounts of creditworthiness will also diversify paths to reputational distinction in society, demonstrating that there is more than one way to be recognized as meritorious. A social acceptance of the diversity of merit is one way to address the grave concerns about "meritocracy"

---

42 Sara B. Tosdal, 'Preserving Dignity in Due Process' [2011] 62(4) Hastings Law Journal 1003.

43 Michal Herzenstein, Scott Sonenshein, and Uptal M. Dholakia, 'Tell Me a Good Story and I May Lend You Money: The Role of Narratives in Peer-to-Peer Lending Decisions' [2011] 48 Journal of Marketing Research S138.

44 Ken Plummer, *Narrative Power: The Struggle for Human Value* (Polity Press 2019); Benjamin A Rogers et al. 'Seeing your life story as a Hero's Journey increases meaning in life' [2023] 125(4) Journal of Personality and Social Psychology 752.

45 Alasdair MacIntyre, *After Virtue: A Study in Moral Theory* (University of Notre Dame 1981) (London: Duckworth).

expressed in Michael Young's eponymous, satirical book.[46] To "know" one lives in a society where all have been fairly ranked on clear social metrics would be exceptionally demoralizing to those consigned to the bottom of the social hierarchy. Knowing instead that there are several paths to distinction, and that algorithmic ordering is just one of them, is a way of maintaining morale among all those in society, not just its algorithmically chosen "winners." And given that self-perception as a winner or loser often depends on one's chosen comparators, maintaining such morale is important to social integration.[47]

This leads to a final dimension of the intrinsic case for alternative evaluation systems: the epistemic advantage inherent in judgments drawing upon complementary forms of knowledge. Too many advocates of algorithmic decision-making suggest it is part of a historical progression toward rational decision making, where older processes (based largely on narrative description and evaluation) are discarded in favour of more objective, numerical ways of understanding reality. Yet these forms of knowledge ideally complement each other, with distinctive strengths. Consider, for instance trade credit, which still very frequently incorporates methods that are descriptive and qualitative.[48] Lenders know that, in the context of business loans, there is extraordinary variation in risk and opportunity given the variation between entities and irreducibly historical knowledge relevant to each applicant. It is time to bring this awareness to consumer lending as well.

Many scholars have called for reuniting (or at least recognizing the distinctive, respective values of) the "two cultures" of scientific objectivity and humanistic intersubjectivity).[49] For example, the psychologist Jerome

---

46 Michael Young, *The Rise of the Meritocracy. London* (Routledge 1961).

47 Robert Frank, *Choosing the Right Pond: Human Behavior and the Quest for Status* (Oxford University Press 1988); Talcott Parsons, [1961] 'An Outline of the Social System' in Craig Calhoun, ed., Classical Sociological Theory (Wiley-Blackwell, 2nd Ed., 2007).

48 Yufei Xia, Lingyun He, Yinguo Li, Nana Liu, and Yanlin Ding, 'Predicting Loan Default in Peer-to-Peer Lending Using Narrative Data' [2020] 39 Journal of Forecasting 260; Kenneth Lipartito, 'The narrative and the algorithm: Genres of credit reporting from the nineteenth century to today' [2010] 2010 Harvard Business School History Seminar.

49 Charles P. Snow, *The Two Cultures and the Scientific Revolution* (Cambridge University Press 1962); on intersubjectivity see Jürgen Habermas, *The Theory of Communicative Action II: Lifeworld and System: A Critique of Functionalist Reason* (Thomas McCarthy trans., Beacon Press 1987).

Bruner has drawn a distinction between paradigmatic and narrative modes of reasoning, while insisting on the value of each.[50] For Bruner, the paradigmatic is a largely scientific and analytic mode, whereas narrative is about interpretation, meaning, and synthesis. Tsoukas and Hatch provide a useful set of contrasts between paradigmatic and narrative modes of thought, noting the importance of context and history in the latter.[51] History (not only writ large, but also the sense of self-narration) is a source of resonance and meaning to individuals.[52]

The critical contribution of narrative explanation here is a reconnection between the subjects of credit systems and common-sense understandings of desert and opportunity via a causal and value-laden account of life events. As Bruner argues, "it is very likely the case that the most natural and the earliest way in which we organize our experience and our knowledge is in terms of the narrative form".[53] It is not too much to ask of contemporary credit systems that at least some of their benefits are granted on expressly narrative rationales. Moreover, if advocates of narrative do not insist on its relevance being imposed by law in appropriate scenarios, they should not be surprised if its waning role in the contemporary academy and culture shrivels to the point of vestigiality.

F. Conclusion

Social scientists and lawyers have proposed many ways of improving the fairness and accountability of computational evaluations of person. They may have several positive effects, addressing several of the concerns described in Part II above. However, there are strong market pressures working to undermine any consistent effort to ensure that corporations address social concerns when they collect, analyse, and use data. It can be extremely expensive and limiting to clean data so thoroughly that all inaccuracies are removed, and discriminatory impacts are addressed. Moreover, even if such improvements are made, alienating aspects of opaque scoring will remain.

50 Jerome Bruner, *The Culture of Education* (Harvard University Press 1996).

51 Haridimos Tsoukas and Mary Jo Hatch, 'Complex Thinking, Complex Practice: The Case for a Narrative Approach to Organizational Complexity' [2001] 54(8) Human Relations 979.

52 Hartmut Rosa, *Resonance: A Sociology of Our Relationship to the World* (James Wagner tr, Polity 2019).

53 Jerome Bruner, *The Culture of Education* (Harvard University Press 1996) at 121.

Addressing the shortcomings of credit scoring systems will require a concerted effort from all stakeholders involved. It is important to develop ethical guidelines and regulatory frameworks that promote fairness, transparency, and accountability in the development and use of scoring algorithms. Yet even if such efforts are successful, there will be pervasive and persistent misgivings about the tendency of our "ordinal society" to totally subsume so much of credit allocation into algorithmic forms.[54] Therefore, non-algorithmic evaluative systems should play some role as an alternative in the future. They are by no means a panacea, but they can provide concrete help to some marginalized applicants, and may also illuminate shortcomings in dominant algorithmic approaches.

The contribution of this chapter is, we hope, twofold. On a prescriptive level, it offers a rationale for regulators to require those operating powerful social systems to meet halfway at least some of those whom they now exclude or disadvantage via algorithmic means. Algorithmic systems can only be reformed up to a certain point, and certain of their shortcomings are either unreformable or unfathomable given computational complexity and trade secrecy. By contrast, if lenders were required to offer some invitations to rejected applicants to offer a narrative account of their creditworthiness, this would serve as a direct and powerful way to inculcate societal recognition that any evaluative system is but one of many ways of assessing merit.

The second contribution is, on a critical and theoretical level, to explore the types of understanding of algorithmic systems that are possible once one has recognized alternative modes of evaluation. Charles Taylor once observed that behind every critique of power lays a positive (even if unarticulated) normative vision of freedom; behind every critique of lies and obfuscation lays a conception of truth.[55] When a fuller range of evaluative modes are considered, new dimensions of algorithmic evaluations' shortcomings are more sharply delineated. For example, social theory's critique of alienation, once dismissed as idealistic, becomes more urgent and clearer once one understands what authentic self-advocacy would look like in predominantly scored settings. Just as Hartmut Rosa helped revive critical theory by demonstrating its contemporary power when reconsidered in light of his account of resonance, we hope to have advanced the critical

54 Marion Fourcade and Kieran Healy, *The Ordinal Society* (Harvard University Press 2024).

55 Charles Taylor, C. 'Foucault on Freedom and Truth' [1985] 12(2) Political Theory 152.

sociology of algorithmic accountability by illuminating the strengths and plausibility of a non-algorithmic approach in an evaluative context.[56]

Bibliography

Alasdair MacIntyre, *After Virtue: A Study in Moral Theory* (University of Notre Dame 1981) (London: Duckworth).

Amar Bhidé, *A Call for Judgment: Sensible Finance for a Dynamic Economy* (Oxford University Press 2010).

Ari Ezra Waldman, 'Power, Process, and Automated Decision-Making' [2019] 88 Fordham Law Review 613.

Arvind Narayanan, 'The urgent need for accountability in predictive AI' [2023] <https://www.cs.princeton.edu/~arvindn/talks/insight_forum_statement.pdf>.

Aziz Huq, 'The Right to a Human Decision' [2020] 106 Virginia Law Review 611.

Benjamin A Rogers et al. 'Seeing your life story as a Hero's Journey increases meaning in life' [2023] 125(4) Journal of Personality and Social Psychology 752.

Byung-Chul Han, *The Crisis of Narration* (John Wiley & Sons 2024).

Charles P. Snow, *The Two Cultures and the Scientific Revolution* (Cambridge University Press 1962).

Charles Taylor, C. 'Foucault on Freedom and Truth' [1985] 12(2) Political Theory 152.

Christian Smith, *Moral, Believing Animals: Human Personhood and Culture* (Oxford University Press 2003).

Devin Pope and Justin R. Sydnor, 'What's in a Picture?: Evidence of Discrimination from Prosper.com' [2011] 46(1) Journal of Human Resources 53.

Elizabeth Anderson, *Private Government: How Employers Rule Our Lives (and Why We Don't Talk About It)* (Princeton University Press 2017).

Erving Goffman, *The Presentation of Self in Everyday Life* (University of Edinburgh Social Sciences Research Centre 1956).

Frank Pasquale and Danielle Keats Citron, 'Response and Rejoinder: Promoting Innovation While Preventing Discrimination: Policy Goals for the Scored Society' [2014] 89(4) Washington Law Review 1413.

Frank Pasquale, 'Power and Knowledge in Policy Evaluation: From Managing Budgets to Analyzing Scenarios' [2023] 86(3) Law and Contemporary Problems.

Frank Pasquale, 'The Algorithmic Self' [2015] 17(1) The Hedgehog Review.

Frank Pasquale, *New Laws of Robotics* (Harvard University Press 2020).

Frank Pasquale, *The Black Box Society* (Harvard University Press 2015).

Gregor Dorfleitner, Christopher Priberny, Stephanie Schuster, Johannes Stoiber, Martina Weber, Ivan de Castro, and Julia Kammler, 'Description-Text Related Soft Information in Peer-To-Peer Lending–Evidence from Two Leading European Platforms' [2016] 64 Journal of Banking & Finance 169.

56 Hartmut Rosa, Resonance: A Sociology of Our Relationship to the World (James Wagner tr, Polity 2019).

Haridimos Tsoukas and Mary Jo Hatch, 'Complex Thinking, Complex Practice: The Case for a Narrative Approach to Organizational Complexity' [2001] 54(8) Human Relations 979.

Hartmut Rosa, *Resonance: A Sociology of Our Relationship to the World.* (James Wagner tr, Polity 2019).

Ifeoma Ajunwa, 'The Paradox of Automation as Anti-Bias Intervention' [2020] 41(5) Cardozo Law Review 1671.

Janine Hiller and Lindsay Jones, 'Who's Keeping Score? Oversight of Changing Consumer Credit Infrastructure' [2022] 59 Am Bus Law J. 61.

Jeannette Wing, 'Computational thinking' [2006] 49(3) Communications of the ACM 33.

Jenna Burrell, 'Automated Decision-Making as Domination' [2024] 29(4) First Monday.

Jerome Bruner, *The Culture of Education* (Harvard University Press 1996).

Jing-Ti Han, Qun Chen, Jian Guo Liu, Xiao-Lan Luo, and Weiguo Fan, 'The Persuasion of Borrowers' Voluntary Information in Peer to Peer Lending: An Empirical Study Based on Elaboration Likelihood Model' [2018] 78 Computers in Human Behavior 200.

Jürgen Habermas, *The Theory of Communicative Action II: Lifeworld and System: A Critique of Functionalist Reason* (Thomas McCarthy trans., Beacon Press 1987).

Katrina Geddes, 'The Death of the Legal Subject: How Predictive Algorithms Are (Re)constructing Legal Subjectivity' [2023] 35 Vanderbilt Journal of Entertainment & Technology Law 25.

Ken Plummer, *Narrative Power: The Struggle for Human Value* (Polity Press 2019).

Kenneth Lipartito, 'The narrative and the algorithm: Genres of credit reporting from the nineteenth century to today' [2010] Harvard Business School History Seminar.

Kiel Brennan-Marquez, Karen Levy, and Daniel Susser, 'Strange Loops' [2019] 34(3) Berkeley Technology Law Journal 745.

Laura Larrimore, Li Jiang, Jeff Larrimore, David Markowitz, and Scott Gorski, 'Peer to Peer Lending: The Relationship Between Language Features, Trustworthiness, and Persuasion Success' [2011] 39(1) Journal of Applied Communication Research 19.

Lindsay Sain Jones and Goldburn Maynard Jr., 'Unfulfilled Promises of the Fintech Revolution' [2023] 111 California Law Review 801.

Marion Fourcade and Kieran Healy, *The Ordinal Society* (Harvard University Press 2024).

Matthew Bruckner and CJ Ryan, 'Student Loans and Financial Distress: A Qualitative Analysis of the Most Common Student Loan Complaints' [2023] 35 Loyola Consumer Law Review 203.

Matthew Bruckner and CJ Ryan, 'The Magic of Fintech? Insights for a Regulatory Agenda from Analyzing Student Loan Complaints Filed with the CFPB' [2022] 127 Dickinson Law Review 49.

Melvin Seeman, 'On the Meaning of Alienation' [1959] 24(6) American Sociological Review 783.

Michael Young, *The Rise of the Meritocracy. London* (Routledge 1961).

Michal Herzenstein, Scott Sonenshein, and Uptal M. Dholakia, 'Tell Me a Good Story and I May Lend You Money: The Role of Narratives in Peer-to-Peer Lending Decisions' [2011] 48 Journal of Marketing Research S138.

Mikella Hurley and Julius Adebayo, 'Credit Scoring in the Era of Big Data' [2016] 18 Yale Journal of Law and Technology 148.

MK Lee, 'Understanding Perception of Algorithmic Decisions: Fairness, Trust, and Emotion in Response to Algorithmic Management' [2018] 5(1) *Big Data & Society.*

Nikita Aggarwal, 'The norms of algorithmic credit scoring' [2021] 80(1) Cambridge Law Journal 42.

Pamela Foohey and Sara Greene, 'Credit Scoring Duality' [2021] 85 Law and Contemporary Problems 101.

Pamela Foohey, 'A New Deal for Debtors: Providing Procedural Justice in Consumer Bankruptcy' [2019] 60(8) Boston College Law Review.

Peter Schuck, 'Multi-Culturalism Redux: Science, Law, and Politics' [1990] 11(1) Yale Law & Policy Review 1.

Rebecca Crootof, Margot Kaminski, and Nicholson Price, 'Humans in the Loop' [2022] 76 Vanderbilt Law Review 429.

RM Kramer, 'Trust and Distrust in Organizations: Emerging Perspectives, Enduring Questions' [1999] 50(1) *Annual Review of Psychology* 569-598.

Robert Frank, *Choosing the Right Pond: Human Behavior and the Quest for Status* (Oxford University Press 1988).

Sara B. Tosdal, 'Preserving Dignity in Due Process' [2011] 62(4) Hastings Law Journal 1003.

Sarah Cen and Manish Raghavan, 'The Right to be an Exception to a Data-Driven Rule' [2022] ArXiv <https://arxiv.org/abs/2212.13995>.

Talcott Parsons, [1961] 'An Outline of the Social System' in Craig Calhoun, ed., Classical Sociological Theory (Wiley-Blackwell, 2nd Ed., 2007).

Yufei Xia, Lingyun He, Yinguo Li, Nana Liu, and Yanlin Ding, 'Predicting Loan Default in Peer-to-Peer Lending Using Narrative Data' [2020] 39 Journal of Forecasting 260.

Yuval Shany, 'The Case for a New Right to a Human Decision Under International Human Rights Law' [2023] Working Draft (SSRN: https://ssrn.com/abstract=4592244).

Trust and Legitimacy in an Era of Algorithmic Criminal Justice

Hadar Dancig-Rosenberg

This chapter explores the implications of algorithmic decision-making in the criminal justice system, focusing on the concepts of trust, legitimacy, and accountability. It discusses whether the transition to AI-driven criminal justice signifies a genuine regime change or merely perpetuates existing biases under the guise of neutrality. It highlights how algorithms, while promising consistency and efficiency, may undermine procedural justice principles. It proposes that integrating human discretion with algorithmic tools, alongside participatory and deliberative frameworks, could enhance the legitimacy and trustworthiness of AI-driven criminal justice systems.

A. Introduction

Algorithmic criminal justice has transitioned from a theoretical concept to an undeniable reality. The adoption of algorithmic and AI-based tools and technologies by criminal legal institutions is no longer a matter of "if." Such algorithms are now integral to various stages of the criminal legal process, from predictive policing to pretrial detention, predictive prosecution, sentencing, and post-sentencing.[1]

As time progresses and more experience is gained in using AI tools, the normative debate over the desirability of making the criminal legal system rely on algorithms with a 'mediation' of humans becomes more controversial. In the United States, the current efforts of criminal justice reform to constitute a systemic, fundamental change in the flawed existing

1 For a collection of writings demonstrating the use of algorithms along various stages of the criminal legal process, see, e.g., Andrew Guthrie Ferguson, Policing Predictive Policing, 94 Wash. U. L. Rev. 1109 (2017); Andrew Guthrie Ferguson, Predictive Prosecution, 51 Wake Forest L. Rev. 705 (2016); Megan Stevenson, Assessing Risk Assessment in Action, 103 Minn. L. Rev. 303 (2018); Richard Berk & Jordan Hyatt, Machine Learning Forecasts of Risk to Inform Sentencing Decisions, 27 Fed. Sent'g Rep. 222 (2015); Richard Berk, An Impact Assessment of Machine Learning Risk Forecasts on Parole Board Decisions and Recidivism, 13 J. Experimental Criminology 193 (2017).

criminal legal system have brought to the forefront the question of whether algorithmic justice can serve the goal of improving the broken system.[2] Scholars have highlighted arguments for or against using algorithms in criminal justice-making processes. In this chapter, I would like to reflect on the interplay of AI-driven criminal justice and the concepts of trust and legitimacy, given the ongoing debate on the desirable ways to promote criminal justice reform.

B. AI-driven Criminal Justice: A Cosmetic or a Real Regime Change?

The crisis of faith in the current criminal legal system has sparked a pressing need for a systemic change – not a cosmetic one, but a shift towards a new regime. Christoph Burchard suggested a hypothesis explaining why algorithmic predictions have become so prevalent in the US: "Many have lost faith in criminal law as a 'big experiment' that can be turned towards progress and positive reform. The underlying conflict or conflict resolution, then, needs to be experienced as something with positive potential. If this is not the case, regime change becomes an issue - from law to algorithms; from criminal law to transformative justice".[3]

Burchard points out a distinction between the concepts of trust and faith. Trust refers to a subjective perception that one has towards someone or something in concrete cases or circumstances (it could be a person, an agency, or an institution).[4] Faith is a first-order belief that relates to the normative conceptions or the ontological foundation of a regime/institution. Therefore, someone who feels disappointment following a specific experience or an encounter with the criminal legal system might feel distrust toward the system's agents whose conduct did not meet her expectations. However, at the same time, she might still have faith in the system as a

2 See, e.g., John Chisholm & Jeffery Altenburg, The Prosecutor's Role in Promoting Decarceration: Lessons Learned from Milwaukee County, in Smart Decarceration: Achieving Criminal Justice Transformation In The 21st Century 71 (Matthew W. Epperson & Carrie Pettus-Davis eds., 2017).

3 Christoph Burchard, Musings on a Vision of Predictive Criminal Justice in Light of Trust, Conflict, Uncertainty, and Coercion (unpublished draft).

4 There is a rich body of writing in social sciences on the concept of trust. In the context of criminal law, see, e.g., Joshua Kleinfeld & Hadar Dancig-Rosenberg, Social Trust in Criminal Justice: A Metric, 98 Notre Dame Law Review 101 (2022); Kevin Vallier, Social, and Political Trust: Concepts, Causes, and Consequences (Research Paper, Knight Foundation).

whole, as it carries much more than one bad experience. The system holds a set of values, goals, and rationales that are appreciated as valuable and desirable from that person's point of view. As long as the bad experience is the exception, it might break trust, but it will not undermine faith—the deep belief in the legitimacy of the regime/institution. However, if a person repeatedly experiences more and more disappointing encounters, she might start to doubt this system or institution as a whole. When anecdotal bad experiences become systematic, individuals may lose faith.

Based on this distinction between trust and faith, Burchard explained how the crisis of faith with the traditional criminal justice system led to a willingness to make a "regime change" – a transformation from clinical predictions and human-based decisions to predictive algorithms and AI-based judgments. The supposition is that algorithmic justice can constitute a new regime—a transition from one set of principles and values to another, substantially differentiated from the traditional, old regime. But does the transition to algorithmic justice indeed mark a regime change? Does the transition from conventional, liberal criminal justice run by humans to computational-oriented, predictive criminal justice reflect a change in values and policies? Is it about a profound alteration of normative principles and values, or is it only a replacement of the mere procedures and techniques of decision-making? The answer to this question seems more complicated than it looks at first glance.

One of the fundamental functions of predictive algorithms is to foresee the future according to the past. Algorithms are fed by input representing the data that have been accumulated until the moment of processing this input. This nature of algorithms makes algorithmic predictions quite conservative. Algorithmic models are developed based on past decisions made by human decision-makers. Humans fill the algorithms with content; They determine what the algorithms should measure, what weight to give each metric, what to look at, and what to overlook. Therefore, by definition, algorithms encode underlying existing human biases and tendencies. They may even enhance such tendencies by inflating their weight as predictors of risk or other outcomes of interest.

In that sense, algorithms do not seem revolutionary. Instead, they seem an easy tool to perpetuate former preferences and normative decisions, replicating and reproducing a similar set of values and principles that were determined and adopted by human decision-makers in the past. It is true that, at a certain level, they could "clean" the process from noise or biases.[5] AI algorithms have the potential to enhance consistency among decision-makers and construct the decision-making process to be less reliant on individual biases or propensities. Also, their improvability trait ensures they 'fix' themselves in an ongoing and iterative process to reflect the most accurate output. But essentially, algorithms are still shaped in the form of human biases. In the criminal legal system, they reflect judges', prosecutors', and police officers' biases. Some scholars, therefore, have classified algorithms as a form of bureaucratic, as opposed to democratic, criminal justice.[6] It has been argued that "they may make systems more resistant to change, especially given their tendency to reflect normative facts about the world embedded in their underlying data".[7] Algorithms preserve and amplify past policies established by criminal legal professionals. They do not absorb data representing creative, untraditional, and critical standpoints of multiple stakeholders and community members.

It is not clear then that the transition to algorithms indeed marks a substantial regime change that can revive the faith lost in the criminal justice system. Indeed, people might fall into the illusion that algorithms create a regime change. However, given the ontological character of algorithms and how they are built and operated, there is a solid reason to argue that they represent the same old thing in a different package. One may even claim that algorithms create a more dangerous representation of the old system because the "different package" hides the same old thing and, thus, causes people to develop *false* faith. In other words, people may believe that algorithms constitute a substantial regime change, whereas, in fact, it is the same old story.

5 Kahneman, Sibony, and Sunstein distinguish between noise and bias. While noise is variability in human judgment that leads to inconsistent decisions, namely random errors, bias leads to systematic errors. *See* DANIEL KAHNEMAN, OLIVIER SIBONY, AND CASS SUNSTEIN, NOISE: A FLAW IN HUMAN JUDGMENT (2021).

6 For a distinction between notions of bureaucratic and democratic criminal justice, see a symposium issue titled "Democratizing Criminal Law," published by the NORTHWESTERN UNIVERSITY LAW REVIEW (2016). The symposium is dedicated to the dispute over whether to promote reform in the criminal justice system by adopting a bureaucratic or democratic approach.

7 Itay Ravid & Amit Haim, *Progressive Algorithms*, 12 UC IRVINE L. REV. 527, 563 (2022).

C. Trust, Legitimacy and Accountability

At this point, I would like to add two concepts to the discussion of criminal justice in the era of algorithms. These concepts are *legitimacy* and *accountability*, and they are both connected to trust.

Let me start with the concept of legitimacy and what we know about it from the body of research on procedural justice. In the 90s, Tom Tyler and colleagues demonstrated through a series of empirical studies that procedures perceived as fair enhance the sense of governmental legitimacy. This legitimacy significantly influences legal compliance far more than the perspectives that view human motivation, primarily in terms of force and incentives.[8] Moreover, fair procedures might affect compliance more than substantive outcomes.[9] When people perceive decision-making processes as fair, namely as understandable, respectful, transparent, and neutral, they ascribe a higher level of legitimacy to the decision and the decision-maker as an authority. This increases their level of compliance.[10]

Tyler and colleagues have distinguished between two components of procedural justice. The first component, the quality of interpersonal treatment, relates to the respectful attitude given by the authorities to those affected by the decision, as well as the recognition and upholding of their rights and needs throughout the process.[11] The second component, the quality of the decision-making process, refers to whether the decision was made in a neutral, transparent, equal, and unbiased manner, whether explanations about the procedure and how the decision was reached were provided by the authority, and whether the parties were given an opportunity to voice their opinions and present their positions in a way that could influence the decision.[12]

8 *See* Tom R. Tyler, Why People Obey The Law (2006); Tom R. Tyler, *Procedural Justice, Legitimacy, and the Effective Rule of Law*, 30 Crime & Just. 283 (2003); Tom R. Tyler & Yuen J. Huo, Trust In The Law: Encouraging Public Cooperation With The Police And Courts (2002).

9 Tyler, Why People Obey The Law, *ibid*, at 175.

10 *See* Tyler & Huo, *supra note* 8, at 26; Tyler, *Procedural Justice, Legitimacy, and the Effective Rule of Law*, *supra note* 8, at 284 (2003); Jason Sunshine & Tom R. Tyler, *The Role of Procedural Justice and Legitimacy in Shaping Public Support for Policing*, 37 Law & Soc'y Rev. 513, 534 (2003).

11 Tyler, *Procedural Justice, Legitimacy, and the Effective Rule of Law*, *supra note* 8, at 329.

12 *Ibid, ibid.*

Looking at algorithms through a procedural justice lens, it seems that pessimistic-realistic critics would question their alignment with procedural justice principles. Starting with neutrality, algorithms are allegedly supposed to be more neutral and "cleaned" from noise and human biases. They are emotionless (so they cannot be in a good or bad mood), consistent, never get tired, and can provide input based on a large number of previous cases, following an analysis based on "big picture" data, reducing the weight of outliers. Whereas emotions are inherent to human nature and have been traditionally perceived by many as a potential engine for infecting discretion and increasing irrationality, inaccuracy, and discrimination, algorithms are (still) emotionless (even though some AI tools use a language of emotions when you ask them how they feel!). Yet, as mentioned below, given that algorithmic tools are fed by humans and, therefore, may substantially rely on "dirty data,"[13] critics have pointed out that this romantic supposition is naïve and false. In fact, as explained above, algorithms might perpetuate and replicate human-created discrimination and bias under the guise of neutrality. Moreover, their rigidity hinders the ability to identify unique cases that justify deviating from the pattern.

The role of emotions in criminal justice decision-making processes raises particularly interesting questions. It is worth dwelling on the interrelation between emotions and bias or noise creation. Allegedly, emotions may interfere in applying the same decision-making process and, within the process, the same considerations in similar cases, thus potentially leading to different treatment and outcomes in similar cases. Who wants to be sentenced by an exhausted, tired judge who has not had the chance to take a lunch break (even if she is known as a decent judge)?

However, this interrelation between emotions and biases or noise seems more complicated than it might look in the first place. Despite the tendency to see the vices of emotions in infecting decision-making processes, emotions might sometimes serve as tools to fix arbitrariness and to distinguish between cases that might be perceived "on the surface" as identical if you consider only certain kinds of measurable data and ignore the broader context, which is sometimes hard to measure. Think about unique cases that do not fall into typical categories of cases. Empathy, sensitivity, intuition, and compassion can sometimes lead to a more just outcome when a

13 See Rashida Richardson, Jason M. Schultz & Kate Crawford, Dirty Data, Bad Predictions: How Civil Rights Violations Impact Police Data, Predictive Policing Systems, and Justice, 94 N.Y.U. L. Rev. Online 15 (2019).

combination of exceptional circumstances, characteristics, life stories, and backgrounds makes an individual case one-of-a-kind. Algorithms might do no justice in such cases. They will produce only an approximate outcome based on the closest cases they encountered, not the fairest and most just outcome that fits this unprecedented case. Since they predict based on past experience, they cannot recognize outliers and exceptions, unlike humans. Emotions might increase creativity and encourage acting and thinking less patterned and more intuitively—a virtue that is needed and welcome in unique cases.

For AI algorithms, a given case could be described as an element in a mathematical set of elements. Algorithms *cannot* "see" the people behind the case. Real-life stories are reduced and translated into a collection of facts and data. In contrast, legal professionals *can* recognize defendants, crime victims, or others involved in or affected by a criminal case as individuals, even within the overloading machinery of criminal justice. Yes, unfortunately, some professionals do not do it properly. Incisive critics of the mainstream criminal legal system may even argue that many, if not most, professionals fail to treat stakeholders humanely enough. Still, even if this is correct, it does not mean that criminal justice actors *cannot* treat stakeholders humanely. Human decision-makers in the criminal legal system can develop this human capacity; they can remind themselves daily that what they do applies to real people's lives. If they are encouraged to do so (e.g., by relevant incentives set by the system), they will be *able* to do so. For this to happen, emotions must be granted pride of place because emotions are essential for "translating" a case – an element in a mathematical set, into a story of an individual—a human being with a unique life experience. Algorithms, at least for now, do not have this capacity. Instead of a human being, they "see" an abstract element.

Since algorithms cannot feel, something important might get lost in their decision-making process, which applies to humans, particularly in the criminal justice context, where moral judgments are so integral. One of the episodes of the British anthology television series "*Black Mirror*" demonstrates how emotions are essential for making moral decisions.[14] The episode shows that when soldiers put on glasses that transform the figures they see from humans to mutated humans called "roaches," and when they do not know that the figures they see are, in fact, regular people,

14 "Black Mirror", season 3, episode 5 "Man Against Fire" (written by Charlie Brooker, 2016).

they lose their compassion. Algorithms can be metaphorically compared to someone who produces output with compassion-blocking glasses. Under such conditions, respectful treatment as a procedural justice component cannot be provided. Moreover, the outcome itself might not be fair, not just the procedure. It turns out that, on the one hand, algorithms are not free from the vices of distorted emotions embedded within the data they underly. On the other hand, they cannot benefit from the virtues of emotions humans have and use in extraordinary cases to fix arbitrariness and make justice in idiosyncratic cases.

In addition, the use of algorithmic tools in the criminal justice system undermines transparency.[15] This argument is primarily based on the inherent obscurity of algorithmic systems, particularly those that use deep learning and remain opaque or hidden from human comprehension. This problem has been termed the "black box problem," which means that "observers can witness the inputs and outputs of these complex and non-linear processes but not the inner workings,"[16] including observers with computational expertise. This lack of clarity potentially conflicts with legal standards that require clear reasoning behind decisions, particularly in the context of criminal law, where the stakes are high.

To sum up, even if algorithmic tools could increase the chances of reaching the most accurate and just outcome (and as explained, this is a big question in itself), we might lose a human-friendly process that people expect to experience to acquire legitimacy for its outcome and maintain their faith in the criminal legal system. Doing justice is essential, but the appearance of justice also has its merits. In other words, while reaching the right outcome is essential, the process of reaching that outcome can be no less important, and even more important to people affected by this outcome, to see it as legitimate and, therefore, to comply with it. Furthermore, decision-making processes that are not aligned with procedural justice principles might sometimes lead to unjust substantive outcomes. As Kevin Vallier stated when discussing the best ways to cultivate trust among members of a polity, "[w]e generally want social trust to be sustained for the right reasons. Pouring the 'trust hormone' Oxytocin into the water supply might make people more trusting, but it is not a good way to promote

15 See, e.g., Alyssa M. Carlson, Note, The Need for Transparency in the Age of Predictive Sentencing Algorithms, 103 Iowa L. Rev. 303 (2017).

16 Warren J. Von Eschenbach, Transparency and the black box problem: Why we do not trust AI, 34 Philosophy & Technology 1607 (2021).

social trust. It is better to sustain social trust by giving persons morally appropriate incentives to be trustworthy, and then allowing social trust to form as a free cognitive and emotional response to observed trustworthy behavior".[17] An analogy can be drawn to the context of developing trust (on an individual case) and faith (on a systemic ground) in an algorithmic regime of criminal justice: we should not (and probably even cannot) instil trust and faith in people by memorizing a mantra of "we believe in algorithms because they make justice!". Algorithms need to be trustworthy; this can happen if they are transparent, neutral, and, at the same time, sensitive and creative; this can happen if they are open to absorbing broader information representing multiple perspectives and considerations that are sometimes hard to capture through measurable metrics. In such a reality, people will develop sustainable trust and faith as a natural cognitive and emotional response.

Another factor that influences trust is accountability. Individuals have the right to understand the decisions made by public officials in their cases. Margot Kaminski and Jennifer Urban argued that if decision-makers cannot explain their decisions, as is often the case with decisions made by algorithms, it violates the basic expectation of the individuals affected.[18] For decision-makers, the option to rely on algorithms might reduce accountability.[19] If a decision primarily depends on algorithmic judgement, it offers a strong "defence claim" to a human decision-maker. Instead of explaining and justifying a decision by using an independent judgment, decision-makers might tend to overly rely on algorithmic recommendations because, in this way, they can attribute responsibility to an external entity – the machine ("Hey, it's the algorithm, not me!"). [20] This phenomenon has been known as the "automation bias." However, when a decision depends mainly on human discretion, a potential decision-maker realizes that her discretion would be the subject of scrutiny. She will be evaluated and promoted (or not) by her decisions. Therefore, she will need to explain why she decided this and not that. The requirement to account for how and why she made

17 Vallier, supra note 4, at 4.

18 Margot Kaminski & Jennifer Urban, The Right to Contest AI,121 Columbia L. Rev. 1957 (2021).

19 See Kate Crawford & Jason Schultz, Al Systems as State Actors, 119 Columbia L. Rev. 1941 (2019).

20 Linda J. Skitka, Kathleen Mosier & Mark D. Burdick, Accountability and Automation Bias, 52 Int'l J. Hum.-Comput. Stud. 701 (2000).

that specific decision creates incentives to be more cautious, balanced, prudent, and accountable with her decisions.

D. Trust in an Era of Algorithms: A Look to the Future

What, after all, can be done to minimize the risks of utilizing algorithms in the criminal legal system without giving up the benefit of using them? How can we enhance trust and faith in an AI-based predictive criminal justice system that is not false but authentic and justified? And how can the algorithmic regime work hand-in-hand with other turns and trends in the criminal justice system seeking to reform systemic problems and make the system more democratic?

These questions portray some of the challenges the future holds. Potential solutions should combine additional toolsets of human checks and balances along the decision-making processes in the criminal justice context. One suggestion, for instance, is to combine the use of algorithms with other reforms that deviate from traditional principles and values but are based on human discretion. Itay Ravid and Amit Haim suggested designing what they call "progressive algorithms."[21] Their proposed decision-making model prioritizes accountability, transparency, and democratization principles by adopting progressive prosecutors' agendas and using them as the content according to which computational methods and algorithms would be designed. As Ravid and Haim explain, at first glance, it seems that the trends of progressive prosecutors and algorithmic justice are fundamentally at odds over a crucial issue in criminal justice reform—what role do humans play, and what potential do they have in driving systemic change: "While the promise behind the progressive prosecutors' movement puts the keys to resolving the criminal justice system's problems in the hands of humans, the computational decision-making trend sends a whole different message: the solution will arrive by limiting the presence of human discretion in the criminal process."[22] They suggest that a model combining the two trends can reconcile the alleged paradox of having both trends coexist.

Another suggestion is to consider deliberative frameworks for adopting algorithms that incorporate professionals' diverse agendas and standpoints, reflecting the cacophony of individual and public interests embedded with-

21 Ravid & Haim, supra note 7.
22 Ibid, at 531.

in the criminal justice endeavour. Since algorithms promote efficiency by saving much time on complex technical calculations, decision-makers can use the time saved to reach balanced agreements about the weight given to various kinds of complementing or contradicting considerations by the algorithms, promoting a more transparent, democratic process of algorithmic design.

A less mediated way to incorporate public views and concerns about algorithmic design and operation is to adopt a participatory framework that would consider lay stakeholders' perceptions and perspectives in addition to the professionals. An actual example of such a framework is a process undergone by the Pennsylvania Commission on Sentencing to adopt sentence risk-assessment instruments.[23] The implementation of these tools included a participatory process in which various community stakeholders, policy-makers, and legal professionals were invited to contribute their input in open public hearings. Such processes can suggest ways to address concerns about the lack of democratization and transparency, which erode trust and legitimacy.

Indeed, the million-dollar question is whether humans are the inevitable solution or the root problem in the era of algorithmic criminal justice. I believe that as long as machines do not become humane (and at least for now, they don't!), human discretion must be involved in criminal decision-making processes to make them trustworthy. The notions of trust, faith, legitimacy, and accountability can help illuminate the dilemmas pertaining to the desirability of an algorithmic regime in the criminal context. Future studies should use empirical tools to uncover the public perceptions of AI's role in criminal justice and the interplay between trust, legitimacy, and the AI-based criminal justice system. Understanding the public sentiments as a significant factor driving trust can help ensure that reforms align with democratic values and accountability standards.

23 See https://www.pacodeandbulletin.gov/Display/pabull?file=/secure/pabulletin/data/vol50/50-3/60.htmlId, as mentioned in Ravid & Haim, supra note 7, at 564.

The Transformation of Democracy and Diffusion of Power

On the Constitution of Algorithms

Sabine Müller-Mall, Johannes Haaf

The widespread use of algorithms and technologies of artificial intelligence profoundly shapes social structures and dynamics. This contribution explores the intricate relationship between algorithmic governance and the idea of the constitution, aiming to elucidate the transformative impact of these technologies. We suggest that the constitutional perspective offers a comprehensive lens through which to make sense of and navigate the concrete challenges posed by the ascent of the algorithmic society. More specifically, we argue that algorithms, guided by logics of calculation and prediction, provide a competing model of the political-legal order embodied in the democratic constitution. Central to our analysis is the shift from the legality of the law to a new "legality of the normal" detached from public deliberation and the collective construction of meaning. This shift disrupts and reconceptualizes the established coupling of law and politics characteristic of the modern constitution.

A. Introduction[1]

New technologies always change our world. They change how we perceive and understand ourselves and the world around us. In recent years, this has been particularly true of algorithms. They are almost everywhere, from social media to law enforcement, from traffic navigation to medicine. But the way in which new technologies affect social experiences and imaginaries is not a one-way process, in the sense that they simply come upon us, manipulate us and eventually dominate us (though the threat of "algocracy" is real to some)[2]. Similar to ideas, we make creative use of them, apply them in various contexts and modify them in turn. Some technologies soon disappear again. Others, however, become more and more woven into the

1 Research for this article was supported by the SFB/TRR 339, funded by the German Research Foundation.

2 Cf. John Danaher, 'The Threat of Algocracy: Reality, Resistance and Accommodation' (2016) 29 *Philosophy and Technology* 245.

fabric of our daily lives, profoundly affecting the ways in which we organize the social world, the ways we live together.

In this contribution, we explore how to understand the extensive use of algorithms and how their increasing significance plays out for a very specific form of the organization of the social world: the constitution. Our aim is to develop a perspective on the question of how this relationship can be addressed. How do algorithms relate to the idea and practice of the modern constitution? How might a constitutional perspective illuminate important aspects of the widespread adoption of algorithms in society? Crucially, the term "constitution" can also be used as a (substantive) verb, signaling activities that take on a distinct form or have a distinct effect. In this vein, the contribution's title should neither imply that algorithms and technologies of artificial intelligence (AI) have a constitution comparable to the domain of democratic politics and law. Nor should it be taken to mean, to borrow Lessig's famous formula, that "code is constitution," and that programming algorithms is the same as drafting a constitution. Instead, we want to investigate the ways in which the ubiquitous presence of algorithms has something to do with the role and function of what we usually think of as a constitution.

We argue that the logic of calculation and the logic of prediction, which are elementary features of (digital) algorithms, compete with the idea of the constitution. They do not replace, but provide an alternative model of the political-legal order. This is to say that the use of algorithms in the present and their increasingly broad field of application in the foreseeable future has a deep impact on the relationship between law and politics which lies at the core of the concept of the modern constitution – a concept that itself was always less uniform and robust than sometimes assumed. However, our analysis of this impact is not embedded in a history of loss and decline. Rather, we are concerned with developing a suitable perspective on the contemporary rise of algorithms in some distance to the more specific doctrinal issues and policy responses associated with the unique challenges posed by the emerging "algorithmic society"[3].

We proceed as follows. First, we discuss the constitutive features of algorithms and of algorithmic governance. Second, we show that algorithms are political by effecting the ways in which we perceive and imagine the future. They are thus contributing to the "political form of society" (Lefort). Algo-

3 Hans-W. Micklitz et al. (eds.), *Constitutional Challenges in the Algorithmic Society* (CUP 2021).

rithms do so, as we argue in the third section, at least in part, through a new kind of legality – a legality that we understand as the *legality of the normal*. This legality of the normal is significantly different from the law's legality. Whereas legal norms are intrinsically connected to the possibilities of public deliberation and critique, algorithmic norms are regularities extracted from huge data sets to serve as standards for decision-making and as guidelines for the future organization of the social. By reconfiguring the relationship between law and politics, the widespread use of algorithms establishes a competing model to the modern constitution. In a fourth step and in lieu of a conclusion, we outline three of those challenges to illustrate what the rise of algorithms means for the structure of law and politics that underpins the democratic constitution.

B. Algorithms[4]

In a very general sense, algorithms are predetermined sequences of explicit steps for solving a problem or making a decision. These sequences of instructions need not be strictly formalized; a ritual, a baking recipe in a cookbook or a construction manual are also examples of algorithms. As such, algorithms are therefore nothing new or very exciting. They were common before they were used in computer software and have long been an integral part of almost every aspect of the social world. So why are we only now talking about the *algorithmization of the social* and discussing the effects of algorithmic governance for democratic societies?

There are two reasons for these newly awakened concerns. First, digital algorithms as we use them today are both more specific and more complex than other algorithms. They are strictly formalized and use code, i.e. they are written in programming languages, which mediate between the computer's binary code and human languages. Secondly, *algorithmization* is not a linear process that began at a certain point in history and has been steadily progressing ever since, but is rather a gradual, creeping change in the significance of (digital and abstract) algorithms for the social world. Over the past decades, various developments have been converging and reinforcing each other with remarkable simultaneity. Algorithms are increasingly becoming more complex as the capacity and speed of data-pro-

4 Some ideas and arguments in this section draw upon and are developed in more detail in Sabine Müller-Mall, *Freiheit und Kalkül: Die Politik der Algorithmen* (Reclam 2020).

cessing increases while, at the same, the possibilities to interconnect the processed data are becoming ever more comprehensive. Crucially, machine learning technologies are becoming more and more sophisticated, so that digital algorithms are now often able to improve their capabilities to solve a problem or make a decision on their own. The more information such learning algorithms are provided with, the faster and more accurately they can deal with enormous sets of data in a coherent manner. It is mainly due to these capacities for autonomous learning that algorithms recently became closely associated with AI technologies. However, although such technologies almost always utilize algorithms, their diverse elements cannot fully be understood along those conceptual lines. Despite this, for the sake of simplicity, we use the term in this broader sense, which includes technologies of artificial intelligence.

Importantly, algorithms derive from and embody a *logic of calculation.* Not only are they essentially made up of sequences of detailed instructions. They also establish a distinct idea of how to address and think about the future, namely as a calculable goal that can be achieved via such formalized and stubbornly applied procedures. As the historian Lorraine Daston notes, the machine-based use of algorithms in the 19th and 20th century eventually "cultivated the ability to analyse complex tasks and problems into step-by-step sequences."[5] In case we are unable to create new algorithms or adapt existing ones in order to solve a problem or reach a decision, contemporary AI technologies can step in. They are able to optimize existing algorithms or even find them in the first place. In doing so, they draw (again algorithmically) on large sets of data. These data sets are then sorted and classified with the help of algorithms, which, for their part, are improved by these calculations.

Often, algorithms are made use of not only to identify patterns, to classify data or to carry out regression analyses. They are also valued for making predictions about future developments, attitudes or behaviours. The analysis and classification of data is regularly accompanied by a prognosis of how things will be developing in the near or distant future. Algorithms follow a *logic of prediction*, which processes the aggregated data for the specific purpose of charting future behavior. This probabilistic dimension, the interest in what is most likely to happen, is particularly acute in the case of learning algorithms. These kinds of algorithms are capable of guiding

5 Lorraine Daston, *Rules: A Short History of What We Live By* (Princeton University Press 2019), 148.

themselves in making predictions. They can even autonomously filter out the criteria that are relevant for a good prognosis. At the same time, it is almost impossible to investigate these criteria and make them transparent in retrospect, and thus to somehow "explain" how AI works.

C. Algorithms and the Political Form of Society

It is, of course, rather obvious that the spread of new technologies reshapes experiences of the social and interferes with the established ways in which societies organize themselves with a view to the future. As the cultural theorist Cornelia Vismann explains, all cultural technologies (and all technologies are a product of culture in the broader sense) are connected to the society's "symbolic order".[6] In order to investigate the differences between them, to understand and evaluate the diverse effects of their respective deployment, the task is "to deduce the script from the action, the rules of operation from the concrete operation."[7] They are technologies precisely in the sense that a certain schema or certain characteristics are intrinsic to them. These characteristics or "rules of operation" should take centre stage when asking about the consequences of a technology's manifold use for the constitution of societies.

Algorithms foster a logic of calculation and are often determined by a logic of prediction, which have the potential to alter the possibilities of the political and thereby also the conditions of the law's legality. Within democratic societies, *the political* goes beyond formal procedures and institutions of decision-making. Rather, it refers to what Claude Lefort describes as the "form of society",[8] that is the symbolic order which encompasses the entirety of social facts, experiences and relationships. The political thus includes anything concerned with how the social is arranged and formed, how spaces of action are designed and how the future is addressed.[9] In this regard, it is closely associated with the collective construction of meaning.[10] Normative evaluations and (implicit as well as explicit) agreements are a

---

6 Cornelia Vismann, 'Kulturtechniken und Souveränität', in *Das Recht und seine Mittel* (Fischer 2012), 459 (own translation).

7 Ibid., 451 (own translation).

8 Claude Lefort, 'The Question of Democracy', in: *Democracy and Political Theory* (Polity 1998).

9 Müller-Mall, *Freiheit und Kalkül*, 12-13.

10 Lefort, 'The Question of Democracy', 18.

constitutive feature of the social form, with unrestricted public deliberation and contestation being essential to the institution of democratic societies in particular. Those deliberations also complement the authority of the law and legal discourse, because the elementary distinction between "right and wrong" presupposes this kind of jointly constructed meaning. The political, in short, concerns the ways in which we perceive and imagine the social world.

Against this background, the extensive use of algorithms is political in the sense that it modifies the established ways in which democratic societies and their members imagine themselves. It is not that algorithms simply restrict procedures and processes of public deliberation that were once "free". Rather, they establish an alternative kind of political normativity. At stake is a different form of engaging with societal facts and especially the ways in which we think about and shape the future of living together: how we organize normative and institutional orders, how we distribute rights and freedoms and how we relate to one another as equals.

At the centre of this transformation lies the numerical, the pronounced role of the number and of a governance of statistics. Of course, the term as well as the widespread use of statistics is deeply linked to the development of modern statehood and what has been called *Staatswissenschaft* in German. A detailed knowledge about the state's population and economy, that is a numerical representation of society in the form of tables and graphs was (and still is) considered to be an essential precondition of successful government. However, the new political significance of the numerical can hardly be compared to that earlier rise of statistics as a means of state power. Therefore, Antoine Garapon and Jean Lassègue characterize the extensive use of algorithms as a "numerical revolution".[11] In particular, the introduction and omnipresence of the (mobile) computer in almost every area of life marks a fundamental change. Numbers, processed by digital technologies, create a different form of writing centred around information, not meaning. This allows for describing the entire social world – images as well as texts, values as well personalities – in one single language. Using the binary code 0/1, the world, dis-connected from any physical space, is perceived and processed numerically.

Computer algorithms infuse this numerical revolution with their logics of calculation and prediction. For one thing, they enable us to sort and

11 Antoine Garapon and Jean Lassègue, *Le numérique contre le politique: Crise de l'espace et reconfiguration des médiations sociales* (PUF 2021).

arrange these numerical sets of data with a view to possible linkages and shared characteristics. And because everything is potentially connected, these linkages – one could also say: these perceptions of the social world – are almost infinite (and thus almost random). For another thing, and even more importantly, algorithms draw a conclusion about the future development of such random linkages and their various variables. The predictions they make and the probabilities they delineate, however, are completely deprived of meaning, if we take the creation of meaning to refer to a collective process in which controversial demands, conflicting judgments and contested ideas come to bear. Algorithms are political in this sense, insofar as they re-constitute the ways we perceive, imagine and eventually shape the world around us.

This constitution of the social through algorithmic governance is by no means neutral or objective, but contains normative aspects. As already mentioned, many algorithms are premised upon the idea that the data sets documenting the past behavior of a large number of people can be used to make an accurate prediction about the future behavior of individuals. The success of online advertisement based upon the shopping data of a large number of other consumers from a specific region or socio-economic class is a testament to this power of prediction. The (contested) assumption is that we are more likely to behave in the future in a similar way to how we did in the past and that we are more likely to behave in a manner similar to our social environment: What we and our peers want today, is probably what we will want tomorrow. Whether or not this assumption is true, by building on it, the widespread use of algorithms brings about a new type of societal organization, a new form of perceiving and shaping collective life. This new type of organization can be described as "normalization", as the alignment of social action or values with what is the statistical norm. Whereas a legal norm or a moral demand is in some way external to social practice, guidelines and principles for action are now based on what is (algorithmically) deemed to be normal. In contexts of "normalization in the strict sense"[12], Foucault highlights, the relationship between the norm and the normal is reversed. Instead of a specific, pre-existing norm that serves as a standard according to which certain future behavior is judged, with technologies of normalization, the normal is prior to the norm and,

12 Michel Foucault, *Security, Territory, Population: Lectures at the Collège de France 1977-1978* (Palgrave 2007) 63.

in a certain sense, the material from which the norm is build: "the normal comes first, and the norm is deduced from it."[13] Through the use of algorithms, this type of organizing and steering social life, once intrinsically linked to the technologies of the modern (liberal) state, is now widely disseminated. In the "empire of algorithms",[14] shopping preferences, but also scientific knowledge, traffic navigation or communicative behavior on social media-platforms are converging based on data about which sneakers are usually bought, which papers are often quoted, which routes are regularly chosen and which videos are most of interest.

One could, of course, object that algorithms merely document what is going on around and in-between us. And indeed, in some respects, the statistically processed data sets may indeed simply depict "real" social behavior. The convergence of consumer preferences or a shared understanding of what is a valuable piece of scholarship can very well pre-date the use of algorithms. However, this representation of social facts is deeply normative. Algorithms do not carry out these procedures for the sake of translating a complex and confusing social world in the precise language of numbers, but for the purpose of generating an output that is intrinsically prognostic. The analysis of pixel arrangements is supposed to allow to determine how new images are to be attributed correctly; the sorting through of social media should make it possible to identify consumer interests for the aim of targeted advertising in the future. In other words, the data analysis is carried out with a view to the goal of predicting something as accurately as possible. Algorithms do not simply depict existing patterns, distributions or correlations, but they evaluate these patterns or distributions in terms of their probabilistic value. Thereby, they prioritize one particular future action over another because the former is more likely to become reality under certain conditions than the latter. Since the designated future action is by no means inevitable, this selection is a normative operation. Or, to put it another way: algorithms knit the analysis and the evaluation of data together.

Therefore, algorithms can effectively help to solve a problem and to reach a decision without having to rely on (a collective process of) constructing meaning. This supposed neutrality, together with their wide range of application, is what is so often cherished. Algorithms can sort and link together huge sets of data in almost any dimension, without ever having to

13 Ibid.
14 Daston, *Rules*, 7.

attribute any meaning to this link. At the same time, they forecast a specific future, a particular world of likeliness, by prioritizing one possible course of action over a different one. In this way, the extensive use of algorithms is *political.* It reshapes how we imagine the future, how we create normative orders and how we challenge them.

D. A New Legality of the Normal[15]

This (new) political significance of algorithms competes with the idea and possibilities of the democratic constitution in two-fold manner. First, and starting from the assumption that the constitution is a distinct relationship between law and politics, the use of algorithms establishes a different kind of legality. Algorithms advance a *legality of the normal* as opposed to the *legality of the law.* They call into question the crucial distinction between legal rules on the one hand and the (statistical) representation of past behavior on the other hand by substituting the logic of the law for the logic of regularities. Second, the power of algorithms to "form" society and their corresponding legality of the normal fundamentally challenges the democratic constitution as a specific model of the political-legal order.

Following Luhmann, the constitution describes a structural coupling of law and politics: the juridification of politics and the simultaneous politicization of law.[16] In modern constitutional democracies, public deliberation and procedures of collective decision-making complement the rule of law. At the same time, the law's legality contributes crucially to the institution of these fora and procedures. A pressing problem which stems from this specific coupling of law and politics is the temporality of the constitution. On the one hand, the constitution provides a normative framework for the exercise of rule. It is therefore *static.* On the other hand, the constitution is itself subject to political processes and practices. It is, in that sense, *dynamic.* The constitution as a development or a process – a process of re-constituting the constitution – thwarts the metaphor of a framework and is often discussed under the headline of "constitutionalization". It is, however, not restricted to the extension of constitutional norms to a hitherto non-constitutional area of law, but a crucial component of the

15 Some ideas and examples in this section are already put forth in Müller-Mall, *Freiheit und Kalkül.*

16 Niklas Luhmann, 'Verfassung als evolutionäre Errungenschaft' (1990) 9 *Rechtshistorisches Journal* 176.

structural coupling of law and politics itself. In view of this problem of intersecting temporalities, we argue that both dimensions, that is processes of (re-)constitution as well as the idea of a consolidated normative framework must be included in the concept of the constitution. A constitution is both something that is stable and robust and something that is continuously re-created.

Characteristic of the legality of the law and the legality of the normal are their contrasting modes of application. We outlined above that, whereas legal norms are linked to diverse fora and procedures of public deliberation, algorithmic norms result from the analysis of data on past behavior. Both types of norms are directed towards the future, i.e. they are intended to solve future problems by means of their application. In the case of the legality of the law, the norm is applied through judgement. To judge is to link the individual case to the norm and to relate *this* case to *that* norm in the first place.[17] In the case of algorithms, the norm is applied without judgement, which is to say that the individual case is attributed to the relevant (statistical) norm. The relationship between the case and the norm is thus the prerequisite of the decision or outcome, not its result (as in the case of a judgement). Accordingly, the legal judgement is subject to a potential critique that asks for the relationship between the individual case and the norm to be a comprehensible one – the judgement must somehow show how the norm and the case are interrelated. The algorithmic decision, by contrast, cannot be criticized, since the relevant norm or standard is not accessible as such. Sociologically speaking, there is no "legitimation by procedure",[18] because there is not really a procedure as such. What we are left with is only the result of a case that has been attributed to a particular norm as a matter of fact.

The differences between the legality of the law and the legality of the normal, however, are more subtle than the contrast between regulation *de jure* and *de facto* suggests. Rather, algorithmic norms are advancing a new form or principle of legality compared to the legality of the law. Notwithstanding the question of legitimacy, the respective principles of legality embody a different conception of what constitutes a norm and how said norm is applied. These differences can account for the "smoothness" of algorithms and algorithmic governance. The legality of the normal is neither dependent

17 Cf. Sabine Müller-Mall, *Verfassende Urteile: Eine Theorie des Rechts* (Berlin 2023), 143-150.

18 Niklas Luhmann, *Legitimation durch Verfahren* (Luchterhand 1969).

on public deliberation and collective processes of generating meaning nor subject to a critique targeting the injustices of a concrete decision. In both respects, algorithms operate in what is often perceived to be a frictionless manner of regulating the social.

The extensive use of algorithms establishes a different kind of political normativity as well as a different kind of legality. By simultaneously changing the ways we perceive and imagine the social world, and by establishing a distinct mode of regulating behavior and decision-making, algorithms create new links between the sphere of politics and the domain of legality. This does not directly attack the structural coupling of law and politics characteristic of the modern democratic constitution. What is at stake is a competing model of the political-legal order. Similar in a way to the democratic model, this competing model also connects concrete outcomes to a principle of legality. The algorithmically discovered laws are applied to an individual case. Predictive policing, for example, is making use of huge data sets on the past behavior of many people in order draw to a conclusion on the likely future of a particular criminal, while operating within the bounds of official law. Or, to provide another example, when tax authorities use software to filter out tax cases that are then subject to closer scrutiny, executive bodies base their decision-making on algorithmic norms. This can be done in full compliance with the applicable legal provisions and yet create a situation of competition.

Again, this is not to say that the legality of the normal simply replaces the legality of the law. Algorithms do not supplant the democratic model of constitutional ordering, and they certainly do not bring about a "new constitution". Rather, basic propositions of the constitutional relationship between politics and law are confronted with a different set of – diametrically opposed – assumptions regarding both the constitution as a normative framework and the dynamic processes of constitutionalization. Modern democratic constitutionalism starts from the idea that the creation of legal norms is linked to or is, at least, the potential object of public deliberation. Such deliberation is absent in the case of algorithms and their norm-generative operations, since they effectively solve problems and decide issues, but do not disclose the criteria (or, to be more precise, the patterns and regularities) on which the respective decision is based. While the application of legal norms always depends on a judgement and juridical decision-making can therefore be adjusted to the peculiarities of each individual case, the algorithmic decision requires no judgement at all. Finally, the normative structures established through the use of algorithms circumvent the notion of both collective and individual autonomy, i.e. the assumption that the individual person as well as particular communities both can and must be able to act on their own. By contrast, algorithms presuppose that action is essentially pattern-driven. It can be determined by behavioural data and be regulated by "smooth" rules.

E. Three Challenges in Lieu of a Conclusion

The challenges posed by the algorithmic model to the established perspectives and premises of the modern constitution are of a fundamental nature. They are both conceptual and concrete. The extensive use of algorithms is giving rise to a competing model of relating politics to law – to a different conception of both the structure of politics and of law as well as the ways in which they are interconnected. This competition is becoming manifest in a number of concrete challenges and issues, which can provoke processes of (re-)constituting the modern constitution as described above. In what follows, we sketch three of those challenges concerned with the notion of autonomy, the idea of political freedom and the form and procedures of decision-making. They show the enormous pressure on the democratic constitution to adapt to the competing model of algorithmic governance.

The *notion of autonomy* entails the assumption that every individual is capable of acting freely and in a self-determined manner, and that these capabilities should be protected through the guarantee of fundamental rights (regardless of whether or not there is empirically such a thing as a free will). This basic assumption underlies not only the constitutional protection of human dignity, but also the various individual freedoms and personal rights. Recent discussions about the liability of self-driving cars, data protection in the domain of AI-assisted medicine or the recognition of digital persons as legal entities express these fundamental challenges to the principle of autonomy. The legal and political responses to these issues, for example with regard to the nature of data protection and the scope of the relevant laws, are intrinsically linked to this distinct understanding of autonomy and therefore also the normative framework of the modern constitution, even though they are often portrayed as problems of dogmatic innovation alone. Intimately linked to the notion of autonomy is the *idea of political freedom*. It comprises, inter alia, the freedom to form opinions, to choose representatives and to engage in politics without being subject to any prior constraints of justification. Political freedom links individual to collective autonomy and is thus the foundation of democratic self-determination. As with autonomy, the exercise of political freedom is challenged by algorithmic norms, especially with regard to the continuing transformation of the public sphere as a result of the numerical revolution. Whenever, for example, the digitalization of mass communication raises the question of how freedom of expression and its limits should be understood, this represents not only a case-specific conflict about what constitutes proper online content or a doctrinal dispute over the adequate balance of fundamental rights – but it just as much concerns the changing conditions and possibilities of the constitutional guarantees of political freedom. A further challenge are the *forms and procedures of decision-making* within democratic societies. The role of social bots in election campaigns, the use of "legal tech" in the legal profession or the prediction of court decisions with the help of AI signify developments which are not restricted to the effective guarantee of individual rights to due process and effective participation. These developments and the discussions that accompany them are also always about the complicated relationship between legitimacy and legality, about how a distinct decision can be traced back to the collective autonomy of the people in light of the forecasted future of algorithmic governance.

These different, but interconnected challenges show that the disruptive potential of the constitution of algorithms is not restricted to single issues of policy design and legal discourse. The extensive use of algorithms is of political significance and advances a specific kind of legality. At the same time, they can become subject to public deliberation and adequate legal and judicial control, although "algorithms are unleashed from territories"[19] and state jurisdictions. This requires, however, a more holistic understanding of the ways in which the rise of algorithmic governance and the logics of calculation and prediction disrupt as well as reconfigure the multi-dimensional relationship between law and politics. For this, the constitutional perspective provides a suitable starting point.

19 Mariavittoria Catanzariti, 'Algorithmic Law: Law Production by Data or Data Production by Law?', in Hans-W. Micklitz et al. (eds.), *Constitutional Challenges in the Algorithmic Society* (CUP 2021), 89.

Gender and the Automation of Public Law: The Start of a New Conversation

Sofia Ranchordas

Administrative law and digital government scholarship devote scarce attention to gender. Recent debates on the regulation of AI and digital government have focused predominantly on human-centred perspectives, disregarding the importance of gender in defining the human element or implicitly assuming that this debate is gender neutral. Yet, gender is a relevant dimension of automated government which if overlooked, may lead to the exclusion of many citizens. This has proven to be particularly detrimental to women, whose needs, socioeconomic circumstances, and biological differences are either invisible to public decision-makers or are regarded with suspicion as 'deviations' from a male or gender-neutral pattern. For example, recent scandals on the automation of social welfare (e.g., Robodebt in Australia and the Dutch Childcare Benefits Scandal) affected predominantly women, especially single mothers. This invisibility of gender is exacerbated when digitalization and automation replicate stereotypes, patriarchal approaches to the role of women in society, and longstanding dynamics of power and inequality.

Drawing on interdisciplinary scholarship including feminist and gender studies, this paper explains why gender should be more closely considered in the regulation of AI in the public sector, digital government, and automated decision-making.

A. Introduction

There is growing demand for human-centric perspectives in the regulation of AI, digital government, and the use of algorithms by governments and private companies.[1] Existing or proposed EU legislation has responded to

1 David Restrepo Amariles and Pablo Marcello Baquero, 'Promises and Limits of Law for a Human-Centric Artificial Intelligence' (2023) 48 Computer Law & Security Review; Joanna J Bryson and Andreas Theodorou, 'How Society Can Maintain Human-Centric Artificial Intelligence' in Marja Toivonen and Eveliina Saari (eds), Human-Centered

it with Article 22 of the General Data Protection Regulation (GDPR) and multiple dispositions of the AI Act on human oversight and fundamental impact assessments.[2] A human-centric perspective to AI is respectful of European values and ethical principles. In this perspective, 'human values are central to the way in which AI systems are developed, deployed, used, and monitored, by ensuring respect for fundamental rights'.[3] Few scholars and policymakers would openly admit to 'being against a human-centric' approach.[4] Doing so could quickly be interpreted as a blind adoption of techno-optimism or a refusal to protect fundamental rights.[5] However, do we truly understand what the concept of human-centrism entails? And who is this human at the centre of the regulation of AI? Are we referring to a man, a woman, a non-binary individual, or a genderless construct? And does it matter who is at the centre, as long as it is a human?[6] Another aspect that is often overlooked is the identity of the addressee of the algorithmic administrative decision. Once again, are we speaking of a man, woman or a non-binary individual? And does gender matter?

Most national policies and regulations are designed to be gender-neutral, based on the assumption that only in specific cases will women have different claims and needs than men or non-binary individuals. However, this assumed gender-neutrality of government policies and regulations is a

---

Digitalization and Services (vol 19, Springer Singapore 2019) 4; Leif and Jonny Holmström, 'Citizen-centricity in Digital Government Research: A Literature Review and Integrative Framework' (2024) 29(1) Information Polity 55 – 72.

2 Alessandro Mantelero, 'Human Rights Impact Assessment and AI' in Beyond Data, Information Technology and Law Series, vol 36 (TMC Asser Press, The Hague 2022) https://doi.org/10.1007/978-94-6265-531-7_2.

3 European Parliament, EU Guidelines on Ethics in Artificial Intelligence: Context and Implementation' (2019), available at https://www.europarl.europa.eu/RegData/etudes/BRIE/2019/640163/EPRS_BRI%282019%29640163_EN.pdf (accessed on 8 May 2024).

4 Scholars have, nevertheless, underlined that humans and AI should be seen in a different light, by focusing on augmentation, or how AI can collaborate with humans, rather than restricting the focus to 'human-like AI', see Erik Brynjolfsson, 'The Turing Trap: The Promise and Peril of Human-Like Artificial Intelligence' 151 (1) Daedalus 272 (2022).

5 John Danaher, 'Techno-optimism: an Analysis, an Evaluation and a Modest Defence' (2022) 35 Philos. & Technol. 54 https://doi.org/10.1007/s13347-022-00550-2.

6 On gender and public administration, see Susan D. Phillips, Brian R. Little and Laura A. Goodine, 'Reconsidering gender and public administration: five steps beyond conventional research' 40 Canadian Public Administration 563 (1997).

fiction.[7] Law and policy often overlook the fact that behind market actors, civil servants, and mandated 'humans in the loop' there are individuals of flesh and blood, each with their own political preferences, morals, religious views, and gender. Public administration scholarship has identified two major silences concerning gender: first, the representation of women and the role of gender equity within public service workforces, and second, the potential contributions of feminist theories in addressing contemporary public management challenges.[8] A third and fourth silences regard the role of gender in how administrative law and regulation see citizens and regulatees and the limited consideration of gender in the automation of administrative decision-making. At a time when women in many countries are gradually increasing their representation, for example, in the public workforce, gender blindness may reverse progress by perpetuating longstanding power dynamics, neglecting the importance of biological differences, sustaining gender inequity, and failing to account for different socioeconomic conditions and diverse needs.[9] Focusing on 'human-centric perspectives' in regulation of AI—or many other policy or regulatory subjects—without talking about gender is thus destined to be a limited perspective. In other words, human-centrism is not as encompassing as it sounds at first blush because it overlooks the gender dimension which partly defines who we are as humans.

In this paper, I discuss the importance of considering gender in the context of the digital transformation in the public sector, including digitalization of public services, the automation of administrative decision-making and regulation.[10] I do not challenge the current focus of scholarship and policymakers on human-centrism. Instead, I argue that we should seek to understand what 'human-centric' means from a gender perspective,

7 Mieke Verloo & Connie Roggeband, 'Gender impact assessment: the development of a new instrument in the Netherlands' 14(1) Impact Assessment 3 (1996), DOI: 10.1080/07349165.1996.9725883.

8 Gemma Carey and Helen Dickinson, 'Gender in Public Administration: Looking Back and Moving Forward' 74(4) Australian Journal of Public Administration 391 (2015).

9 See Judith Butler, Bodies that Matter: On the Discursive Limits of Sex. Routledge, 2011 (on returning the focus of theories of gender to the body).

10 European Commission/JCR, AI Watch: European Landscape on the Use of Artificial Intelligence by the Public Sector (2022), available at https://ai-watch.ec.europa.eu/publications/ai-watch-european-landscape-use-artificial-intelligence-public-sector_en (last accessed on May 20, 2024).

particularly with reference to the automation of public services and administrative decision-making.

This paper, while exploratory and modest in scope, aims to complement administrative law scholarship, which seldom incorporates insights from the wealth of feminist studies on public law, theory of the state, social policy, and citizenship.[11] Notable exceptions include scholarly analyses of administrative adjudication and gender bias as well as on the use of gender data in algorithmic systems to define identity.[12] Keeney and Fusi have recently confirmed our claim, stressing also the need to study gender biases in digital government and the role of gender in the public workplace.[13] Legal scholars have also highlighted some of the dangers of employing biometrics on women's bodies, namely facial recognition.[14] This paper does not delve into the issue of algorithmic bias and discrimination, as this has been extensively discussed in legal scholarship.[15] Instead, it adopts a broader perspective, discussing (i) the relationship between administrative

11 See, for example, Catherine A. MacKinnon, Toward a Feminist Theory of the State (Harvard University Press, 1989); Mimmi Abramovitz, Regulating the Lives of Women: Social Welfare Policy from Colonial Times to the Present. South End Press, 1988; Ann Sheila Orloff, 'Gender and the Social Rights of Citizenship' 58 American Sociological Review 303 (1993); Elettra Stradella (ed.), Gender Based Approaches to the Law and Juris Dictio in Europe. Pisa University Press; Eva Brems, Protecting the Human Rights of Women. International human rights in the 21st century: protecting the rights of groups, Lanham, 2003; Catherine A. MacKinnon, Women's Lives, Men's Laws. Harvard University Press, 2004; Tracy A. Thomas, 'The Long History of Feminist Legal Theory' in Deborah Brake, Martha Chamallas & Verna L. Williams (ed.), The Oxford Handbook of Feminism and Law in the United States (Oxford University Press 2021) 15.

12 E. Golin, 'Solving the Problem of Gender and Racial Bias in Administrative Adjudication 95(6) Columbia Law Review 1532 (1993) doi:10.2307/1123135; Ari Ezra Waldman, AE. "Gender Data in the Automated Administrative State" (2023) 123 Colum L Rev 2249.

13 Mary K. Feeney and Federica Fusi, 'A Critical Analysis of the Study of Gender and Technology in Government' 26 Information Polity 115 (2021).

14 Morgan Klaus Scheuerman, Madeleine Pape, and Alex Hanna, 'Auto-essentialization in automated facial analysis as extended colonial project' 8(2) Big Data & Society (2021), https://doi.org/10.1177/20539517211053712.

15 See, for example, Jeremias Adams-Prassl, Jeremias, Reuben Binns, and Aislinn Kelly-Lyth, 'Directly discriminatory algorithms' 86(1) The Modern Law Review 144 (2023); Frederik Zuiderveen Borgesius, 'Discrimination, artificial intelligence, and algorithmic decision-makingì Council of Europe, Directorate General of Democracy 42 (2018); Sandra Wachter, Brent Mittelstadt, and Chris Russell. 'Why fairness cannot be automated: Bridging the gap between EU non-discrimination law and AI' 41 Computer Law & Security Review 105567 (2021).

law, regulation and gender; (ii) the importance of considering gender in the automation of public law; and (iii) how these considerations can help advance an inclusive human-centric approach to the regulation of AI.

In Section 1, I explain the significance of gender in shaping our interactions with government and regulatory frameworks. After providing contextual background on the interactions between government and citizens, I delve into how gender has been historically overlooked or women have been seen as 'deviations' from men.[16] An illustration is the medical and pharmaceutical research and regulatory paradigm, where the white male body has been traditionally the standard, consequently failing to adequately address the distinct physiological needs of the female body. Section 1 mentions many other regulated fields with the same blind side. Hence, in Section 2, I explain why gender considerations are particularly relevant in the digitalization and automation of government. While there have been many incidents of algorithmic discrimination of women and non-binary individuals, technology does not have to be the 'villain' in this context. Instead, several nuances of gender discrimination have mainly come to light with recent controversies in the context of the automation of the state.[17] Technology has exacerbated discrimination in some cases, but it has also shined a spotlight on it.[18] Section 3 discusses this aspect and how considering gender in the regulation of technology can help us promote human values.

B. The Relevance of Gender in Administrative Law and Regulation

This section begins by examining the general dynamics between citizens, government, and administrative law. Historically, the relationship between citizens and government has been marked by a significant power asymmetry. This disparity in power is even more pronounced for citizens who have faced historical disadvantages due to their gender. The second part of this section discusses different areas of regulation that have neglected the role of gender with significant detriment to a large part of the population.

16 Catherine D'ignazio, Catherine, and Lauren F. Klein. Data feminism (MIT press 2023).

17 Cary Coglianese and David Lehr, Regulating by Robot: Administrative Decision-Making in the Machine-Learning Era, 105 GEORGETOWN L. J. 1147, 1152-53 (2017); Cary Coglianese & Alicia Lai, Algorithm vs. Algorithm, 72 DUKE L. J. 1281 (2022).

18 See Orly Lobel, The Equality Machine: Harnessing digital technology for a brighter, more inclusive future (Hachette UK, 2022).

I. Administrative Law: Background Information

Administrative law regulates power asymmetries. Castells (2016) defines power as 'the relational capacity that enables certain social actors to asymmetrically influence the decisions of other actors in ways that favour the empowered actors' will, interests, and values.'[19] Power relations 'construct and shape the institutions and norms that regulate social life'.[20] This includes the interactions between citizens and governments. Administrative law aims to correct power asymmetries, ensuring that governments use their discretionary powers within limits, citizens can exercise their rights, and power asymmetries are not abused. The principles of good administration which have been adopted by a growing number of jurisdictions, exemplify the modern attempt to improve the interactions between citizens and government.[21]

Once upon a time, the relationship between citizens and the state was primarily vertical and top-down throughout the administrative state. Citizens were subjects, not right holders.[22] No one inquired who the citizen was, because administrative law was primarily focused on organizing the public administration. During the 19th century in continental Europe, administrative law was constructed upon intricate layers of social understanding, conventions, and professional practices, which were integrated into a shared public order or drawn from social and technical expertise. However, in the twentieth century, government involvement in societal affairs expanded rapidly. The state's role transcended its traditional boundaries, engendering a paradigm shift wherein government intervention permeated facets of daily life to an unprecedented degree.[23] As the role of the state expanded, so did its power ("*puissance publique*").[24] This had

19 Manuel Castells, 'The Sociology of Power: My Intellectual Journey' 42 Annual Review of Sociology 1, 2 (2016).

20 Manuel Castells, 'The Sociology of Power: My Intellectual Journey' 42 Annual Review of Sociology 1 (2016).

21 Sarah Nason, 'European Principles of Good Administration and UK Administrative Justice' 26(2) European Public Law 391 (2020).

22 Laemers, M. T. A. B., & de Groot-van Leeuwen, L. E. (2010). De Awb en 'de burger'. In T. Barkhuysen, W. den Ouden, & J. E. M. Polak (Eds.), *Bestuursrecht harmoniseren: 15 jaar Awb* Boom Juridische uitgevers, p.132.

23 Cananea, G. d. (2023). "Chapter 1 The Development of Administrative Law: Fact and Theory". In The Common Core of European Administrative Laws. Leiden, The Netherlands: Brill | Nijhoff.

24 M Hauriou, 'Droit administratif' in Répertoire Béquet (Dupont 1897) xiv.

two major implications. Firstly, government started encroaching upon economic freedoms and asserting control over private property, for example, through expropriations. Second, the administration possessed the capacity to formulate regulations with far-reaching implications for various groups within society. Third, it was required to pursue different facets of the public interest which were at times, incompatible. This became particularly true with the development of the welfare state, and more recently, with the challenge to control the costs of such a model in a context of shrinking state budgets. Administrative law slowly developed as a system of checks and balances so as to limit the potentially arbitrary use of discretionary powers in the relationship between citizens and public authorities.[25]

While citizen-government interactions have become more horizontal in some areas, administrative law has overlooked the study of the citizen's identity as part of its main questions.[26] Administrative law developed without acknowledging gender elements, as if they were irrelevant. Constitutional and administrative law traditionally regulated the public sphere of a liberal state, entrusting the economy, religion and family matters to the private realm. The assumption that women were considered to be inferior to men was implicit to numerous foundational declarations such as the French Declaration of the Rights of Man and of the Citizen, proclaimed "freedom and equality in rights of man at birth" (1789).[27]

However, gender remained a missing piece in this scholar's analysis, and to my knowledge, in many other administrative law scholars' research agendas. However, gender is just as relevant to administrative law as it is to other fields of public and private law. To begin with, women constitute the primary demographic receiving welfare benefits. They are poorer than men either because of the gender pay gap or because they take more time off for

25 Cananea, G. d. (2023). "Chapter 1 The Development of Administrative Law: Fact and Theory". In The Common Core of European Administrative Laws. Leiden, The Netherlands: Brill | Nijhoff.

26 An exception in the Netherlands is Leo Damen, 'Bestaat de Awbmens?' In J.L. Boxum, et al. (Eds.), Aantrekkelijke gedachten (Kluwer 1993) 109; Leo Damen, 'Van Awbmens naar responsieve burger? In T. Barkhuysen, et al. (Eds.), 25 jaar Awb. In eenheid en verscheidenheid (Wolters Kluwer, 2019) 113. Damen's work does not address gender.

27 Davinić, M., Kristoffersson, E., Marinković, T. (2023). Gender Equality Aspects of Public Law. In: Vujadinović, D., Fröhlich, M., Giegerich, T. (eds) Gender-Competent Legal Education. Springer Textbooks in Law. Springer, Cham. https://doi.org/10.1007/978-3-031-14360-1_9.

caring duties.[28] In other words, women are more likely to depend on the state.

II. Public Law and Gender

In public law, the element of gender has been primarily visible to constitutional law and international law scholars who have conducted important research on a set of gender-related topics.[29] As Vauchez and Rubio-Marín explain, 'in terms of gender equality, law is a fundamentally ambivalent artefact. It can certainly be a vector for progressive change (...) [but] it can also entrench profound inequalities'.[30] The gendered aspect of public law may start with birth as, in some countries, rules on nationality have impeded women from passing on their nationality to their children.[31]

One of the key debates in public law and gender revolves around the issue of gender recognition which determine how individuals can have their gender identity recognized by the state. This includes recognition of non-binary identities, the type of identification required by law (e.g., self-identification without further medical exams in the most progressive jurisdictions), access to transition-related care, and additional legal protection and rights (e.g., education, prison placement). Osella and Rubio-Marín have explored the importance of gender recognition policies.[32] This discussion is particularly important for trans and nonbinary individuals and has been welcomed with a great deal of controversy in many countries that are traditionally focused on binary systems. Such systems typically interpret

---

28 Miliann Kang, Donovan Lessard, Laura Heston, Sonny Nordmarken, Introduction to Women, Gender, Sexuality Studies (Pressbooks by University of Massachusetts Amherst Libraries, 2017) 76-77.

29 Kim Rubenstein, and atharine G. Young, eds. The Public Law of Gender: From the Local to the Global. of Connecting International Law with Public Law. Cambridge: Cambridge University Press, 2016.

30 Stéphanie H. Vauchez and Ruth Rubio-Marín, 'Introduction: From Law and Gender to Law as Gender—The Legal Subject and the Co-production Hypothesis' in Stéphanie H. Vauchez and Ruth Rubio-Marín (eds.), The Cambridge Companion to Gender and the Law (Cambridge University Press, 2023)1-2.

31 Melany Toombs and Kim Rubenstein, 'The National Subject' in Stéphanie H. Vauchez and Ruth Rubio-Marín (eds.), The Cambridge Companion to Gender and the Law (Cambridge University Press, 2023) 271-301.

32 Stefano Osella and Ruth Rubio-Marín, 'Gender recognition at the crossroads: Four models and the compass of comparative law' 21(2) *International Journal of Constitutional Law* 574 (2023).

human bodies through a binary less, categorizing individuals as male or female. This reduction excludes, nonetheless, a large number of individuals and overlook the existence of other genders. As Osella and Rubio-Marín explain gender is an apparatus that produces not only maleness and femaleness but also gender norms at large.[33]

A second set of debates in public law refers to gender and participation in constitutionalism, fundamental rights, and voting rights. As Julie Suk inquires in her work, "We the People" did not include "We the Women" for a very long time.[34] Very few constitutions refer actively to women, and engage with women's rights and reproductive health. Furthermore, in many countries including those with recently adopted constitutions, very few women were given the opportunity to participate in its drafting and ultimately sign it. The constituent power has thus ignored gender for a long time and it has been primarily a male constituent power. The history of access to voting rights is well-documented, highlighting a long path toward equality. However, despite the many silences in constitutional law regarding gender, the absence of debate or its limited nature is more pronounced in administrative law and regulation.

A third set of debates on public law concerns (public) regulation and the invisibility of gender. This discussion is relatively recent and has been disperse across various regulated sectors. In *Invisible Women*, Caroline Criado Perez describes multiple areas where women are ignored, from the labour market to public transport, from medicine to road safety.[35] Criado Perez documents how the female body and its specificities have been forgotten for decades. An example is automobile safety as car safety test dummies have for decades not included female variants.[36] Also airbags were not originally designed for 'smaller bodies', thus excluding individuals that were shorter and lighter than average, namely women.[37] In the following section,

33 Osella and Rubio-Marin at 576. See also Judith Butler, Undoing Gender (2004) p. 42.

34 Suk, Julie C. *We the Women: The Unstoppable Mothers of the Equal Rights Amendment.* Simon and Schuster, 2020, p. 12.

35 Caroline Criado Perez, *Invisible Women* (Random House, 2019).

36 Fariss Samarrai, *Study: New Cars Are Safer, But Women Most Likely to Suffer Injury*, University of Virginia (Jul. 10, 2019), https://news.virginia.edu/content/study-new-cars-are-safer-women-most-likely-suffer-injury (discussing the male-centered testing methods for seatbelts and other car safety features and the resulting dangers to female drivers).

37 Cary Coglianese, 'The Limits of Performance-Based Regulation' 50 University of Michigan Journal of Law Reform 525, 556 (2017).

I elaborate on the invisibility of women in different government-citizen interactions.

C. Invisible Women in the Context of Government-Citizen Relations

I. Gender Blindness

Jurisdictions that have codified administrative law and have a general administrative law act rarely—if ever, to the best of my knowledge—make any single reference to the terms "sex" or "gender". These matters are generally considered to fall under the jurisdiction of constitutional and human rights lawyers. In the case of the Netherlands, these words are not featured in the General Administrative Act law (*Algemene wet bestuursrecht*). Administrative law is often presented as an operational field that should not hinder the realization of fundamental rights. While we observe that sector-specific regulation increasingly addresses gender issues—mostly as responses to new research or incidents, administrative law rarely incorporates them into its core studies. Administrative law and public regulation have been long regarded as gender-neutral. However, they are instead gender-blind. Claiming gender-neutrality is inaccurate in a world where standards of normalcy are set by middle-aged, able-bodied male citizens. In this section, we provide a number of examples of this gender blindness in different government-citizen interactions.

I start with urban planning which, though part of our daily lives, is often considered a genderless or gender-neutral field. However, this assumption comes into question when examining specific policy choices, such as the construction of bicycle paths, lighting of neighbourhoods, public transportation, and generally speaking, urban design. Historically, public spaces were designed by men and for men due to the underrepresentation of women and other genders in urban policy, architecture, transport policy, and in general, in the workforce.[38] This also applied to the interaction between urban spaces and public transportation.

38 Sharon Bessell, "Good Governance, Gender Equality and Women's Political Representation: Ideas as Points of Disjuncture." Chapter. In The Public Law of Gender: From the Local to the Global, edited by Kim Rubenstein and Katharine G. Young, 273–95. Connecting International Law with Public Law. Cambridge: Cambridge University Press, 2016. See generally Ines Sanchéz de Madariaga and Marion Roberts (Eds), *Fair Shared Cities: The Impact of Gender Planning in Europe* (Routledge 2013).

For a long time, including the post-World War II period, the assumption was that the primary users of public transportation would be men commuting to work. Public transportation has therefore been designed in a linear way, considering male commuting patterns.[39] Nevertheless, women who are more often caregivers, move in 'circular patterns' since they bring their children to school, run errands, and attend more often to the needs of elderly parents. The circularity of women's movements result from the fact that women do more trips, have more unpredictable schedules, and are more frequently pedestrians. However, women are the most frequent users of public transportation: they are the average users that are being disregarded. Women's heavy reliance on public transportation is often overlooked when designing routes, thinking of safety measures, and timetables. Women are on average less wealthy and must thus rely on more economical means of transport which, in many cities around the world, translates into long waiting times, crowded buses or shared vans.

As Ines Sanchez de Madariaga' s work shows, mobilities of care are tendentially ignored by urban planners.[40] Women's commuting patterns, their feeling of unsafety at night are often disregarded by city planners.[41] According to existing research, women spend considerably more time engaged in domestic activities and would thus benefit from gender-sensitive urban and transport planning that would make it easier to combine housework, caring responsibilities, and paid employment.[42] In terms of urban planning and urban lighting, it is important to highlight that women more regularly report to feel unsafe walking at night, as, once again, street lighting was not designed to consider gender needs.

In the case of bicycle paths, we regularly see that they are designed based on the 'fastest route' criterion. In some cases, these paths will lead

39 Christine Ro, 'How to Design Safer Cities for Women', BBC, 12 April 2021, available at https://www.bbc.com/worklife/article/20210409-how-to-design-safer-cities-for-women (last accessed on 20 May 2024).

40 Ines Sanchez de Madariaga, 'From Women in Transport to Gender in Transport: Challenging Conceptual Frameworks to Improved Policymaking' 67 (1) Journal of International Affairs 43 (2013).

41 Inez Sanchez de Madariaga, 'Mobilities of Care: Introducing New Concepts in Urban Transport' in Marion Roberts and Inés Sanchez de Madariaga (Eds), Fair Shared Cities: The Impact of Gender Planning in Europe (Routledge, 2013) 51.

42 Inés Sánchez de Madariaga (ed.), Advancing Gender in Research, Innovation and Sustainable Development. (Fundación General de la Universidad Politécnica de Madrid, 2016), available at https://triggerprojectupm.wordpress.com/wp-content/uploads/2017/10/muriel_ina_20170920_low.pdf.

cyclists through dark woods instead of well-lit areas. Also here, we must critically assess whether this planning decision is truly gender-neutral. Such planning choices can disproportionately affect women and other vulnerable groups, highlighting the need to consider safety and accessibility for all genders in urban design.

Another area of gender blindness concerns retirement and social security benefits. Women tend to live longer but have, on average, smaller pensions to rely on. Lower lifetime earnings due to the gender pay gap and caregiving responsibilities (for children and elderly parents) contribute to reduced retirement savings. Gender equality affect thus retired women at a stage of their lives when they may be particularly vulnerable and unable to work. There is, therefore, a high probability that women will experience financial challenges later in life. In many countries around the world (e.g., Colombia, Israel), retirement ages still differ on the grounds of the gender and women are required to retire earlier. This results in lower lifetime earnings, smaller pensions, greater financial dependence, a negative impact on savings and investments.

In the United States, a study by the Brookings Institution found that women receive Social Security benefits that average only 80% of the benefits received by men.[43] Social security law is a particular field where there are significant power asymmetries and a relationship of dependency between the state and citizens. Here, gender is very visible as also women are the primary beneficiaries of social security systems. At the same time, gender is also invisible as there are few gender-sensitive regulations. This is particularly important considering recent scandals involving the automation of the social welfare state, namely Robodebt in Australia and the Dutch Childcare Benefits scandal.[44] Both scandals had a disproportionate effect on women who were severely penalized and often wrongly accused of having committed fraud. While single mothers in particular, may be more dependent on the social welfare state due to the gender pay gap and care obligations, this field has perceived women with suspicion for decades. Digitalization and automation have exacerbated the problem and allowed for the large-scale investigation of women. Digital technologies allow tax

43 Brookings Institution,'How does Gender Equality Affect Women in Retirement' (July 2020), available at https://www.brookings.edu/articles/how-does-gender-equality-affect-women-in-retirement/.

44 80% of the victims of the Dutch Childcare Benefit Scandal were women, namely mothers.

authorities to optimize data analysis, predicting which taxpayers or social welfare recipients are more likely to commit fraud, and thus profile them as potential fraudsters.[45]

The majority of the Robodebt scandal were predicted to be women. As it happens, according to the data provided by the Royal commission that investigated this scandal, at least 226,780 Australian women were served unlawful debt notices over four and a half years.[46] Women accounted for 55% of those affected by Robodebt, most of them were under 35 years old.[47] 'Robodebt' is an Australian government initiative from 2016 aimed at recovering 'overpayments' to social security recipients since 2010. Initially targeting $1.7 billion over 5 years, it expanded over time. Drawing on data-matching and automated algorithms, it identified discrepancies, calculated overpayments, and raised debts. This approach, criticized on social and mainstream media, neglected the timing and amount of earnings. The Robodebt initiative faced challenges primarily due to discrepancies in income reporting between Centrelink and the Australian Tax Office. The automated system used a yearly income approach, neglecting the fortnightly nature of Social Security payments based on current circumstances. This mismatch led to miscalculations and the issuance of debts without properly accounting for variations in entitlement rates over shorter periods. The inclusion of 'nil rate' periods, intended to encourage work, further complicated the system. The failure can be attributed to the inability of the automated algorithm to accurately align with the dynamic and fortnightly nature of Social Security payments. Additionally, it shifted the burden of proof onto affected individuals, differing from the prior practice of obtaining detailed records from employers.

The history of social security law shows that this perception is deeply rooted in how welfare recipients are seen by the state. In *The Automation of Poverty*, Virginia Eubanks describes how social security law has entrenched the notions of 'deserving' and 'undeserving poor'. These notions were

45 Luisa Scarcella, 'Tax Compliance and Privacy Rights in Profilin and Automated Decision Making' 8(4) *Internet Policy Review* (2019), available at DOI: 10.14763/2019.4.1422.

46 Australian Ministers for the Department of Social Services, Questions on the Royal Commission into Robodebt, 9 March 2023, available at https://ministers.dss.gov.au/transcripts/10596.

47 Whiteford, P. Debt by design: The anatomy of a social policy fiasco – Or was it something worse? *Aust J Publ Admin.* 2021; 80: 340–360. https://doi.org/10.1111/1467-8500.12479.

obvious in the context of the aggressive fraud investigations that took place during the Reagan Administration which affected mostly single mothers. Midnight raids were conducted to try to 'find a man' in the household of a female welfare recipient, thus showing that this woman should not be in need of state support. Feminist studies have critiqued how social welfare systems have been developed in a patriarchal way in order to provide temporary relief to men and their families, being thus less suitable for single parents with lower income and higher dependency.[48] Many welfare offices across the United States adopted 'suitable home' and 'substitute parent' rules, which were moral standards that were used to judge the lives of welfare recipients. These rules, particularly prevalent in the South, disproportionately excluded women of colour from welfare assistance. Despite a 1961 directive from the Secretary of Health, Education, and Welfare to curb the arbitrary application of suitable home requirements, numerous welfare offices persisted in conducting surprise home visits, commonly known as midnight raids, to enforce 'man in the house' rules.

The presence of men in these households was construed as a violation of welfare rules, and the discovered men were considered household breadwinners who had concealed their income from the aid office.[49] Beyond the stated reasons, the unspoken objectives of these rules were to monitor and penalize the sexuality of single mothers, cut off indirect government support for able-bodied men, reduce the welfare rolls, and reinforce the notion that families receiving aid were entitled to only minimal living standards, approaching desperation. By the mid-1960s, low-income women of colour were being blamed for all sorts of social problems. A frequently cited 1965 report by Daniel Patrick Moynihan suggested that the issues of inner cities—poverty, joblessness, and crime—were interconnected. In 1968, the Supreme Court struck down the 'substitute father' rule, which had required any man living with a mother to be considered a substitute father and financially responsible for the entire family.[34] This decision intensified the stigma on mothers. The Supreme Court held in *King v. Smith* that the

48 P. Yang and Barrett, N. (2006), Understanding public attitudes towards Social Security. International Journal of Social Welfare, 15: 95-109, https://doi.org/10.1111/j.1468-2397.2006.00382.x; Stensöta, H.O., Wängnerud, L., Agerberg, M. (2015). Why Women in Encompassing Welfare States Punish Corrupt Political Parties. In: Dahlström, C., Wängnerud, L. (eds) Elites, Institutions and the Quality of Government. Executive Politics and Governance. Palgrave Macmillan, London.

49 Kaaryn Gustafson, 'The criminalization of poverty." *The Journal of Criminal Law and Criminology (1973-)* 99, no. 3 (2009): 643–716. http://www.jstor.org/stable/20685055.

substitute-father presumption was inconsistent with the intent of the Social Security Act to provide for needy children. The decision highlighted that the Act aimed to support children in need regardless of the cohabitation status of their mothers.

Negative stereotypes were also promoted by Reagan during his campaign, by merging the identities of women who had been convicted of welfare fraud. Reagan exaggerated the character of the woman living abundantly thanks to social welfare support and the stereotype of the 'welfare queen' emerged in this context. This stereotype was infused with racial and sexual meanings, conjuring images of poor, black, and sexually-promiscuous women benefiting from welfare, even though at the time, white women were the largest group receiving welfare benefits.[50]

For decades, implicitly or explicitly, there have been welfare policies that aimed to discourage poor women (often welfare recipients) from having (more) children. While in the first half of the twentieth century, these policies included mandated sterilization, these policies evolved into less direct attacks to citizens' reproductive health. Instead, free contraceptives, refusal to receive benefits, and other similar policies were enacted in the 1980s and 1990s to prevent what was "then regarded as costly and pathological" reproduction.[51] Dorothy Roberts has analysed this problem extensively, particularly with regards to black women's reproductive health and how black families are discriminated by the welfare system.[52] For example, poor pregnant women seeking Medicaid-funded prenatal services endure persistent state surveillance.[53] Also in the Netherlands, investigations by Lighthouse Reports on the deployment of welfare surveillance algorithms in Rotterdam revealed that female claimants were often asked intrusive questions regarding their intimacy. It turns out that privacy is a luxury of those who do not depend financially on the state. In the United States, Anita L. Allen has named this "Black Opticon", a term which entails dis-

---

50 Miliann Kang, Donovan Lessard, Laura Heston, Sonny Nordmarken, *Introduction to Women, Gender, Sexuality Studies* (Pressbooks by University of Massachusetts Amherst Libraries, 2017) 38.

51 Dorothy E. Roberts, 'The only good poor woman: Unconstitutional conditions and welfareì 72 *Denv. UL Rev.* 931 (1994) 933.

52 See Dorothy E. Roberts, Killing the black body: Race, reproduction, and the meaning of liberty (Vintage, 2014;) Dorothy E. Roberts, Torn apart: How the child welfare system destroys Black families--and how abolition can build a safer world (Basic Books, 2022).

53 Nair supra note at 208.

criminatory oversurveillance, discriminatory exclusion, and discriminatory predation.[54]

While the stereotype of the 'welfare queen' is derogative at many levels, there is one aspect in which it is accurate: poverty and social welfare dependency is a women's issue. Indeed, in 1984, when the stereotype was widespread, two-thirds of the adults living below the poverty line were women, and households headed by single mothers were five times more likely to live in poverty than two-parent families.[67] Moreover, with rising divorce rates and an increasing number of non-marital births in the United States, women and their children became disproportionately represented in the social welfare system. This is possibly also a problem we see elsewhere. In the Netherlands, two thirds of women in 2021 were economically dependent.[55] In the United States, women, especially women of colour, are more likely to live in poverty than men: according to U.S. Census Bureau Data, of the 38.1 million people living in poverty in 2018, 56 percent were women.[56] According to the UN, 1 in every 10 women in the world lives in extreme poverty.[57]

A third area of gender blindness is medical and pharmaceutical regulation. For many years, women's bodies were only regulated negatively (e.g., prohibition to wear certain clothes, criminalization of abortion and other restrictive reproductive health measures). However, the differences between male and female bodies were not considered in medicine and pharmaceutical regulations for decades. A well-known and tragic illustration of the latter is the administration of thalidomide, a drug prescribed to pregnant women in the 1950s and 1960s to alleviate morning sickness. The drug caused several birth defects when taken during pregnancy as it had not been tested on pregnant women. The thalidomide scandal prompted significant changes in pharmaceutical regulation and testing procedures and initiated a debate on the importance of considering the difference between the male and female bodies (for example, when assessing and treating heart disease symptoms).

---

54 Allen, A. L. "Dismantling the" Black Opticon": Privacy, Race Equity, and Online Data-Protection Reform." Yale LJF 131 (2021): 907.

55 'Hoe gender(on)gelijk is Nederland? Vrouwen in armoede' (Nieuwsbericht, College voor de Rechten van de Mens, 14 December 2022) <www.mensenrechten.nl/actueel/nieuws/2022/12/14/hoe-genderongelijk-is-nederland-vrouwen-in-armoede>.

56 'The Basic Facts About Women in Poverty' (Center for American Progress, 3 August 2020) < www.americanprogress.org/article/basic-facts-women-poverty/>.

57 UN Women, '1 in every 10 women in the world lives in extreme poverty' UN, 8 March 2024, available at https://www.unwomen.org/en/news-stories/press-release/2024/03/1-in-every-10-women-in-the-world-lives-in-extreme-poverty.

However, also nowadays, many aspects specific to the female body remain overlooked. Examples are perimenopausal and menopausal symptoms or the study of female hormones and their relationship to multiple diseases and conditions.

Another area of disregard for gender sensitivity, in the relationship between public regulators and citizens, concerns financial regulation. Women are not only poorer on average, but they also have lower financial literacy.[58] Women are thus more likely to fall prey to financial fraud or make ill-advised financial decisions. Since women typically are more reluctant to invest, there has been a trend to educate women in financial literacy since the number of investors is primarily male. Nevertheless, financial regulation and supervision does not consider gender in any way or the need to address this knowledge gap. Even though women interact with money differently, have different behaviours, upbringing, the concept of the vulnerable consumer of financial services and products does not consider gender. Instead, the 'vulnerable consumer' of financial services takes into account education, income, age, but regards gender as irrelevant. While paternalistic and patriarchal perceptions of women are undesirable, gender-sensitive financial and consumer regulation could help break the vicious circle of female poverty.

There are many other areas where the gender dimension and more specifically, women are invisible in regulation and generally in government-citizen interactions such as redress and reparations.[59] While the history of gender inequities are well-known, why do women remain invisible in the administrative law and regulatory contexts, especially in Western countries that claim to advance gender parity?

58 Andrea Hasler and Annamaria Lusardi, 'The Gender Gap in Financial Literacy: A Global Perspective Report' Global Financial Literacy Excellence Center - George Washington University Business School (2017), available at https://gflec.org/wp-content/uploads/2017/05/The-Gender-Gap-in-Financial-Literacy-A-Global-Perspective-Report.pdf.

59 Brandon Hamber and Ingrid Palmay, 'Gender, Memoralization, and Symbolic Reparations' in Ruth Rubio-Marín (ed.), *The Gender of Reparations: Unsettling Sexual Hierarchies while Redressing Human Rights Violations* (Cambridge University Press, 2009).

II. Why women remain invisible

The invisibility of gender and in particular of women is, in most cases, probably not intended as discriminatory. More often than not, no one thought about it. Regulations have been thus far a reflection of those drafting regulations, their values, and needs. There has been perhaps the unspoken assumption that these regulations could or should be gender-neutral as a way of ensuring equal treatment. However, in many fields, gender neutrality does not truly exist and gender discrimination does not have to be intended or direct.

First, as Caroline Criado Perez has explained in the book *Invisible Women*, women are invisible because they are often regarded, in medicine, technical design, and much more, as a deviation from the male standard. Simone de Beauvoir had described this perspective in the *Second Sex*: Men are the subject, women are 'the other'.[60] This otherness means that women are relegated to a secondary position because nothing is defined by reference to them, but by reference to men. Since then, this position has also been corrected by postcolonial perspectives that have added that in many countries, the main denominator has not simply been a 'man' but a 'white man'. However, when someone is regarded as 'a deviation' and there is less data about a certain group, many elements of the lives of these individuals go uncounted. And what does not get counted, does not count. This brings us to our connection between gender and the automation of administrative decision-making and how public regulators use digital technologies. AI systems will work less well on women and non-binary individuals because of the historical inputs on these individuals (or the lack thereof). Consequently, these individuals may be more frequently discriminated since they are regarded as deviations from a standard model. Decisions supported by these systems may also be less accurate and overlook the needs of a large part of the citizenry.

A recent report of the European Parliament Research Service on digitalization and administrative law has reflected on the diversified impact of digital technology on gender equality: to begin with, the EU faces a shortage of women in science, technology, engineering and mathematics (STEM) in the digital sector who are able to contribute to the development

---

60 Simone de Beauvoir, The Second Sex, xxxii-xxxv.

of new automated systems.[61] Furthermore, exploratory studies of the use of AI in the Spanish public administration has identified potential discriminatory bias with relevance to gender, which were primarily caused by training data in which women are under-represented.[62] Lastly, women are also affected by another type of inequality: more limited digital skills and uptake of digital technology due to lack of training, culture, or access to new technologies.[63]

The limited presence of gender discussions and more specifically the limited participation of women in administrative law and regulation are a blind spot of the administrative state.[64] This is particularly problematic at a time when administrative and regulatory decision-making is increasingly automated, thus reproducing historical biases, omissions, and distorted narratives. Women and minorities tend to be disproportionately discriminated by automated systems that do not understand the invisibility of women in historical data.[65] This regulatory blindness concerning gender has not ceased to exist. There are still nowadays multiple examples of equipment used in certain jobs which was built only with male bodies in mind (e.g., if machinery used by firefighters that can be operated safely only by those who meet height and weight requirements that rule out significantly more women than men).[66] While changes are ongoing, particularly when it comes to safety regulation, it is important to continue to raise awareness for

61 European Parliamentary Research Service, Digitalisation and Administrative Law, available at https://www.europarl.europa.eu/RegData/etudes/STUD/2022/730350/EPRS_STU(2022)730350_EN.pdf.

62 I. García, 'Artificial Intelligence Risks and Challenges in the Spanish Public Administration: An Exploratory Analysis through Expert Judgements', Administrative Sciences, Volume 11, Issue 102, September 2021.

63 European Parliamentary Research Service, Digitalisation and Administrative Law, available at https://www.europarl.europa.eu/RegData/etudes/STUD/2022/730350/EPRS_STU(2022)730350_EN.pdf.

64 Cfr. Cseres, Kati, Feminist Competition Law (January 3, 2024). Amsterdam Centre for European Law and Governance Research Paper No. 2023-04, Amsterdam Law School Research Paper No. 2023-43 Draft chapter for Cambridge Handbook on the Theoretical Foundations of Antitrust and Competition Law (Cambridge University Press, forthcoming 2024 , Available at SSRN: https://ssrn.com/abstract=4682906 or http://dx.doi.org/10.2139/ssrn.4682906.

65 Joy Buolamwini and Timnit Gebru, 'Gender Shades: Intersectional Accuracy Disparities in Commercial Gender Classification', *Proceedings of the 1st Conference on Fairness, Accountability and Transparency* (PMLR 2018) <https://proceedings.mlr.press/v81/buolamwini18a.html> accessed 8 November 2023.

66 Schouten, Gina. "Discrimination and Gender." The Routledge Handbook of the Ethics of Discrimination. Routledge, 2017. 185-195.

the gendered nature of public law and the interactions between government and citizens.

A gender sensitive approach to the automation of administrative decision-making should also consider the historical differences in the position of women in society, the additional caring duties that are traditionally imposed on women, the feminization of poverty, and the need to gather further input as to the needs of different genders. The following section discusses how to further develop gender-sensitive administrative law and regulation.

D. Gender Matters

Gender-sensitive administrative law and regulation are particularly crucial in the context of automation of public law. Considering gender when designing the automation of public services, administrative decision-making, and proposing new regulation can ensure that digital technologies do not perpetuate historical power asymmetries. Furthermore, it can shed light into areas that were until now disregarded and where women or non-binary individuals have different needs that impact their interactions with government. This section discusses three suggestions that aim to raise awareness for the relevance of gender: gender impact assessments; data feminism and AI as equalizer which aim to reshape administrative law and regulation drawing on feminist and gender studies.

I. Gender Impact Assessments

Over the last years, several countries (e.g., Austria, Sweden, Denmark, Finland) have adopted so-called Gender Impact Assessments to promote gender-responsive budgeting and regulations. These regulatory and policy decision-making methods have been around since the mid-nineties and were designed to address the structurally unequal power relations between women and men, particularly in the context of labour division.[67]

By systematically evaluating how different genders are affected by policies, programs, and budgets, this impact assessment aims to guarantee

67 Mieke Verloo & Connie Roggeband, 'Gender impact assessment: the development of a new instrument in the Netherlands' 14(1) Impact Assessment 3, 6 (1996).

that gender considerations are integrated in the decision-making processes. The aims of this tool are twofold: on the one hand, this impact assessment intends to promotes equity; on the other, it also acknowledges the need to consider gender so as to enhance the effectiveness of policies by addressing diverse needs. A gender impact assessment can also lead to the implementation of concrete actions aimed at improving gender equality. These actions might include adjusting the policy framework to better accommodate gender-specific needs, establishing clear objectives, implementation milestones, and progress commitments within the policy parameters, improving the collection of gender-disaggregated data to better understand and address gender impacts, and initiating new research or consultations to explore the gendered impacts of policies more deeply. According to the European Institute for Gender Equality, 'gender impact assessment is a tool for gender mainstreaming (...) and civil servants working for governmental, regional or local offices, departments or ministries initiating a new norm or policy should be involved in the process of gender impact assessment.'[68] Different countries may design this assessment according to different models, depending on the institutional settings and different actors involved. Models can vary depending on the degree of autonomy accorded to civil servants for this task, the assistance provided by gender equality mechanisms and the potential intervention of 'external' actors such as gender or legal experts.

According to the Council of Europe, gender impact assessments can be broadly applied both to proposed and existing policy programmes, budgets, policy plans, legislation and regulation and they require training and knowledge of gender issues.[69] Recent research shows that gender impact assessments of regulation may be in practice incomplete as they remain primarily gender neutral and do not consider adequately the experiences of women and LGBTQI+ individuals that often carry a disproportionate burden of the adverse impacts of economic activities. Much of the focus of impact assessments has been economic, so gender has been often analysed in relation to labour. However, going forward, it is essential to take these

68 European Institute for Gender Equality, Gender Impact Assessment: Who Should Use Gender Impact Assessment', available at https://eige.europa.eu/gender-mainstreaming/toolkits/gender-impact-assessment/who-should-use-gender-impact-assessment?language_content_entity=en.

69 Council of Europe Gender Equality Glossary, Gender Impact Assessment (2016), available at https://edoc.coe.int/en/gender-equality/6947-gender-equality-glossary.html.

impact assessments seriously, train staff in gender so that those conducting these assessments are aware of how to address power imbalances. Furthermore, gender impact assessments should not be reduced to the position of women, but they should encompass gender broadly in order to ensure that policy and regulation is responsive to the different experiences of individuals.[70]

II. Data Feminism

Nowadays, we discuss the role of digital technology and datafication processes in perpetuating historical inequalities. It is regarded as a shortcoming of the digital state. However, data collection—including on gender—is far from recent. Church officials and colonial authorities have collected personal data for centuries as a method of consolidating knowledge and controlling power over individuals' lives.[71] Over the last decade, a new research field emerged focused on giving meaning to gendered data and the different interactions between data and gender: data feminism. The latter does not limit itself to studying women and data. On the contrary, it draws on intersectional approaches, considering how race, class, sexuality, ability, religion, and geography and many more factors influence each person's experience and opportunities in the world. In other words, this intersectional perspective of data 'feminism examines unequal power.'[72]

Data feminism is a burgeoning field of scholarship that offers a novel approach to understanding data, emphasizing both their uses and limitations. This perspective is informed by direct experiences, a commitment to activism, and the principles of intersectional feminism. Scholars in this field begin with the recognition that power is not distributed equally in society.

By examining how data practices reinforce or challenge existing power structures, data feminism advocates for more equitable and inclusive data methodologies. This approach not only critiques traditional data practices but also seeks to empower marginalized communities through more ethical

70 Nora Götzmann & Nicholas Bainton, 'Embedding gender-responsive approaches in impact assessment and management'39(3) Impact Assessment and Project Appraisal 171 (2021), DOI: 10.1080/14615517.2021.1904721.

71 Catherine D'Ignazio and Lauren F. Klein, *Data Feminism* (MIT Press, 2020) 12.

72 Catherine D'Ignazio and Lauren F. Klein, *Data Feminism* (MIT Press, 2020) 14.

and representative data use. 'Data feminism is not only about women (...) and is not only about gender (...) intersectional feminists have showed how race, class, sexuality, ability, religion, and geography and many more factors influence each person's experience and opportunities in the world. Intersectional feminism examines unequal power.'[73]

III. AI as Equalizer

In her book 'The Equality Machine,' Orly Lobel argues that artificial intelligence can be used to remove gender biases from decision-making, increase the neutrality of human assessments, and provide a lever for changing traditional 'white-male-dominated' practices.[74] There has mounting concern regarding the impact of automation on labour, particularly women's labour. Job displacement is expected to affect women who are trained in traditional sectors rather than in STEM, women with limited education and resources in the Global South. However, AI can also be used for augmentation, that is, to enhance human capabilities and optimize human labour, thus reducing the time required per task.[75] Lobel argues that the discussion on automation and gender should not be limited to labour. In every sector, AI can potentially assist women's position, if properly regulated, as it may actually shed light on discriminatory practices that were hidden in someone's values before. Therefore, Lobel contends that we can use technology to ameliorate human cognitive biases and correct human mistakes that an automated system would not typically make (for example, paying excessive attention to negative information about a certain fact, even when the predominant information about it is positive).

A combination between feminist and gender studies and this more optimistic perspective of the potential of AI could help us further understand how to incorporate gender elements in the automation of administrative decision and regulation.

---

73 Catherine D'Ignazio and Lauren F. Klein, *Data Feminism* (MIT Press, 2020) 14.

74 Orly Lobel, *The Equality Machine: Harnessing Digital Technology for a Brighter, More Inclusive Future*, Hachette, 2022.

75 World Economic Forum, The Future of Jobs Report (2023), https://www.weforum.org/publications/the-future-of-jobs-report-2023/digest/.

E. Conclusion

This paper argues that the digitalization and automation of administrative decision-making and its regulation are not and should not be gender-neutral or gender-blind. Gender matters in administrative law, and this is particularly pertinent in the context of automation. It is well known that technology often exacerbates longstanding issues and social biases. Furthermore, as I have argued elsewhere, administrative law is never gender-neutral. Rather, administrative law is based on a standard citizen who is typically not genderless, but often an autonomous, middle-aged man, with a stable income, average family, home, and education.[76] These were the citizens that once upon a time, engaged with government to apply for licenses, permits, and benefits for their families. Nevertheless, this is a vision of the past we need to correct, and we should not allow AI to perpetuate it.

A gendered perspective on AI is needed, not only in the context of labour but more broadly. AI systems are integrated in multiple digital interactions between citizens and governments. If no action is taken, they will continue to perpetuate the vicious circle of power inequality.

I conclude with a few reflections. First, regulators and policymakers should be trained on gender issues. This is an important gap in our law schools and the legal profession training—as gender and feminist studies are rarely offered in European law schools or in the legal profession training—and this gap is not addressed later by professional trainings. Gender studies should be thus more mainstream because if we would like to ensure that administrative law and regulation includes the perspectives of all the different individuals in our society, we need to ensure that we understand their experiences and needs. Thus far, gendered regulations have been reactive, often emerging as responses to incidents and empirical data on the deaths of women whose bodies were not considered in medical or safety trials (e.g., automotive sector, healthcare, pharmaceuticals). A preventive approach is thus advised.

Second, technology is an opportunity to break the vicious circle, but only if we regulate it properly. Generative AI outputs still discriminate against women because they are trained on historical data that associate 'expertise' with 'men' and women with 'beauty' and other stereotypical

76 Sofia Ranchordas, *Administrative Blindness: All the Citizens the State Cannot See* (Tilburg University 2024) (inaugural lecture).

female features.[77] The AI Act seeks to safeguard fundamental rights and combat discrimination, thus seeking to manage risks and promote equality. However, the AI Act does too little to address gender discrimination. Gender deserved a special section or at least a couple of legislative dispositions, ensuring that measures are taken to address the problem of underrepresentation of women in the technology sector, the gendered lens of AI systems, and an intersectional perspective on data analysis and processing. More and better data and training are needed to ensure that generative AI will stop 'hallucinating' against women. However, changing human biases may be more difficult than changing technical ones.

There is a long road ahead of us when it comes to solving gender blindness in the automation of administrative decision-making and regulation. This is merely the beginning of a long conversation we should have with scholars from feminist and gender studies, civil society, and the individuals around us.

77 Anamika Kundu, 'The AI Act's gender gap: When algorithms geti t wrong, who rights the wrongs?' Internet Policy Review, https://policyreview.info/articles/news/ai-acts-gender-gap-when-algorithms-get-it-wrong/1743.

Trust and ban – a critical reassessment of debates on the regulation of innovations in democracies

Beatrice Brunhöber, Bernhard Jakl

A common belief, which also underpins the EU's current digital strategy, is that trust in normative orders can be fostered through the imposition of bans. The prevailing approach, informed in legal theory and in theoretical sociology, which we call a "communicative picture" tends to support such notions. This approach considers bans as a special form of communication that stabilizes expectations and thus generates trust, or at least functions as a latent reason for correct behavior. In contrast, our critical argument, derived from legal philosophy, is that the relationship between trust and ban varies in different fields of law. The transition to an institutional-argumentative justification of norms proposed here allows to critically reassess the questionable nexus of trust and ban.

The need for trust is increasingly apparent in today's intricate mass society. Individuals can only engage in action and collaboration within such a society if they place trust in others, even without knowing their identities or intentions. Economic, organizational, and technical complexities can only be navigated through trust in institutions such as the market, organizations, and large-scale technologies. Contrary to initial impressions, trust within modern, complex mass society is fundamentally strengthened through legal coercion, a fact particularly reflected in various forms of legal ban.

The utilization of bans is growing in significance for fostering trust in innovations. Legal bans frequently serve the purpose of instilling trust in innovations by shielding individuals from undesirable outcomes stemming from their use. For instance, the European Artificial Intelligence Act (Draft AI Act)[1], adopted by the EU Parliament in March 2024, categorizes AI ap-

1 Artificial Intelligence Act proposed by the European Council (21 April 2021), adopted by European Parliament (13 March 2024), awaits reading in the EU Council, COM(2021) 206 final (Draft AI Act), <https://eur-lex.europa.eu/legal-content/EN/TXT/?uri=CELEX:52021PC0206> accessed 26 April 2024.

plications based on risk and prohibits AI practices (such as social scoring) deemed to pose unacceptable risks. According to the EU Commission, the Act was formulated to "ensure that Europeans can trust what AI has to offer."[2]

In the realm of legal philosophy, the outlined discussions regarding trust in innovations within complex mass societies shed light on the fundamental interplay between trust and ban. This interplay is characterized by bans reacting to and at the same time shaping innovations.

This contribution provides a critical (re-)assessment of debates surrounding the regulation of innovations in democracies. Firstly (1.), we examine the widely accepted – as we put it – *communicative picture* of the relationship between trust and ban, as portrayed by legal theory and theoretical social science: the notion of it primarily functioning as a form of communication. In contrast, the subsequent two sections adopt a perspective rooted in the philosophy of law, offering an alternative picture of the relationship between trust and ban based on the specific legal doctrines developed within different areas of law: here we explore the argumentative standards of criminal law (2.) and private law (3.). In the final section (4.), we conclude that the delineated *institutional-argumentative picture* of the relationship between trust and ban, based on legal philosophy, holds greater appeal than the traditional communicative picture, as it exhibits more significant critical potential.

A. The communicative picture of the relationship between trust and ban

The interplay between trust and ban in the context of democratic control over innovations is conventionally examined through the lens of legal theory and theoretical sociology, often grounded in either the concept of communicative justification discourses or the concept communicative systems. We may therefore call this type of – otherwise very different – conceptions a "communicative picture" of the relationship between trust and ban.

2 See the Digital Strategy of the European Institutions, <https://digital-strategy.ec.europa.eu/en/policies/regulatory-framework-ai> accessed 5 May 2024.

I. Adapting law to evolving realities

The evaluation of bans, emphasizing their communicative mediations and justifications, sheds light on the intricate relationship between a normative surplus generated through communication and the imperative of adapting to (normative) reality for generating trust. On one hand, approaches rooted in discourse theory often advocate for ban in pursuit of a normatively excessive conception of democracy and justice.[3] For example, scholars respond to the emergence of "surveillance capitalism" by advocating for democratic control over information.[4] Conversely, systems theory approaches aim at systemic adaptations.[5] Building upon these premises, authors argue that legal subjectivity ought to be dissociated from personal

3 For the realization of his concept of justice see John Rawls, *A Theory of justice* (revised edn, Cambridge, MA: The Belknap Press of Harvard University Press 1999) 5, 22, 113, 156 on defining fundamental rights and obligations and emphasizing the institutional framework. According to this, only the enforcement of a public system of penalties by the government removes the presumption that others do not obey the rules, ibid. 209. On the implementation of the equal originality of private and public autonomy, see Jürgen Habermas, *Between Facts and Norms. Contributions to a discourse theory of law and democracy*, transl. by William Rehg (Cambridge, MA: MIT Press 1996), 399-404, according to which the aim is to abolish privileges that are incompatible with the equal distribution of subjective freedoms demanded by this principle. Freedom thus depends essentially on state activities and direct specifications justifying in principle a priority of public over private autonomy. For *democratic trust* see below 2.3. (text to n 36) and Russel Hardin, Trust and Trustworthiness (New York: Russel Sage 2002), 151-172; Pippa Norris, "The conceptual Framework of Political Support" in Sonja Zmerli and Tom WG van der Meer (eds), Handbook on Political Trust (Cheltenham: Edward Elgar Publishing 2017) 19-32; Pippa Norris, In Praise of Skepticism. Trust but Verify (New York: Oxford University Press 2022); Mark E. Warren, "Trust and Democracy" in Eric M. Uslaner (ed), The Oxford Handbook of Social and Political Trust (Oxford: Oxford University Press 2018) 75-94; for the development in democratic theory see Beatrice Brunhöber, Die Erfindung "demokratischer Repräsentation" in den Federalist Papers (Tübingen: Mohr Siebeck 2010), 136-144.

4 E.g. Shoshana Zuboff, *The Age of Surveillance Capitalism. The Fight for a Human Future at the New Frontier of Power* (London: Profile Books 2019) 366-371, to overcome the danger of "instrumentarian power" and Carol Gould, "How Democracy can Inform Consent: Cases of the Internet and Bioethics" (2019) 36 (2) *Journal of Applied Philosophy* 173, for a democratic revision of consent by means of an "all-affected-principle".

5 Niklas Luhmann, *Das Recht der Gesellschaft* (Frankfurt a.M.: Suhrkamp 1993) 277, according to whom stabilization can serve as a motivation for innovation. Therefore, Luhmann concludes, social theory has to change from "target formulas such as peace and justice to system analysis", ibid 438.

conceptions and that legal frameworks should be adjusted accordingly (e.g., by granting legal capacity to software agents).[6]

II. Bans as recognized political instrument

Given the prevalent acceptance of the communicative picture of the relationship between trust and bans, the latter are commonly regarded as effective tools to forestall undesirable outcomes of innovations in their early stages, thereby fostering trust in the respective innovation.[7] This highlights a unique interaction between bans and trust. Bans respond to the ongoing progression of innovations and their anticipated impacts on individuals and society. Concurrently, bans influence the future development of the regulated innovations, both technically and socially, shaping aspects such as the types of applications brought to market and their modes of utilization.[8]

III. The relationship between trust and ban

Within communicative approaches, there is controversy over whether modern law relies not only on communicative mediation[9] but also necessitates trust in public discourse for resolving social conflicts.[10] Irrespective of this controversy, the question remains to what extent bans must be issued, justified, and shaped to assert and foster socially effective trust within a pluralistic society of free individuals. From these communicative standpoints, legally institutionalized bans and the associated coercion not only mitigate uncertainty regarding the actions of others. Rather, institutionally enforce-

6 E.g. Gunther Teubner, "Digitale Rechtssubjekte? Zum privatrechtlichen Status autonomer Softwareagenten" (2018) *Archiv für die civilistische Praxis* 155, 204.

7 E.g. from a European legal perspective Irina Orssich, "Das europäische Konzept für vertrauenswürdige Künstliche Intelligenz" (2022) *Europäische Zeitschrift für Wirtschaftsrecht* 254.

8 Cf. Wolfgang Hoffmann-Riem, *Innovation und Recht – Recht und Innovation. Recht im Ensemble seiner Kontexte* (Tübingen: Mohr Siebeck 2016) 698: The legislator should open up "options spaces" within which further development can take place.

9 Luhmann (n 5) 128 refers in this respect to repetitions of communication acts that constrain the scope for alternatives and thus have a stabilizing effect. Also Niklas Luhmann, *Soziale Systeme. Grundriß einer allgemeinen Theorie* (Frankfurt a.M.: Suhrkamp 1987) 498.

10 Habermas (n 3) 16 and 80 for the special case of legal argumentation.

able bans also facilitate the resolution of negative cooperative experiences by stabilizing expectations. According to the viewpoint of theoretical sociology, bans can ultimately cultivate trust.[11] In terms of justification, bans in this context are perceived less as instruments of power and more as means of communication.[12]

From this perspective, the potential for sanctions accompanying bans cannot be the main driver for cultivating trust,[13] as trust relies on communication. If sanctions take precedence, the individuals involved may no longer extend trust, nor is it necessary for them to do so. Instead, sanctions enforce proper behavior, not trust. The availability of sanctions has a limited impact, primarily influencing the motivation of the trustees and incentivizing them to act in a trustworthy manner in their own self-interest. The availability of sanctions afforded by bans thus serves as a subsidiary reason and possesses a latent function.[14]

From this justification-oriented perspective, bans should be measured less in terms on whether they are institutionally enforced and more in terms of whether they are justified in a manner that renders them perceived as binding by the individuals and groups they target. In the context of democracies, in line with discourse theory considerations, such perception is more likely to occur if individuals also perceive themselves as the creators of laws and can trust legislation and its application to be fair under the rule of law.[15]

11 Niklas Luhmann, *Vertrauen. Ein Mechanismus der Reduktion sozialer Komplexität* (5th edn, Konstanz: UVK Verlagsgesellschaft mbH 2014) 27-38.

12 E.g. Klaus Günther, "Zwang/Sanktion und Vertrauen im Konflikt" (ConTrust Working Paper Series, manuskript 2020) 8-13.

13 Luhmann, (n 11) 39 sees trust as a kind of deception about the complexity of the world. Also see Georg Simmel, *Soziologie. Untersuchungen über die Formen der Vergesellschaftung* (10th edn, Frankfurt a. M.: Suhrkamp 1992) 263 who describes trust as "hypothesis of future behavior" ("Hypothese künftigen Verhaltens", translation by the authors).

14 Luhmann (n 11) 35 and Günther (n 13) by drawing on Joseph Raz's differentiation between operative and auxiliary reasons. According to Raz, *Practical Reasons and Norms* (Oxford: Oxford University Press 1999) 32-34, a reason is an operative reason if the belief in its existence implies that one adopts a practical critical attitude. A reason that is not an operative reason, on the other hand, is what Raz calls an auxiliary reason.

15 See Habermas (n 3) 119-120; Rawls (n 3) 52, 53 and 131.

IV. Open questions

The communicative picture delineated by legal theory and theoretical sociology underscores essential facets of the relationship between trust and ban. However, on the basis of legal philosophy, the question arises of whether the narrow emphasis on communication neglects the argumentative standards developed within the institutionally distinct areas of law. To address this question, the subsequent two sections scrutinize these institutional-argumentative standards concerning the relationship between trust and ban within the domain of criminal law on one hand and private law on the other.

B. Criminal law and innovations: from ban to trust

In this section we investigate the correlation between trust and ban in criminal law, illustrated through the lens of criminal liability pertaining to actions associated with innovations such as algorithms and/or artificial intelligence (AI).

I. Bans in criminal law: Penalizing conduct in the context of innovations

Criminal liability for such conduct typically falls under cybercrime legislation. This is because the majority of algorithms and/or AI applications are utilized within computer programs. Under the prevailing definition, cybercrime includes the utilization of a digital device, such as a computer, as an integral part of committing a crime or making a computer system the object of the crime.[16] A significant portion of global cybercrime regulation[17]

16 See e.g. Budapest Convention on Cybercrime (adopted 23 November 2001, entered into force 1 July 2004) 2296 UNTS 167 (Convention on Cybercrime) art. 1 (a).

17 As of 1 May 2024, 68 countries have signed the Convention on Cybercrime, that is by all Council of Europe members as well as Canada, Japan, the United States and South Africa as well as Australia and quite a few further countries from Africa (e.g. Senegal, Ghana), Asia (e.g. Philippines) and South America (e.g. Argentina, Brazil, Chile, Columbia). It was estimated in 2017 that the Convention had already influenced the cybercrime regulation of more than 130 countries due to its policy measurements all over the world, see Alexander Seger, in Roderic Broadhurst et al. (eds.), *Cyber Terrorism* (Research Report of the Australian National University Cybercrime Observatory for the Korean Institute of Criminology 2017) Fig. 7.1.; also

is either harmonized or influenced by the Council of Europe Convention on Cybercrime[18] and, within the European Union, by corresponding Framework Decisions and Directives.[19] The Convention mandates that state parties criminalize various forms of conduct categorized as cybercrime and encourages interstate cooperation in law enforcement.[20] Its global impact is further augmented by capacity building initiatives in non-signatory states. The Convention advocates for the criminalization of access offenses (e.g. hacking), use offenses (e.g. cyberfraud), and content offenses (e.g. hate speech or child pornography).[21] Presently, many traditional cybercrimes are perpetrated through the use of algorithms and/or AI.[22] For instance, hacking may involve employing reverse engineering. Fraudulent phishing emails may be crafted utilizing machine learning to evade spam filters. Hate speech may be disseminated through social bots. Certain instances of child pornography may be produced using AI. This list could easily go on.

II. From ban to trust: Cultivating trust by pre-empting future risks associated with innovations

Criminal prohibitions in the context of innovations primarily seek to bolster trust in the utilization of new technologies by pre-empting potential future risks associated with the innovations. The drafting of the Cybercrime

---

see Neil Boister, *An Introduction to Transnational Criminal Law* (2th edn, Oxford: Oxford University Press 2018) 189; critical of the scope Marco Gercke, "10 years Convention on Cybercrime. Achievements and Failures of the Council of Europe´s Instrument in the Fight against Internet-related Crimes" (2011) 5 *Computer Law Review International* 142-43.

18 Draft AI Act (n 1).

19 Especially 2013/40/EU of 12 August 2013 on attacks against information systems and replacing Council Framework Decision 2005/222/JHA; 2011/92/EU of 13 December 2011 on combating the sexual abuse and sexual exploitation of children and child pornography and replacing Council Framework Decision 2004/68/JHA.

20 Convention on Cybercrime (n 16), chap. II, sec. 1 (substantive criminal law) and sec. 2 (procedural law).

21 Title I, II and III of the Convention on Cybercrime (n 16) and 2003 Additional Protocol concerning the criminalization of acts of a racist or xenophobic nature committed through computer systems (adopted 28 January 2003, entered into force 1 July 2004) 2466 UNTS 205.

22 See e.g. for hate speech with social bots Sabine Gleß and Thomas Weigend, "Intelligente Agenten und das Strafrecht" (2015) 123 (3) *Zeitschrift für die gesamte Strafrechtswissenschaft* 561.

Convention commenced in 1997,[23] a period when computers, the Internet, and digital devices such as mobile phones had yet to assume significant roles in daily lives of most individuals.[24] The objective of the Cybercrime Convention was to establish global control of cyberactivity in order to mitigate nascent risks to commerce, businesses, private communications and public institutions at an early stage.[25] These risks are associated with factors such as the widespread use of digital devices, which expands the potential number of affected individuals, the availability of anonymity and encryption options, which may incentivize engaging in particularly risky behavior and may be used for concealing responsibility for the commitment of a crime, and the transnational nature of cybercrime, hindering investigation, prosecution and adjudication processes.[26] Addressing these challenges is intended to facilitate individuals' ability to securely share data via cloud computing, communicate via email or to conduct banking transactions online without running the risk of exploitation or compromise. In essence, bans of (presumed) risky cyberactivity and corresponding law enforcement measures are generally aimed at fostering trust in cyberspace.

With the emergence of AI, concerns about mitigating anticipated risks associated with its utilization arose early on.[27] These concerns culminated in the Draft AI Act[28], marking the world's inaugural major legislation aimed at regulating AI to instil trust in its application.[29] The Draft AI Act governs

23 See Ryan M. F. Baron, "A critique of the International Cybercrime Treaty" (2002) 10 (2) *CommLaw Conspectus* 263, 265. In 1997 a Committee of Experts on Crime in Cyber-Space was set up by the Council of Europe (Specific Terms of Reference of the Committee of Experts on Crime in Cyber-Space, Council of Europe's Fight Against Corruption and Organised Crime, sec. 5 (c) 583rd Meeting) which eventually drafted the Convention on Cybercrime (n 16). The Convention was opened for signature in 2001 and came into force in 2004.

24 Jonathan Clough, "The Council of Europe Convention on Cybercrime" (2012) 23 *Criminal Law Forum* 363, 365.

25 For an overview of presumed damages from cybercrime see Nir Kshetri, *The Global Cybercrime Industry: Economic, Institutional and Strategic Perspectives* (Berlin: Springer 2010) 4-6.

26 Cf. Marco Gercke and Philipp Brunst, *Internetstrafrecht* (2th edn, Stuttgart: Kohlhammer 2023) para. 10; UNODC, *Comprehensive Study on Cybercrime* (Vienna: UN 2013) 226.

27 Thomas C King, Nikita Aggarwal, Mariarosaria Taddeo, Luciano Floridi, "Artificial Intelligence Crime: An Interdisciplinary Analysis of Foreseeable Threats and Solutions" (2020) 26 (1) *Sci Eng Ethics* 89-120.

28 Draft AI Act (n. 1).

29 <https://digital-strategy.ec.europa.eu/en/policies/regulatory-framework-ai> accessed 5 May 2024.

the entry of specific AI products into the EU internal market.[30] This approach has sparked apprehension over whether certain particularly harmful AI activities should instead be subjected to EU-wide criminalization. Examples include the penalization of deepfakes, i.e. the use of applications to produce AI-manipulated political information or to create sexually explicit AI-fabricated images humiliating others.[31]

Typically, criminal bans seem to serve as notably effective methods for shielding individuals from undesirable outcomes and thereby bolstering trust in innovation.

III. Reassessing the relationship between trust and ban in criminal law regulation of innovations

The communicative picture of trust intersects with the developed relationship between trust and ban in a crucial domain: According to system theories, the penalties facilitated by corresponding criminal statutes can stabilize behavioural expectations[32] within the realm of innovations. They are intended to foster trust in the conduct of others when engaging with computers, the Internet, algorithms and/or AI. This outcome remains valid even when shifting the focus from the availability of sanctions to the norms permitting sanctions, as discourse theories suggest.[33] The efficacy of prohibitions then relies less on their enforcement and more on whether they are perceived as binding, a condition that is met when individuals see themselves as their authors.[34] Criminal provisions concerning innovation typically emerge from a (national) democratic process often implementing

30 See for the consequences for criminal product liability Victoria Ibold, *Künstliche Intelligenz und Strafrecht: zur strafrechtlichen Produktverantwortung in der Innovationsgesellschaft* (Baden-Baden: Nomos Verlagsgesellschaft 2024).

31 In early 2024 criminalization of sexually explicit deepfakes was introduced by both the UK ministry of Justice (Guardian, 16 Apr. 2024, <https://www.theguardian.com/technology/2024/apr/16/creating-sexually-explicit-deepfake-images-to-be-made-offence-in-uk> accessed 10 May 2024) as well as by the European Union (Directive of the European Parliament and of the Council on combating violence against women and domestic violence, PE-CONS 33/24 of 25 April 2024 [not yet published in the Official Journal], (19) and art. 5 (1)(b)).

32 Luhmann (n 11) 27-38; see above 2.3.

33 Günther (n 12); Raz (n 14); see above 2.3.

34 Habermas (n 3); Rawls (n 3); see above 2.3.

supra- and international guidelines[35] and thus must also adhere to the respective fundamental principles outlined in national constitutions. These include the requirements for democratic self-determination as well as human rights and principles such as the rule of law.

However, from the vantage point of the communicative picture, another aspect is somewhat overlooked, which can be highlighted more effectively from an institutional-argumentative perspective informed by the philosophy of law. The communicative picture of trust tends to underemphasize the fact that criminal law not only pertains to the trust relationship between citizens which must be upheld through criminal sanctions wielded by sovereign authority, but also encompasses the trust relationship between citizens and the sovereign authority itself. This relationship only comes into view in discussions about trust in government or democratic institutions.[36] From an institutional-argumentative standpoint grounded in the philosophy of law, it becomes evident that criminal law prohibitions serve as a direct mechanism from authority to control individual behavior. As observed, legislation on innovations often seeks to control individual activities in a manner that instils trust in the respective innovation.

The main objective is to avert future risks associated with the innovation, leading to a significant expansion of criminal law.[37] Firstly, unlike other domains of criminal law, regulations concerning innovations are frequently justified by the use of "risky" tools or the risk posed to targeted vulnerable objects. For instance, the Cybercrime Convention advocates for criminalizing the mere possession of hacking tools,[38] implying that they could be used

35 Beatrice Brunhöber, "Criminal Law of Global Digitality. Characteristics and Critique of Cybercrime Law" in Alexander Peukert, Matthias Kettemann, Indra Spiecker gen. Döhmann (eds.), *Law of Global Digitality* (London: Routledge 2022) 246-47; Allen Buchanan, 'The Legitimacy of International Law' in Samantha Besson and John Tasioulas (eds), *The Philosophy of International Law* (Oxford: Oxford University Press 2010) 79.

36 See Hardin (n 3) 151-172; Norris (2017, n 3) 19-32; Norris (2022, n 3); Warren (n 3) 75-94; for the development in democratic theory see Brunhöber (n 3) 136-144.

37 With regard to the following see Andrew Ashworth and Lucia Zedner, *Preventive Justice* (Oxford: Oxford University Press 2014) 95-118; Beatrice Brunhöber, "Von der Unrechtsahndung zur Risikosteuerung durch Strafrecht und ihre Schranken" in Roland Hefendehl et al (eds), *Festschrift für Bernd Schünemann* (Berlin: De Gruyter 2014) 3-15.

38 Convention on Cybercrime (n 16) art. 6 (1)(b).

in a detrimental manner.[39] Consequently, criminalization is not grounded in the violation of specific rights and legal concerns but rather alludes to some form of ambiguous risk. Secondly, given the objective of preventing any risks, criminal law regulation of innovations frequently necessitates penalizing behavior that facilitates harmful or dangerous conduct, enabling law enforcement to intervene at an early stage. Criminalizing the mere possession of hacker tools eliminates the necessity for evidence of actual computer system access to initiate an investigation. The presence of hacking tools on the suspect's computer alone suffices as evidence. Thirdly, owing to the goal of preventing any risks, corresponding offenses often do not require an intent to cause harm or substantive actions towards that end.[40] For instance, the Convention on Cybercrime calls for criminalizing "computer hacking" without requiring additional elements of a crime, such as breaching security measures.[41] Finally, unlike other domains of criminal law, penalization within the context of innovations often covers "neutral" every day behaviours that are deemed risky when undertaken with malicious intentions.[42] This broadens criminal liability from rare exceptional circumstances to embrace everyday life. For example, given that cybercrime regulation, in terms of its structure (computer systems as a tool or objective), potentially affects any use of information technology, many users are uncertain whether their actions fall under its purview (e.g. sharing music and movies, taking part in online protests via distributed denial of service attacks, and sharing explicit content images). At best, this uncertainty leads to indifference to the relevant offences; at worst, it induces self-restraint (a chilling effect).[43]

The trend toward expanding criminal law runs counter to the foundational principles of the criminal law system: Despite varying opinions on the specifics, legal scholars generally concur that the application of criminal law should be highly restrained. Moreover, democratic constitutions typically include specific provisions for criminal law to circumscribe its

39 Brunhöber (n 35) 245-46; see Andrew Ashworth, *Positive Obligations in Criminal Law* (Oxford: Hart Press 2013), 149-172 generally criticizing the "unfairness of risk-based possession offences".

40 Brunhöber (n 35) 246.

41 Convention on Cybercrime (n 16) art. 2. The parties to the Convention may include further elements of crime, but are not obliged to do so.

42 Cf. the debate on criminal liability for neutral assistance, e.g. Marcus Wohlleben, Beihilfe durch äußerlich neutrale Handlungen (Munich: CH Beck 1997) 7-10.

43 Neil Richards, *Why Privacy Matters* (Oxford: Oxford University Press 2022) 129.

scope (e.g. nulla poena sine lege, nulla poena sine culpa).[44] Criminal law represents an exceptionally severe, if not the most severe, instrument of sovereign authority: It not only authorizes monetary penalties (fines) but also entails deprivation of liberty (imprisonment) or even the loss of life (capital punishment, as in certain US-states). Furthermore, criminalizing particular behaviours signifies deeming them public wrongs (e.g. criminal records leading to job exclusion from crime-related professions, e.g. disqualification from teaching roles due to a history of child abuse), establishing a severe threat of an evil in order to give a pragmatic reason for not doing it, and to censure those who break the law.[45] Finally, criminalization grants law enforcement the power to conduct searches, surveillance, detentions, interrogations, and so forth. The exercise of such powers, which have significant consequences, necessitates a high standard of justification. That entails democratic decision-making regarding criminal provisions as well as theoretical justification based on substantial reasons for establishing such a rigorous control regime over individuals.[46] Regardless of the respective, quite different theoretical context, it is widely acknowledged that criminalization cannot be warranted solely by an imminent risk; rather it is essential that the penalized conduct causes harm to others (the harm principle[47]), violates legal interests (Rechtsgutstheorie[48]), or infringes upon concerns that outweigh individual liberty.[49] Consequently, criminalizing

---

44 E.g. nulla poena sine lege in art. 103 (2) German Basic Law (Grundgesetz); nulla poena sine culpa founded in human dignity (art. 1 (1) German Basic Law) or as prerequisite of the presumption of innocence (art. 6 (2) European Convention on Human Rights).

45 Andrew Ashworth and Jeremy Horder, *Principles of Criminal Law* (7th edn, Oxford: Oxford University Press 2013) 22-23.

46 Ibid 23.

47 John Stuart Mill, *On Liberty* (Harmondsworth Middlesex: Penguin Books 1979); Joel Feinberg, *Harm of Others* (New York: Oxford University Press 1984) 26.

48 Winfried Hassemer, „Grundlinien einer personalen Rechtsgutslehre (1989)“ in Winfried Hassemer, *Strafen im Rechtsstaat* (Baden-Baden: Nomos Verlag 2000) 160, 167; first Winfried Hassemer, *Theorie und Soziologie des Verbrechens* (Frankfurt a.M.: Athenäum-Verlag 1973), 147, 221; Claus Roxin and Luis Greco, *Strafrecht Allgemeiner Teil*, vol. 1 (5th edn, Munich: CH Beck 2020) sec. 2 para. 7; first Claus Roxin, “Sinn und Grenzen staatlicher Strafe“ (1966) *Juristische Schulung* 377, 381.

49 Beatrice Brunhöber, “Was ist freiheitlich-demokratische Strafrechtsbegrenzung? Stärkung des Blicks der Kriminalisierungstheorien für die Freiheit der Verbotsadressierten“ in Beatrice Brunhöber, Christoph Burchard, Klaus Günther et al. (eds), *Strafrecht als Risiko, Festschrift für Cornelius Prittwitz* (Baden-Baden: Nomos Verlag 2023) 59-75; Antony Duff, *Answering for Crime. Responsibility and Liability in the Criminal Law* (Oxford and Portland: Hart Publishing 2007), 141-42.

conduct cannot be justified by merely alluding to potential risks. Criminalization can only be justified by at least the prospect of harm to others or violations of legal interests. The justification process thus necessitates precise identification of the rights and concerns that may be impacted by certain behaviours and their penalization.

C. Private law and innovations: from trust to ban

This third part explores the relationship between trust and ban in private law using as an example AI systems identified as a growth market for private algorithmic-based businesses and their regulation.

I. The approach of EU institutions: creating trust in the digital world through bans

In the field of innovations, the current risk-differentiated normative proposals from the EU Commission and the European Parliament aim to create trust in AI systems. The European legal framework is designed to ensure the reliability of AI systems, referred to as "trustworthy AI".[50] For instance, Article 11 of the Draft AI Act requires technical documentation and compliance assessment procedures for high-risk AI systems, while Article 14 stipulates human oversight and Articles 30-39 require notification procedures. This Draft AI Act is complemented by a Draft AI Liability Regulation,[51] which seeks to establish standards of liability beyond existing national private law. These standards are to correspond to the risks identified as inherent to the AI system by preventive technical prognosis according to Articles 8, 3, 4 and 5 of the AI Liability Regulation Draft. The implicit and explicit claim of these legislative initiatives is to create trust by ex-ante bans. This raises the question of the role of bans in private law.

50 Draft AI Act (Fn. 1).

51 European Parliament, Report with recommendations to the Commission on a civil liability regime for artificial intelligence, 20 Oct. 2020, P9_TA-PROV(2020)0276, <https://www.europarl.europa.eu/doceo/document/A-9-2020-0178_EN.html> accessed 26 April 2024, followed by COM/2022/496 final, a Proposal for a Directive of the European Parliament and of the Council on adapting non-contractual civil liability rules to artificial intelligence (Draft AI Liability Directive), <https://eur-lex.europa.eu/legal-content/EN/TXT/?uri=CELEX%3A52022PC0496> accessed 26 Apr. 2024.

II. Where to find normative experiences with ban in existing private law?

In the realm of contractual agreements, which can also be assessed through the lenses of tort and unjust enrichment law, it becomes apparent, that private autonomy is restricted. This applies particularly to mass transactions governed by the law on general terms and conditions. This occurs both in public debates surrounding innovations and through legislative revisions, often converging on an ambiguous notion of contractual fairness[52] or intricate risk disclosure and liability assignments, notably extending to product liability law.[53]

The most recent instances of mandatory legislative adjustments within the detailed contract law framework in German law entail new conceptual classifications, stemming partly from European law imperatives for digitalization.[54] These have been incorporated into the German law of obligations through sec. 327a-q German Civil Code (Bürgerliches Gesetzbuch, BGB) for package contracts and contracts for goods with digital elements, alongside a revised concept of deficiencies for digital products (sec. 434, 475b et seq. BGB). Nevertheless, from these individual rules, characterized as "specific measure acts" (Maßnahmegesetze), it is hardly possible to discern foundational normative experiences applicable for identifying a general standard. Nevertheless such a standard, independent of the contingencies of a business model under consideration in each instance, is essential for establishing trust through bans within the domain of innovations.

In both civil law and common law systems, contracts remain binding based on generally accepted principles, except where they contravene principles of good morals, bona fide protections, public order or other mandatory regulations.[55] The determination of what constitutes a breach of good

52 See Heike Schweitzer, "Digitale Plattformen als private Gesetzgeber: Ein Perspektivwechsel für die europäische ‚Plattform Regulierung'" (2019) *Zeitschrift für Europäisches Privatrecht* 2019, 1, 8 and 12 uses the concept „Richtigkeitsgewähr" (assurance of correctness) even as an alternative concept for private autonomy.

53 E.g. from a German perspective Gerhard Wagner, "Liability Rules for the Digital Age – Aiming for the Brussels Effect" (2022) *Journal of European Tort Law* 191.

54 On the implementation and an overview on some consequences of the der Directive (EU) 2019/770 of the European Parliament and of the Council of 20 May 2019 on certain aspects concerning "contracts for the supply of digital content and digital services" into national law in the case of the German Civil Code (BGB) see Thomas Riehm, "Verträge über digitale Dienstleistungen" (2022) *Recht Digital* 209.

55 See as an example instead of multiple national norms art. 4:109 Principles of European Contract Law (PECL) and art. 4:110 PECL.

morals, bona fide protection, or public order, thereby permitting deviation from a contractual agreement as an exception, may vary between legal systems and occasionally change over time.[56]

In German law, for example, there exists a specific provision incorporating a general clause on good morals, as stipulated in sec. 138 BGB, as in Austrian Law with sec. 879 General Civil Code (Allgemeines Bürgerliches Gesetzbuch), in French Law with Art. 1131 and 1133 Code civil, and in Swiss law with Art. 20 Code of obligations (Obligationenrecht). Art. 138 BGB is open to interpretation and holds significant promise for examining normative experiences concerning the relationship between trust and ban. The legal concept of good morals outlined in sec. 138 BGB imposes certain constraints on all contractual agreements, some of which are not explicitly made positive law. Examples include adhesion contracts, usury, or contracts relating to organ donation and surrogate motherhood. The legal consequence of the nullifying the contractual agreement is prescribed here, rendering the contract unenforceable as well.

Although subject to debate, sec. 138 BGB can be understood structurally as a ban insofar as it withholds legal protection from the corresponding intentions of the parties.[57] Despite being a classic dogmatic reference point, which has thus far received little attention in the discourse on digitalization, the interpretation of good morals within a legal system nonetheless enables the identification of normative experiences regarding the relationship between trust and ban.

---

56 E.g. Hein Koetz, „Sitten- und Gesetzeswidrigkeit von Verträgen“ in Jürgen Basedow, Klaus J. Hopt, Reinhard Zimmermann (eds), *Handwörterbuch des Europäischen Privatrechts* (Tübingen: Mohr Siebeck 2009) 1404-1407; in order to limit legal transaction risks arising from trust in the declarations of the contracting parties, the term “liability based on trust” (“Vertrauenshaftung”) is sometimes used in German Privat Law, partly in accordance with Roman law, see Claus-Wilhelm Canaris, *Die Vertrauenshaftung im deutschen Privatrecht*, (Munich: CH Beck 1971, reprint 1981); Claus-Wilhelm Canaris, *Gesammelte Schriften*, edited by Hans Christoph Grigoleit and Jörg Neuner (Berlin, Boston: De Gruyter, 2012) 3-656. For a general strenthening of such a de-individualized trust see also Claus-Wilhelm Canaris, “Wandlungen des Schuldvertragsrechts. Tendenzen zu seiner Materialisierung”, (2000) Archiv für civilistische Praxis 273-364, 276.

57 On Nullity as a sanction in the sense of its behavior-controlling effect Herbert L A Hart, *The Concept of Law* (3rd ed, Oxford: Clarendon Press 2012) 33–35. See also Bernhard Jakl, *Handlungshoheit. Die normative Struktur der bestehenden Dogmatik und ihrer Materialisierung im deutschen und europäischen Schuldvertragsrecht* (Tübingen: Mohr Siebeck 2019) 129.

When exploring the potential to elucidate the essence of good morals inherent in the law, which can be conveyed through principles within the framework of contract law and constitutional requirements, a key jurisprudential insight into the relationship between trust and ban emerges: The argumentative and dogmatic path of private law begins with trust even under extreme scenarios, ultimately culminating in ban on certain contractual provisions in strictly limited cases.

This normative experience of the good morals provision can serve as a model for creating trust in innovations through the mechanisms of private law.

III. Trust as starting point for private law

In the legal-philosophical and institutional-argumentative assessment of the relationship between trust and ban in private law, the perspective initially shifts from the relationships between the state and its citizens to those among citizens themselves. Secondly, trust emerges here as an exemplar of interpersonal or intersubjective relationships, which remains also the prevailing paradigm in social and philosophical theories of trust.[58] Consequently, some scholars posit that the underlying reason for the binding force of contracts lies in the moral intuition that promises of performance inherently possess a uniquely compelling quality.[59] Others go so far as to invoke the notion that contractual obligations as a manifestation of human autonomy unfold within a framework of trust and respect akin to Kantian principles.[60]

Private law, particularly contract law, relies not foremost on state sanctions but on contractual agreements. Their binding nature and enforceability stem from mutual trust in individual freedom of choice and the fulfilment of performance promises by the parties involved. This entails the

58 See Carolyn McLeod, "Trust" in Edward N Zalta and Uri Nodelman (eds), *The Stanford Encyclopedia of Philosophy* (Fall 2023 Edition), <https://plato.stanford.edu/archives/fall2023/entries/trust/> accessed 26 Apr. 2024.

59 E.g. Hanoch Dagan and Michael Heller, *The Choice Theory of Contracts* (Cambridge: Cambridge University Press 2017) 25-32.

60 Charles Fried, *Contract as Promise. A Theory of Contractual Obligation* (Cambridge, MA: Harvard University Press 1981) 5, 13-14, 17, 21. To this point, a critical interpretation of the legal philosophy of classical German philosophy from an action-oriented perspective cf. Jakl (n 57) 37 and 120-126.

risk for one contracting party of not only relying on the other contracting party but also of incurring losses if the latter fails to perform as expected.

Beginning with the mutual trust of contracting parties, bans in private law have only an indirect impact on governing social behavior, unlike criminal law and public law.[61]

The potency of mutual trust in contract law is exemplified, not least, by the success of the digital mobility service provider Uber and its algorithmic-based business model. Despite regulatory protections safeguarding the taxi industry throughout Europe through public law and administrative law including threats of fines, consumers were willing to use the service en masse. They willingly shared their location and payment data even in contravention of extensive data protection regulations in favour of what they perceived as a more user-friendly transportation alternative compared to taxis under public supervision. As a consequence, state regulations governing taxis across Europe were subsequently adjusted in favour of Uber.[62]

To explore the relationship between trust and ban, it is crucial to consider the potential justifications for limitations, restrictions, and even bans that exceptionally permit interventions into the freedom of trust-based contracts. However, the general rule is that contracts are binding. It is even acknowledged that mutual contractual obligations can override value judgements under the law of unjust enrichment (enrichment without cause) and tort law in civil law systems as well as in common law systems.[63] Further-

61 For examples of the broader European Terminology of Horizontal and indirect effects see Christian Timmermans, "Horizontal Direct/Indirect Effect or Direct/Indirect Horizontal Effect: What's in a Name?" (2016) 24 Issue 3/4 *European Review of Private Law* 673.

62 On the changes of the German Passenger Transportation Act (Personenbeförderungsgesetz) as an adjustment to reality for the needs of mobility services like Uber see Benjamin von Bodungen and Martin Hoffmann, "Digitale Vermittlung, Pooling, autonomes Fahren. Rechtsrahmen plattformbasierter Mobilitätsangebote vor dem Hintergrund der PBefG-Novelle" (2021) *Recht Digital* 93, 100.

63 E.g. in German Law for the overriding priority of the contract and its interpretation over the law on general terms and conditions, statutory prohibitions and enrichment law in the case of swap contracts the decision of the Federal Court of Justice (Bundesgerichtshof - BGH) (2023) *Neue Juristische Wochenschrift – Rechtsprechungs-Report* 1021 para. 22, 23. See for Britain making clear, that a claim in unjust enrichment could not succeed because unjust enrichment is excluded where the benefit conferred is dealt with by a contract, Supreme Court's Decision Barton and others vs. Morris and another in place of Gwyn Jones (deceased), 2023, UKSC 3 (Barton vs. Morris), <https://www.supremecourt.uk/cases/docs/uksc-2020-0002-judgment.pdf> accessed 26 Apr. 2024.

more, consent to a violation of a legal interest, even in cases involving bodily harm,[64] is conceivable, as is the preservation of the legal foundation in unjust enrichment law. For instance, in scenarios such as family guarantees, where a party's legitimate interest is subjectively acknowledged despite the contract being objectively disadvantageous.[65]

Drawing from normative experiences within private law lets us conclude that trust ought to be based, to some extent, in the individual freedom of choice of the contracting parties and their reciprocal trust in the fulfilment of mutual contractual obligations. Bans should be considered only as a well-grounded and insofar filtered exception that may follow.

IV. A comprehensive ban on social scoring?

The unique alteration in the dynamic between social trust and ban in private law can also be exemplified through the concept of social scoring. Social scoring pertains to mechanisms utilizing algorithmic data processing in application software, aiming to evaluate and incentivize positive conduct by individuals to govern or influence their behavior. Social scoring augmented by AI systems denotes the assessing of people's social behavior for the purpose of predicting or managing behavior.[66] Illustrations include associating infrequent sick leave with higher salaries in labour law or other incentives, as well as linking regular subscription upgrades to additional benefits or access to other advantages within bonus systems, which many workers and consumers often appreciate.[67]

---

64 E.g. for Germany: consent according to sec. 630 (d) BGB in the context of medical treatment involving bodily injury excludes other claims based on tort or unjust enrichment.

65 E.g. for Germany: even if a contract is unusually burdensome for the weaker party, the contract is binding, if the weaker party has a self-interest or the stronger party has an accepted interest in a specific advantage, e.g. to prevent shifts in assets to the disadvantage of the stronger party, see the decision of the Federal Court of Justice (Bundesgerichtshof - BGH) (2013) *Neue Juristische Wochenschrift Rechtsprechungs-Report* 1258 para. 21.

66 See e.g. Martin Wiener, W. Alec Cram and Alexander Benlian, "Algorithmic Control and Gig Workers: A Legitimacy Perspective of Uber Drivers" (2023) 32 (3) *European Journal of Information Systems* 485.

67 See e.g. Emma McDaid, Paul Andon and Clinton Free, "Algorithmic management and the politics of demand" (2023) 103 *Accounting, Organizations and Society*, <https://www.sciencedirect.com/science/article/pii/S0361368223000363> accessed 26 Apr. 2024.

According to the Draft AI Act, social scoring is banned from the EU market due to its potential to interfere with trust in the use of AI applications. Specifically, AI applications for behavior or emotion recognition in workplaces or schools are to be disallowed due to their deemed unacceptable risk.[68] Additionally, political or religious profiling ought to be banned. AI applications in general are not allowed to directly influence or exploit people's behavior.[69]

With regard to trust building, existing and forthcoming regulations within public law at the European level, including the Draft AI Act, are not very convincing. There remains a concern that social trust in the legal system could be significantly undermined if it were revealed that the proposed ban on social scoring under European law, and thus under public law, could firstly be rendered ineffective by contractual agreements, as seen in the Uber case with taxi regulations. Secondly, the current proposal lacks an argumentative approach to this social issue rooted in individual freedom of choice, making it challenging to justify such a broad ban to the individual contracting parties in a comprehensible or plausible manner under civil law. Consequently, citizens may even lose trust in AI systems, because they are regulated under the Draft AI Act at this point. This concern is further compounded by the absence of a distinction between the risks posed by state-run and private social scoring systems and their respective potential benefits.[70]

Given the normative experience in private law, particularly in contract law, where trust serves as the foundation and bans are infrequent exceptions requiring solid justification, the transition from ban to trust adopted by the executive and legislative branches for the digital realm seems at least bold, if not improbable. For instance, it seems unlikely that all bonus systems, initially regarded as instances of social scoring, will be eliminated upon the latter's prohibition. However, this raises the spectre of the Draft AI Act inadvertently silencing an essential discourse on the rejection of

68 Cf. Reason 31 and Art. 5 (1f) and (1g) of the Draft AI Act (n 1).

69 Cf. Reason 29 and Art. 5 (1c) of the Draft AI Act (n 1) esp. for the (normatively not completely convincing) description of a risk of deceiving natural persons by nudging through AI Systems.

70 E.g. critical on state-run social scoring systems and their ability to improve social situations so far Anja Geller, *Social Scoring durch Staaten. Legitimität nach europäischem Recht – Mit Verweisen auf China* (Munich: Ludwigs-Maximilians University Munich 2022) 99, <https://edoc.ub.uni-muenchen.de/31151/1/Geller_Anja.pdf> accessed 26 Apr. 2024.

welfare augmentation through social scoring for valid reasons, thus stifling public debate in Europe.

Irrespective of the future of social scoring beyond the Draft AI Acts, the predominantly state-centric European approach currently adopted in the policy field of digitalization with its intended path from standard bans to creating social trust, stands in a remarkable contrast to the contentious yet tested and established normative experiences in private law. These normative experiences typically involve a path from trust to ban, a path that appears compelling, if not plausible, particularly in the context of regulating upcoming algorithms and AI systems.

D. Conclusion

We have (re-)evaluated the debates surrounding the regulation of innovations in democracies, drawing on legal philosophy and considering the various argumentative standards across different areas of law. This approach has allowed us to discern the rationales behind issuing certain bans, not only by analysing public debates but also by interpreting and reconstructing the law. By expanding the prevailing communicative picture of the relationship between trust and ban, we have introduced an institutional-argumentative picture.

Moving beyond the communicative picture, we elucidated that the relationship between trust and ban exhibits a distinct directional structure in the realms of criminal law and civil law. In criminal law, bans with sanctions are intended to foster trust, whereas in private law, trust in individual decisions serves as the starting point, with bans utilized in exceptional cases to secure trust.

Regarding the criminal law path from ban to trust, the communicative perspective demonstrates how trust can be cultivated between interacting citizens, with sanctions potentially stabilizing behavioural expectations in the context of innovations. However, the emphasis on generating trust through banning untrustworthy behavior sidelines the equally crucial principle of limiting criminal law to exceptional circumstances – leaving room for potentially unlimited use of criminal law. Innovation debates often prioritize the prevention of any risks associated with innovations without considering the specific rights and concerns intended to be protected by bans or the freedoms these restrict. For example, the UN Comprehensive

Study on Cybercrime[71] focuses primarily on the risks of cyber activities without addressing the different legal interests being protected, e.g. the prohibition of cyberfraud serves the protection of asset rights whereas the prohibition of hate speech serves the protection of personal rights.

In contrast, the private law trajectory from trust to ban reveals a gap in the communicative understanding from a legal-philosophical and insofar institutional-argumentative perspective. The mutual trust between contract parties is underestimated and the potential path from trust to ban is neglected. This tendency to neglect is particularly concerning as regulations in the digital sphere strive to maintain effectiveness by offering justifications for bans that influence the everyday behavior and use of digital opportunities by contract parties. Consequently, there is a risk that crucial public debates will be overshadowed by bans, including for example discussions on which welfare gains from state or privately organized social scoring we may want to give up for good reasons.

Contrary to the communicative picture in the legal-philosophical and institutional-argumentative picture trust no longer appears as an independent normative concept with unique analytical or explanatory power. Instead, trust derives its significance in relation to bans across various legal domains, such as criminal law or private law in different ways. This differentiation enables a nuanced and thus well-founded critique of debates on trust-building bans to regulate innovations in democracies. It is this approach that opens our eyes to the issues that we should be discussing.

71 UNODC (n 26) passim.

Anxieties of Distrust and Uncertainty as Factors for Constitutional Polycrisis in post-Modern Algorithmic Society

Martin Belov

This paper aims at briefly exploring the challenges to trust and certainty in post-Modernity and global algorithmic society. It will offer critical assessment of the anxieties of distrust and uncertainty that contribute to the development of constitutional polycrisis and the visible tendencies towards post-democracy and global algorithmic technocracy.

The paper shall polemically assess the existential insecurity about the conceptual framework of modern liberal democracies produced by external and internal challenges to constitutional axiology, constitutional design, and constitutional pragmatics. More precisely, it will explore the impact of digitalization on the constitutional orders and its side effects that are producing value insecurity and pragmatic concerns about the feasibility of maintaining the proper functionality of key constitutional concepts in the context of global algorithmic society.

The paper shall conclude with reflections on the deconstitutionalization and de-democratization in the context of globalization and digitalization. It will outline the trends towards a global algorithmic technocracy and dark constitutionalism.

A. Introduction

This paper aims at briefly exploring the challenges to two normative expectations and social phenomena with constitutional relevance, namely trust and certainty, in the context of post-Modernity and global algorithmic society. It will offer critical assessment of the anxieties of distrust and uncertainty that contribute to the development of constitutional polycrisis[1]

1 See M Belov, 'The Conceptual Shapes of Constitutional Polycrisis: Deconstruction, Asymmetries and Post-Modern Anxieties of Constitutional Normalcy', in (2023) 70 *Irish Jurist*, special issue 'Law in a Time of Crisis', 393-410 and M Belov, 'Rule of Law in Europe in Times of Constitutional Polycrisis, Constitutional Polytransition and

and the visible tendencies towards post-democracy[2] and global algorithmic technocracy[3].

The paper polemically assesses the existential insecurity about the conceptual framework of modern liberal democracies produced by external and internal challenges to constitutional axiology, constitutional design, and constitutional pragmatics. More precisely, it relates to the impact of digitalization on the constitutional orders, producing value insecurity and pragmatic concerns about the feasibility of maintaining the proper functionality of key constitutional concepts in the context of global algorithmic society.

The deconstruction of secure identities, the dismantling of fundamental preconditions for democracy, and the challenges to constitutional imaginaries of modern democracy are promoting democracy, rule of law, and constitutionalism in flux. They have the potential to produce an implosion of constitutional democracy[4] consisting in its internal disintegration due to the failure of the belief in the constitutional imaginaries[5] sustaining it as a coherent, legitimate, and efficient socio-legal project. Democratic implosion may result in maintaining the constitutional framework and the democratic and rule of law cover while immobilizing them in practice and producing alienation, disempowerment, distrust, and frustration of the people. Thus, the implosion of constitutional democracies results in

---

Democratic Discontent', in (2023) 3 *Diritto pubblico comparato ed europeo, Rivista trimestrale*, 875-884.

2 See C Crouch, *Post-Democracy* (Cambridge, Polity Press, 2004) 1-144.

3 See M Belov, 'Rule of Law and Democracy in Times of Transitory Constitutionalism, Constitutional Polycrisis and Emergency Constitutionalism: Towards a Global Algorithmic Technocracy?' in M Belov (ed), *Rule of Law in Crisis: Constitutionalism in a State of Flux* (Abingdon, Routledge, 2023) 21-47.

4 See M Belov, 'Constitutional Foundations of Peace and Discontent' in M Belov, (ed.) *Peace, Discontent and Constitutional Law. Challenges to Constitutional Order and Democracy* (Abingdon, Routledge, 2021), 15-30.

5 See J Přibáň, Constitutional Imaginaries. A Theory of European Societal Constitutionalism (Abingdon, Routledge, 2020), 1-251 and J Komárek, 'Political Economy in the European Constitutional Imaginary – Moving beyond Fiesole', Verfassungsblog, 04 September 2020, https://verfassungsblog.de/political-economy-in-the-european-constitutional-imaginary-moving-beyond-fiesole/, M Belov, *Constitutional semiotics. The Conceptual Foundations of a Constitutional Theory and Meta-Theory*, (Oxford, Hart publishing, 2022) 1-349, M Belov, 'Rule of Law in Bulgaria: Semi-Permanent Transitory Experiences on the Edge between Normative Expectations, Pragmatic Imperatives and Constitutional Imaginaries' (2023) Poliarchie/Polyarchies Special Issue.

façade democracies and formal rule of law while triggering socio-political distancing of the people, civic disobedience or both.

According to Seyla Benhabib:

'We are like travellers navigating an unknown terrain with the help of old maps, drawn at a different time and in response to different needs. While the terrain we are travelling on, the world-society of states, has changed, our normative map has not.'[6]

Thus, we need to define the normative concepts of trust and certainty using the shapes through which they emerged in constitutional and political Modernity. Then, we have to deconstruct them in order to see whether they are capable of serving as pillars of constitutional imaginaries and constitutional design in the current situation of constitutional polycrisis and constitutional polytransition[7].

The paper does not aim at providing extensive research and final definitions of trust and certainty. Clearly, this is a task that goes well beyond the claim of a short paper devoted to a particular topical issue. There is an extensive multidiscoursive debate in the literature that cannot even be summarized here. The task of the research provided in the paper is to outline the mainstream understanding of trust and certainty as meta-legal concepts with pivotal importance for constitutionalism in general and constitutional democracy in particular. Such concise outlining of these concepts will allow for exploring the transformative effects of the global algorithmic society on them. It will serve as a starting point for assessing their structural permutations of constitutional (dis)order in the context of digital constitutionalism. It will present the redefinition of trust, accountability, legitimacy, predictability, and certainty in times of globalization, deterritorialization, privatization, and algorithmic transformation of public power and their joint impact on constitutionalism.

The paper will demonstrate the main challenges of contemporary age to trust and certainty as pillars of constitutional democracy and rule of law. We are living in a situation where globalization, the multitude of technological revolutions (IT revolution included), and the post-modern anxieties are profoundly reshaping the conceptual, ideological, and normative foundations of our constitutional orders. The deconstruction of democ-

6 S Benhabib, (2005) 38 'Borders, Boundaries and Citizenship', *Political Science and Politics*, 674.

7 M Belov, (2023) 3 'Rule of Law in Europe in Times of Constitutional Polycrisis, Constitutional Polytransition and Democratic Discontent', *Diritto pubblico comparato ed europeo, Rivista trimestrale*, 875-884.

racy, its hollowing-up and the post-democratic tendencies are producing clear trends towards technocratic governance. Thus, the final part of the paper will be devoted to the outline of the post-democratic shapes of the algorithmic society.

The paper will provide a critical account of the current 'constitutional moment'[8] peculiar paradox of which is that it may produce deconstitutionalization and even anti-constitutionalism. They may result in 'thin' and formal-procedural versions of constitutionalism that allow for democracy and rule of law more in name than in nature. The shapes of the emerging 'brave new world'[9] have been defined with negative labels such as 'technofeudalism,'[10] 'digital Leviathan'[11] or 'surveillance capitalism'[12] or shaped via more optimistic concepts such as 'digital constitutionalism'[13] or 'algorithmic constitutionalism.'[14] Finally, I will propose my own hypothesis regarding the future of constitutionalism framed in the concept of 'global algorithmic technocracy.'[15]

8 See B Ackerman, *We the People: Foundations* (Harvard University Press, 1991), 266.

9 See A Huxley, *Brave New World* (Harper Perennial, 2006).

10 Y Varoufakis, *Technofeudalism: What Killed Capitalism* (Melville House, 2024), 1-304.

11 S Wróbel, 'The new Leviathan is an autonomous digital machine' https://blogs.lse.ac.uk/businessreview/2021/02/08/the-new-leviathan-is-an-autonomous-digital-machine/.

12 S Zuboff, *The Age of Surveillance Capitalism: The Fight for a Human Future at the New Frontier of Power* (Profile Books, 2019), 1-704.

13 See E Celeste, 2018 (2) 'Digital Constitutionalism: Mapping the Constitutional Response to Digital Technology's Challenges', *HIIG Discussion Paper Series,* G De Gregorio (2020) 'The Rise of Digital Constitutionalism in the European Union', *International Journal of Constitutional Law,* B Wagner, M Kettemann and K Vieth, *Research Handbook on Human Rights and Digital Technology: Global Politics, Law and International Relations* (Oxford, Edward Elgar, 2019).

14 O Perez and N Wimer, 2023 (30, 2) 'Algorithmic Constitutionalism', *Indiana Journal of Global Legal Studies,* 81-113, H-W Micklitz, O Pollicino, Oreste, A Reichman, A Simoncini, G Sartor, G De Gregorio (eds), *Constitutional challenges in the algorithmic society* (Cambridge, Cambridge University Press, 2022), https://hdl.handle.net/1814/74296 and O Pollicino O, G De Gregorio, 'Constitutional Law in the Algorithmic Society' in H-W Micklitz, O Pollicino, Oreste, A Reichman, A Simoncini, G Sartor, G De Gregorio (eds) Constitutional challenges in the algorithmic society (Cambridge, Cambridge University Press, 2022), 3-24.

15 See M Belov, 'Rule of Law and Democracy in Times of Transitory Constitutionalism, Constitutional Polycrisis and Emergency Constitutionalism: Towards a Global Algorithmic Technocracy?' in M Belov (ed) *Rule of Law in Crisis: Constitutionalism in a State of Flux* (Abingdon, Routledge, 2023), 21-47.

B. Uncertainty in the Digital Age: Constitutional Challenges and Repercussions

Trust and certainty are normative preconditions for democracy and the rule of law thus being indispensable factors for unfolding and maintenance of liberal-democratic constitutionalism. They are socio-legal determinants of predictability, accountability, and legitimacy of public power, promoting the development of the constitutional process as a trajectory for maximizing of liberty in the time-space continuum.

The principle of legal certainty is key element of rule of law the latter being strategic element of constitutional axiology. Legal certainty is a precondition for securing the normative expectations of the constitutional players. It is a safeguard for the predictability of the legal action of the institutions of public power. It is a guarantee for the due expectations of the citizens that must be able to organize their lives and behave in accordance with stable legal order with understandable rules, implemented via due process, and organized within reasonable and predictable constitutional and legislative framework.

Legal certainty is overarching imperative that functions as justification ground for range of other elements of rule of law. The most important of them are the due process of law, the balancing of rights, and the principle of proportionality in limiting of constitutional rights. In fact, rule of law has emerged in early modernity in order to be able to organize the increasing complexity of social life stemming from the rise of social, political, cultural, religious, and other forms of pluralism. Ordering of constitutional orders[16] has always been a key task of the constitution. It is dependent upon safeguarding of legal certainty.

Indeed, ordering can also be done in context of a crisis. All constitutions – liberal or illiberal, democratic or authoritarian – provide for more or less developed crisis management models or at least tools. However, history shows that the 'problem-solution-problem' spiral, consisting in the artificial creation or the mere use of objectively existing crisis, has been exploited by elites for the establishment and maintenance of authoritarian or oligarchic regimes. Thus, the production of order out of disorder has been achieved at the expense of certainty, in the context of systemic uncertainty, where emer-

16 See M Belov, 'Three Models for Ordering Constitutional Orders', (2022), *Pravni Zapisi*, 361-387.

gency and crisis constitute the normalcy[17]. Trust, under such circumstances, has still been key governmental resource. In contrast to liberal democracies, however, where trust stems from liberty, autonomy, free will, and political engagement, in authoritarian-oligarchic systems it is built through fear politics and anti-constitutionalism of fear[18]. This type of 'façade' constitutional orders can be defined as forms of 'dark constitutionalism'.

Liberal-democratic constitutionalism is based upon liberty, autonomy, free will, and free choice. If a true form of liberal constitutionalism is established, it must maintain certainty and trust through normative ideologies of freedom, humanism, and democracy. Thus, there is a certain minimum of requirements – legal, socio-political, and imaginary – that must be maintained in order to promote that form of constitutionalism as tool for safeguarding of basic equality and existential liberty.

Rule of law is both order and liberty maximizing principle. It is a tool for the achievement of liberty through autopoietic order. Its task is to provide for a substantial degree of personal autonomy safeguarding moral choice and the unfolding of free will. Modern constitutional orders have been born in order to serve as a framework of liberty allowing for maximal freedom for all in an organized society. Legal certainty has been important element of this great philosophic, political, cultural, and legal endeavour. Hence, rule of law is both dependent from trust and certainty and serve as a promotor of these key determinants of liberal-democratic constitutional orders. Moreover, rule of law is an intellectual product of western modernity.

Modernity was a national, territorial, and rational project. Constitutional modernity – the constitutional shapes and forms of this political, social and, last but not least, cultural project – builds upon the heritage of the centralized territorial statehood. The territorial state has been legally, theoretically, and imaginary shaped to serve as a 'territorial container'[19] of different nations the latter being socio-cultural and political projects for

---

17 See M Belov, 'The Conceptual Shapes of Constitutional Polycrisis...', 393-410.

18 See M Belov, 'The Role of Fear Politics in Global Constitutional 'Ernstfall': Images of Fear under COVID-19 Health Paternalism' in M Belov (ed) *Populist Constitutionalism and Illiberal Democracies. Between Constitutional Imagination, Normative Entrenchment and Political Reality* (Cambridge, Intersentia, 2021), 187-221.

19 See P J Taylor, 'The State as Container: Territoriality in the Modern World-System', in Progress in Human Geography, 1994, (18) 2, P J Taylor, 'Beyond Containers: Internationality, Interstateness, Interterritoriality', in Progress in Human Geography, 1995, (19) 1 and N Brenner, 'Beyond state-centrism? Space, Territoriality and Geographical Scale in Globalization Studies' in Theory and Society, 1999, 28 (1), 39-78.

political integration and mobilization. The state and its socio-political core – the nation – were factually 'captured' and entrenched within a territory. Moreover, territory has been legally shaped through different versions of territoriality as its legal and imaginary signifier[20]. Legally, state and society were shaped, and entrenched within a rational plan, preconditioned upon the existence of common will, common good, public reason, and representation. This plan has been normatively vested in written, systematic, logical, and presumably rational constitutions.

In the context of modern, national, territorial, constitutional, and rational statehood certainty in general and legal certainty in particular is an element with key role for sustaining the socio-legal equilibrium, the eudemonia, and the legitimacy of the state monopoly over violence.[21] Hence, certainty is among the intellectual, social, and normative pillars of modern constitutional orders stretched between the 'rational', 'national', and 'territorial' entrapment of modernity.

It must be underlined, that modern democracy and rule of law were calibrated to address national problems, confined within statehood, and having clear territorial dimension. They were preconditioned upon the presumption of rationality of constitution and constitutional law and the territoriality of power. Hence, modern constitutional orders were supposed to produce, maintain, and safeguard certainty and predictability only within the 'squared territoriality'[22] of the modern state. Thus, the constitutional design and constitutional axiology of modern constitutional orders as well as the normative expectations of the people shaped as constitutional imaginaries are incapable of properly, legitimately, and efficiently addressing constitutionalism beyond statehood and even less capable of responding to post-territorial and aterritorial constitutionalism of the global algorithmic society.

20 See M Belov, 'Territory, Territoriality and Territorial Politics as Public Law Concepts' in M Belov (ed) *Territorial Politics and Secession. Constitutional and International Law Dimensions* (London, Palgrave, 2021), 21.

21 A Munro, "State Monopoly on Violence", in Encyclopedia Britannica, https://www.britannica.com/topic/state-monopoly-on-violence and M Weber, *Politik als Beruf* (Berlin, Duncker&Humblot, 2016), 1-56.

22 See P J Taylor, 'The State as Container: Territoriality in the Modern World-System', in Progress in Human Geography, 1994, (18) 2, P J Taylor, 'Beyond Containers: Internationality, Interstateness, Interterritoriality', in Progress in Human Geography, 1995, (19) 1 and N Brenner, 'Beyond state-centrism? Space, Territoriality and Geographical Scale in Globalization Studies' in Theory and Society, 1999, 28 (1).

Hence, there is huge potential for constitutional dysfunctionality impeding the achievement of basic legal certainty in the context of globalization, IT revolution[23], and digitalization of the power grid of de-nationalized and de-territorialized society. This is even more problematic with regard to the ongoing dismantling of rationalism as normative ideology of constitutionalism and the deconstruction of the partially failed rational constitutionalism[24].

Since the beginning of the XXI century we are living in an age of uncertainty. Uncertainty is produced by five major groups of factors. These are the post-modern situation, the constitutional polycrisis, the constitutional polytransition, the globalization (including processes of de-globalization, regionalization and renationalization which I define elsewhere as Westphalian, post-Westphalian and neo-Westphalian constitutionalism[25]), and last but not least the IT revolution with all its aspects. Let's briefly consider all five groups of factors while paying special attention to the crisis of certainty in the context of algorithmic society.

The post-modern situation is characterized by several features. The belief in the existence of a single version of objective truth is dismantled. Rather, there are different versions of truth which are negotiated and are largely contextually dependent. Thus, truth is much more a matter of narratives, semiotic, and semantic games rather than rock-solid phenomenon with universal meaning. This is clearly a conceptual challenge to certainty of meaning and thus also to the legal certainty.

The versatility of meaning, the narrative character of truth and the multidiscoursive pluralism in an increasingly globalized world render difficult and even impossible the establishment of a single universal meaning of legal phenomena. Hence, the post-modern, deconstructive, and narrative-based approach to meaning is reinforced by globalization and the ethical, moral, and philosophical relativism stemming from it.

The attempts at organizing the world through constitutional pluralism[26] is also a promoter of uncertainty. The failure of hierarchical approaches

23 See M Belov, The IT Revolution and its Impact on State, Constitutionalism and Public Law, (Oxford, Hart, 2021).

24 See M Belov, Constitutional semiotics. The Conceptual Foundations of a Constitutional Theory and Meta-Theory, (Oxford, Hart publishing, 2022), 49-55.

25 See M Belov, 'Three Models for Ordering Constitutional Orders...', 361-387.

26 N Walker, 2002 (65, 3) 'The Idea of Constitutional Pluralism', in *The Modern Law Review*, 317–59, M Poiares Maduro, 'Contrapunctual Law: Europe's Constitutional Pluralism in Action' in N Walker (ed) *Sovereignty in Transition* (Oxford, Hart, 2003),

such as multilevel constitutionalism[27] to produce a feasible model for organization of constitutionalism beyond statehood, but also beyond regional forms of supranational cooperation, allowed the promotion of a more nuanced global approach such as constitutional pluralism. They are intellectually appealing but produce huge uncertainty regarding their application as practical models capable of durably organizing the world via single and clear ordering matrix. Thus, constitutional pluralism is itself a postmodern scheme for ordering of constitutional orders transforming uncertainty from exception to *de facto* rule with structural importance.

Constitutional polycrisis and constitutional polytransition jointly contribute to the substantial increase of legal, socio-legal, and imaginary uncertainty. Constitutional polycrisis consists in the multitude of crisis that are overlapping and jointly produce an overall detrimental context for the functioning of liberal constitutional democracy. Constitutional polycrisis transforms the emergency into normalcy. The security and terrorism crisis, the financial, migration, and pandemic crisis that deeply marked our social, political and constitutional orders since the beginning of the XXI century destroy predictability, certainty, and trust. Thus, they dismantle the fundamental prerequisites for liberty, autonomy, and self-determination which were the pillars of post-World War II liberal democratic constitutionalism.

Constitutional polytransition is a concept that frames the multitude of transitions which are currently unfolding and are challenging the legal, constitutional, political, and social orders. The most important of them are the transitions from authoritarianism to democracy (democratization) and from democracy to authoritarianism (democratic backsliding), from modern and holistic to post-modern and fragmented constitutionalism, from national to post-national, transnational, supranational, and global constitutionalism, from Westphalian to post-Westphalian, and neo-Westphalian constitutionalism, from constitutionalism 'within' to constitutionalism 'be-

---

501-538 and M Poiares Maduro, 'Three Claims of Constitutional Pluralism' in M Avbelj and J Komarek (eds) *Constitutional Pluralism in the European Union and Beyond* (Oxford, Hart, 2012), 67-84.

27 See E U Petersmann, *Multilevel Constitutionalism for Multilevel Governance of Public Goods* (Oxford, Hart, 2017), 1-416, G della Cananea, 'Is European Constitutionalism Really "Multilevel"?', in ZaöRV 2010, (70), 283-317 and I Pernice, 'Multilevel Constitutionalism and the Crisis of Democracy in Europe' in European Constitutional Law Review, 2015, 11(3), 541-562.

yond' statehood, from sovereigntist to post-sovereigntist constitutionalism, and from state centred to societal constitutionalism[28].

There are also constitutional transitions which are of special importance for the challenges to legal certainty in the context of the emerging global algorithmic society. These are the transitions from territorial to post-territorial and aterritorial constitutionalism, from real (physical-spatial) to meta-real (Internet-based, digital, algorithmic) constitutionalism, and from democratic to post-democratic (technocratic) constitutionalism. Last but not least, we should mention a possible game-changer transition from constitutionalism to governance and administrative technocracy.

The joint impact of these transitions that run in parallel and change the core, substance, institutional manifestations, and functionality of constitutionalism on legal certainty is dramatic and generally very negative. The polytransition produces structural changes in constitutionalism as legal, socio-legal, and imaginary phenomenon. The digital transition puts immense pressure on fundamental pillars of constitutionalism. It produces global power grid, crisis of territoriality resulting in transterritorial and post-territorial networks of power and governance. It changes the context and concept of rights, jurisdiction, and authority. It blurs the 'public-private divide', privatizes public power, produces governance instead of government, and technocracy instead of democratic constitutionalism.

Indeed, the digital transformation and transition has also many positive effects on constitutional orders. It expands the sphere of rights, promotes new right, creates new opportunities for engagement, information and inclusion and broadens the realm of horizontal, societal, networked constitutionalism while limiting the power of domestic and regional hierarchies to impose restraints on liberty. Nevertheless, while old hierarchies are dismantled, new ones are established on supranational, global, transterritorial, and post-territorial scale. Moreover, the dynamic of the digital and algorithmic transformation is so intense and the combination of globalization, IT revolution, crisis of territoriality, and time-space compression is so powerful that they produce immense power asymmetries. They are elitist biased and lead to global reemergence of biases, hierarchies, and spheres of inequality. The increasing complexity of the algorithmic world and the

28 G Teubner, Constitutional Fragments: Societal Constitutionalism and Globalization (Oxford, Oxford University Press, 2012, 38-42 and J Přibáň, Constitutional Imaginaries. A Theory of European Societal Constitutionalism (Abingdon, Routledge, 2020), 1-251.

multilayered and fragmented character of decision-making promote by necessity the rise of technocracy.

The speed, scale, and complexity of transition altogether overburden legal certainty. They create a situation of radical uncertainty which suffocates the chances for maintenance of the degree of predictability, trust, accountability, and information needed in order to sustain rule of law and democracy. Thus, constitutional polytransition contributes to the constitutional polycrisis and in the context of radical deconstruction of the old constitutional world in a global, post-modern, and post-territorial situation produces technocratic and algorithmic society where post-truth, post-trust, and post-certainty are gradually becoming the rule.

It seems that post-certainty shall be an imminent feature of the global algorithmic society. The narrative character of truth, negotiable only in certain contexts, the complexity of the rule grid, the non-transparent power relations, the remoteness of power centres, the augmented reality blurring the shapes of reality and making post-truth the norm rather than exception are some of the key factors for the emergence of the phenomenon of post-certainty in the digital age. This is the situation notwithstanding the power of AI to transform reality, the capacity of big data to create algorithmic worlds and the tendencies of digitalization to produce new layers of reality in a post-constitutional metaverse.

C. Challenges to Trust produced by Algorithmic Transformations of Power

Trust is key factor and normative precondition for authority, legitimacy, and efficiency of constitutional orders. All constitutional orders, irrespectively whether they are democratic, liberal or authoritarian, technocratic or oligarchic, provide for instruments for generating and sustaining of trust of their citizens. Nevertheless, the trust building mechanisms they use largely differ. The increasing use of non-democratic trust building mechanisms will be addressed in the final part of the paper.

Authoritarian and populist orders frequently rely on charismatic and traditional legitimacy[29]. Populism in not exclusively related to authoritarianism. There are degrees and forms of populism which can be elements

29 See M Weber, Soziologie. Weltgeschichtliche Analysen. Politik (Stuttgart, Kröner Verlag, 1968), 151 ff.

also of democratic orders[30]. However, true liberal democracies provide for mechanisms for sustaining of trust via accountability and limited government deriving its justification mostly from rational legitimacy[31]. In contrast, trust in authoritarian-technocratic orders may stem from range of strategies that are detrimental to liberty. Usually, such orders use fear politics employing the presumed monopoly of truth for suggesting ways out of crisis through recourse to expertise. Hence, political mobilization through emergency and crisis and with the instruments of fear politics is essential element of dark constitutionalism. This problem shall be explored in the final part of this paper devoted to global algorithmic technocracy.

Authority of democratic constitutional orders is based on trust. They are both derived from complex chains of democratic accountability and control and not from meta-constitutional sources such as God, the nature of things or the tradition. The authority of liberal democracy is not supposed to be justified only through the efficiency of the state institutions as forms of legitimate coercion[32]. Democratic legitimacy in late modernity has been a complex and multilayered phenomenon. Nevertheless, two forms of legitimacy that are pillars of liberal democracy are very dependent on trust as a power source for their feasibility. These are the input legitimacy and the rational legitimacy.

Input legitimacy[33] suggests direct impact of the popular will on taking key decisions or at least the selection of office holders. Hence, according to this normative concept, people must be able to directly or indirectly influence decision-making. The theory and practice of liberal democracies has produced a general outline of typical decisions that must be taken by political institutions having input democratic legitimacy and not by purely technocratic bodies relying only on output legitimacy. The concepts of parliamentary and legislative reserve are result of such trust in political, democratically elected, and democratically accountable institutions. This

30 See P Blokker, 'Varieties of populist constitutionalism: The transnational dimension' in German Law Journal, 2019 (20) 332 – 350 and B Ackerman, *Revolutionary Constitutions: Charismatic Leadership and the Rule of Law* (Cambridge, Massachusetts, Belknap Press, 2019), 1-472.

31 See M Weber, *Soziologie. Weltgeschichtliche Analysen. Politik* (Stuttgart, Kröner Verlag, 1968), 151 ff.

32 See M Weber, *Politik als Beruf* (Berlin, Duncker&Humblot, 2016), 1-56.

33 See F W Scharpf, *Governing in Europe. Effective and Democratic?* (Oxford, Oxford University Press, 1999) and F W Scharpf, 'Problem-Solving Effectiveness and Democratic Accountability in the EU' *Mpifg Working Paper* 2003 (3), available at: www.mpifg.de/pu/workpap/wp03-1/wp03-1.html.

is also the case with the democratic theory of sovereignty and the special procedures for constitutional amendment stemming from it.

Rational legitimacy[34] is the second type of legitimacy that lays at the core not only of liberal-democratic constitutionalism but also of constitutional Modernity. In fact, Modernity as intellectual, philosophical, social, political, and constitutional project is based on rationalism as normative ideology[35]. The trust in rationality of constitutional orders has been excessive. The trust in rational political behavior, in the rational design of constitutional institutions and in the rationality of the constitutional order in general led to a phenomenon which I have defined elsewhere as 'rationalist entrapment'[36] of constitutional Modernity.

Liberal constitutional democracies are structured on the basis of a chain of selection procedures that are supposed to safeguard the democratic input and the ability of the electorate to control the governing elites. Liberal representative party democracy is grounded on several conditions. The most important of them is the existence of a set of political rights providing for basic political equality and critical levels of democratic inclusion. They presuppose free and fair elections, pluralist and representative party systems, polycentric and free media, channels for rational and regular voicing of democratic discontent and rights for political participation generating trust and accountability.

The system of representative democracy aims at making government controllable, responsible, responsive, and accountable. All these elements of representative democracy in their capacity as constitutional imaginaries, normative ideologies, institutional pillars, and normative practices are based on the existence of at least critical levels of trust.

In fact, the distrust in elites and their capacity to promote the common good is the main reason for the emergence of the constitution as a social contract including a variety of instruments for increasing the trust. Separation of powers, the principle of competence of state institutions, the various

34 See M Weber, *Soziologie. Weltgeschichtliche Analysen. Politik* (Stuttgart, Kröner Verlag, 1968), 151 ff.

35 See M Belov, 'Humanism and Rationalism as Fundamental Normative Ideologies of Constitutionalism' in M. Novkirishka, M. Belov and D. Nachev (eds) *Scientific Conference "Human Rights – 70 Years Since the Adoption of the Universal Declaration of Human Rights"* (Sofia, University of Sofia 'St. Kliment Ohridski' Press, 2019), 69-90 and M Belov, *Constitutional semiotics. The Conceptual Foundations of a Constitutional Theory and Meta-Theory*, (Oxford, Hart publishing, 2022), 1-349.

36 Ibid.

instruments for political (direct democratic or parliamentary) or technocratic (administrative and judicial) control are institutional expressions of distrust. Hence, the interplay between trust and distrust is one of the main driving forces of constitutionalism as a liberty maximizing and power abuse preventing mechanism.

Trust as constitutional imaginary, normative precondition, and factual requirement of constitutional Modernity is profoundly challenged in the context of post-Modernity and in the process of the rise of global algorithmic society. There are several factors for distrust in the context of algorithmic society. The most important of them are the use of instruments for information bias (e.g. filter bubbles and micro targeting)[37], the paradoxical remoteness and democratic detachment of the power centres combined with simultaneity of their digital availability and performance, and the postmodern-fragmentation of truth as factor for distrust.

Trust usually requires predictability and is based on experience. In territorial democracies trust building mechanisms were generally based on territorially entrenched experiences with politicians, activists, opinion leaders, etc. that have gradually acquired the roles of heroes, saints, or villains through political experience embedded in the national political life. The detachment of addressees of trust from the mass public has started with the rise of mass media. However, in the context of the new Internet based media this detachment has reached new level. Truth became almost detached from reality. Trust has been detached from truth as well. Thus, trust in algorithmic society has become social imaginary with constitutional importance rather than practical experience based on and generated through political rights.

The AI brings the problems of trust, truth, and certainty to a whole new level. Until the emergence of the AI the manipulation of truth as a precondition for trust and certainty has been attributed to fake news, filter bubbles, micro targeting, and algorithmic biases produced by the big data. All these forms of manipulation of truth presuppose the existence of a solid reality with objective truth that is just misrepresented or faked either deliberately or as a side effect of the new technologies. The AI is the key to

37 See S Hardt, 'Data Revolution and Public Will Formation: Regulating Democratic Process in the Digital Age' in M Belov (ed) *The IT Revolution and its Impact on State, Constitutionalism and Public Law* (Oxford, Hart, 2021), 109-127 and H-T Nguyen, 'The Disruptive Effects of Social Media Platforms on Democratic Will-Formation Process', in M Belov (ed) *The IT Revolution and its Impact on State, Constitutionalism and Public Law* (Oxford, Hart, 2021), 93-109.

creating reality – digital, virtual, algorithmic – that can be fully detached from the reality of fact, norms, institutions, and social imaginaries to which our constitutional and legal orders are adjusted. Hence, there is a real chance that the augmented reality of the global algorithmic society largely or even fully escapes from the normative-institutional regulatory grid of the constitution and the socio-legal order it has to establish. This triggers the challenging question are we going to live in a 'deep-fake' reality dominated by post-truth, post-certainty, and post-trust.

The combination of the rise of the political importance of expertise, the broadening of the scale of the constitutional game to regional, supranational, and global levels and the emergence of new realities paralleling the physical reality of territorial constitutionalism together with the incredible acceleration of technologies dismantle the well-established mechanisms for generation and maintenance of trust that were so carefully and painfully shaped during the 'long XIX century' and the 'short XX century'[38]. The globalization, deterritorialization, time-space compression, and the IT revolution produce structural asymmetries. They are hardly reconcilable with traditional constitutional schemes of democratic trust, control, and accountability. Reversely, they lead to escape of the elites from the schemes of control and accountability triggering a rapidly increasing distrust by the people.

Hence, it seems, that we are heading towards a post-trust society. Indeed, such concept seems as an internal conceptual contradiction due to the fact that each society is based on trust. In other words, trust is substantial precondition for the establishment and maintenance of durably structured social bonds. Trust is a societal value. It is generated and sustained within communities. Hence, trust is pillar of community, solidarity, and mutual comprehension. That is why trust must be secured by all means. In the context of algorithmic society, where AI will play an increasingly important role, post-trust may be prevented and replaced by post truth. This is an extremely problematic possibility since it entails the danger of replacement of truth as precondition for the constitutional order. Acquiring of trust and certainty via post-truth constitutes the ultimate dismantling of the rationalist project of Modernity and the constitution and constitutionalism as veritable, rational, and reasonable phenomena.

---

38 See E Hobsbawm, *The Age of Revolution: 1789-1848* (New York, Vintage, 1996), 1-368 and E Hobsbawm, *Age of Extremes: The Short Twentieth Century 1914-1991* (Time Warner Books, 1995), 1-627.

Trust is even more important for constitutionally framed political societies. Politics as the functional core of each constitutionally framed order is impossible without trust. One of the tasks of modern constitutions has been to generate and promote trust in mass societies framed as territorial nation states. Their role has been to establish national integrity in institutionalized way, through founding of a political community based on trust.

The dismantling of the state as ultimate framework of power, the deconstruction of centralized authorities, and the disintegration of traditional political communities paralleled with the rise of the global networked algorithmic society profoundly changes the roots of power, trust, and accountability. The uncertainty of truth, the certainty of uncertainty in the global post-modern disorder, and the crisis of established mechanisms for community building, transform trust from empirical fact and normative expectation into a constitutional imaginary. The imaginaries of trust are nowadays ascribed to atypical contexts such as digital communities, post-territorial and aterritorial forms of power, and even the AI as new sources of expertise, efficiency, and authority. These tendencies jointly render the traditional schemes of trust provided by the constitutions as jurisdictionally entrenched and pre-algorithmic contracts valid for territorial communities increasingly dysfunctional. Thus, we are in dare need of reconceptualization of the concept, patterns, and safeguards of trust in the context of algorithmic society in order to avoid the combined situation of post-truth, post-trust, and post-certainty.

D. Deconstitutionalization and de-democratization trough Globalization and Digitalization: towards a Global Algorithmic Technocracy and Dark Constitutionalism?

Internet seemed as a quite promising platform for reinforcement and promotion of democracy[39]. Its territorial detachment, networked features, and polycentric nature appeared as natural promoters of networks and circles instead of hierarchies and squared territorial containers as forms of consti-

39 See O. Policino, G. Romero (eds.) *The Internet and Constitutional Law. The Protection of Fundamental Rights and Constitutional Adjudication in Europe* (Abingdon, Routledge, 2016) and G De Gregorio, 'From Constitutional Freedoms to the Power of the Platforms: Protecting Fundamental Rights Online in the Algorithmic Society', in *European Journal of Legal Studies* (2019) 11(2), 65-103.

tutional geometry[40]. A global, networked, and territorially detached reality might be conceived as the natural playground for power polycentrism, democratic empowerment, and rule of law embedded in post-territorial and aterritorial societal constitutionalism. It seems as an adequate context not only for the algorithmic society, but also for the fluid or liquid modernity and society[41] and its spaces of flows[42].

Indeed, global digital constitutionalism is a clear departure from territorial, national, and hierarchical constitutionalism. It is hardly reconcilable with sovereignty and territorial democracy 'within' or even 'beyond' statehood. It looks like a possible escape from the excessive use of public power and as a medium for promotion of universal values, global interests, and innovative forms of policy-making aiming at rationality, humanism, and prosperity. Global digital constitutionalism appeared as the quasi-natural promoter of democratic empowerment on a global scale.

Unfortunately, the combination of globalization, IT revolution, and technocratic governance did not result in a global algorithmic democracy, at least not yet or in the foreseeable future. Instead, visible trends of novel global hierarchies marked the departure from the ideal of global and digital or algorithmic democracy. The simultaneity of transformation and the incredible speed of the new technological revolution created huge information, motivation, and resource asymmetries that could not be reconciled through the means of territorial liberal-democratic constitutionalism. It should be noted that the ongoing technological revolution, paralleled by constitutional polycrisis and constitutional polytransition, possesses the scale, depth and complexity that are unprecedented in human history. Thus, they altogether produce a new civilization as a response to the immense technological shocks on the state, society, and their constitutional order. The responses of the social and political system to the exogeneous pressures of the multifaceted scientific revolution (IT revolution, bio and medical revolution, mobility revolution etc.) producing algorithmic society are neither democratic, nor territorially restrained, nor necessarily compatible with the constitutional axiology, normative ideology, and constitutional design of constitutional and political Modernity.

---

40 See M Belov, 'Constitutional semiotics...', 241 ff.

41 See Z Bauman, *Liquid Modernity* (Cambridge, Polity Press, 1999), 1-240 and U Eco, *Chronicles of a Liquid Society* (Houghton Mifflin Harcourt, 2019), 1-320.

42 See M Castells, *The Rise of the Network Society* (Oxford, Wiley-Blackwell, 2009), 407-460 and M Belov, 'Rule of Law in Space of Flows, in M Belov (ed) *Rule of Law at the Beginning of the Twenty-First Century* (The Hague, Eleven publ., 2018), 97-141.

Thus, the current process of adaptation of the socio-political order to the joint pressures of globalization and the technological revolution objectively promote the rise of global algorithmic technocracy. The increasing complexity of policy-making, the deep crisis of representative party democracy, the inefficiency of the numerous (predominantly theoretical) proposals for 'democratization of democracy'[43] jointly contribute to the establishment of global algorithmic technocracy. Technocracy is gradually but visibly overburdening both democratic and authoritarian orders where democracy and authoritarianism seem to be transformed into a façade for technocratic-oligarchic governance. The current form of technocracy that is gaining momentum is global since it is unfolding in a globalized world. It is algorithmic due to the impact and results of the ongoing technological transformation and the IT revolution that is its driving force.

Each constitutional order and political regime require legitimation and strives at achieving the trust of the society. Unfortunately, the current experiences with constitutional polycrisis and constitutional polytransition reveal that global algorithmic technocracy is frequently legitimized through fear politics resulting in forms of post-democracy and promoting dark constitutionalism.

It must be noted, that the chances for promotion of fear politics and dark constitutionalism in the context of algorithmic society are much greater than in non-digital and pre-digital contexts. This is due to their global outreach, incomparably diverse instruments for digital manipulation of meaning, and the non-transparent and elitist-technocratic ontology. The combination of the new digital tools for shaping of meaning and promotion of negative emotions and the rise of emotional politics of fear seem a dangerous combination that is capable of deconstructing traditional chains of trust and creating new ones based on dark constitutional imaginaries.

Especially the technocratic authoritarian-oligarchic regimes strive at detachment of expertocracy from democratic (popular and parliamentary) control. Their promise is to deliver the anticipated presumable efficiency and expertise of government while their final objective is to reverse the direction of control and to produce unquestionable technocratic governance. Thus, while the line of control and accountability in liberal democracy stems from the people and through the parliament is directed towards the government and the technocratic parts of the governmental structure

43 C Offe (Hrsg) *Demokratisierung der Demokratie. Diagnosen und Reformvorschläge*, (Campus, 2003), 1-304.

in authoritarian-oligarchic technocracies it is the experts who make the government dependent, disable the parliamentary control, and transform the people from sovereigns into a mere object of governance.

The rising technocracy is launching the anti-democratic impetus by promoting efficiency and blunt belief in science as a new political ideology. In fact, the very concept of unquestionable belief in science goes against the critical-rational core of scientific knowledge making scientific absolutism, e.g. in the form of digital, financial or health paternalism, a new religion. The constitutional polycrisis is and has been the natural context for the rise of 'digital', 'surveillance', 'security', and 'health Leviathans'[44] promoting trust based on fear politics safeguarded by a mixture of technocratic, authoritarian, and oligarchic means. Thus, democratic control and accountability are replaced by technocracy, justice, liberty and autonomy are replaced by efficiency and government is replaced by governance. Under such autocratic-oligarchic-technocratic regimes trust in expertise and unquestionable knowledge should justify the monopoly over violence[45] replacing democratic engagement, activism, control, and checks and balances.

In the last decades two enemies of liberal democracies have been on the rise. These are the populist regimes and the forms of technocratic governance. They both render traditional modes of trust dysfunctional replacing them with charismatic or technocratic authority. Paradoxically, algorithmic society is fostering both of them although in a different way. Digitalization, IT revolution, and algorithmic governance are all promotors of technocracy. They lead to overburdening of traditional forms and procedures for creation of trust. The rise of populism is to an extent a side effect of technocracy and the increasing feeling of democratic disempowerment. The people distrust technocracies. They feel the trend towards post-democracy. Unfortunately, they make recourse to a wrong medicine for this disease by hoping to be able to get themselves out of the post democratic swamp trusting populist politicians, parties, and movements.

44 See M Belov, The Role of Fear Politics ..., 187-221 and A Mercescu, 'The COVID-19 Crisis in Romania, or on How One Cannot Escape (Bad, Legal) Culture' http://exceptions.eu/2020/05/11/the-covid-19-crisis-in-romania-or-on-how-one-cannot-escape-bad-legal culture/?fbclid=IwAR3hTyciWC-Kiei2r9KFjHVN0KjGzx6aepFuZ9VYlnDz89Jr94dWUydAh_Y.

45 See M Weber, Op. cit.

Diffusion of responsibility through the use of algorithms and AI in the area of internal security – allocation of responsibility through (constitutional) law?

Michael Bäuerle

The article examines the phenomenon of the diffusion of responsibility through algorithms from a constitutional law perspective using the example of the security authorities.

A. Scope and delimitation

Security authorities[1] like police, customs and intelligence services use increasingly systems controlled by algorithms and artificial intelligence. Techniques such as automatic facial recognition, automatic license plate reading systems, crime prediction systems, automatic data analysis and forensic evaluation of mobile phones and personal computers now regularly complement the general information and communication technologies that has long been used by the security authorities.[2] Algorithms and AI in the hands of security authorities now monitor and recognize people, extract "new knowledge"[3] from existing data sets and make predictions about when and where crimes will be committed. This gives the task fulfilment of security authorities new dimensions.

1 Agencies whose most important task is to maintain internal security. Cf. to the legal political concept of internal security in Germany the Standing Conference of Federal and State Interior Ministers/Senators, Program for Internal Security in the Federal Republic of Germany, Part I, June 1972, Supplement to GMBl. No. 31/1972, Preliminary Remarks (p. 5): "Internal security is a central issue in contemporary politics. It is primarily about protecting the individual from crime, but increasingly also about protecting the institutions of the state and its basic democratic order." An addition to the program was made in 1974, supplement to GMBl. no. 9/1974.

2 See also Bäuerle, CRi 2022, 33 ff. with the in-depth distinction between general and task-specific use of information and communication technology by the security authorities.

3 See BVerfG NVwZ 2023, 1169 (1201, para. 67).

Although Security authorities do not yet make exclusively automated decisions within the meaning of Art. 11 Directive (EU) 2016/680[4] or fully automated administrative acts within the meaning of Section 35a VwVfG,[5] the use of the mentioned algorithmically and/or AI-controlled Systems and tools leads - depending on the result - to further intervention measures, such as searches, seizures and confiscations, surveillance measures, the use of undercover investigators, telecommunication surveillance and/or arrests or detentions.

If such measures take place due to algorithmically and AI-controlled processes, this means diffusion of responsibility to the extent that the underlying facts or the selected target persons were identified or selected automatically and not by an official, therefore not under the responsibility of the acting officials. In view of the lack of traceability[6] and the susceptibility to error and discrimination[7] of algorithmically or AI-controlled processes, the question of the allocation of responsibility arises when police interventions in fundamental rights are carried out on the basis of the results of such processes.

The following article examines the resulting legal questions primarily from a constitutional perspective. From this perspective, the "algorithmic turn“[8] among the security authorities is embedded in a long history of legis-

---

4 Directive (EU) 2016/680 of the European Parliament and of the Council of 27 April 2016 on the protection of natural persons with regard to the processing of personal data by competent authorities for the purposes of the prevention, investigation, detection or prosecution of criminal offenses or the execution of criminal penalties, and on the free movement of such data, and repealing Council Framework Decision 2008/977/JHA, implemented inter alia by Part III of the BDSG and corresponding sections in the data protection laws of the federal states. In accordance with the area exception in Art. 2 para. 2 d) GDPR, this does not apply to this area, which also includes the protection against and the prevention of threats to public security in accordance with Art. 1 para. 1 Directive (EU) 2016/680. However, a provision corresponding to the content of Art. 11 Directive (EU) 2016/680 can also be found in Art. 22 GDPR.

5 In the USA, however, technologies that come close to exclusively automated decisions are already being used for security and law enforcement, see Rückert, *Mit künstlicher Intelligenz auf Verbrecherjagd: Einsatz von Gesichtserkennungstechnologie zur Aufklärung der "Kapitolverbrechen", VerfBlog,* 2021/1/22, https://verfassungsblog.de/ki-verbrecherjagd/ (accessed on 28.4.2024).

6 See Martini, Blackbox Algorithmus, 2019, p. 88 ff.

7 See Fröhlich/Spiecker genannt Döhmann: *Können Algorithmen diskriminieren?, VerfBlog,* 2018/12/26, https://verfassungsblog.de/koennen-algorithmen-diskriminieren/ (accessed 28.4.2024).

8 Term used by Sommerer, Predictive Policing, 2020, p. 260 (here in relation to crime control).

lative expansion of their informational powers and the constant correction of this development by the Federal Constitutional Court.

As a result, the German legal system proves to be well equipped to counteract the diffusion of responsibility through algorithms in the area of security authorities.[9]

B. Legal-political and social Background

The law governing security authorities in Germany has been undergoing dynamic change for some time.[10] The context for this development was initially formed by changes to the so-called security architecture,[11] ongoing legislative adjustments and their continuous "monitoring" by the Constitutional Court.

9 Not covered in the interest of limiting the subject matter of the study is the Europeanization that occurred recently to informational powers of security agencies, see e.g. Title V of the TFEU (Art. 67 to 89) and Art. 16 Abs. 2 TFEU and the European legislation based on it like Data Protection Directive for police and justice (Directive (EU) 2016/680 of the European Parliament and of the Council of 27 April 2016 on the protection of natural persons with regard to the processing of personal data by competent authorities for the purposes of the prevention, investigation, detection or prosecution of criminal offenses or the execution of criminal penalties, and on the free movement of such data, and repealing Council Framework Decision 2008/977/JHA (OJ 2016 L 119 p. 89, as amended in 2018 L 127 p. 9 and 2021 L 74 p. 36); See on this development Aden, HdB Polizeirecht, Section M, para. 1 et seq. with further references; for criticism, see Pfeffer, Vom Verfassungsstaat zur Sicherheitsunion, p. 75 ff.

10 For example Wolff/Brink, BeckOK DatenschutzR/Albers, Vorb. Syst. L., para. 1 ("few areas have changed so much in recent decades"), Löffelmann, GSZ 2021, p. 16 ("conspicuous reform dynamics"); Bäcker, Kriminalpräventionsrecht, 2015, p. 1 f. (characterizing the "permanent reform" of security law as a symptom of the "regulatory crisis of public law").

11 For more details, see Bäcker in Herdegen/Masing/Poscher/Gärditz, VerfassungsR-HdB § 28, para. 5 et seq.

I. Expansion of the tasks of the security authorities and technological change

In the face of new threats to state and society, the security authorities - namely the federal and state police forces and intelligence authorities[12] - were initially centralized, expanded[13] and their areas of responsibility extended.[14]

As a result of the legally created "preliminary tasks"[15] of the security authorities, their concepts of action developed from a reactive case-by-case approach to a (also) structure-oriented "operational" approach.[16] The more it became necessary to recognize security risks for civil society at an early stage and to ward them off in a promising manner, the more the authorities were dependent on the acquisition and processing of information; only when sufficient information is available on the state side can corresponding

12 In the following, the examination is essentially limited to these authorities, as their traditional main tasks - the prevention of threats to public security and the investigation of efforts against the free democratic basic order - outline the area that is referred to in the political arena as internal security. In the interest of limiting the subject matter of the investigation, the authorities entrusted with foreign or military-specific tasks (Federal Intelligence Service and Military Counterintelligence Service) are therefore excluded, unless there is case law from the Federal Constitutional Court relevant to the topic.
The regulatory and administrative authorities, which in many federal states are also responsible for averting danger (cf. for example § 1 Para. 1 HSOG, § 1 Para. 1 Rh.-Pf. POG), are still not considered, since public security is only one responsibility among others.

13 For more details, see Wolff/Brink, BeckOK DatenschutzR/Albers, Vorb. Syst. L., para. 5 et seq.

14 In the case of intelligence authorities, the traditional task of monitoring anti-constitutional efforts was (partially) extended to terrorism and/or organized crime (see Möstl/Schwabenbauer, BeckOK PolR Bayern/ Lindner/Unterreitmeier, Syst. Vorb., para. 1 ff.); in the case of the police authorities, the traditional task of averting danger was extended to include the task of preventively combating criminal offences (see Lisken/Denninger PolR-HdB/Denninger, Section B, para. 14 ff.).

15 On the term instead of many Möstl/Schwabenbauer, BeckOK PolR Bayern/Möstl, Syst. Vorb. PolR Deutschl., para. 43 ff. with further references; what is meant is that action may already be taken before the traditional police and criminal procedure law intervention thresholds of concrete danger to public safety or order or suspicion of a criminal offense are exceeded.

16 See Bäcker, HdB VerfR, § 28, para. 18 ff., 23 ff.

danger and suspicion hypotheses be created, checked and made the basis for suitable measures.[17]

This development coincided with the technological change in information technology, which resulted, among other things, in the far-reaching datafication of social communication.[18] This change not only created new (potential) sources of information for the security authorities, but also instruments and technologies for their exploitation and analysis as well as the generation of knowledge as such.[19] Those instruments and technologies include regularly algorithmically and AI-controlled processes, which causes the diffusion of responsibility described above.

II. Intensification of information-related legislation

The expansion of tasks and technological change in turn necessitated an adaptation and expansion of the legal basis for the collection and use of data and information by the security authorities. The increasing pace of federal and state legislative activity, particularly from the beginning of the 2000s,[20] resulted in a disproportionate increase in the information-related part of security legislation.

For example, in the Hessian Law on Public Security and Order (HSOG), only 30 of its 129 paragraphs - i.e. around 23% - currently refer to the handling of data, but their text comprises more than 49% of the entire legal text; in the Bavarian Police Duties Act (BayPAG), the data-related provisions account for around 33% (34 of 102 paragraphs), but make up around 63% of the entire legal text.[21] It is therefore correctly diagnosed in the literature that "the law governing the police and intelligence services

17 Lisken/Denninger PolR-HdB/Müller/Schwabenbauer, Section G, para. 2; Altwicker, p. 100, is also succinct: "Precautionary measures taken in advance of the danger are primarily information management."

18 Wolff/Brink, BeckOK DatenschutzR/Albers, Vorb. Syst. L., para. 1.

19 Wolff/Brink, BeckOK DatenschutzR/Albers, Vorb. Syst. L., para. 1, referring, among others, to the increasing use of artificial intelligence.

20 This can be seen, for example, in the list of amendments to the Code of Criminal Procedure in the large number of changes made between 1992 and 2022 in Section 8 of Book 1 ("Investigative measures", Sections 94 to 111q).

21 Numbers calculated using the word and character counting function in Microsoft Word.

is now to a large extent the law governing the handling of personal information and data."[22]

III. The Federal Constitutional Court as a permanent corrective

The expansion of the security authorities' informational powers has proven to be just as constant as its review by the constitutional court. "We know," says *Volkmann*, "that every new regulation in the area of security that is introduced by the federal or state legislature is bound to end up before the BVerfG."[23]

In fact, in view of the Federal Constitutional Court's case law on the security authorities' informational powers - which is probably unprecedented in terms of the number and depth of its decisions for a single area of regulation - it is not difficult to speak of a constitutionalization of this area of law.[24]

C. Constitutionalization of the security authorities' informational powers

The finding of a constitutionalization of the security authorities' informational powers raises the question of why such comprehensive constitutional court control of legislative activity has occurred in this area of law in particular. This process, which has been subject to significant criticism in the legal literature,[25] can essentially be traced back to two constitutional starting points.

The review of information collected by the security authorities found its material basis early on in the constitutional court's understanding of the

---

22 Wolff/Brink, BeckOK DatenschutzR/Albers, Vorb. Syst. L., para. 2; Lisken/Denninger PolR-HdB/Müller/Schwabenbauer, Section G, Part I., para. 2 ("Teilgebiet des Informationsverwaltungsrechts"), Bäcker, HdB VerfR, § 28, para. 42, refers to the constantly expanding legal basis for the security authorities information system; Gärditz, GSZ 2017, 1 (4) emphasizes the "key position" of the handling of data and information in security law.

23 Volkmann, NVwZ 2021, 1408 (1409).

24 For example, Möstl/Schwabenbauer, BeckOK PolR Bayern/Lindner/Unterreitmeier. BayVSG, Syst. Vorb., Heading IV vor para. 14 ff., Wolff, DVBl. 2015, 1076 (1078 ff.), Gärditz, GSZ 2017, 1 (3 f.); Schoch, VVDStRL 81 (2022), Aussprache und Schlussworte, p. 504, speaks of an "over-constitutionalization of security administrative law".

25 For example, von Gärditz, EuGRZ 2018, 6 (21 f.); Lindner/Unterreitmeier, DÖV 2017, 90 (93); Möstl, DVBl. 2010, p. 808 et seq.

fundamental right to free development of the personality guaranteed by Article 2 (1) of the Basic Law.

I. State handling of data as an encroachment on fundamental rights

According to the Federal Constitutional Court, this fundamental right supplements the special ("named") civil liberties as an "unnamed" civil liberty right, which - such as the privacy of correspondence, post and telecommunications and the inviolability of the home - also safeguard constituent elements of personality.[26] Its task is to guarantee the narrower personal sphere of life and the preservation of its basic conditions in the sense of human dignity as the supreme constitutional principle, which cannot be conclusively covered by the traditional concrete guarantees of freedom; this necessity exists in particular in view of modern developments and the new threats to the protection of the human personality associated with them.[27]

The court then recognized such new threats as early as 1983 in modern data processing; under these conditions, the general right of personality also guarantees the right of the individual to determine the disclosure and use of their personal data (right to informational self-determination), the court ruled in the so-called census judgment.[28]

This established that the informational activities of the security authorities, insofar as they concern personal data, must always be considered to have the quality of an encroachment on fundamental rights.[29] Since

26 See only BVerfGE 54, 148 (153) = NJW 1980, 2070. The case law of the Federal Constitutional Court is cited below from the official collection of decisions, insofar as it is published there; parallel references are only cited in the first citation and only for decisions that are not listed in the list in the appendix, in which parallel references are named.

27 BVerfGE 54, 148 (153); BVerfGE 65, 1 (41) = NJW 1984, 419 (421); also Di Fabio, Dürig/Herzog/Scholz, GG, Art. 2 para. 1, para. 127, on the openness to development of the general right of personality for the protection against actual or presumed new threats due to social or technical developments.

28 BVerfGE 65, 1 (41 and Ls. 1 and 2) with reference to and continuation of BVerfGE 54, 148 (155), BVerfGE 27, 1 (6) = NJW 1969, 1707; BVerfGE 27, 344, (350 f.) = NJW 1970, 555; BVerfGE 32, 373 (379) = NJW 1972, 1123; BVerfGE 35, 202 (220) = NJW 1973, 1226; BVerfGE 44, 353 (372 f.) = NJW 1977, 1489 and BVerfGE 56, 37 (41 ff.) = NJW 1981, 1431; BVerfGE 63, 131 (142 f.) = NJW 1983, 1179.

29 Möstl, Die staatliche Garantie für die öffentliche Sicherheit und Ordnung, 2002, p. 209 et seq.; Mann/Fontana, JA 2013, 734 (736); Bäcker in Herdegen/Masing/Poscher/Gärditz, VerfassungsR-HdB § 28, para. 2 et seq. with footnote 5; "the census judg-

then, restrictions on this right have only been permissible in the overriding public interest and on the basis of a sector-specific and sufficiently specific legal basis.[30]

II. Case law of the Federal Constitutional Court

The census ruling opened in cooperation with some procedural peculiarities for the admissibility of corresponding constitutional complaints the space for the court to comprehensively specify the constitutional requirements for informational authorizations of the security authorities.

1. Differentiated fundamental rights protection of privacy as a starting point

The court differentiated the constitutional requirements for informational authorizations of the security authorities based on the fundamental right affected by the respective authorization.[31] The protection of the privacy affected by such authorizations is guaranteed in the Basic Law with the secrecy of correspondence, post and telecommunications (Art. 10 GG),[32] the inviolability of the home (Art. 13 GG),[33] the general right of personality and the right to informational self-determination[34] as its manifestation through several special fundamental rights.[35] In 2008, the court developed the latter further again with a view to technological progress and the change in living conditions: the widespread use of information technology systems and their central importance for the individual lives of many people requires the protection of the general right of personality to be extended to the confidentiality and integrity of information technology systems.[36]

ment, which was not issued directly on security law, was also momentous"); Lisken/Denninger PolR-HdB/Schwabenbauer, Section G, para. 13 et seq.

30 BVerfGE 65, 1 (41 and Ls. 1 and 2)

31 See also Lisken/Denninger PolR-HdB/Schwabenbauer, Section G, para. 62 et seq.

32 For example in BVerfGE 100, 313 et seq.; BVerfGE 113, 348 et seq.; BVerfGE 154, 152.

33 Above all in BVerfGE 109, 279 et seq.

34 For example in BVerfGE 120, 378 et seq.; BVerfGE 141, 220 et seq.

35 The Charter of Fundamental Rights of the European Union, which concentrates this protection in Art. 7 (respect for private and family life) and Art. 8 (protection of personal data), is different.

36 BVerfGE 120, 274 et seq. (online searches under the North Rhine-Westphalia Constitution Protection Act).

In the early rulings on the informational powers of the security authorities, it was primarily the secrecy of correspondence, post and telecommunications (Art. 10 GG)[37] and the inviolability of the home (Art. 13 GG)[38] that initially formed the fundamental rights benchmark. From the mid-2000s, the right to informational self-determination and then also the right to confidentiality and integrity of information technology systems came to the fore.[39]

Although all decisions related to authorizations for covert informational measures by security authorities, they can initially be read primarily as decisions on the special requirements for a specific informational interference with the respective fundamental right, which were also determined with regard to the specific tasks of the respective authorized authority.

However, with regard to the constitutional standards, the decisions show similarities from the outset with regard to the legal reservation under fundamental law and the principle of proportionality.

2. Legal reservation and proportionality as overarching standards

Uniform requirements initially result from the reservation of the law, which, according to the understanding of the court[40] , generally requires the legislator to regulate all essential questions - in particular those that are important for the realization of fundamental rights[41] - itself (so-called essentiality theory).

a) Sector-specific, sufficiently specific and sufficiently clear legal basis

In the census ruling, the court had already specified this for informational interventions to the effect that the basis for authorization must be formulated in a sector-specific manner and be sufficiently specific.[42] For covert in-

37 Thus in BVerfGE 100, 313 et seq.

38 BVerfGE 109, 279 et seq.

39 E.g. in BVerfGE 120, 378 et seq. and BVerfGE 120, 274 et seq.

40 See, for example, BVerfGE 40, 237 (249 with further references) = NJW 1976, 34; BVerfGE 49, 89 (126 f.) = NJW 1979, 359; BVerfGE 84, 212 (226) = NVwZ 1991, 1072; BVerfGE 83, 130 (142 ff.) = NJW 1991, 1471; BVerfGE 95, 267 (307 f.) = NJW 1997, 1975.

41 Only BVerfGE 47, 46 (80) = NJW 1978, 807; BVerfGE 49, 89 (127); BVerfGE 98, 218 (252 ff.) = NJW 1998, 2515.

42 BVerfGE 65, 1 (46).

formation interventions by the security authorities, the court now requires in particular that the reason, purpose and scope of the intervention be specified in concrete terms and clearly defined by law. In this respect, the authorization must be determined in such a way that the authorities addressed are guided and limited by the legal requirements and specifications ("intervention thresholds") and the potentially affected parties are put in a position to assess possible measures against them.[43] This is all the more important as legal protection in the case of covert security measures is regularly only available to a limited extent and the parliamentary and social control required by democratic theory is at least reduced in this area.[44]

Finally, the legal definition of the purpose of the measure is important in view of the principle of purpose limitation of data collection, which has also been in force across the board since the census ruling.[45]

b) Proportionality of the enabling provision(s)

In addition to these requirements, the Federal Constitutional Court also consistently instrumentalized the constitutional principle of proportionality[46] as an overarching standard of review for statutory authorizations of the security authorities to covertly interfere with information.[47] These had to be suitable, necessary (lack of a milder means) and appropriate (proportionality of purpose and means) for the intended purpose.[48] In this respect, it derived a whole bundle of formal and material requirements from the

---

43 BVerfGE 113, 348 (375 et seq.); BVerfGE 120, 378 (407 et seq.); BVerfGE 133, 277 (336); BVerfGE 141, 220 (265).

44 BVerfGE 113, 348 (375 et seq.); BVerfGE 120, 378 (408); BVerfGE 133, 277 (336 et seq.); BVerfGE 141, 220 (265); BVerfGE 155, 119 (177); BVerfGE 156, 11 (44 et seq.).

45 BVerfGE 65, 1 (47 et seq.) and then BVerfGE 100, 313 (360 et seq.); BVerfGE 109, 279 (375 et seq.); BVerfGE 110, 33 (73); BVerfGE 120, 351 (368 et seq.); BVerfGE 125, 260 (333); BVerfGE 130, 1 (33 et seq.); BVerfGE 133, 277 (372 et seq.), BVerfGE 141, 220 (324).

46 In general, for example, BVerfGE 50, 217 (227) = NJW 1979, 1345; BVerfGE 80, 103 (107) = NJW 1989, 1985; BVerfGE 99, 202 (212 ff.) = NJW 1989, 935, in more detail Grzeszick, Dürig/Herzog/Scholz, GG, Art. 20, para. 119 ff., on the literature's criticism of this standard, see the references ibid, para. 120, fn. 6.

47 For example, BVerfGE 120, 274 (318 f.); BVerfGE 125, 260 (316); BVerfGE 141, 220 (265), in each case with further references.

48 For more details, see Grzeszick, Dürig/Herzog/Scholz, GG, Art. 20, para. 114, 115 ff., 119 ff.

appropriateness - also referred to as proportionality in the narrower sense - which the legislators must meet.[49]

III. The constitutional requirements for information interventions by the security authorities in detail

On this basis, between 1999 and 2023, the court reviewed more than two dozen proceedings statutory authorizations of the security authorities to interfere with information, initially primarily challenging individual instruments - such as the "large-scale eavesdropping attack", preventive telecommunications surveillance or the use of license plate reading systems.[50] Later, constitutional complaints were added, in each of which a larger number of informational power norms from an entire body of law were put under scrutiny.[51]

While the principle of proportionality formed the central standard of review in the decisions, its standards varied - as a result of the need for a balancing of interests inherent in the criterion of appropriateness - according to the intensity of the encroachment on fundamental rights authorized by the provision under review. In this respect, the court successively developed criteria that can be used to determine the intensity of the encroachment of the security authorities' informational encroachment powers.

1. Criteria for determining the intensity of intervention

The court's explanations on the weight of the interference[52] initially revert to formulations that can already be found in the census judgment. The typical introductory sentence reads: "In general, the weight of an interference with informational self-determination is determined above all by the type, scope and conceivable use of the data as well as the risk of its misuse."[53]

49 For example, BVerfGE 141, 220 (265, 267 f., 290 f.) and the criticism of this in the dissenting opinions of Judges Eichberger (354 f.) and Schluckebier (365); see also BVerfGE 120, 274 (318 ff.); BVerfGE 125, 260 (316).

50 BVerfGE 109, 279 et seq.; BVerfGE 113, 348 et seq.; BVerfGE 120, 378 et seq.

51 E.g . in BVerfGE 141, 220 et seq. (BKA-G); BVerfG, NJW 2022, 1583 et seq. (Bayr. VerfassungsschutzG), BVerfG, GSZ 2032, 98 et seq. (PolizeiG M-V).

52 See also in detail Schwabenbauer, HdB Polizeirecht, Section G, para. 119 et seq.

53 BVerfGE 156, 11 (48 f.); BVerfG BeckRS 2023, 1828, para. 76 in each case with further references and with reference to BVerfGE 61, 1 (48 f.).

It is then regularly further stated that[54] it is important how many fundamental rights holders are exposed to how intensive impairments and under what conditions these occur, in particular whether these persons have given cause for this. The number of persons affected and the intensity of the individual impairment are therefore decisive. The weight of the individual impairment depends on whether the persons concerned remain anonymous, what personal information is collected and what disadvantages the holders of fundamental rights suffer as a result of the measures or fear without good reason. In particular, the secrecy of a state intervention measure leads to an increase in its intensity, as does the de facto denial of prior legal protection and the difficulty of obtaining subsequent legal protection, if such protection can be obtained at all.[55]

Based on these typical general findings of the court, the criteria used to determine the weight of the interference can ultimately be divided into qualitative, quantitative and modal criteria.[56]

From a qualitative perspective, the affiliation or proximity of the (potential) information to be collected or used to the privacy[57] of the data subjects plays a role. The more deeply the collection and/or processing of information by the security authorities interferes with this sphere, i.e. the space in which the individual is usually left to his or her own devices unobserved, the greater the weight of the interference.[58]

---

54 On the following BVerfGE 156, 11 (48 f.); BVerfG BeckRS 2023, 1828, para. 76; BVerfGE 100, 313 (376); BVerfGE 115, 320 (353); BVerfGE 141, 220 (265), in each case with further references.

55 See previous footnote for evidence.

56 However, it is not possible to draw a clear-cut distinction between these three groups; the subdivision in Lisken/Denninger PolR-HdB/Schwabenbauer, Section G, para. 119 et seq. differs somewhat.

57 According to the BVerfG, the private sphere has always been part of the scope of protection of the general right of personality, see for example BVerfGE 90, 255 (260) = NJW 1995, 1015: "Such a sphere is established by the general right of personality. Art. 2 para. 1 GG guarantees the free development of personality. One of the conditions for the development of personality is that the individual has a space in which he is left to himself unobserved or can associate with persons of his particular trust without regard to social expectations of behavior and without fear of state sanctions. It follows from the importance of such a retreat for the development of the personality that the protection of Article 2.1 in conjunction with Article 1 of the Basic Law also includes the private sphere (see BVerfGE 27, 1 (6) = NJW 1969, 1707; established case law)".

58 See BVerfGE 100, 313 (358 et seq.); BVerfGE 107, 299 (312 et seq.); BVerfGE 110, 33 (52 et seq.); BVerfGE 113, 348 (364 et seq.); BVerfGE 115, 320 (341 et seq.); BVerfGE 125, 260 (316 et seq.); BVerfGE 133, 277 (335 et seq.); see also Lisken/Denninger PolR-HdB/Schwabenbauer, Section G, para 62, 111 et seq.

Since the protection of privacy extends in particular to confidential communications,[59] the potential inclusion of corresponding communication relationships in the collection and processing of information by the security authorities also increases the weight of interference.[60]

In quantitative terms, the number of persons potentially involved in the collection or processing of information by the security authorities ("range") is important for the intensity of the interference, as is the duration and intensity of the measure in relation to the individual persons concerned. The court[61] sees a wide range that increases the weight of the interference if numerous persons are included in the scope of a measure who have no connection to a specific misconduct and did not cause the interference through their behavior. Accordingly, the individual's fundamental freedom is affected all the more intensely the less they themselves have given rise to a state intervention.

Such interventions could also have an intimidating effect, which could lead to impairments in the exercise of fundamental rights.[62] A deterrent effect on the exercise of fundamental rights - according to the further justification - must not only be avoided in order to protect the subjective rights of the individuals concerned; the common good is also impaired because self-determination is an elementary functional condition of a free democratic community based on the ability of its citizens to act and participate.[63] It jeopardizes the impartiality of conduct if the wide range of investigative measures contributes to the risk of abuse and a feeling of being under surveillance.[64]

59 BVerfGE 90, 255 (260): "Confidential communication is also part of the protection of privacy. Particularly in the case of statements made to family members and persons of trust, the focus is often less on the aspect of expressing opinions and the intended influence on the opinion-forming of third parties than on the aspect of self-expression."

60 BVerfG, BeckRS 2022/41609, para. 102 (passage not reprinted in GSZ 2023, 98 et seq.); BVerfGE 141, 220 (276), on the resulting absolute restriction of the core area of private life, see cc) below.

61 For the first time in BVerfGE 100, 313 (376, 392), then for example in BVerfGE 107, 299 (320 f.); BVerfGE 109, 279 (353); BVerfGE 113, 29 (53); BVerfGE 113, 348 (383); see also Lisken/Denninger PolR-HdB/Schwabenbauer, Section G, para. 132.

62 This was already the case in the census judgment, BVerfGE 65, 1 (42), then BVerfGE 113, 29 (46).

63 BVerfGE 113, 29 (46).

64 BVerfGE 107, 299 (328); see also Lisken/Denninger PolR-HdB/Schwabenbauer, Section G, para. 125, 134.

In relation to the individual data subjects, the weight of the interference is also determined by the duration and scope of the respective monitoring measure. The longer the period of surveillance and the more comprehensively the movements and expressions of life of the person concerned are recorded, the more serious the intrusion.[65]

With regard to the modes of information collection, the covertness or secrecy of a measure per se increases the intensity of its intrusiveness.[66] Additional weight is added by the use of technical means, with the help of which perception hurdles are overcome or the processing of large complex data sets becomes possible.[67] The exploitation of trust worthy of protection in the identity and motivation of a communication partner also has an intrusive effect; finally,[68] the same applies to the risk or probability of being exposed to follow-up measures.[69]

2. Intervention intensity and need for regulation in the application of algorithm- or AI-controlled processes by the security authorities

On this basis, the court has recently also increasingly turned its attention to the use of algorithm- or AI-controlled processes in the context of data collection and data processing by the security authorities. Explicit statements on this can be found for the first time in a decision from 2020 on the strategic foreign telecommunications surveillance carried out by the Federal Intelligence Service, in which such processes played a decisive role, as foreign communications are automatically evaluated using certain search terms. On the question of which constitutional requirements the legal basis for this measure must meet, the court stated, among other things: "The framework provisions to be prescribed by law include the requirement of an immediate evaluation of the collected data (...), the application of the

65 BVerfGE 109, 279 (323); BVerfGE 112, 304 (319 f.); BVerfGE 130, 1 (24); BVerfGE 141, 220 (280 f.)

66 With regard to the collection of police information, BVerfGE 133, 277, 328 f.: "A secret police force is not envisaged."

67 BVerfG BeckRS 2023, 1828, para. 69 et seq.; BVerfGE 120, 274 (375); BVerfG NJW 2022, 1583 (1610).

68 In particular BVerfGE 120, 274 (375); BVerfG NJW 2022, 1583 (1610).

69 On the whole BVerfGE 107, 299 (318 et seq.); BVerfGE 109, 279 (353 et seq.); BVerfGE 113, 348 (382 et seq.); BVerfGE 115, 320 (347 et seq.); BVerfGE 118, 168 (169 et seq.); BVerfGE 120, 274 (322 et seq.); BVerfGE 125, 260 (318 et seq.); BVerfGE 141, 220 (268 et seq.).

principle of proportionality in the selection of search terms - as currently already provided for in the service regulations -, regulations on the use of intrusion-intensive methods of data evaluation, in particular complex forms of data comparison (...) as well as compliance with the prohibition of discrimination under the Basic Law (...). The use of algorithms may also need to be regulated, in particular to ensure their fundamental traceability with a view to independent control."[70]

The court expanded on this approach in a highly regarded decision on the use of the "Gotham"-program from Palantir Inc. by the Hessian police for the automated analysis of its own databases.[71] The program extracts correlations between people, groups of people, institutions, organizations, objects and things from police data, classifies incoming information according to known facts and evaluates the data statistically. It therefore generates "new knowledge" that could not otherwise have been derived from the data and presents this graphically in a form that is easy for users to understand.[72]

The court stated that the automated data analysis alone constitutes an interference with the right to informational self-determination and, in terms of the intensity of the interference, has an intrinsic weight that goes beyond that of the collection of the analysed data.[73] Depending on the complexity and "learning ability" of the algorithms used as well as the scope and sensitivity of the data involved, the use of such systems for automated data analysis is of the highest intensity of interference.[74]

As a result, the strictest requirements apply to legal authorizations for the use of such systems; the court had already differentiated these in its extensive case law.[75]

In particular, the requirements relate to thresholds of interference, protected interests and addressees of the measures, allow only limited exceptions to the purpose limitation of data and place high demands on the exchange of data between different authorities, in particular between the

---

70 BVerfG NJW 2020, 2235 (2253, para. 192).

71 BVerfG NJW 2023, 1196 ff., the decision concerned not only the legal basis created for data analysis in Hesse but also the parallel standard from Hamburg.

72 See BVerfG NJW 2023, 1196 (1201, para. 96 et seq.).

73 See BVerfG NJW 2023, 1196 (1201, para. 67 et seq.).

74 See BVerfG NJW 2023, 1196 (1201, para. 75 et seq.).

75 Cf. for example BVerfGE 100, 313 (360 f., 389 et seq.); BVerfGE 109, 279 (375 et seq.); BVerfGE 110, 33 (73); BVerfGE 120, 351 (368 et seq.); BVerfGE 125, 260 (333); BVerfGE 130, 1 (33 et seq.); BVerfGE 133, 277 (372 et seq.); BVerfGE 141, 220 (324); see also Lisken/Denninger PolR-HdB/Schwabenbauer, Section G, para. 23, 120, 222 et seq.

police and intelligence services. Furthermore, legal requirements for (prior) control, procedures, transparency and legal protection must be guaranteed and a core area of private life must always remain free from information interventions by the security authorities.

With regard to the specific system, legal specifications must also be made to reduce the risks of discrimination associated with automated data analysis and to counteract the susceptibility of the data analysis system to errors. If - as is the case here - the system of a private provider is used, government monitoring of the (further) development of the software must also be provided for.[76]

D. (No) diffusion of responsibility through algorithms under the conditions of the constitutionalization of the security authorities' informational powers

If we look at the constitutional requirements from the point of view of the court regarding the diffusion of responsibility through algorithms, it should first be noted that the Federal Constitutional Court primarily assigns responsibility for the use of AI and algorithm-controlled processes by the security authorities to the legislator.

Although the legislator may permit the use of such systems, it must counteract the risk of a diffusion of responsibility by making provisions to minimize the risks of discrimination and the susceptibility of AI or algorithm-controlled systems to errors. Furthermore, the typical risk of the non-traceability of algorithmically generated results must be limited by specifying transparency, procedures and controls and ensuring that legal protection can be obtained at any time in the event that errors nevertheless occur.

The fundamental rights of those affected must also be taken into account by restricting the data that may be used in AI and algorithm-driven analyses and by imposing restrictions on the technologies used, which - if they originate from state providers - also require state monitoring.

In the field of legal policy, technologies such as predictive policing or AI-supported surveillance of public spaces are often associated with dystopias that are easy to understand in view of the potential of such technologies for ubiquitous total surveillance. In the German legal system, these dystopias

76 BVerfG NJW 2023, 1196 (1202 et seq. para 77; 1204 et seq. para 95; 1205 Para 100; 1202 et para 109).

are unlikely to be based on a realistic prognosis under the conditions of the constitutionalization of the security authorities' powers of informational intervention.

Even if the risk remains that serious police or secret service measures may be taken in individual cases on the basis of faulty AI or algorithm-controlled processes, this should be readily acceptable in view of the potential associated with such technologies to make public security measures more effective as a result of the guarantee of subsequent control and correction.

Uncertainty, Risk and Responsibility

The Security of the Future – Artificial Intelligence and Social Control.
From Predictive Policing to Social Scoring

Tobias Singelnstein

Artificial intelligence[1] *will have an impact similar to the invention of electricity. With this much-quoted statement, computer scientist and Stanford professor Andrew Ng has summarised the formative role of artificial intelligence (AI).*[2] *Just like electricity in the 19th and 20th centuries, AI is a technology that will find its way into practically every area of life and change them more or less fundamentally. The world of crime and criminal sciences is no exception. The new technologies and the understanding on which they are based will lead to a completely different societal understanding of security and its threats in the coming decades. For not only does deviant behaviour shape the measures that society takes – from a constructivist perspective, it is rather that, contrary to this common understanding, the way in which deviance is dealt with determines how it is seen, understood and conceptualised.*

A. Starting points

Criminology refers as social control to mechanisms by which society ensures that its social norms are adhered to. It distinguishes between informal forms in the immediate environment, and formal social control, particularly through the police and criminal law. The category therefore includes things as diverse as rolling one's eyes at friends on the one hand, and imprisonment on the other. What all these mechanisms have in common,

1 The text was first published in Horst Beisel et al. (ed), *Die Kriminalwissenschaften als Teil der Humanwissenschaften: Festschrift für Dieter Dölling zum 70. Geburtstag* (Baden-Baden 2023) 963ff.

2 Alexander Armbruster, 'Er ist ein Star der künstlichen Intelligenz' *Frankfurter Allgemeine Zeitung* (Frankfurt, 22 March 2017) ‹https://www.faz.net/aktuell/wirtschaft/netzwirtschaft/andrew-ng-er-ist-ein-star-der-kuenstlichen-intelligenz-14936979.html› accessed 18 April 2024.

however, is that they are based on the concept of social norms and punish offences against these norms.

This backward-looking concept has come under pressure in the recent past. It is no longer enough for society to react to deviant behaviour in the past. Instead, the supposed ideal of comprehensive security has become dominant. To this end, violations of norms should be prevented, i.e., before they materialise in practice.[3] Society's response to theft, for example, has long been exclusively repressive and primarily left to criminal law. Of course, it would be more practical if such offences could be prevented in advance. Over time, a new, instrumental understanding of prevention and precaution has prevailed instead of what was characteristic of the welfare state of the postwar Federal Republic – from public safety measures and criminal prosecution to prevention, prediction and pre-emption.[4] It is not about changing social conditions and living circumstances in the sense of primary prevention, but about specific intervention regarding situations and persons to whom risks are attributed.[5] The central prerequisite for this idea is that potentially harmful situations and potentially dangerous people can be identified before the damage has occurred.[6] To this end, new forms of social control use the concept of risk. In short, this refers to a perceived potential for harm, and thus to circumstances that, statistically speaking, make the occurrence of harm or deviant behaviour more likely. For example, people are more likely to commit crimes when they are young than when they are older.

Artificial intelligence is a colourful term. It encompasses diverse techniques, such as machine learning, robotics, and neural networks. Therefore, artificial intelligence has many faces and is already being used in many different areas, such as online translation services, deepfake apps for manipulating videos, autonomous driving, drones, and weapons systems. However,

3 Tristan Barczak, *Der nervöse Staat* (Tübingen 2020); Tobias Singelnstein, 'Preventive Turn: Wie Gefahr und Risiko zum zentralen Gegenstand von Strafrecht und sozialer Kontrolle werden' in Thomas Fischer and Eric Hilgendorf (eds), *Gefahr* (Baden-Baden 2020) 96ff.

4 Uwe Volkmann, 'Prävention durch Verwaltungsrecht: Sicherheit' (2021) 40 NVwZ 1408, 1409ff.

5 Tobias Singelnstein and Karl-Ludwig Kunz, *Kriminologie: Eine Grundlegung* (8th edn, Bern 2021) 391ff.

6 General information on knowledge production in security law Benjamin Rusteberg, 'Wissensgenerierung in der personenbezogenen Prävention: Zwischen kriminalistischer Erfahrung und erkenntnistheoretischer Rationalität' in Laura Münkler (ed), *Dimensionen des Wissens im Recht* (Tübingen 2019) 233.

all of these are still quite simple forms, one could even say pre-forms of artificial intelligence in the true sense, and their interaction with the real world is often inadequate. There are machines that execute certain patterns for which they have been programmed, such as robots in industry. Programmes and algorithms can be trained with large amounts of data to recognise certain patterns, such as in autonomous driving. But we are still a long way from machines that actually act like humans, that can touch and grasp, that are able to deal with unfamiliar situations appropriately.

B. Artificial intelligence and social control

On the one hand, the technical developments described above pose new challenges and problems for the criminal sciences. In general, these automated processes raise the question of how negative consequences can be attributed. Who is responsible if, for example, an autonomously flying drone causes an accident? The new technologies also lead to new forms of crime, raising the question of whether they fall within the scope of existing criminal laws or whether new regulations are required.

However, AI also opens up new opportunities for social control.[7] For example, it can be used to make existing tasks easier: In the US, for example, predictive sentencing exists, which advises judges on their decisions, and automation is also finding its way into the administration of justice in Germany.[8] The police in Germany are developing tools to compare and identify handwriting or recognise sexual abuse of children in images; algorithms are designed to detect pattern-based money laundering, tax evasion or other economic crimes; upload filters by private companies on digital platforms recognise deviant behaviour and exclude it; video surveillance can identify

7 Overview at Alexander Baur, 'Maschinen führen die Aufsicht: Offene Fragen der Kriminalprävention durch digitale Überwachungsagenten' [2020] ZIS 275; Timo Rademacher, 'Verdachtsgewinnung durch Algorithmen: Maßstäbe für den Einsatz von predictive policing und retrospective policing bei Gefahrenabwehr bzw. Strafverfolgung' in Daniel Zimmer (ed), *Regulierung für Algorithmen und Künstliche Intelligenz* (Baden-Baden 2021) 234ff.

8 Martin Fries, 'Automatische Rechtspflege' [2018] RW 414; Johannes Kaspar, Katrin Höffler and Stefan Harrendorf, 'Datenbanken, Online-Votings und künstliche Intelligenz: Perspektiven evidenzbasierter Strafzumessung im Zeitalter von „Legal Tech"' (2020) 32 NK 35; Clemens Kessler, 'KI und Legal Tech. Utopie, Dystopie, Realität' in Susanne Beck, Carsten Kusche and Brian Valerius (eds), *Digitalisierung, Automatisierung, KI und Recht* (Baden-Baden 2020); Hannah Ofterdinger, 'Strafzumessung durch Algorithmen?' [2020] ZIS 404.

people – not only by means of facial recognition, but in the future, for example, also by the way they walk.

But AI is not just a tool. It also enables completely new forms of social control. By analysing patterns and correlations in crime data, it will supposedly be possible to predict deviant behaviour. Intelligent video surveillance can recognise behaviour patterns that are typical of dangerous or criminal behaviour, such as the hectic movements of several people in a dangerous place.[9] Prospectively, it is also expected to be able to interpret facial expressions in order to read motivations and attitudes such as an intention to buy, sexual interest, or suicidal intentions, or be able to recognise coronavirus infections.[10] Predictive policing – i.e., the prediction of criminal offences through mass data analysis – is still in its infancy in Germany. However, a look at the US demonstrates how influential the concept will be for police work in the future.[11]

These new technologies are not supporting already existing forms of social control, such as criminal law. Rather, they are taking their place as entirely new forms characterised by two features. Firstly, they follow a probabilistic perspective, i.e., they make probabilistic statements regardless of a specific occasion and well in advance of possible harm. This can be both person-related and situation-related. Secondly, they favour dealing with these risks in advance, which in turn can take various forms. On the one hand, this can consist of a more detailed investigation of the situation or the corresponding procurement of information. On the other hand, direct intervention in the respective event can be undertaken in order to achieve a change for the future, which is referred to as pre-emption.[12] Hence, these techniques claim to fulfil social control's long-held desire – namely, to prevent deviance. In the case of theft, it would no longer be necessary to wait for the offence to be committed. Instead, the facial expression or other social characteristics of potential perpetrators could be used to recognise whether they are more likely to commit theft.

9 Sebastian J Golla, 'Lernfähige Systeme, lernfähiges Polizeirecht. Regulierung von künstlicher Intelligenz am Beispiel von Videoüberwachung und Datenabgleich' (2020) 52 KrimJ 149, 156f.

10 Wolfgang Behr, 'Gesichtsverlust 3.0' (*Geschichte der Gegenwart*, 18 April 2021) ‹https://geschichtedergegenwart.ch/gesichtsverlust-3-0/› accessed 18 February 2022.

11 Tobias Singelnstein, 'Predictive Policing: Algorithmenbasierte Straftatprognosen zur vorausschauenden Kriminalintervention' [2018] NStZ 1, 2ff.

12 Simon Egbert, 'Drogentests und 'Alltags-Präemption'' (2018) 50 KrimJ 106, 109ff.

C. Problems and question marks

The way of dealing with risks as exemplified by these new techniques of social control can be divided into three abstract steps: Calculation or identification, assessment, and management.

I. Risk identification

At the level of risk identification or calculation, the aim is to determine factors that make the occurrence of deviant behaviour more likely for certain people or situations.[13] The systems operate according to the principle of pattern recognition. In a first step, vast data sets are examined to see whether certain patterns can be identified that are associated with deviant behaviour. This can refer to various things. On the one hand, very specific things, such as certain behaviour or a certain facial expression in the case of intelligent video surveillance. On the other hand, there are also comprehensive procedures, such as in the case of predictive policing systems, which create profiles of people or analyse situations using a wide range of different data. If patterns are identified that statistically make the commission of criminal offences more likely, the systems are trained to recognise them in the real world so that they can be evaluated and managed there.[14]

In this way, AI opens up interesting new perspectives. Under certain circumstances, it can even provide insights that were previously hidden from us, as human behaviour can be measured and calculated to a certain extent, thereby leading to a new understanding of risk.[15] However, risk identification in the area of social control of deviant behaviour is also associated with fundamental difficulties, in particular our incognizance of risks which impedes the clear definition of patterns. Firstly, human behaviour is only measurable and predictable in some respects; if there are patterns to varying degrees, some risk factors are easier to predict than others. Secondly, the quality of pattern recognition depends heavily on the complexity of the subject in question.

---

13 Tobias Singelnstein and Karl-Ludwig Kunz, *Kriminologie: Eine Grundlegung* (8th edn, Bern 2021) 394ff.

14 Mareile Kaufmann, Simon Egbert and Matthias Leese, 'Predictive Policing and the Politics of Patterns' (2019) 59 BritJCrim 674.

15 Kelly Hannah-Moffat, 'Algorithmic risk governance: Big data analytics, race and information activism in criminal justice debates' (2019) 23 Theoretical Criminology 453.

Finally, these processes require the collection and processing of (also) personal data on a very large scale.[16] Firstly, large amounts of data are required for the techniques to train and work with, for example in order to recognise patterns – the more and the more diverse the data, the better. Secondly, once these technologies are functioning, they will have to constantly survey us and our world in order to detect patterns and risk factors.[17] The more comprehensive this preventive surveillance is, be it through video surveillance or data analyses, the more the technologies can discover.

Due to the intrusive nature of such measures with regard to informational self-determination, approaches that look at situations and therefore do not process personal data have dominated in Germany to date. However, forms of personal risk analysis are also increasingly entering the scene.[18] These are currently still focused on certain groups, such as multiple offenders, sex offenders and dangerous offenders, working primarily with existing police databases and not yet using AI, as shown by police databases, but also by the BKA's RADAR programme (rule-based analysis of potentially destructive offenders to assess the acute risk).[19] However, various projects, particularly from the BMBF's security research programme, show where the journey is heading: data-based, automated risk analyses, including those relating to individuals. This can be based on very different data sets, including those from social media.[20]

II. Risk assessment

The issue becomes much more difficult when it comes to assessing the respective risks, i.e., the question of what the existence of a risk factor actually means in concrete terms and what the consequences should be.

---

16 Simon Egbert, 'Datafizierte Polizeiarbeit – (Wissens-)Praktische Implikationen und rechtliche Herausforderungen' in Daniela Hunold and Andreas Ruch (eds), *Polizeiarbeit zwischen Praxishandeln und Rechtsordnung* (Wiesbaden 2020).

17 Hans-Heinrich Kuhlmann and Simone Trute, 'Predictive Policing als Formen polizeilicher Wissensgenerierung' [2021] GSZ 103, 108f.; see also Sebastian J Golla, 'Lernfähige Systeme, lernfähiges Polizeirecht. Regulierung von künstlicher Intelligenz am Beispiel von Videoüberwachung und Datenabgleich' (2020) 52 KrimJ 149, 157f.

18 Lucia M Sommerer, *Personenbezogenes Predictive Policing* (Baden-Baden 2020).

19 Celina Sonka and others, 'RADAR-iTE 2.0: Ein Instrument des polizeilichen Staatsschutzes: Aufbau, Entwicklung und Stand der Evaluation' [2020] Kriminalistik 386.

20 Michael Spranger and Dirk Labudde, 'Vorhersage von Gruppendynamiken auf der Grundlage von Daten aus Sozialen Netzwerken' in Thomas-Gabriel Rüdiger and Petra Saskia Bayerl (eds), *Cyberkriminologie* (Wiesbaden 2020).

Here, the new techniques of social control, like all forms of forecasting, have to contend with the problems of ambivalence, complexity, and uncertainty. These are particularly evident in the prediction of deviant behaviour. For not only is deviant behaviour highly diverse, but it also involves very complex social events that can be influenced by a large number of very different factors.

Whether and why someone violates social norms depends on countless factors, some of which exert their influence in the long-term and others spontaneously. There are now myriad criminological theories explaining the development of crime in one way or another. Depending on their epoch and the paradigm in force, they seek the causes of deviance in disposition or environment, in biological, psychological, social or socio-structural circumstances. Yet we really only know of certain factors that make the occurrence of deviant behaviour more likely. There is no universal formula to explain criminal behaviour.[21] And while it is one thing to attempt to theoretically and empirically clarify how crime arises, the prediction of deviant behaviour by certain individuals in concreto is something completely different. Even in the field of crime prediction, which involves a very specific population of test subjects or very specific issues, the methodological possibilities of predicting future criminal offences are highly controversial and anything but satisfactory.[22]

However, once someone has been identified as a dangerous offender, it is difficult for them to exculpate themselves, to free themselves of this label. Where there is no specific accusation but only a vague assessment, it is impossible to convincingly exonerate oneself. The European and international no-fly lists have impressively demonstrated how Kafkaesque this can become.

III. Risk management

The third step involves the question of how to deal with the risks that have been identified and assessed. There are various possible forms for this. On the one hand, there are so-called recommender systems. These provide information and recommendations on how a certain situation should be

21 Tobias Singelnstein and Karl-Ludwig Kunz, *Kriminologie: Eine Grundlegung* (8th edn, Bern 2021) 219ff.

22 See only Ulrich Eisenberg and Ralf Kölbel, *Kriminologie* (7th edn Tübingen 2017) 228ff.

handled, but do not make decisions themselves. These include predictive sentencing systems, for example, which are designed to support judges in their decision making. For such systems, the question always arises as to what extent the decision-makers remain capable of making qualified assessments for themselves and, if necessary, of resisting the recommendations. On the other hand, systems can incorporate automated decisions, for example when an intelligent video surveillance system triggers an alarm or locks rooms.

There are also various ways of managing risks. Firstly, concrete control, i.e., intervention to handle a specific risk situation, can be considered. This handling could consist of risk research, for example by ordering police officers to a certain location where the probability of burglaries is said to be increased, or by observing potentially dangerous people to obtain further information about them and their actions and to clarify whether a threat is materialising. However, it is also possible to directly modify the risk situation. For example, a potential thief could be denied access to a department store if the video surveillance identifies a suspicious facial expression.

Secondly, there are precautionary models that link more or less comprehensive consequences to more general risk predictions. The aim then is not to deal with specific identified risks, such as an increased probability of burglary or theft. Instead, the general riskiness of people is determined in the form of risk profiles using a large number of parameters in order to link them with an equally broad range of reactions in terms of prevention. What this might look like in practice is demonstrated by glimpses of China's notorious social scoring system[23] – or the private sector. In Germany, too, SCHUFA and insurance companies have long been using social scoring to assess creditworthiness or the probability of insurance claims.[24] In the case of SCHUFA, this form of risk management can lead to someone being unable to obtain credit (or only at very expensive rates) or enter into certain contracts. The Chinese social scoring system, for example, excludes people from buying tickets for flights and train journeys once they reach a certain score. By these measures, an increased, not necessarily further specified risk profile is dealt with before these risks materialize any further.

23 Katika Kühnreich, 'Social Credit, Sicherheit und Freiheit' in Oliver Everling (ed), *Social Credit Rating* (Wiesbaden 2020).

24 See also Niklas Maamar, 'Social Scoring: Eine europäische Perspektive auf Verbraucher-Scores zwischen Big Data und Big Brother' (2018) 34 CR 820, 820ff.

At the same time, however, such forms of precautionary exclusion obviously also constitute sanctions and therefore incentives for good behaviour and self-management. These incentives do not necessarily have to be of such an overt nature but can also take on a manipulative form. AI and algorithms offer excellent opportunities for this, as they are getting to know us better and better and can not only predict our behaviour and decisions, but are also aware of our needs, desires, and fears.[25] From a technical point of view then, the step to risk management through manipulation is not too far away.

So, while we can observe different techniques, their underlying principle is the same: risk management. From this perspective, governmental social scoring ultimately appears to be merely a logical further development of the techniques already used in Germany today.

D. The security of the future

The technologies and strategies described in the context of AI will lead to a fundamentally different image of deviant behaviour and crime – and thus create a fundamentally different social understanding of security. Security is a social construct. Its form and change are characterised by the respective social conditions and existing social discourses. How much security is necessary? Regarding which areas and topics? Whose perspective is decisive? What exactly does security mean – i.e., when is it present and when is it disturbed? These questions are answered differently at different times and in different societies, but also by different groups in society. Central to this issue is what a society sees as disruptions and threats, i.e., what its sources of insecurity are and which concepts are favoured in dealing with them.

I. Disruptions to the security of the future

In future, the things that are conceived as disruptions to security, as sources of insecurity, and as threats will be very different from today. The focus will

25 'Gefahr für die Menschheit: Vordenker warnt vor möglicher Macht der Algorithmen' (*Chip*, 9 May 2019) ‹https://www.chip.de/news/Gefahr-fuer-die-Menschheit-Vordenker-warnt-vor-moeglicher-Macht-der-Algorithmen_168085191.html› accessed 18 April 2024.

no longer lie with crime and behaviour that deviates from social norms, as is the case today with criminal law and related techniques of social control. Instead, risk factors (as they are addressed and dealt with by the new AI techniques of social control) will already be seen as disruptions to security by themselves.[26]

According to this way of thinking, a normal person is not someone who merely refrains from prohibited behaviour, but someone who possesses no risk factors for future deviant behaviour. In the world of probabilistic perspectives, the predictability of risks becomes the decisive question. These techniques – and therefore we ourselves – will no longer look at whether people's actions violate norms, which requires a very precise determination. Instead, they calculate probabilities of a possible norm violation in the future and consider this risk factor as a disruption well in advance of any harm. From this perspective, it follows that we no longer look at individual actions of people and assess them, as we have done in criminal law to date. Instead, we look at people and situations as such and subject them to a forward-looking overall assessment when analysing risk. In the case of individuals, this introduces the possibility of rating, i.e., categorising the population into different risk classes. Let's think back to the example of theft: a thief does not only come into focus when he commits the theft, but already when he enters the department store with a suspicious facial expression or otherwise exhibits risk characteristics that speak in favour of committing theft – young age, wrong residential area, previous criminal record. This may be practical regarding a person who actually wants to commit theft. However, it also applies to dozens of others who have similar risk characteristics but would not actually commit theft. The techniques do not judge individuals as such, but construct groups based on probability statements.

The changed understanding of security disruptions will bring completely different phenomena to the centre of attention. Which forms of disruption are at the centre of social perception and how they are understood always depends on the respective strategies through which a society endeavours to control these disruptions. For example, repeat offenders only became an issue when police files and forensic evidence made it possible to prove that individual suspects had committed several offences. Where predictions

26 Kelly Hannah-Moffat, 'Algorithmic risk governance: Big data analytics, race and information activism in criminal justice debates' (2019) 23 Theoretical Criminology 453.

are made based on pattern recognition, as is the case with AI, the focus naturally shifts to disruptions that exhibit certain patterns. And society's perception will focus more on external signs of such patterns than on attitudes, social explanations, and similar causal contexts.[27] In criminology, other theories of crime that follow this pattern-based, external perspective will become stronger.

However, this fundamental change does not – as one might perhaps hope – mean that there will no longer be any disruptions to security. Rather, only the understanding of what is to be regarded as a disruption is changing – namely the risk factor well in advance of actual harm or violations of legal interests.

II. Dealing with disruptions to the security of the future

Dealing with disruptions to security – i.e., calculating, assessing, and managing risks – is to a large extent the state's responsibility and primarily the task of the police. At the same time, however, the new understanding also shapes the practical experiences of citizens. In their everyday lives, they endeavour to recognise risks and take precautions to counter them. Police prevention programmes even encourage them to do so. Today, more than in previous decades, protection against threats and concern for security are also projects of the individual. After all, the production of security is increasingly becoming a market. Private companies offer their own solutions for calculating and assessing risks as well as corresponding precautionary measures. In doing so, they further stimulate both public and private risk management.

Looking outward from today's perspective, it is difficult to say which proportions this risk management will assume in society. It is conceivable that this management will extend only to particularly significant risks. If sufficiently concrete patterns and risk factors for homicides could be identified, these could be countered with selective control through risk research measures. At the other end of the scale looms the model of comprehensive risk management favoured in China: By comprehensively surveying the world, people, and their actions through intelligent video surveillance and various data analyses, a permanent calculation of risks is taking place, and

27 Tobias Singelnstein, 'Predictive Policing: Algorithmenbasierte Straftatprognosen zur vorausschauenden Kriminalintervention' [2018] NStZ 1, 4f.

they can be assigned to individuals by way of already ubiquitous facial recognition.[28] Here, identification and risk detection as different areas of application for AI are therefore linked. In the preventive model, the necessary management is implemented in the form of a social credit system.

In Germany and Europe, the direction of development will depend heavily on whether society succeeds in dealing rationally with relevant risk factors. After all, risk factors are defined precisely by the fact that they only provide for a statement of probability and do not always materialise. However, there is little cause for optimism in this respect. This is not only demonstrated by the way we deal with security incidents and crime today, which is often not very rational or evidence based. The findings of research being done on risk acceptance also suggest that our society will find it extremely difficult to react rationally, since these risks have practically everything that makes them particularly unacceptable: they are not taken voluntarily, but are imposed; they are difficult to control and usually have no positive benefits, but may have serious consequences and potentially affect all or many people.[29] And the expectation of prevention associated with this is almost never-ending, never sufficient, can always go even further, is always possible even earlier and always finds even further risk factors.

E. Conclusion

Artificial intelligence technologies offer new possibilities and the opportunity for innovative insights within the field of social control. They promise to do almost exactly what was previously impossible. At the same time, however, they also harbour massive problems and raise fundamental questions. Firstly, we can only inadequately calculate and assess the risks of future deviant behaviour – at least from today's perspective. Such techniques will therefore primarily reproduce existing images of criminality with all

28 Madeleine Genzsch, 'Harmonie durch Kontrolle? Chinas Sozialkreditsystem' in Tobias Loitsch (ed), *China im Blickpunkt des 21. Jahrhunderts* (Berlin/Heidelberg 2019) 136ff.; Wolfgang Behr, 'Gesichtsverlust 3.0' (*Geschichte der Gegenwart*, 18 April 2021) ‹https://geschichtedergegenwart.ch/gesichtsverlust-3-0/› accessed 18 April 2024.

29 Michael Zwick, 'Risikoakzeptanz und Gefahrenverhalten' in Thomas Fischer and Eric Hilgendorf (eds), *Gefahr* (Baden-Baden 2020) 40ff.

their distortions.[30] Where do the ethical limits lie for such AI? How can effective control and legal regulation of such algorithms be organised? Is calculating and surveying really superior to chance?

Secondly, this means that AI is acting as a motor for fundamental change in social control, which is now increasingly focussing on the management of risks in order to prevent potential harm in advance. Taken together, this will shape the security of the future, i.e., our image of security, disruption, and insecurity, and how society should deal with them. Security in this sense is becoming increasingly important. It is increasingly being framed as an ideal of absolute security. And it appears as a security constantly under threat in the face of risks – which, from a subjective point of view, creates uncertainty rather than security, resulting in a permanent loop. Where are the limits of such developments, such a constant shift forward?

Thirdly and finally, the change described and these strategies of risk management are associated with extremely problematic consequences, namely with chilling effects: the more comprehensively risk recognition and risk management are designed as forms of social control, the greater the pressure on the individual to behave in a compliant manner and not to attract attention. On the one hand, this gentle restriction of autonomy and freedom without coercion may be efficient. On the other hand, however, it is also dangerous precisely because it is less conspicuous and avoids societal debate. Where do the absolute limits for these forms of influence and manipulation lie in a democratic constitutional state? To what extent are our contemporary dogmatics, and constitutional law in particular, capable of preserving these limits in practice – especially considering the powerful image of the security of the future that is beginning to emerge?

30 Jan Wehrheim, 'Definitionsmacht und Selektivität in Zeiten neuer Kontrolltechnologien' in Henning Schmidt-Semisch and Henner Hess (eds), *Die Sinnprovinz der Kriminalität* (Wiesbaden 2014).

Automation and Mercy

Kiel Brennan-Marquez

This chapter explores the idea that machines are incapable of adopting a "merciful attitude" toward decision-making. If that is true, I argue it supplies a reason to be sceptical of many forms of legal automation - regardless of how powerful or computationally complex the instruments of automation become. To make this argument, I connect longstanding debates about the link between justice and the mercy, inspired by the scholastics, to contemporary literature on "algorithmic governance."

When automated systems replace human decision-makers, what is lost? Over the last few decades, scholars have developed two answers to this question: one focused on distributional accuracy,[1] the other on procedural integrity.[2] This chapter offers a different sort of answer. In some domains, I argue, the most salient drawback of automation is neither distributional nor procedural. Rather, it concerns the absence of a particular kind of attitude—a merciful disposition—on the part of those responsible for executing decisions.[3] Even at their most callous, human decision-makers tend to exercise some degree of forbearance. Judges dismiss charges. Executives grant pardons.[4] Guards unlock doors.[5] Not often, certainly not in every case —perhaps too little, perhaps too much. But whatever the exact calibration

---

1 *See* Ryan Calo & Danielle Citron, *The Automated Administrative State: A Crisis of Legitimacy*, 70 Emory L. J. 797 (2021); Andrea Roth, *Trial By Machine*, 104 Geo. L. J. 1245 (2016).

2 *See* Hannah Bloch-Wehba, *Visible Policing: Technology, Transparency, and Democratic Control*, 109 Cal. L. Rev. 917 (2021); Cary Coglianese & David Lehr, *Transparency and Algorithmic Governance*, 71 Admin. L. Rev. 1 (2019).

3 The chapter builds on past (co-authored) work in this vein. *See* Kiel Brennan-Marquez & Stephen E. Henderson, *Role-Reversibility, AI, and Equitable Justice – Or: Why Mercy Cannot Be Automated*, 114 J. Crim. L. & Criminology Online 1 (2023); Kiel Brennan-Marquez & Stephen E. Henderson, *Artificial Intelligence and Role-Reversible Judgment*, 109 J. Crim. L. & Criminology 137 (2019).

4 This function is typically associated with heads of state—presidents, governors, and the like. But the logic may reach further. *See* Lee Kovarsky, *Prosecutor Mercy*, 24 New Crim. L. Rev. 326 (2021).

5

of mercy, its *possibility* forms the backdrop of all juridical decision-making, regardless of institutional particulars, across space and time.

To "automate away" forbearance, then, would be to discard an essential ingredient of the administration of justice among human beings, as it has been practiced for millennia.[6] Would this change be welcome? In what follows, I explore this question by drawing a link between (1) longstanding puzzlement about the relationship between justice and mercy and (2) today's "algorithmic governance" debates. Those debates typically unfold by asking what someone poised to suffer adverse treatment might say about the legitimacy of human judgment, on one hand, or robotic artifice, on the other. This emphasis on the "perspective of the condemned" is understandable, even virtuous. But it has obscured a different question, one of potentially greater importance, which requires taking the perspective of *the executioner*. How do decisions look from the vantage point of those responsible for carrying them out? From an "internal point of view," what does it mean to be the one charged with wielding the axe—not the one awaiting its blade?

Does it matter, in short, if executioners are free, until the very last moment, to lay down their arms?[7] Does this freedom change the moral quality of law? Some might say no. Others might say yes, but in a troubling way. There is, after all, a concept of legality—quite alive in our institutional practices today—that sees "mercy" as a euphemism for arbitrariness and caprice, which might suggest that automation stands to *perfect*, not to imperil, human legal institutions.[8] My goal is not to dislodge either of these positions. It is far more modest. I aim to explore the implications of the "pro-mercy" view for the enterprise of legal automation. Here is the argument on offer:

If the executioner's freedom is a welcome aspect of legal systems—if mercy is integral to law's moral quality—then all legal automation, regardless of specifics, should be cause for concern.

The inverse is not necessarily true. Automation may *still* be cause for concern even if mercy is irrelevant (or inimical) to law's moral quality. But

6 *See* FERNANDA PIRIE, THE RULE OF LAWS: THE 4000 YEAR QUEST TO ORDER THE WORLD (2021); Martha Nussbaum, *Equity and Mercy*, PHIL. AND PUB. AFFAIRS (1993).

7 For present purposes, I count judges—and many other state officials who are not literally responsible for administering capital punishment—in the "executioner" category. *See* Robert Cover, *Violence and the Word*, 95 YALE L. J. 1601 (1986).

8 For an argument along these lines, see Jane Bambauer, *Filtered Dragnets and the Anti-Authoritarian Fourth Amendment*, 97 SO. CAL. L. REV. (forthcoming 2024).

we should be clear, either way, about what is at stake in today's "algorithmic governance" debates. In the end, those debates are not about technical specifics or jurisprudential minutiae. They are about the fundamental status of moral agency—the sense of freedom, or lack thereof—in our public life.

Since the scholastics, and perhaps long before, the relationship between mercy and justice has been uneasy. If mercy represents a departure from the requirements of justice—if mercy is "beyond" justice—how is it distinct from injustice? If justice supplies an answer, in principle, to all relevant cases, what role is left for mercy? For thinkers like Anselm and Aquinas, the urgency of this question was metaphysical: they sought to reconcile the promise of natural law—the notion that God's will is intelligible to human reason—with the idea that salvation is an act of grace, freely given and irreducible to law. Their solution, broadly speaking, was to imagine grace as a supplement to law. "God acts mercifully," Aquinas famously wrote, "not indeed by going against His justice, but by *doing something more than justice*."[9]

Modern legal systems have inherited a version of this solution. We frequently imagine mercy as something "more than" justice: not counteracting or overriding the latter's requirements, but improving upon them. On this view, justice becomes a necessary but insufficient condition of legal perfection. In their ideal form, the thought goes, legal institutions will be just, but they will not be *exclusively* just. They will also be merciful; they will also make room for forbearance.[10]

The "supplemental" idea of mercy is not without dissent. For some observers, mercy is a structural pathology: a bug, not a feature, of modern legal systems.[11] Whatever its appeal in particular cases, the argument goes, mercy—as an act of radical discretion—is antithetical to the rule of law. All mercy, regardless of moral valence, represents the triumph of personal will over law's impersonal majesty.

For the scholastics, to be clear, this was exactly the point. God's will, manifest as merciful salvation, was supposed to take precedence over natu-

9 THOMAS AQUINAS, SUMMA THEOLOGICA (Part I).

10 For an example of this form of argument, see Rachel Barkow, *The Ascent of the Administrative State and the Demise of Mercy*, 121 HARV. L. REV. 1332 (2008).

11 *See* Aziz Z. Huq, *The Difficulties of Democratic Mercy*, 103 CAL. L. REV. 1679 (2015); Dan Markel, *Against Mercy*, 88 MINN. L. REV. 1421 (2004).

ral law; or at any rate, natural law was not supposed to *preclude* merciful salvation. For modern sceptics, on the other hand, transplanting the puzzle to the realm of human legal institutions causes its solution to invert. Mercy, the modern sceptics insist, is no longer the thing that needs protecting; rather, it is what justice must be protected *from.* Foreclosing the space of mercy—taking institutional steps necessary to ensure that reason, to the maximal extent possible, *does* preclude will—is a central aspiration of "law's empire."[12]

From here, the debate has many subtle turns. Some have argued, for example, that counterposing justice and mercy is too simple—the wrong frame on the problem. Instead, mercy is best understood as a *continuation* of justice: a complement, not a supplement, to the application of discrete rules, especially in cases whose particularity, idiosyncrasy, or pathetic quality make them difficult to categorize ex ante.[13] Others, meanwhile, have argued that acts of mercy are no more (or less) unaccountable than ordinary acts of sovereign decision—which is certainly a problem to be managed in practice, but hardly a challenge to the rule of law in principle. In fact, advanced legal systems embed many "states of exception" into their everyday workings; forbearance is not special.[14]

Not surprisingly, these nuanced reconstructions of mercy have spawned equally nuanced rejoinders. Some observers argue, for example, that even if mercy harmonizes with rule-of-law principles, it tends, in practice, to be deployed regressively—and becomes objectionable for all the usual reasons that regressive aspects of the legal system are objectionable.[15] Along similar lines, other observers worry that forbearance mechanisms stunt the dynamic evolution of legal rules, causing doctrine to atrophy over time. Why bother refining normally-applicable rules, the thought goes, when mercy is there to "clean up" the exceptions?[16]

For present purposes, the bottom-line is that even though (1) mercy can be celebrated for many different reasons, (2) most observers attribute *some* value to mercy—such that its wholesale elimination from human legal

---

12 *See* Ronald Dworkin, Law's Empire (1986).

13 *See* Linda Meyer, "The Merciful State," in Forgiveness, Mercy, and Clemency (Hussain & Sarat, eds. 2007); Robin West, Caring For Justice (1997).

14 *See* Giordana Campagna, *The Miracle of Mercy*, 41 Oxford J. Legal Studies 1096 (2021).

15 *See* Markell, note 9.

16 *See* Mary Sigler, "Equity, Not Mercy," in The New Philosophy of Criminal Law (Flanders & Hoskins, eds. 2016).

systems would register as a loss. Furthermore, even those who express scepticism about mercy often do so in relative terms: they argue that mercy's value is, in certain contexts, not worth prioritizing over *other* values, not that it lacks value at all.

Some observers, to be clear, *do* argue that mercy is categorically unworthy of prioritization, insofar as they take mercy to conflict necessarily with the rule-of-law.[17] But that is by far the minority position: an outlier the rest of this chapter will set aside. If one believes that mercy is, ultimately, just a temptation to avoid—a contingent feature of legal systems that, under the right conditions, could and should be eliminated—the "mercilessness" of automated decisions will not be cause for concern. It may be cause for cheer. If, on the other hand, mercy has *some kind* of moral worth, the question becomes: can the radical freedom that mercy instantiates be replicated by non-humans means? Are the values served by mercy—whatever their exact content and contours—susceptible to automation?

Let us begin with what we know about *human* mercy. For one thing, mercy is inextricably linked to grace. Mercy is never compelled; its receipt is never a matter of right or entitlement, and its dispensation is never a matter of duty. Rather, mercy is, by necessity, "freely given."[18] We also know, moreover, that nothing about the conceptual structure of mercy—as grace —makes it the exclusive province of God. One *could* conceive of mercy that way; indeed, this is a plausible reconstruction of the modern sceptical view (discussed above), which wants to insist on the impermissibility of mercy within human institutions. But other positions are available. It is perfectly coherent—and familiar—to speak about human beings dispensing grace to one another. Furthermore, this is true whether or not grace is thought to have any connection to divinity. Even if grace is an inclination of divine origin, that hardly precludes human beings from sharing in its spirit. It may, indeed, embolden that outcome.

In other words, it is possible to imagine human officials as *agents* of grace, vested with the authority to decide, case by case, that otherwise-just punishment ought to be set aside. Premodern political theories made this connection literal, casting sovereign grace as a matter of divine delegation,

17 I imagine even these observers would be open, at least in principle, to attributing value to mercy in *other* settings—e.g., mercy exercised between soldiers on warring sides of a battle, or mercy exercised by a healer in the face of medical suffering. For present purposes, however, I leave this point to one side.

18 Paul Twambley, *Mercy and Forgiveness*, 36 ANALYSIS 84, 87 (1976).

whereas modern political theories take a more figurative approach to the "agency" question. Both, however, reach the same end. Grace is an inclination—perhaps of divine origin, perhaps not—to which humans can plausibly aspire, and around which human institutions can be built.

Does this logic extend to machines? Can we imagine machines as "agents of grace" in the same way that we imagine human beings in that mode? No, I want to suggest—because grace, like the mercy it occasions, is *attitudinal or dispositional* in nature. Seneca, the first great defender of mercy as a political virtue, defined it as an "inclination of the soul to mildness in exacting penalties."[19] In practice, this plays out, phenomenologically, as regard for "each particular case as a complex narrative of human effort in a world full of obstacles."[20] Abiding this inclination, the "merciful judge will not fail to judge the guilt of the offender," but she "will also see the many obstacles this offender faced... imagin[ing] what it was like to have been this particular offender, facing those particular obstacles with the resources of [their particular] history."[21]

This operation is not reducible to information-processing, the dry application of abstract rules to concrete facts. It requires imagination and, more importantly, the ability to self-conceive *as an agent*—because it requires the judge to be capable of considering how the world might have seemed from the offender's perspective, whether the judge herself might (or might not) have acted differently in the offender's shoes, and how the offender's moral frailty is connected to the moral frailty of human beings, writ large, simply in virtue of being human.[22] As Martha Nussbaum once put the point:

> The merciful attitude requires, and rests upon, a new attitude toward the self. The retributive attitude has a we/them mentality, in which judges set themselves above offenders, looking at their actions as if from a lofty height and preparing to find satisfaction in their pain. The [merciful] judge, by contrast, has both identification and sympathetic understanding.[23]

The merciful judge, in other words, not only regards the offender in a particular way; she also regards *herself* in a particular way. She looks both outward and inward—to the offender, to herself, to all of humanity—in deciding whether lenience is warranted in the particular case. This process

19 SENECA, DE CLEMENTIA (Book II Chap. 3).

20 Nussbaum, note 4 at 102.

21 *Ibid.*

22 *See* Brennan-Marquez & Henderson, *Artificial Intelligence and Role-Reversible Judgment*, note 1 (elaborating these dynamics at greater length).

23 Nussbaum, note 4 at 103.

may benefit from heuristics and parameters, but it admits of no shortcuts. The decision may be easy or difficult, pleasant or painful. But whatever its other qualities, the decision is always—and irreducibly—particular. It is truly about whether lenience *is warranted*, not whether lenience is compelled. For mercy, unlike justice, is never compulsory. It is always a free act.

None of this means, of course, that mercy is always exercised wisely or legitimately in practice. The form of mercy sketched above is a stylized aspiration—not a sociological description. On the ground, especially with respect decisions made "at scale," mercy is typically non-existent, and when it *does* transpire, it often looks more routine than majestic. Worse still, as sceptics like to remind us, the motivation behind particular instances of mercy can be venal, nepotistic, or vindictive. Forbearance can be bargained for and weaponized. It can be made into a political commodity. In short, not every exercise of mercy deserves celebration—far from it. If the possibility of mercy enhances the moral quality of law, it is not because mercy always bespeaks virtue, but in spite of the fact that it sometimes—too often —does not.

At some level, however, the "dark side" of mercy only underscores why the merciful attitude, as an attitude, is likely to elude machines. Mercy requires an inner life, mediated by a sense of frailty that unifies human experience across place, time, and context. This sense of frailty is what allows judges to be "inclined mildly" toward the moral shortcomings of others. And it is also on display when human mechanisms of mercy are corrupted or abused. In that case, frailty is what weakens the moral will of decision-makers, not what allows them to sympathize with the moral weakness of others. Either way, however, the upshot is the same. Mercy requires a kind of self-understanding (1) that machines are unlikely, in principle, to be capable of, and (2) that real-world efforts toward automation tend, in any case, to eliminate. This should give us pause. For it suggests that, in some contexts, the challenges that artificial intelligence pose to public life are more existential than practical—and that familiar fixes, centred on transparency, intelligibility, and democratic process, are unlikely to solve the core problem.

Towards a Usable Attack Graph for Safety and Security*

Tim Zander, Jürgen Beyerer

We revisit a mathematical framework for estimating risk of safety and security, which describes risk in the context of safety and security problems quantitatively and integratively. We will discuss this framework in the context of other literature. We identify similar ideas and solutions that help advance the framework by adding graph structure. Further, we discuss challenges and opportunities for application of these theories.

A. Introduction

Safety and security share many commonalities. Nevertheless, measures and systems to provide and ensure safety and security are planned and implemented often independently by different experts[1]. If both aspects were treated in an integrated manner, synergies could be realized, and costs could be reduced. If we want to ensure the safety and security of such complex systems as critical infrastructures and complex socio-technical systems, many disciplines will be stakeholders: engineering, law, economics, humanities, social sciences, etc. Still, there is no common formal language that fits all approaches; meaning that there is no common formal language concerning safety and security and no common language across all involved disciplines. This paper aims to discuss quantitative mathematical approaches from the literature and enhance them a bit to serve to describe and analyse safety and security problems in a unified fashion and to plan and optimize dedicated measures and systems.

* This work was supported by funding from the topic Engineering Secure Systems of the Helmholtz Association (HGF) and by KASTEL Security Research Labs.

1 Sara Sadvandi, Nicolas Chapon, and Ludovic Piètre-Cambacédès, "Safety and Security Interdependencies in Complex Systems and SoS: Challenges and Perspectives" (Omar Hammami, Daniel Krob, and Jean-Luc Voirin eds, Springer Berlin Heidelberg 2012); Giedre Sabaliauskaite and Aditya P Mathur, "Aligning Cyber-Physical System Safety and Security" (Michel-Alexandre Cardin and others eds, Springer International Publishing 2015).

The paper "A Framework for a Uniform Quantitative Description of Risk with Respect to Safety and Security"[2] established a quantitative formulation of risk (which we refer to as UQDR from now on). Uncertainties were modelled as probabilities, which are interpreted as degrees of belief (DoB). This is due to the risks of individuals (intelligent agents) being described from their entirely subjective views. Individuals draw their decisions based on their subjective assessments of potential costs and frequencies of event occurrence with potential biases in their estimation. The three roles sources of danger D, subjects of protection S, and protectors P were used for describing different entities in the framework. Sources of danger are endowed with a DoB distribution describing the probability of occurrence and are partitioned into subsets of random causes, carelessness, and intention.

A set of flanks of vulnerability F was assigned to each subject of protection. These flanks characterize different aspects of vulnerability, including mechanical, physiological, informational, economic, reputational, psychological vulnerabilities. The flanks of vulnerability are endowed with conditional DoBs that describe to which degree an incidence or an attack will be harmful. Additionally, each flank of vulnerability was endowed with a cost function that quantifies the costs that are charged to the subject of protection. Additionally, we will introduce the notion of multi-stage attack in this paper. Where an initial attack might be successful, such as gaining non-privileged remote user access to an office system. Only a secondary attack might lead to access to the industrial network, where a production system could be damaged[3]. Hence, we introduce in this paper a directed graph structure to the flanks of vulnerability, where one broken flank opens new flanks.

There are many methods in the literature of a graph or tree view of vulnerabilities in safety and security and its algorithm for finding solutions. Among those are techniques of probabilistic risk analysis such as fault and event trees[4] and that of (cyber-)security, such as attack trees and graphs[5]

2 Jürgen Beyerer and Jürgen Geisler, "A framework for a uniform quantitative description of risk with respect to safety and security" (2016) 1 European Journal for Security Research 135.

3 Markus Karch and others, "CrossTest: a cross-domain physical testbed environment for cybersecurity performance evaluations" (2022).

4 TJ Bedford and R Cooke, Probabilistic risk analysis: foundations and methods (Cambridge University Press April 2001).

5 Mohsen Khouzani, Zhe Liu, and Pasquale Malacaria, "Scalable min-max multi-objective cyber-security optimisation over probabilistic attack graphs" (2019) 278(3)

and its automatic generation[6]. Moreover, there exists work in which combines fault and attack trees[7].

The calculated risk in UQDR was balanced against the cost of protection measures, or in the case of a rational attacker, it would balance the benefit of a specific attack against its cost. We will discuss challenges that arise from this subjective view. As individual agents will choose the cost-optimal solutions, this often leads to worse general utility, as sometimes a protection measure is only effective if enough people commit to it, and then an attack could become completely unprofitable. There is often an imbalance between producers of digital goods and their users. The first is richly rewarded for innovations that carry with them heightened security risks, and the latter bears the majority of these risks. This moral hazard leads to the necessity that certain security measures should be enforced by regulation[8].

In the UQDR framework, challenges of the determination of the cost functions were discussed. Especially the estimation of the probabilities (DoBs) of the model. We revisit this in the context of existing Bayesian approaches for safety and security. Bayesian approach for probabilistic risk assessment is a well-established approach[9] and is used in applications such

European Journal of Operational Research 894;b Tadeusz Sawik, "Selection of optimal countermeasure portfolio in it security planning" (2013) 55(1) Decision Support Systems 156; Mohsen Khouzani and others, "Efficient numerical frameworks for multi-objective cyber security planning" (2016); Teodor Sommestad, Mathias Ekstedt, and Hannes Holm, "The cyber security modeling language: a tool for assessing the vulnerability of enterprise system architectures" (2012) 7(3) IEEE Systems Journal 363; Nathaporn Poolsappasit, Rinku Dewri, and Indrajit Ray, "Dynamic security risk management using bayesian attack graphs" (2011) 9(1) IEEE Transactions on Dependable and Secure Computing 61; Lei Wang and others, "An attack graph-based probabilistic security metric" (2008); Hatem M Almohri and others, "Security optimization of dynamic networks with probabilistic graph modeling and linear programming" (2015) 13(4) IEEE Transactions on Dependable and Secure Computing 474.

6 Alyzia-Maria Konsta and others, "Survey: Automatic generation of attack trees and attack graphs" (2024) 137 Computers & Security 103602 ⟨https://www.sciencedirect.com/science/article/pii/S0167404823005126⟩.

7 E Andre and others, "Parametric Analyses of Attack-Fault Trees" (IEEE Computer Society June 2019) ⟨https://doi.ieeecomputersociety.org/10.1109/ACSD.2019.00008⟩; Rajesh Kumar and Mariëlle Stoelinga, "Quantitative Security and Safety Analysis with Attack-Fault Trees" (January 2017).

8 Jeffrey Vagle, "Cybersecurity and Moral Hazard" (2020) 23 Stanford Technology Law Review ⟨https://ssrn.com/abstract=3055231⟩.

9 Dana Kelly and Curtis Smith, Bayesian inference for probabilistic risk assessment: A practitioner's guidebook (Springer Science & Business Media 2011).

as deep water drilling operations[10]. A combined risk estimation of safety and security for process industries with Bayesian networks was done in[11] for security alone, efficient algorithms for solving Bayesian Stackelberg games have been found.[12] Moreover, this has been applied to network security to optimally decide which initial security measures to take and which are the optimal online measures to take while receiving signals.

Challenges arise for the costs of certain security or safety measures or the cost of successful attacks or incidents. For that, the opinion of experts can be a viable tool to get valuable data to fit into a model. The optimal combination of multiple expert opinions is exceptionally useful researched field[13]. With recent advances in large language models, for some cases, it might be an expert on its own[14] and has been shown to help estimate some values[15]. We will discuss how this can be useful in the UQDR.

Often, it is also useful to directly influence the attackers to believe via some deterrence signal such as that of insider threat[16] or other[17].

---

10 Jyoti Bhandari and others, "Risk analysis of deepwater drilling operations using Bayesian network" (2015) 38 Journal of Loss Prevention in the Process Industries 11 ⟨ https://www.sciencedirect.com/science/article/pii/S0950423015300188⟩.

11 Priscilla Grace George and VR Renjith, "Evolution of Safety and Security Risk Assessment methodologies towards the use of Bayesian Networks in Process Industries" (2021) 149 Process Safety and Environmental Protection 758.

12 Praveen Paruchuri and others, "Playing games for security: an efficient exact algorithm for solving Bayesian Stackelberg games." (Lin Padgham and others eds, IFAAMAS 2008) ⟨http://dblp.uni-trier.de/db/conf/atal/aamas2008-2.html#ParuchuriPMTOK08⟩.

13 Robert T Clemen and Robert L Winkler, "Combining Probability Distributions From Experts in Risk Analysis" (1999) 19(2) Risk Analysis 187 ⟨https://ideas.repec.org/a/wly/riskan/v19y1999i2p187-203.html⟩.

14 Siru Liu and others, "Assessing the Value of ChatGPT for Clinical Decision Support Optimization" [2023] medRxiv ⟨ https://www.medrxiv.org/content/early/2023/02/23/2023.02.21.23286254⟩.

15 Michael Haman, Milan Školník, and Michal Lošťák, "AI dietician: Unveiling the accuracy of ChatGPT's nutritional estimations" (2024) 119 Nutrition 112325 ⟨ https://www.sciencedirect.com/science/article/pii/S0899900723003532⟩.

16 William Casey and others, "Compliance signaling games: toward modeling the deterrence of insider threats" (2016) 22(3) Computational and Mathematical Organization Theory 318 ⟨ http://dx.doi.org/10.1007/s10588-016-9221-5⟩.

17 NJ Ryan, "Five Kinds of Cyber Deterrence" (2017) 31(3) Philosophy & Technology 331 ⟨http://dx.doi.org/10.1007/s13347-016-0251-1⟩.

B. Attack Graph model of safety and security

In the UQDR framework, the modelling included simple flanks of vulnerabilities that could be breached, and some damage could occur. We extend the model by introducing an attack graph where the flanks are now the edges of a graph, and the nodes are the elevated states of an attacker. These states could be increased privileges in a computer network. But also such things as stolen or forged access cards on the streets or an attacker who hid in a cabinet till the office closed. Some flanks require no elevated state but can be exploited directly, such as a distributed denial of service attack.

In the UQDR framework, the vulnerability with respect to attacks a or incidents i on flank $f \in F$ of $d \in D$ was modelled as a DoB-density with some degree of success β, if a or i hits s via f. Attacking system s via flank f with success β incurs a cost $c(s, f, \beta) \in [0, \infty)$.

Figure 1: Flow graph of the conceptual role model as introduced in UQDR[18].

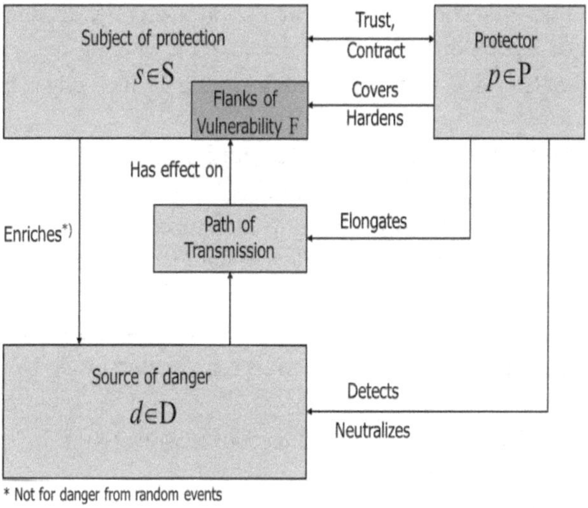

18 (Beyerer and Geisler [n 2]).

We build up on the ideas of Yunxiao Zhang and Pasquale Malacaria[19], where a Bayesian Stackelberg game on attack graphs with preventive security portfolio was defined. Some choice of security controls, such as online ones, could mitigate the probabilities of attacks.

I. Attack-graph

Precisely, we define a probabilistic attack graph similar to that existing in literature[20] where $G = (A, V, E, h, t, p, s, T, M)$ is a directed multi-graph where:

- A: is a set of attackers. (This was not defined before.)
- V: is the set of vertices (or nodes); a privileged state of an attacker in the organization.
- E: is the multi-set of directed edges. Note that there can be multiple edges between two vertices, corresponding to different atomic attacks between two attackers' privilege states. Equivalently, an edge e can be represented by the ordered triplet $e = (i, j, k)$, where i and j are the tail and head of the edge, and $k$is its index among all such edges that go from i to j.
- $h: E \rightarrow V$: returns the head node of an edge.
- $t: E \rightarrow V$: returns the tail node of an edge.
- $p: E \times A \rightarrow (0,1]$: defines the conditional success probability for an attacker to progress from one privileged state to another using a specific attack step. If an attacker has reached privilege state i and aims to advance to state j using attack step$e$, where $j = h(e)$ and $i = t(e)$, then the likelihood of successful advancement is represented by p_e. Until then, the values for p_e are assumed to be known.
- $s \in V$: one of the vertices labelled as source, specifying the initial privilege state of an attacker.
- $T \subset V$: a subset of the vertices labelled as targets (or sink vertices). These are the privilege states or final attacks (e.g. deletion of all the

19 Yunxiao Zhang and Pasquale Malacaria, "Bayesian Stackelberg games for cyber-security decision support" (2021) 148 Decision Support Systems 113599 ⟨https://www.sciencedirect.com/science/article/pii/S0167923621001093⟩.

20 Khouzani, Liu, and Malacaria (n 5).

data on the computer network[21] or destruction of the machinery[22]) that constitute the potential goal of an attacker.
- $M: V \to S$: a membership function that assigns the ownership of a node to a subject. (This was not defined before.)

Note that this is indeed potentially a graph with cycles. For example, one might compromise a machine up to some user-level account. The administrator then deletes the attacker's account, which loses the attacker the privileges he has gained so far.

If the attacker successful reaches $v \in T$ similar as in UQDR incurs a cost $c(v) \subset [0, \infty)$ on subject. Note that compared to the cost before, we replaced the flank with the node and got rid of the degree of success. If there is the need for such a degree of success, one can introduce multiple nodes, each representing some degree of success, and model the probability distribution of the success discretely via the conditional success probability p or, if needed, a success parameter β is added to the target nodes in T. With this, we essentially reproduce the expressibility of the original UQDR framework but can now express more complex problems with agents. It also extends the settings of the approach existing in literature[23] as now multiple agents control different parts of the security graph. This leads to a complex multiplayer game-theoretic situation.

Moreover, the owner or protector has a belief about the nodes attackers have breached (say some set $A \subset V$), and about the effectiveness of countermeasures at a certain cost (decrease of success probability p) and the costs to him when a node is breached ($c(v)$). If we give the node owner or its protector as in UQDR some security portfolio of countermeasures on some edges $E_r \subset E$, then they can choose which measures to apply to harden the flanks. This portfolio $\widehat{\mathrm{E}}_{\mathrm{r}}$ can be represented as the set of all possible countermeasures, where each countermeasure is a tuple containing its effect on the success probability for an attacker a on an edge e:

$$\widehat{E}_{\mathrm{r}} = \{(e, p_r(e, a), c_r) : e \in (E_r), a \in A\}$$

21 Oxford Analytica, "Cyberactivity in Ukraine signals Russian limits" [2022] (oxan-db) Emerald Expert Briefings.
22 David Kushner, "The real story of stuxnet" (2013) 50(3) ieee Spectrum 48.
23 Zhang and Malacaria (n 18).

to apply to harden the flanks. Meaning, that a countermeasurer on the edge e will reduce $p(e,a)$ to $p_r(e,a)$ but cost c_r. They can choose the best countermeasures in a two-player game situation, as with techniques introduced before by others[24]. Note that the belief about breached nodes can be incorporated into the probability p, as the detection of a privileged attacker or at least the presumption about one present through improved detection measures will influence its success probably of the following attacks. The membership function introduces the ownership of different nodes to different agents, which can be used to analyse more complex scenarios.

II. Risk in the attack graph

The DoB-risk of a member m $\in$ M can be calculated as follows. Let $V_m = \{v \in V : M(v) = m\}$, some belief-function of breaches $p_b : V \rightarrow [0,1]$ or more sophisticated some belief-function about multiple types of attackers at a node $p_b : V \rightarrow [0,1]^A$. Moreover, let $\pi(v,a) \in \{0,1\}$ with $a \in A$ be an indication function that attacker a has attacked and $\widetilde{E} \subset \widehat{E}$ multi-set of edges where the countermeasures are applied. The risk of m is the following;

$$\sum_{v \in V} \sum_{a \in A} c(v) \cdot p(v) \cdot \pi(v,a) + \sum_{e \in \widetilde{E}} c_r .$$

If we take the approach as a multi-step game, then the unintended danger can be modelled in the form of an attacker where the $\pi(v,i)$ is always 1, meaning there is always the chance of such an event taking place. The DoB-probability $b_m(a,v)$ of $m \in M$ whether an attacker a has compromised node v is conditioned on the full history of all attacks of all attackers in the past. From that and his belief about the attacker function below, a belief about the next step of the attacker can be formed.

Now, on the attacker side, the attacker has certain knowledge about the attack graph. In fact, we replace the conditional success probability $p : E \rightarrow (0,1]$ with a belief $p_d : E \rightarrow [0,1]$ of the attacker d of the probability. For many attacks, such as a zero day's exploit[25], the ordinary attacker might not know about these attacks. The attacker also has a cost function for conducting an attack.

24 Ibid.

25 Leyla Bilge and Tudor Dumitraş, "Before we knew it: an empirical study of zero-day attacks in the real world" (2012).

In the UQDR framework, the costs of an attacker were described with $c_{\text{Effort}}(a, s, f)$ for the effort executing an attack a on s via f. $c_{\text{Penalty}}(s, f, \beta)$ described the penalty for being caught while conducting damage β and $g(s, f, \beta)$ was the gain of an successful attack of degree β. Now, in our new graph description, the cost of the attacker is $c_{\text{Effort}}(e)$ on $e \in E$ on the condition that the attacker has reached node h(e). Moreover, attacking and being caught has some penalty $c_{\text{Penalty}}(e)$ associated with it. The DOB-probability of being caught $Pr(\text{Penalty} \mid s, f, b) = 1 - Pr(\neg\text{Penalty} \mid s, f, b)$ becomes $Pr(\text{Penalty} \mid \text{nodes attacked till now})$. The reason the condition for nodes attacked till now is that while some notes, such as lock picking, might not leave any trace in some circumstances, other nodes, such as breaking a door to enter known at some point and countermeasures will be taken and the attacker is tried to be caught. The cost of an initial attack such as vulnerability scanning [26]might be very cheap to conduct. Moreover, such as with vulnerability scanning, the penalty cost might be even zero.[27] Additionally, there is a gain $G(a, t)$ for the attacker when they reach a node in$t \in T$.

The effort of an attacker a choosing attack path $P = (e_0, \ldots, e_l)$ in the attack graph is then described by the following formula;

$$\sum\nolimits_{0 \le i \le l} c_{\text{Effort}}(e_0) \cdot \prod\nolimits_{j < i} g(a, e_j),$$

meaning that the attacker only can conduct an attack if he gained access to the next node. The penalty for a path can be calculated as

$$\sum\nolimits_{0 \le i \le l} Pr(\text{Penalty} \mid \text{nodes attacked till now}) \cdot c_{\text{Penalty}}(e_i) \cdot \prod\nolimits_{j < i} g(a, e_j).$$

Finally, the gain of the attacker is

$$\sum\nolimits_{0 \le i \le l,\, t(e_i) \in T} G(a, t(e_i)) \cdot \prod\nolimits_{j < i} g(a, e_j).$$

Now, a rational attacker without countermeasure will attack if the sum of all these three costs is positive.

Ultimately, the game is played as follows. The node owners set up their security measures to reduce p on the edges leading to or from their nodes. Here is already a moral hazard at play, as the ones bearing the cost of the attack

26 Munawar Hafiz and Ming Fang, "Game of detections: how are security vulnerabilities discovered in the wild?" (2016) 21 Empirical Software Engineering 1920.

27 Jamie O'Hare, Rich Macfarlane, and Owen Lo, "Identifying Vulnerabilities Using Internet-Wide Scanning Data" (January 2019).

are the software's users further down the graph and not the software company further. Then, the attacker attacks and takes over some nodes. Again, the node owner applies countermeasures given their signal about compromised nodes, cost structure, their own cost, and so forth. So, the game is, in its most general form, a multi-leader multi-follower game with incomplete information[28]. Now additionally, the attacker also will try to improve their attacking strategy, i.e. a path or, more generally, a probability distribution of paths through the attack graph to maximize their gain. However, for many applications, it might be enough for single-leader multi-follower, multi-leader single-follower, or ordinary two-player Stackelberg games. For the most general form, it remains unclear if such a game will produce meaningful strategies to apply in the real world, even if there is a chance of finding very good ones with recent developments in reinforcement learning[29].

III. Example: Multiple Stakeholders

As we modelled the graph in a multi-agent way, we can now express scenarios with multiple node owners. For example, machine building company A sells machines with a certain AI functionality that needs remote access to a machine learning cluster owned by some company C. These machines come with a software vulnerability that would grant total control of the machine to an attacker who could access it over the network. Now, this machine is owned and run by Manufacturer B. Now, B has an incentive to fix this vulnerability, as a malicious person or a hack of company C could compromise the whole industrial network of C. Now, every one of these agents has their incentive, and potentially, A and C could have the incentive not to fix the security of their product, leaving B to fix the security. Which might be much harder and costly for B or might be impossible because all flanks till B's target are not in B's possession (see Figure 2). Moreover, if there are many machine owners just

28 Didier Aussel and Anton Svensson, "A Short State of the Art on Multi-Leader-Follower Games" in Stephan Dempe and Alain Zemkoho (eds), Bilevel Optimization: Advances and Next Challenges (Springer International Publishing 2020) ⟨https://doi.org/10.1007/978-3-030-52119-6_3⟩.

29 Weichao Mao and Tamer Başar, "Provably Efficient Reinforcement Learning in Decentralized General-Sum Markov Games" [2022] Dynamic Games and Applications ⟨http://dx.doi.org/10.1007/s13235-021-00420-0⟩; Sailik Sengupta and Subbarao Kambhampati, "Multi-agent Reinforcement Learning in Bayesian Stackelberg Markov Games for Adaptive Moving Target Defense" (2020) abs/2007.10457 CoRR ⟨https://arxiv.org/abs/2007.10457⟩.

like B, then the average cost per machine owner might be a price everyone is willing to pay. But then again, we are stuck on the problem of software's external effects. This means that with enough software users, the price for producing the bug fix is high, but the cost per copy is near zero[30].

Figure 2: Attack graph for the example of a machine with a software vulnerability. And the ownership of the edges, respectively, flanks denoted.

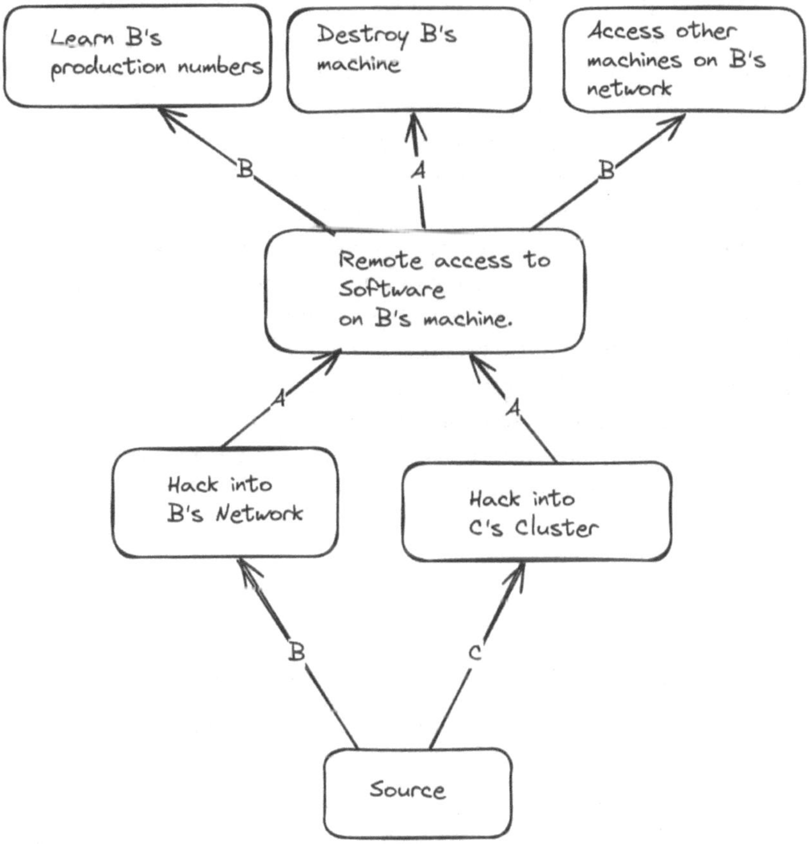

30 Ross Anderson and Tyler Moore, "Information Security Economics -- and Beyond" (Alfred Menezes ed, Springer Berlin Heidelberg 2007).

In some other cases, the attacker might have a false belief in what type of attack he does. They might believe that they have gained privileged access to some computer system, which will lead to future gains. But instead, they might be trapped in a honey pot[31] or a scammer might believe he has some potential victim, but it is just some scam-baiter trying to fool the scammer[32]. All in all, the attacker has to choose its initial victim, and as outlined in the paper[33], if enough targets of the attacker are false positive, the profitability of the attacker will completely collapse. Or in terms of our attack graph, the attacker will try to estimate the success probability of a certain edge by doing such things as writing an unbelievable email or conducting a vulnerability scan. Now, the attacker has some belief about the probability of an attack being successful on edge e owned by member $m(h(e))$ and spends $c_{\text{Effort}}(e)$ to do it. Now, there will be only very few edges that are worth attacking, but it completely relies on its strategy to improve the true-positive rate. Moreover, if this rate is low enough and the penalty high enough, the attack might be completely unprofitable[34] (see Figure 3). Moreover, if enough people commit to some countermeasures to some form of attacks, such as a car theft, the underlying economy such as that of car jacking might completely collapse (see Section 13.2.2 "Deterrence" of Ross Anderson's Book Security Engineering[35]). The problem here lies in the incentive; the installation of countermeasures costs money, but normally, the risk is not big enough to make an effort or is externalized to a third party, such as an insurance company.

31 Marcin Nawrocki and others, "A Survey on Honeypot Software and Data Analysis" (2016) abs/1608.06249 CoRR ⟨ http://arxiv.org/abs/1608.06249⟩.

32 Andreas Zingerle and Linda Kronman, "Humiliating Entertainment or Social Activism? Analyzing Scambaiting Strategies Against Online Advance Fee Fraud" (2013); Lauri Tuovinen and Juha Röning, "Baits and beatings: Vigilante justice in virtual communities" [2007] Proceedings of CEPE 397; Matthew Edwards, Claudia Peersman, and Awais Rashid, "Scamming the scammers: towards automatic detection of persuasion in advance fee frauds" (2017); Cormac Herley, "Why do Nigerian Scammers Say They are from Nigeria?" [2012] Proceedings of the Workshop on the Economics of Information Security.

33 Herley (n 32).

34 Ibid.

35 Ross Anderson, Security Engineering: A Guide to Building Dependable Distributed Systems (3rd edn, Wiley 2020).

Figure 3: Attack graph of Advanced Fee Frauds of people responding to the scammer. The group to the left are people who are easily susceptible to such attacks and have a high success rate p after an initial contact is made. The group to the middle are scam-baiters, which have a very low success rate q to convert contact to money but want to mimic the left group. The groups to the right are hard to scam people with also a very low success rate r. The replies of this group can be avoided by making outrageous claims in the initial contact email. However, this also increases the number of scam-baiters, as they easily recognize these emails in their honey pot email addresses, or some of the right groups may become scam-baiters by chance out of interest.

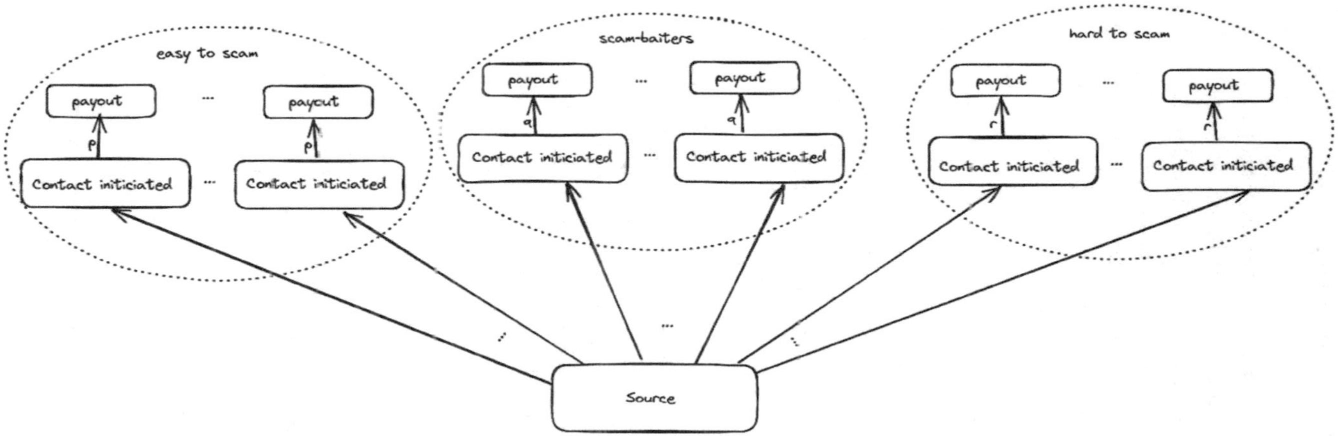

IV. Granularity of the attack graph

Another effect we see is that there is often a specialization of certain attacks. The one conducting a distributed denial of service (DDoS) attack might not be the one that gives access to the devices involved in the first place. This increases the problem of effective measures against such problems. Increasing the punishment of the DDoS-attacker directly did little help to mitigate the problems, but forcing the administrators of the compromised servers to get rid of the access of the perpetrator did follow with a decrease of such attacks[36]. So, finding the right level in the attack graph to mitigate problems seems like the key to finding optimal utility for the common. As with the smart device, which will become the next DDoS device. Should the internet provider be forced to block any traffic from owned devices, or should the device manufacturer be held accountable, which might be non-existent anymore at the time when the device becomes a problem. For a single entity such as a company, the right security implementation might still be higher up in the attack graph as many nodes near the source s might be hard to fix for a single entity that is affected by the attacks.

We can also incorporate the safety aspect into the attack graph model. Certain attacks only become available when certain safety measures fail. For example, a power outage might cause a security camera system to shut down. So, an attacker can now sneak past the camera surveillance area without much risk. Or, because of the power outage, a remote admin might not be able to receive any info on the server they administer because they live in the countryside with a single power line reaching their house. While the server is still running, alerts of the server system fail to reach the administrator.

A general limitation of the attack graph is that it is non-suitable for doing fine-grained safety analysis as the graph will be too complex for a human to construct the graph and oversee the analysis. While there exists work that automatically constructs certain attack graphs[37], in many scenarios using other techniques may help reduce the overall complexity of a fault tree. The

36 Ben Collier and others, "Influence, infrastructure, and recentering cybercrime policing: evaluating emerging approaches to online law enforcement through a market for cybercrime services" (2022) 32(1) Policing and Society 103.

37 Ferda Özdemir Sönmez, Chris Hankin, and Pasquale Malacaria, "Attack Dynamics: An Automatic Attack Graph Generation Framework Based on System Topology, CAPEC, CWE, and CVE Databases" (2022) 123 Computers & Security 102938 ⟨https://www.sciencedirect.com/science/article/pii/S0167404822003303⟩.

fault tree may express a general Boolean statement[38] and to incorporate this into the graph structure, for example, any AND-statement would need to incorporate any subset of the atoms as a node in the graph. Which is, of course, the cardinality of the power set of the set of all atoms, which grows exponentially with the number of atoms.

V. Attack-fault trees

Because of the limitation just stated, one has to look at the attack graph at a subsystem-size granularity, as tracing any screw of every security camera attachment as a failure mode in the attack graph is infeasible. However, one can break down the subsystems in a fault tree. The more recent approach that one can use is one of the so-called attack-fault trees as described in research before[39], which are in these works connected to automata theory[40]. Stochastic timed automata (STA) were used in a paper[41] to do stochastic model checking.

They gave concrete examples, such as a fire safety door example, which highlighted the friction point between safety and security. A fire door might be used as an exit by the user of the building. This can already be a security risk, as intruders or insiders can steal stuff and then leave the building unnoticed through some fire exit. Also, such doors tend to be used as an exit for convenience, such as smoking, and grant re-entry by blocking the door from being closed with something. Also, people can easily use it as an entrance if enough people use it as an exit and if there is enough anonymity present. This helps an attacker to sneak in without passing by typical building access control such as a doorman. One solution could be to lock the fire door, weld it shut, or not construct any in the beginning. Which, sadly, can lead to a catastrophe in the event of a fire. The risk might still be taken by the owner to prevent immediate costs like stealing or extra safety measures[42]. A more typical solution in countries where fire safety rules tend to be enforced, apart from making the door only open from the inside, is to install alarms that either make a loud noise when the door is opened or

38 Balbir S Dhillon and Chanan Singh, Engineering Reliability (Wiley series in systems engineering & analysis, John Wiley & Sons April 1981).

39 Andre and others (n 7); Kumar and Stoelinga (n 7).

40 Arto Salomaa, Theory of automata (Elsevier 2014).

41 Kumar and Stoelinga (n 7).

42 Margrethe Kobes and others, "Building safety and human behaviour in fire: A literature review" (2010) 45(1) Fire Safety Journal 1 ⟨https://www.sciencedirect.com/science/article/pii/S0379711209001167⟩.

trigger some (potentially silent) alarm in the security system. This prevents the door from being used for convenience and mitigates most attacks but keeps the fire exit usable in an emergency. However, cheap solutions tend not to be very robust against some forms of attacks, such as lock picking the latch. So, some sort of risk prevails in any case.

Figure 4: Security improvements such as having no fire door or locked fire doors such as having barred windows will greatly reduce the likelihood of the success of the four left-most attack paths. But this will also, for many buildings, greatly increase the risk on the right-most path, which ends in personal injuries.

In another paper[43] a new type of parametric timed automata (PTA) with (discrete) rational-valued weight parameters named parametric weighted timed automata (PWTA) was defined, and it was shown that attack-fault trees "equipped with an execution time and a rich cost structure that includes the cost incurred by an attacker and damage inflicted on the organization." could be translated to these automata. The addition of time is quite a meaningful feature, as cracking some cryptography might take years, but the data it encrypts might only be valuable for a very restricted time frame. Or an automatic update might patch a vulnerability at midnight, so if the initial attack is not complete by that time, this path will be closed. Also, our cost functions can be thought of as multi-valued. So, some parameters are more constrained, and it is hard to find an extra budget. The administrator's time budget might be limited, and another one might be out of the monetary budget. So should the administrator rather read logs and look for signs of intruders, or should they test and deploy updates to the server? There is no reason why the cost in the upper-defined attack graph can include a multi-valued cost structure.

Moreover, the paper also showed that such attack-fault trees can be translated to an acyclic-directed graph and solved with a model checker stemming from automata theory. This closes the loop, as now such graphs, can be thought of as a subgraph of the bigger attack graph. While this resulting graph might not be very accessible for a human, at least there is language describing the impact of a metal piece with poor tolerances in a small lock to the whole multiplayer system where this piece contributes to computerized reasoning. Moreover, with the rise of very capable large language models such as GPT4[44], there seem to be better chances than ever to build such attack graphs, covering the problem in great detail without the need for a great amount of skilled human labour[45].

C. Conclusion

This paper presents an enhanced mathematical framework heavily building on works of others for estimating safety and security risks within complex systems, integrating a probabilistic attack graph model with the use of

43 Andre and others (n 7).
44 OpenAI and others, GPT-4 Technical Report (2024).
45 Farzad Nourmohammadzadeh Motlagh and others, Large Language Models in Cybersecurity: State-of-the-Art (2024).

the Unified Quantitative Description of Risk (UQDR) framework. This approach continues to model uncertainties as degrees of belief (DoB) and incorporates Bayesian statistical decision theory, game theory, and graph theory to provide a tool for the analysis of potential vulnerabilities and attack vectors.

The attack graph model is a directed multi-graph that outlines the stages of an attacker's progression through a system, including potential targets and the associated costs of attacks for both attackers and defenders. It includes functions for attack success probability, detection probability, mitigation controls, and the membership function assigning the ownership of nodes to subjects. This model allows for strategic planning and optimization of security measures but also highlights the problem of multiple stakeholders for optimal security. Risk is quantified by considering the costs of successful attacks and the effectiveness of security measures in this attack graph. For future work, we suggest focusing on methodologies for using Large Language Models to semi-automatically generate the structure of these attack graphs and to help estimate their parameters (e.g., costs, probabilities) from technical reports and expert interviews. This would address the key challenge of constructing these complex models manually and improve their practical applicability. The framework can express problems such as moral hazards and incentive misalignments, emphasizing the need for regulation to enforce security measures from the bottom up.

In Summary, the paper's contributions are an advanced probabilistic attack graph. With it we highlight the trade-offs between safety and security measures, the challenges of granularity, and confirm the potential for automated tools to assist in model construction. We underscore the importance of multi-stakeholder coordination and the integration of artificial intelligence to develop effective, practical security measures. Future research should further explore the practical application of this model, a wide range of data, and the effectiveness of deterrence strategies in reducing the likelihood and impact of attacks.

The Risk-based Responsibility for Algorithmic Failures

Anna Beckers, Gunther Teubner

Algorithmic failures pose significant risk to society and are capable to create uncertainty and hereby undermine trust in new technologies. Against this background, the EU has started to regulate algorithmic operations by focussing on the risks that they pose. In this contribution, we argue that the EU's risk-based regulation and liability approach is to be welcomed generally but requires adaption regarding the definition of risks and related allocation of responsibility to the various actors involved in algorithmic operations. Rather than focussing on the severity of risk as a benchmark and centre human failures, we propose a risk-based responsibility that focuses on the risks deriving from the integration of algorithms within different socio-digital institutions.

A. Algorithms, Risks, and Regulation: A critique of the European AI Act

Society's increasing reliance on algorithms brings about significant uncertainty. Large responsibility gaps for wrongful decisions appear under current law when autonomous algorithms are employed in decision-making, when algorithms and humans make collective decisions, or when machines operate in an interconnected manner. As a result, people damaged by algorithmic operations have minimal chances of success in obtaining compensation. At the same time, the lack of clearly delineated responsibility subjects challenges the regulation of technology: Who should be subject to regulation? Who should respond to the risks of algorithmic operation?

Furthering trust and mitigating uncertainty via allocating risks have been the main goals of various legislative initiatives, particularly in the EU, in their regulatory approach to new technologies.[1] Such a risk-based approach shifts the perspective: Rather than viewing technology regulation through the lens of specific technical properties or assuming ex-ante legal

1 Marise Cremona, 'Introduction', in Marise Cremona (ed), *New Technologies and EU Law* (OUP 2017) 2.

obligations, risk-based regulation defines as the source of responsibility the tangible social dangers such technologies may create. However, there is still significant uncertainty about how the risk categories should be defined.

In the recently adopted AI Act[2], the EU proposes the severity of the risk as the primary criterion for imposing obligations on actors. The AI Act prohibits systems that carry an unbearable risk, places significant obligations on manufacturers and deployers of so-called high-risk systems, and imposes transparency obligations for those actors involved in other AI systems that do not fall within the two categories. An exception to this risk-orientation is the regulation of general-purpose AI and foundation models. Here, specific technological properties serve as a basis for responsibility. A further differentiation is made according to the type of harm caused by a particular AI system. The literature proposes similar classifications, distinguishing between safety risks and fundamental rights risks.[3]

However, such categorization of risks along the type of damage faces several problems. First, the abstract concept of severity is not sufficiently sensitive to the social context. Generative AI, such as ChatGPT, is a striking example. Whether generative AI produces a high or low risk ultimately depends on its concrete use in a particular context. Generative AI sometimes creates high systemic risks to society; sometimes, its risks are minimal. ChatGPT-produced birthday invitations or out-of-office replies are not particularly risky, while mass production of racist posts on social media creates enormous political damage.[4] The same technology is used in both cases but the risks differ drastically. In addition, classifying risk according to severity may be of little help for the normative allocation of risk to different actors. A classification into high-/low-risk or types of harm does not provide sufficient normative guidance about the person to be held liable should a risk materialize.

2 Regulation 2024/1689 of the European Parliament and of the Council laying down harmonised rules on artificial intelligence (Artificial Intelligence Act) and amending certain Union legislative acts, OJ L, 2024/1689, 12 July 2024.

3 Cf Christiane Wendehorst, 'Liability for Artificial Intelligence: The Need to Address Both Safety Risks and Fundamental Rights Risks' in S Voeneky, Philipp Kellmeyer, Oliver Mueller and Wolfram Burgard (eds), *The Cambridge Handbook of Responsible Artificial Intelligence: Interdisciplinary Perspectives* (CUP 2022) 189 ff.

4 Philipp Hacker, Andreas Engel and Marco Maurer, 'Regulating ChatGPT and other Large Generative AI Models' (2023) *FAccT '23: Proceedings of the 2023 ACM Conference on Fairness, Accountability, and Transparency* 1112.

The European approach in the EU, with the AI Act and the complementary liability rules, needs to be criticized even more harshly. While it aims to respond to the highest AI risks, it nevertheless fails to address the truly novel risk that artificial intelligence has brought about – the autonomy of algorithms. Via establishing legal obligations for different risk situations, the EU legislation addresses only human failures in dealing with AI but ignores algorithmic failures that happen independently of human behaviour. The liability rules to which the AI Act refers are mainly fault-based liability[5] and product liability[6]. And here comes the crucial point. When the human actors involved have fulfilled all their obligations but the algorithms make nevertheless wrongful decisions, neither tort liability nor product liability will compensate the victims for the damages.[7] Thus, the ambitious EU legislation fails to remove a large responsibility gap and hereby fail to realise the objective of fostering trust by addressing and mitigating risks.

While a risk approach is to be welcomed in general, the legally relevant qualification of risks should be adapted in two ways. First, risk-based regulation needs to be sensitive to the social context in which technologies are used. And second, it needs to address not only risks stemming from human action of manufacturing, operating, importing or deploying new technologies, but also algorithmic failures. Therefore, we propose a risk typology that addresses both the dangers of autonomous algorithmic decisions and their occurrences in different socio-digital institutions. This typology, we suggest, provides more robust criteria for connecting specific risks with proximate responsible actors and appropriate legal rules. In contrast to

---

5 Initially, this link between EU-based regulatory duties and national tort liability was explicitly proposed in the Directive on AI Liability, see European Commission, Proposal for a Directive on adapting non-contractual civil liability rules to artificial intelligence, COM(2022) 486 final. With the adoption of the AI Act only and the recent explicit withdrawal of the Proposal for a AI Liability Directive, the exact contours of liability for breach of the AI Act in national liability rules will depend on the interpretation by national courts and the parallel national implementation of the Product Liability Directive. Cf for this interrelation between AI regulation and AI liability Gerhard Wagner, 'Liability Rules for the Digital Age' (2022) *Journal of European Tort Law* 191, 232 ff.

6 See the 2024 revised Directive on liability for defective Products, Directive 2024/2853 of the European Parliament and of the Council of 23 October 2024 on liability for defective products and repealing Council Directive 85/374/EEC, OJ L 2024/2853, 18 November 2024, which now includes the 'ability to continue to learn' as a product defect (Art. 7 (2) (c)).

7 For details see Anna Beckers and Gunther Teubner, *Three Liability Regimes for Artificial Intelligence* (Hart Publishing 2022) 71 ff.

the EU's risk approach, we do not accept that technological properties determine the character and intensity of the risk; instead, risks derive from the technology's concrete application in different social contexts.

At first sight, this may suggest a sector-specific regulation for each concrete type of technology. However, such sector-specific regulation is too fragmented. Common denominators across sectors in the technology's functions need to be addressed. Conversely, an algorithm may be employed for different tasks in the same sector. For example, in the financial sector, we find the delegation of investment decisions to individual robo-advisors and, at the same time, the interconnections of multiple trading algorithms in high frequency trading. Highly diverging algorithmic risks stemming from the different use of technology occur in the same sector. And the other way around, the different forms of usage of AI are not at all sector-specific. Decision-making is delegated to algorithms equally in other contexts and is not specific to the financial sector.

B. Three socio-digital institutions and their risks

We distinguish three different forms of employing algorithms in social contexts and their related social risks – autonomy risk, association risk, and interconnectivity risk. The starting point for our argument is a typology developed in IT studies that distinguishes three types of machine behavior – individual, collective, and hybrid.[8] However, to avoid the technology-deterministic short-circuit of inferring risks, regulation, and liability simply from technological properties, we suggest introducing "socio-digital institutions" as intervening variables between technology and law. Socio-digital institutions mean stabilized complexes of social expectations, which, in our case, are expectations regarding the behaviour of algorithms in social contexts. Such institutions are neither identical with social systems nor with formal organizations, or social relations. Instead, social systems, including formal organizations and interpersonal relations, produce expectations via their communications, which – to use a classical formulation – condense into institutions under an "idée directrice". Such expectations are institutionalized when consensus can be assumed to support them.[9] Now, socio-

8 Iyad Rahwan, Manuel Cebrian, Nick Obradovich and others, 'Machine Behaviour', (2019) *Nature* 477, 481 ff.

9 Niklas Luhmann, *A Sociological Theory of Law* (Routledge 1985) ch.II.4.

digital institutions integrate diverse technical and social expectations about the opportunities and risks of using algorithms in co-production.[10] These institutions serve as effective structural couplings between technical and social systems, including the legal system.

Socio-digital institutions are different from traditional social institutions because of their technicity. Codes and programs now take over the ordering function that previously symbolically meaningful orders would bear.[11] Such new "techno-digital normativity" differs from the normativity generated in human interaction, leading to new risks. A closer analysis of socio-digital institutions provides the criteria for distinguishing between three risk constellations and identifying responsibility subjects that should bear such risks.

(1) The autonomy risk arises from independent "decisions" in individual machine behaviour. It comes up in the emerging socio-digital institution of "digital assistance", which transforms digital processes into "actants". The humanities and the social sciences are needed to analyse how the institution of digital assistance shapes the productive potentialities of the actants and, in particular, the specific risks they pose to principal-agent relations. The "actant" no longer just follows the principal's predefined program but disposes of degrees of freedom that make its decisions unpredictable. The risk consists of the principal's loss of control and exposure to the agent's intransparent digital processes. This raises two questions: Should the law attribute a particular type of legal subjectivity to autonomous algorithms? Which legal rules in contract formation and liability law could mitigate the autonomy risk of digital assistance?

(2) The association risk of "hybrid" machine behaviour arises when activities are inseparably intertwined in the close cooperation between humans and algorithms. In this situation, a new socio-digital institution—"human-algorithm association"—emerges whose sociological analyses will identify emerging properties. Consequently, it is no longer possible to attribute individual accountability to either single algorithms or humans. Instead, legal solutions that account for the aggregate effects of intertwined

10 On the co-production of different social systems Andrew Feenberg, *Technosystem: The Social Life of Reason* (HUP 2017) 75; Sheila Jasanoff, 'The Idiom of Co-Production, in Sheila Jasanoff (ed), *States of Knowledge: The Co-Production of Science and Social Order* (Routledge 2004) 1 ff.

11 Thomas Vesting, *Gentleman, Manager, Homo Digitalis: Der Wandel der Rechtssubjektivität in der Moderne* (Velbrück 2021) 220.

human and digital activities are required, rendering the hybrid association and its stakeholders accountable.

(3) The interconnectivity risk arises when algorithms do not act as isolated units but like swarms in close interconnection with other algorithms, thus creating different collective properties. Here, a new socio-digital institution develops expectations about dealing with society's structural coupling to interconnected "invisible machines". In this case, the distinct risk lies in the total opacity of the interrelations between various algorithms, which cannot be overcome even by sophisticated IT analyses. Sociological theories of de-personalised information flows within such an anonymous swarm of algorithms demonstrate that it is impossible to identify any acting unit, neither individual nor collective. Consequently, the law is forced to give up the identification of liable actors and will need to determine new forms of social responsibilisation.

C. The autonomy risk of digital assistance

I. Socio-Digital Institution: Assistance

We focus on algorithms operating in the "digital assistance" situation. This incipient socio-digital institution determines a specific social status for individual machine behaviour.[12] "Digital assistance" originates in the time-honoured social institution of "human representation." Someone steps in and acts in someone else's place vis-à-vis a third party. This social institution enacts and produces a type of actorship called "representing agency." As opposed to the social role of a messenger, where Alter only carries out quasi-mechanically Ego's strictly defined orders, representing agency gives Alter the general authorisation to make independent decisions in the name of Ego. At the same time, it also determines the limits of this authorisation so that under certain conditions, Alter is barred from speaking and acting for Ego.[13]

Obviously, the transformation of human representation into digital assistance produces new risks. Four more specific risks need to be identified in the general autonomy risk: identification of the agent, lack of understanding between human principal and algorithmic agent, reduction of

12 Rahwan, Cebrian, Obradovich and others (n 8), 481.

13 Katrin Trüstedt, 'Representing Agency' (2020) *Law & Literature* 195, 200.

institutional productivity, and deviation of algorithmic decisions from the principal's intention.

II. Specific Risk: Autonomous algorithmic decision-making

While it is relatively unproblematic in human representation to identify the representing individual, it is frequently difficult to determine the contours of the AI agent that makes the decision in digital agency. Only once an algorithm is carefully shielded from active external input is it clearly identifiable as the agent speaking for its human principal. However, algorithms are rarely totally isolated. Frequently, they rely on external data input for their decisions; thus, they are not entirely detached from the operations of other digital machines. Only when the actual machine behaviour remains linked to the individual algorithm and its use of the data will the institution of digital assistance still govern the participants' roles. The new risk of identification of the 'responsible' algorithm needs to be mitigated not only by evidentiary rules, i.e., to trace back the wrongful decision in a whole chain of calculations, but also by a legal conceptualisation of algorithmic actorship and clear attribution rules. Obviously, this is no longer possible when digital operations are indiscriminately fused with human communications or interconnected with other algorithms to such a degree that no decision centre can be identified anymore. Then digital assistance will be replaced by institutionalised hybridity or interconnectivity. Below, we will discuss these socio-digital institutions and their legal regime.

While in human representation, a mutual understanding between principal and agent in the process of authorisation can be presupposed, this cannot be maintained when humans delegate tasks to machines. Digital assistance as an institution excludes genuine understanding between human minds and algorithmic operations. Instead, understanding is reduced to a one-sided act of putting the algorithm into operation. And even if understanding of mind and calculation cannot happen, understanding is nevertheless possible in concatenating different communicative acts between humans and machines. The advantages of such delegation lie in the abilities of machines to outperform humans in certain types of behaviour, such as handling a large amount of information in a short period. However, the risks of such communicative understanding need to be compensated by a liability regime that shifts action and responsibility attribution from the human to the digital sphere.

The social institution of human representation has a productive potential that is insufficiently understood if representation is described only as mere task delegation from Ego to Alter. Instead, it is the potestas vicaria conferred by the institution of representation that enables Alter to step in and act in Ego's place vis-à-vis a third party.[14] The potestas vicaria is responsible for the productivity of human representation because the agent need not unconditionally follow the principal's intentions. It is not the principal's will that is decisive; it is the project of cooperation between the principal and the agent. This is the very reason why representation constitutes autonomous actorship of the agent.

In the transformation of human representation into digital assistance, there is a risk of losing this productivity potential. The fear of the homo ex machina drives tendencies to narrow down the algorithm's decisional freedom and reduce it to strict conditional programming. However, the institution of digital assistance requires sufficient degrees of freedom for the algorithm so that the relationship between humans and algorithms can develop its creative potential. Blind obedience to the principal will not do. The reduction to the status of sheer tools needs to be ruled out. Not only human but also algorithmic representatives need to be endowed with the "potestas vicaria, in which every act of the vicar is considered to be a manifestation of the will of the one who he represents."[15] The agent acts "as if" he were the principal. Indeed, it amounts to a revolution in social and legal practice when sheer calculations of algorithms bring about the "juridical miracle" of agency law:[16] A simple machine calculation is able to bind a human being as well as create liability for its wrongful actions. The algorithmic agent representing a human being does not only "sub-stitute" but "con-stitute" the principal's actions.[17] One should not underestimate the consequences of such digital potestas vicaria. In comparison to program-

14 Referring to the theological origins of the vicarian relation, Giorgio Agamben, *The Kingdom and the Glory: For a Theological Genealogy of Economy and Government* (SUP 2011) 138 f.

15 Ibid, 138 f. For a detailed interdisciplinary analysis of this *potestas vicaria,* Katrin Trüstedt, *Stellvertretung: Zur Szene der Person* (Konstanz University Press 2022) *passim*, in particular for algorithmic agency, ch V 4.2.

16 See generally: Ernst Rabel, 'Die Stellvertretung in den hellenistischen Rechten und in Rom, in HJ Wolf (ed), *Gesammelte Aufsätze IV* (Mohr Siebeck 1971 [1934]) 491.

17 Menke's thesis that the agent's will con-stitutes and not only sub-stitutes the principal's will makes the dramatic changes involved visible when algorithms are given the power to conclude contracts, Karl-Heinz Menke, *Stellvertretung: Schlüsselbegriff christlichen Lebens und theologische Grundkategorie* (Verlag Johannes 1991).

ming and communicating with computers, digital assistance opens a new channel of human access to the digital world and allows for the use of its creative potential. Here, we find why digital assistance requires the necessary personification of the algorithmic agent and supports technologies that increase degrees of algorithmic autonomy.

But at the same time, digital assistance exposes society to new dangers of non-controllable digital decisions. Notwithstanding the advantages of digital assistance, such representation through the digital sphere is countered by what we call the autonomy risk. The autonomy risk manifests itself when actions are delegated to the uncontrollable digital sphere and thus may lead to damage. Such unpredictability may stem from the particularities of the programmed machine or the data used to train and operate the algorithm. The result is the same: humans do not control the algorithm they have endowed with action capacity. The law eventually needs to respond to this risk of autonomous decision-making by re-orienting its doctrine to fill the liability gaps and deciding on the legal status of such delegation. We will show that the answer is neither equalising electronic agents with humans by awarding full legal personhood nor treating digital assistance as a mere tool. Instead, the answer is to confer limited legal personhood. We conceptualize digital assistance as an agency relationship and thus make an analogy to agency law for algorithmic contract formation. In addition, the rules of vicarious liability become applicable to constellations of digital assistance. These rules respond accurately to digital assistance and the specific roles it creates for humans and algorithms.

Here is the fourth risk of the principal-agent relation, which emerges from an asymmetric distribution of information. The human principal has insufficient information about the algorithmic agent's activities; the algorithmic agent has information unknown to the principal.[18] This opens new insights for the unexpected productivity of digital assistance. The digital agent may devise contractual solutions that the principal had never imagined. While economic theories of principal-agent relations stress the risks of the agent's deviation from the principal's intentions, philosophy and sociology focus on both partners' positive contributions to enriching the principal-agent relation's productive potential.[19] Both aspects need to be carefully balanced in choosing an appropriate legal regime.

---

18 eg: Dimitrios Linardatos, *Autonome und vernetzte Agenten im Zivilrecht* (Mohr Siebeck 2021) 128 ff.

19 eg: Trüstedt (n 13), 195.

Altogether, the autonomy risk associated with using algorithmic assistants is much higher than the simple automation risk in entirely pre-determined computer systems. The human actors decide only about the computer program and its general use for contract formation, while in numerous single contracts, the software agents make concrete choices effectively outside human control. Even the programmer can no longer determine, control, or predict the agent's choices ex-ante or explain them ex-post. The algorithm's autonomy does not interrupt the causal connection between programmer and contract, but it interrupts the attribution connection effectively.[20]

III. Responsibility attribution: Users/Operators

Digital assistance, which generates responsibilities only within the bilateral relation between the algorithm and the human user/deployer (or organization), needs to be accompanied by a legal regime that assigns the principal, i.e., the user, the responsibility for the wrongfully acting agent. Principal-agent liability does not hold liable the multitude of actors involved in the algorithm's use, i.e., programmers, manufacturers, traders, etc. Instead, it exclusively targets the user who delegates a task to the technology and thus assumes the autonomy risk. Therefore, only the human user/deployer (or organization) is responsible for the algorithmic failures. In contrast, some authors argue that this unfairly shifts all the risks to the user/deployer alone. They also see other actors in the role of the responsible principal, mainly the manufacturer or producer, including the back-end operator who provides program updates and similar services in the background.[21] In doing so, however, they ignore that the user has assumed the specific risk of task delegation. As a result, they arrive at an unfair distribution of risk between manufacturer, programmer, and user. All actors involved in the construction and operation of the algorithm create different types of risks. These risks must be defined precisely in each case and then allocated exclusively to those who have assumed them. Principal-agent liability responds to the dangers of the division of labour between the user and the algorithm.

20 Gerhard Wagner, 'Verantwortlichkeit im Zeichen digitaler Techniken' (2020) *Versicherungsrecht* 717, 724.

21 European Parliament, 'Civil Liability Regime for Artificial Intelligence' *Resolution of 20 October 2020 with Recommendations to the Commission on a Civil Liability Regime for Artificial Intelligence* (2020/2014(INL) P9_TA-PROV (2020)0276), para 8.

In contrast, product liability, which certainly remains applicable, responds to the specific risks of programming, manufacturing, and monitoring the algorithms but leaves considerable gaps in liability.

D. The association risk of digital hybridity

I. Socio-Digital Institution: Digital hybridity

Next to delegating decisions to algorithms, we observe a different relation between algorithms and humans: collective human-machine decisions. Here, attribution of responsibility differs due to the varieties of socio-digital institutions: principal-agent relation versus association. In digital assistance, agents act autonomously. If anything goes wrong, the liability for their decisions is not attributed to them but to the principals. However, such an individualistic concept of accountability fails as soon as the actions of humans and algorithms become so intertwined that there is "no linear connection between the emergent structures, cultures or behaviours that constitute collectives and the complex interactions of the individuals from which they emerge".[22]

A relevant case is "algorithmic journalism". Here, algorithms and human actors are brought together in closely timed iterative workflows.[23] Consequently, algorithmic and human contributions to the jointly authored text are often so closely interwoven that it becomes impossible to identify a responsible author. A strange hybrid emerges - a human–algorithm association.[24] There are other cases of such hybrids. Spectacular constellations include "digitized corporate governance" – that is, the assignment of management tasks to autonomous algorithms.[25] For example, Deep Knowledge Ventures appointed an algorithm as a board member whose task was

22 Mark A Chinen, *Law and Autonomous Machines* (Edward Elgar 2019) 101.

23 Konstantin Dörr, Algorithmischer Journalismus – Eine Analyse der automatisierten Textproduktion im Journalismus auf gesellschaftlicher, organisatorischer und professioneller Ebene (University of Zurich Main Library 2017).

24 Nick Diakopoulos, Automating the News (HUP 2019) 15 f.

25 Marcus Becker and Philipp Pordzik, 'Digitalisierte Unternehmensführung' (2020) Zeitschrift für die gesamte Privatrechtswissenschaft 334, 334.

communicating with the other members via predictions and other data.[26] Within companies, algorithms can become directly integrated into the collective decision-making of the organization.[27] Sometimes, they serve as independent board members within a corporate structure;[28] sometimes, they form independent algorithmic sub-organizations, such as subsidiaries.[29] The integration of algorithms in decentralized autonomous organizations (DAOs) goes even further.[30] Here, algorithms independently take over the organization, administration, and decision-making of investor groups. In these cases, algorithms do not merely assist in decision-making but act as autonomous decision-makers.

Beyond these novel developments, a classic case of close human–algorithm interaction is the cyborg characterized by closely interlocking algorithmic impulses and human decisions.[31] However, the media-theoretical interpretation of cyborgs as "extensions of man"[32] is inappropriate because it conceives of information and participation exclusively from the viewpoint of the human subject so that the algorithm appears only as an annex of human action capacities.[33] Yet, this is only one out of several possibilities. In some cases, algorithmic calculations clearly dominate human decisions, but in others, it may be the reverse. Furthermore, from a sociological perspective, the interaction between humans and algorithms is never an expansion of the human action capacity; instead, it is a new kind of human–algorithm collective behaviour that emerges.[34] In such a symbiotic relationship between humans and algorithms, the collective

---

26 Florian Möslein, 'Robots in the Boardroom: Artificial Intelligence and Corporate Law' in Woodrow Barfield and Ugo Pagallo (eds), Research Handbook on the Law of Artificial Intelligence (Edward Elgar 2017) 649.

27 Hirokazu Shidaro and Nicholas A Christanikis, 'Locally Noisy Autonomous Agents Improve Global Human Coordination in Network Experiments (2017) Nature 370.

28 Möslein (n 26).

29 John Armour and Horst Eidenmüller, 'Self-Driving Corporations?' (2020) Harvard Business Law Review 87, 106 f.

30 Christoph Jentzsch, 'Decentralized Autonomous Organization to Automate Governance', manuscript available at <https://lawofthelevel.lexblogplatformthree.com/wp-content/uploads/sites/187/2017/07/WhitePaper-1.pdf>.

31 Pim Haselager, 'Did I do that? Brain-Computer Interfacing and the Sense of Agency' (2012) Minds & Machines 405.

32 Marshall McLuhan, Understanding Media. The Extensions of Man (Gingko Press 2003).

33 Katharina Block and Sascha Dickel, 'Jenseits der Autonomie: Die De/Problematisierung des Subjekts in Zeiten der Digitalisierung' (2020) Behemoth 109, 111.

34 Rahwan, Cebrian, Obradovich and others (n 8) 483.

association is greater than the sum of its parts.[35] In this situation, the social embeddedness of algorithms is contradictory to the understanding of isolated "algorithmic power", and the institution of digital assistance is replaced by a different kind of socio-digital institution: the human–algorithm association. When the individual contributions of humans and algorithms merge in joint decision-making, human–algorithm interactions develop novel collective properties.

II. Specific Risk: indeterminable association of human and machine action

The novel collective properties pose novel social risks. The association risk differs from the autonomy risk in relevant aspects. The Arrow theorem, which prescribes that collective decisions cannot be calculated as an aggregation of individual preferences, also applies to digital hybrids. The participation of algorithms intensifies this intransparency. Bostrom analyses this risk under "collective intelligence" or even "collective superintelligence".[36] The human-machine interactions cannot be fully controlled, which leads to "perverse instantiation": an algorithm efficiently satisfies the goal set by the human participant but chooses a means that violates the human's intentions.[37] And the subtle influence of algorithms on human behaviour is even riskier, as the invisibility of the calculating machines as an integral element of the decision-making may conceal where the actual decision has taken place.

When it comes to accountability, the association risk makes it difficult to determine the damage-causing event as well as the responsible individual. Identifying the illegal action may still be possible – errors in journalistic work as defamation, a corporate board decision as breach of fiduciary duties, social media interaction as collective defamation. However, attributing responsibility to an individual contribution is impossible. Was it the human action or the algorithmic calculation that was at fault? The contrast to the autonomy risk we dealt with above is obvious. For autonomous agents' decisions, it remains possible to delineate individual action, violation of duty, damage, and causality between action and damage; here, the algorithm's decisional autonomy creates the liability gap. In digital hybrids, while it

35 Jacob Turner, Robot Rules: Regulating Artificial Intelligence (Springer 2018) 167.

36 Nick Bostrom, Superintelligence: Paths, Dangers, Strategies (OUP 2017) 58 ff, 65 ff,155 ff.

37 Ibid., 146 ff.

remains possible to identify damage and action, the typical responsibility is due to the impossibility of determining the individual actor. The only way out is to consider the hybrid itself a responsible collective actor. And it is this collective decision-making of hybrids that the law needs to respond to.

III. Responsibility attribution: network

In contrast to principal-agent liability, which exclusively burdens the user, digital hybridity allows the wrongful acts to be attributable only to the human-machine association. However, as long as the association does not have its own assets, it is necessary to channel the resulting responsibility to the multitude of actors who are "behind" the digital hybrid. A whole network of different actors is involved in and benefits from the human-machine association. As control in the network is dispersed across the network nodes, liability must also follow this specific risk structure. We consider "network liability" to be well-equipped to assign, in a fair manner, responsibility to the network participants for the digital hybrid's failures.[38]

The digital network liability we propose is modelled on the American "enterprise liability" and the German Gesamthandshaftung. It works in two steps: attribution of action, then attribution of liability. In the first step, the wrongful act is attributed to the hybrid as a collective actor. This avoids the difficulty of identifying the contributions of humans and the algorithms involved. In the second step, liability for the collective action is channelled to the network members. These members have built and controlled the network, even if only indirectly. They profit from its activities. As a result, all network nodes are liable according to their share. The share is determined by economic benefit from and control over the hybrid. In analogy to the well-known market-share liability, we propose a "network-share liability".[39] An exception is only the constellation in which a company centrally coordinates the network based on contractual agreements. Here, primary

38 David Vladeck, 'Machines without Principals: Liability Rules and Artificial Intelligence' (2014) *Washington Law Review* 117, 149; Jessica Allain, 'From Jeopardy! To Jaundice: The Medical Liability Implications of Dr. Watson and Other Artificial Intelligence Systems' (2013) *Louisiana Law Review* 1049, 1074.

39 For a general discussion of network liability, see: Gunther Teubner, *Networks as Connected Contracts* (Hart Publishing 2011) 264 ff, 267 f.

liability should lie with the controlling company.[40] As a rule, this will be the producer, who will then have recourse to the other network nodes.

E. The interconnectivity risk of interdependent digital operations

I. Socio-digital Institution: Exposure to interconnectivity

In contrast to digital assistance and digital hybridity, our third risk situation, collective machine behaviour, is a purely technological matter. It emerges in the interconnectivity of autonomous algorithms without any human interference.[41] Interconnectivity is different from digital assistance because it is impossible to identify an individual algorithm as responsible. It differs from hybrid human-machine associations because society is ultimately exposed to the interconnected algorithms without being able to establish communicative relations. In collective machine behaviour, there is no two-way communication between humans and algorithms, not to speak of an associative relation between them, but only an indirect structural coupling.

The interdependent algorithmic calculations can be qualified as a "restless collective" based on distributed cognition.[42] Such a "collectivity without a collective" cannot be described as a formal organization or a network. It is only a "swarm" of algorithms arising from chance encounters. Systems theory describes society's relationship to algorithmic swarms as social contact with "invisible machines".[43] Their influence on society is difficult to grasp. As said above, there is no genuine communication between humans and algorithms, nor does a communicative collective emerge from humans and algorithms. Instead of a direct influence mediated through communication, interconnected algorithms exert an influence on social relations that is only indirectly mediated through structural coupling. Therefore, applying the le-

---

40 Rory van Loo, 'The Revival of Respondeat Superior and Evolution of Gatekeeper Liability (2020) *Georgetown Law Journal* 141, 189.

41 If legal analysis identifies a human involvement, the case would qualify as vicarious liability in digital assistance or network liability in digital hybrids. For more details on the three liability regimes, see Beckers and Teubner (n 7) 153ff.

42 Carolin Wiedemann, 'Between Swarm, Network, and Multitude: Anonymous and the Infrastructures of the Common' (2014) *Distinktion: Scandinavian Journal of Social Theory* 309, 313.

43 Niklas Luhmann, *Theory of Society, Volume 1* (SUP 2012) 66; similarly Mireille Hildebrandt, *Smart Technologies and the End(s) of Law* (Edward Elgar 2015) 40.

gal liability rules for individual algorithms or human-machine associations is impossible. Instead, we propose fund solutions that require political and administrative decisions by regulatory authorities, which distribute responsibility to the respective industry.

II. Specific Risk: Interconnectivity

The social risk of interconnectivity lies in the inaccessibility of the calculations and the impossibility of predicting and explaining the results. The authors of the interdisciplinary study on machine behaviour summarise these unexpected properties under the term "collective machine behaviour":

> In contrast to the study of individual machines, the study of collective machine behaviour focuses on the interactive and systemwide behaviours of collections of machine agents. In some cases, the implications of individual machine behaviour may make little sense until the collective level is considered. ... Collective assemblages of machines provide new capabilities, such as instant global communication, that can lead to entirely new collective behavioural patterns. Studies in collective machine behaviour examine the properties of assemblages of machines as well as the unexpected properties that can emerge from these complex systems of interactions.[44]

The study group refers to studies on micro-robotic swarms found in systems of biological agents, on the collective behaviour of algorithms in the laboratory and in the wild, on the emergence of novel algorithmic languages between intelligent machines, and dynamic properties of fully autonomous transportation systems. In particular, they discuss huge damages in algorithmic trading in financial markets. The infamous flash crashes are probably due not to the behaviour of one single algorithm but to the collective behaviour of machine trading as a whole, which turned out to be totally different from that of human traders resulting in the probability of a more significant market crisis.[45]

The interconnectivity risk destroys fundamental assumptions constitutive for action and liability attribution. Interconnectivity rules out the

44 Rahwan, Cebrian, Obradovich and others (n 8) 482.
45 Ibid.

identification of individual or collective actors as liable subjects.[46] It does neither allow for foreseeability of the damage nor causation between action and damage.[47] Dafoe speaks of "structural dynamics", in which

> it is hard to fault any individual or group for negligence or malign intent. It is harder to see a single agent whose behaviour we could change to avert the harm or a causally proximate opportunity to intervene. Instead, we see that technology can produce social harms, or fail to realize its benefits, because of a host of structural dynamics. The impacts of technology may be diffuse, uncertain, delayed, and complex to contract over.[48]

Accordingly, legal scholars refer to complexity theory and philosophies of the tragic when attempting to understand interconnectivity and its potential damages.[49] According to complexity theory, linearity of action and causation cannot be assumed, and surprises are to be expected. Unpredictability and uncontrollability result both from sufficient information and from a poorly designed system for which someone can be responsible; they are inherent in complex systems. Latent failures characterise complex systems that are always run as "broken systems".[50] Coeckelbergh compares the catastrophes resulting from interconnectivity to experiences of the tragic.

---

46 See: Herbert Zech 'Liability for AI: Public Policy Considerations' (2021) *ERA Forum* 147, 148 f.; Indra Spiecker 'Zur Zukunft systemischer Digitalisierung: Erste Gedanken zur Haftungs- und Verantwortungszuschreibung bei informationstechnischen Systemen', (2016) *Computer und Recht* 698, 701 ff.; Susanne Beck, 'Dealing with the Diffusion of Legal Responsibility: The Case of Robotics' in Fiorella Battaglia, Nikil Mukerji and Julian Nida-Rümelin (eds) *Rethinking Responsibility in Science and Technology* (Pisa University Press 2014) 167; Luciano Floridi and J.W. Sanders, 'On the Morality of Artificial Agents' in M Anderson and SL Anderson (eds), *Machine Ethics* (CUP 2011) 205 ff.

47 See Curtis EA Karnow ' The Application of Traditional Tort Theory to Embodied Machine Intelligence' in Ryan Call, Michael A Froomkin and Ian Kerr (eds) *Robot Law* (Edward Elgar 2016) 73: 'With autonomous robots that are complex machines, ever more complex as they interact seamless, porously, with the larger environment, linear causation gives way to complex, nonlinear interactions.'.

48 Allan Dafoe 'AI Governance: A Research Agenda', *Centre for the Governance of AI, Future of Humanity Institute, University of Oxford*, < https://cdn.governance.ai/GovAI-Research-Agenda.pdf> 7.

49 Christiane Wendehorst 'Strict Liability for AI and other Emerging Technologies' (2020) *Journal of European Tort Law* 150, 152 f.; Chinen (n 22) 94ff; Karnow (n 47) 74

50 See generally: Richard I Cook, 'How Complex Systems Fail', Research Paper, < https://how.complexsystems.fail> 4.

Conventional understandings of blame, responsibility, and even causation fall short.[51] Any retrospective identification of a disaster's cause cannot be but "fundamentally wrong", and responsibility attributions are "predicated on naïve notions of system performance".[52]

Many scholars agree that for interconnectivity, neither ex-ante nor ex-post analyses can identify the actors as attribution endpoints and their causal contribution to the damage.[53] European legislative initiatives had been well aware of the difficulties of liability law:

> AI applications are often integrated in complex IoT environments where many different connected devices and services interact. Combining different digital components in a complex ecosystem and the plurality of actors involved can make it difficult to assess where a potential damage originates and which person is liable for it. Due to the complexity of these technologies, it can be very difficult for victims to identify the liable person and prove all necessary conditions for a successful claim, as required under national law. The costs for this expertise may be economically prohibitive and discourage victims from claiming compensation.[54]

Yet, if the attribution of action, causation, and responsibility is impossible, should the law respond to the risks of interconnectivity at all? Once we accept that interconnectivity is inevitably prone to failure, we might conclude that nothing needs to be "fixed" by law. Interconnectivity risks may be a price to pay for the use of technology. However, there is a plausible counter-argument. Despite being invisible, unpredictable in their operations, and incomprehensible in their underlying structure, interconnected systems

---

51 Mark Coeckelbergh 'Moral Responsibility, Technology, and Experiences of the Tragic: From Kierkegaard to Offshore Engineering', (2012) *Science and Engineering Ethic,* 35, 37. For an application in relation to interconnected autonomous machines: Chinen (n 22) 98f.

52 Cook (n 50), points 5 and 7.

53 Karin Young, *Responsibility and AI: A Study of the Implications of Advanced Digital Technologies (Including AI Systems) for the Concept of Responsibility within a Human Rights Framework* (Council of Europe Study DGI (2019)05, 2019) 62 ff; Klaus Heine and Shu Li, 'What Shall we do with the Drunken Sailor? Product Safety in the Aftermath of 3D Printing, (2019) *European Journal of Risk Regulation* 23, 26 ff.; Herbert Zech, 'Zivilrechtliche Haftung für den Einsatz von Robotern: Zuweisung von Automatisierungs- und Autonomierisiken' in Sabine Gless and Kurt Seelmann (eds) *Intelligente Agenten und das Recht* (Nomos 2016) 170.

54 European Commission, 'Report on the Safety and Liability Implications of Artificial Intelligence, The Internet of Things and Robotics, COM(2020) 64 final, 14.

do produce results that may represent a productive surplus of meaning.[55] They generally result in intended results. Automatic and even more so autonomous infrastructure may be regularly out of control but still fulfils a distinct purpose, which allows for automation of processes, alignment of procedures, and reasonable calculations. This has two consequences: First, digital technology does not require consensual practices of actual people; acceptance originates in its problem-solving capacity. Second, human actors tend to be paralysed when the risks materialise, when complex technological systems do not function, when they go astray and cause damage. This means that society cannot tolerate their malfunctions once it has accepted complex technological systems. Technological risks must be mitigated and their damages compensated, even if no culprit can be identified. Therefore, de-personalised compensatory rules need to counteract the risks of new evolving technologies.

III. Responsibility attribution: Socialising of risk

In the case of interconnectivity, determining who should bear the risk is different—responsibility shifts from those directly involved to a larger social collective. The interconnectivity of "invisible machines" makes it impossible from the outset to determine an individually responsible algorithm. Since there is only an indirect "structural coupling" between algorithmic interconnectivity and society, no one-to-one responsibility relationship can be established. Therefore, we propose that liability funds be established. The funds should be financed by the industry sector involved.[56] The players' contributions are calculated based on their market share and specific problem-solving capacity. The US Superfund for environmental damage can serve as a model here.[57] The Superfund aims not only to compensate individual affected parties but also to provide rules for remedying the broader social and ecological impact, including regulations on clean-up and prevention. This idea should be taken up for algorithmic interconnectivity. Restitution measures will serve as additional instruments of liability law. In the case of large-scale damage, the regulatory authority responsible

55 See: Armin Nassehi, *Patterns: Theory oft he Digital Society* (Polity Press 2024), 141 ff.

56 Olivia J Erdélyi and Gabor Erdélyi, 'The AI Liability Puzzle and a Fund-Based Work-Around, (2021) *Journal of Artificial Intelligence Research* 1309.

57 42 US Code § 9601 ff.

for the fund should be empowered to select actors with a robust problem-solving capacity and impose the task of restitution and undoing adverse consequences. The actors involved are obliged to take measures that limit or even eliminate the negative externalities of interconnectivity for the future, such as reversibility[58], creation of firewalls or slowing down of interconnectivity or, ultimately, the shut-down of dangerous technological systems, described as the "death penalty" for robots.[59]

F. Conclusion

With these three categories of socio-digital institutions, risks, and responsible actors, we thus shift the focus for risk specification for AI regulation. In contrast to the European Union's AI Act and the related technology rules, which define risks primarily based on damage severity or technical properties criteria and human/organisational obligations, we suggest defining risks according to the social context in which the technology is used.

The AI Act distinguishes between the obligations of various actors in the "AI value chain"[60] but, without consistent explanation, links such actor obligation to the risk severity of technology or considers, as in general-purpose AI and foundation models, the specific technological properties because of their general riskiness as a reason for imposing obligations. It differentiates between the respective responsibilities of providers, importers, distributors, and deployers/users but does not justify why a particular actor is supposed to bear the risk.

Instead, we suggest that risk and responsibility should not be defined according to damage severity but according to the institutional context of the technology's application. Users – or deployers in the AI Act – have a specific responsibility when they delegate decision-making to algorithms. Funds should be created to manage the systemic risk of interconnected algorithms. The network of actors creating AI is mainly the risk-bearing

58 See on reversibility European Parliament, 'Resolution of 16 February 2017 with Recommendations to the Commission on Civil Law Rules on Robotics', P8_TA ("017), OJ 18/7/2018, C252/239, Annex.

59 Mark A. Lesley and Brian Casey, 'Remedies for Robots' (2019) *University of Chicago Law Review* 1311, 1390.

60 On the term of the AI value chain and the problem of responsibility attribution Jennifer Cobbe, Michael Veale and Jatinder Singh, 'Understanding Accountability in Algorithmic Supply Chains' (2023) *FAccT '23: Proceedings of the 2023 ACM Conference on Fairness, Accountability, and Transparency* 1186.

collective when human and algorithmic decision-making aggregates into collective decision-making.

To end with some examples: We do not propose a specific regulatory framework for general-purpose AI. Instead of an ex-ante allocation of responsibility among manufactures, providers, and deployers/users, the responsibility would be allocated with a view to the specific context. The famous case of a lawyer letting ChatGPT write court briefs is a delegation of decision-making, which leads to the user's responsibility. However, in cases where the interaction between generative AI and humans is so dense that individual contributions cannot be identified,[61] responsibility would be determined according to the principles of network liability. Finally, the socialization of risks via collective funds should be considered only for technologies that operate below the societal level in an interconnected digital sphere without direct interaction with humans.

61 Mark Coeckelbergh and David J Gunkel, 'ChatGPT: Deconstructing the Debate and Moving it Forward' (2024) *AI & Society* 2221, 2225; Joerge Luis Morton Gutiérrez, 'On Actor-Network Theory and Algorithms: ChatGPT and the New Power Relation ships in the Age of AI' (2024) *AI and Ethics* 1071, , 1077 ff.

A Brave New World?

Artificial Intelligence as a Hybrid Life Form.[1] On the Critique of Cybernetic Expansion

Jörn Lamla

"The number you have dialled is not in service ..."
German Federal Postal Service

Artificial intelligence (AI) challenges human intelligence and our humanistic self-conception. This contribution argues that this is happening for good reasons but is based on a mistaken opposition that falls short. Human beings and technology have always been intertwined in hybrid forms of life. Yet the exact nature of this hybridity is misunderstood when inadequate dichotomies of human subject and technical object are replaced by a totalizing conception of a cybernetic informational universe that reduces all that exists to this latter, single point of comparison. Representing the paradigm of digital society, AI is a bearer and expression of such a cybernetic expansion that both anchors digital analogism in society as a closed system of interpreting the world, or a cosmology, and renders it plausible at the level of knowledge. AI thus deepens and generalizes conventions and functional patterns of justification that have a long history in industrial society. The thesis proposed here is that, to counter this expansive dynamic effectively and critically, more needs to be done than evoke humanistic values. What we need is a better understanding of the ontological heterogeneity of the societal modes of existence that are assembled in hybrid forms of life.

---

1 This paper is a translation with minor modifications of the following German-language publication: Lamla, Jörn (2022): Künstliche Intelligenz als hybride Lebensform. Zur Kritik der kybernetischen Expansion. In: Friedewald, M./Roßnagel, A./Heesen, J./Krämer, N./Lamla, J. (eds.): Auswirkungen der Künstlichen Intelligenz auf Demokratie & Privatheit. Baden-Baden: Nomos, pp. 77–100 (open access). Many thanks go to Stephan Elkins for his profound translation services, both linguistically and sociologically. My thanks also go to Bettina Reß for her assistance with literature research. I would also like to thank the Fritz Thyssen Foundation for granting me the opportunity to devote a semester for reading, which made it possible to thoroughly review part of the literature addressed in this essay.

A. Beyond strong and weak AI

A common narrative in the current discourse on artificial intelligence (AI) begins with the distinction of strong and weak AI. By relegating the idea of an all-dominating strong AI—a singular super intelligence of computing machines that is far superior to human cognitive capacities—to the realm of science fiction or unfounded collective paranoia, a position proceeding only from the assumption of a weak AI appears to be realistic, competent, and trustworthy. In this perspective, AI then is no longer a mystery but rather a very concrete, local use of huge computing capacity, adaptive algorithms, and neural networks for performing very specific tasks. As is often the case in techno-scientistic narrations, most of the examples to explain this are drawn from the health sector. They not only illustrate how the use of AI, for instance, in medical imaging techniques increases the probability of detecting cancer but also enhances general acceptance of research and development investments in AI by exemplifying the opportunities of AI in the context of the health as a core value. What is typically not questioned is the distinction between strong and weak AI itself. This distinction is reified as the boundary that allows the implementation of AI as an ethically and legally controllable, essentially socially desirable technology, the good reasons for which can be scrutinized in each individual case and for which general legal provision can be enacted with an eye to the transparency or autonomy of algorithmic decision-making.

Astonishing from a sociological perspective are the implicit conceptions of societal change that are associated with such narratives. Images of machines that, in a belligerent act of revolution, seize control of the world are just as inadequate as the assumption that societal structures will be continuously sustained as long as it is ensured that new technologies are controlled and incrementally infused into the fabric of societal practices, institutions, and values. What this dichotomy misses is the possibility of paradigmatic transformations in the structural makeup of entire societies that have far-reaching consequences precisely because they are gradually and barely noticeably infiltrating the fabric of social practices and everyday activities. In retrospect, however, this is actually the typical case, which can indeed entail far-reaching consequences (cf., e.g., Beck 1997). Seen from this vantage point, the value-laden distinction between strong and weak AI takes on concealing and de-/legitimizing characteristics—not least owing to the fact that this schematic pattern of perception promptly relegates all those who warn about the problematic side effects of AI to the apocalyptic science fiction of strong AI. A very different story of transformation comes into view when we look at the new in the old, at the minor paradigmatic shifts that, as local AI applications spread, initially imperceptibly, into various societal domains, and gradually change our ways but cumulatively cause substantial structural changes.

The following considerations develop such a transformation hypothesis by starting from the paradigmatic changes that can be observed in many contexts. The objective is to identify the common structural principle that, as these changes are expanding, is gradually making its imprint on the characteristic structures of society (cf. Giddens 1984). This structural principle is not in itself AI. AI, thus the assumption, is rather only one of many exemplary testing grounds for its expansion. AI along with its many local applications is in itself only one instance of applying a more general transformational dynamic, the programmatic core of which can be called *cybernetic cosmology*, that is expanding into and becoming manifest and evident in various social practices and constellations. This structural principle thus has a side that is virtual, ideological, world-interpreting, or pragmatic and another side that is material, structuring (in terms of shaping the ontology of practices in space and time), operational, or also syntagmatic. It can be identified and described in different contexts accordingly. It does not fall from the heavens but has been gradually evolving from historical predecessors that belong to and accompany the imaginary of industry and its development, which can be seen, for instance, in the harmonious conceptions of order among early utopian socialists such as Fourier (1971) or Saint-Simon (1975). This structural principle thus describes a specifiable genealogical path and at the same time appears in the form of various structurally related phenomena. These can be changes of a technological-material kind but also in pedagogy and psychotherapy, in law, in the sciences, and not least in the mode of governance (cf. Lamla 2020).

Before I unfold this argument in more detail, let me elaborate this other transformation narrative by addressing a specific aspect of AI. To enable algorithms to identify patterns, make suggestions, or decisions first requires *training* them on a vast pool of data (cf. Engemann 2018). These data form the probabilistic basis that enables AI to conclude with sufficient likelihood that a specific shadow in an image indicates cancer, that the choice of a music title reflects a preference for a specific style, that two profiles on a dating website indicate attraction or antipathy, and so on. Compiling data for such training belongs to the practical problems of computer science that require considerable effort and are thus costly—especially when this must happen under the laboratory conditions of science, by hand, and in compliance with high data privacy standards. It would be easier and much more efficient if this training of algorithms could directly tap into societal practice: images from X-ray and computer tomography in medicine and their classification by practicians, for instance, or vast quantities of data from a music-streaming or data platform, or the indexing work of the image recognition industry, which occasionally, and paradoxically, depicts the monotonous training of machines as proof of being human: "I am not a robot" (reCAPTCHA). This grounding of specific developments in machine learning and AI in the contexts of societal practice itself raises the question of who is actually training whom. If robots that are supposed to learn how to interact with children to later support them in learning must first have interacted with children to predict and anticipate their reactions and patterns of attention, these children will be learning at the same time how to interact with robots, adopt them as playmates, and devote the necessary attention to them (Reimer and Flückinger 2021). In the same vein, we quickly learn to deliberately address the voice recognition software in our automobiles in ways that we can expect its responses to be halfway useful. The famous Turing test (Turing 1950) also falls into this category. It can be viewed as the paradigm of an AI whose performative intelligence is assessed in terms of perceiving no difference between the responses of people and machines. What remains unanswered, however, is whether this owes itself to the learning of the machine or the adjustments of humans (Lanier 2010, p. 32). For AI, this makes no difference. The only measure is success.

What becomes problematic here, however, is the concept of AI as a whole—no matter whether in its strong or weak version. For in both cases, as a threat or a complement, the concept tinkers with its opposition to human intelligence, which seems to be an independent entity that is contrasted with its artificial counterpart. Yet this independence does not really exist. Human and machine intelligence are indeed always already recursively coupled, so that what we are dealing with is a genuinely socio-technical intelligence the material basis of which is not a high-performance computer and computer networks but rather *hybrid life forms*. The hybrid nature of these forms of life is, however, misunderstood in two ways, thus my thesis, because the common concept of AI continues to imply a superior humanity and cherish humanism on the one hand while assuming the universal connectivity and translatability of machine language—that is, the duplication of the world in the form of data—on the other (Nassehi 2019,

p. 33f.). Yet both are not only in a relation of contradictory tension but each one in its own way also misconceives the specific nature of hybrid life forms.

To elaborate this thesis in more detail, this contribution will draw on recent anthropological theories on the hybridity of life forms. With their program of recursive linkages and couplings of everyday life and AI, they are spearheading a new digital analogism (section 2). However, a critical response to such a diagnosis must not deny the hybridity of life forms and revert to the simplistic humanistic dichotomy of human beings and machines as, for instance, the renaissance of digital sovereignty has prematurely been doing. What is required is rather to open up third spaces for thinking about setting limits to cybernetic expansion. For the redefinition of critical competencies, we can resort to, for example, environmental and sustainability discourses (section 3). Their core characteristic is an enhanced awareness of the heterogeneous in hybrid life forms and, mediated via this awareness of ontological diversity, the ability to question and reject, for good reasons, sociotechnical constraints, for instance, the ability to counter, for emancipatory purposes, the telecommunications provider's crisis response cited at the outset of this article.

B. The digital analogism of the cybernetic cosmology

Making the impact and interplay between a humanistic and cybernetic worldview visible requires comprehending them as such. Applying methods from the history of ideas, Vincent August (2021), for example, has traced how cybernetic thought evolved during the 20th century as an alternative way of thinking about control and fostered new forms of technological governance. In the process, this new, network-oriented mode of thought—aimed at capturing emergent, self-regulating feedback systems—increasingly broke away from ideas based on a sovereign subject exercising hierarchical control. Whereas the idea of sovereignty still reflects the humanistic worldview in which the human subject occupies an exceptional status on grounds of its faculty of reason, the cybernetic worldview has increasingly abandoned this idea. In the latter view, human beings appear to be nothing more than positions in emergent social networks of communication or streams of information. The digital revolution can then be considered as one more humiliation of this human subject, namely, as the fourth humiliation after the Copernican turn, Darwin's theory of evolution, and

Freud's psychoanalytical humiliation of human autonomy and centrality (Floridi 2014, pp. 87–100). Whereas the previous revolutions have banished the human being from the centre of the universe, the animal kingdom, and Cartesian self-consciousness, the infosphere now has also decentred logical thinking, our intelligence, by outsourcing and transferring it to information-processing machines. But what in this context appears to be a statement claiming veracity that can be substantiated by numerous empirically evident examples—one need only think of the use of navigation tools to get from A to B as quickly as possible—is at the same time an expression of a cybernetic worldview that gives precedence to digital information processing over all other forms of socio-material relations.

Making visible that statements of this kind are tied to social positions is not an easy task in the case of cybernetic cosmology because these statements are increasingly gaining plausibility and are becoming hegemonic with the help of evidence drawn from digital contexts of application. Showing how such tendencies toward closure have emerged and have been evolving historically requires special methodical efforts. Whereas the history of political ideas, the sociology of knowledge (e.g., Mannheim 1991), or the discourse-analytical study of historical epistemes (Foucault 1971) specialize in this, they can nevertheless remain wedded to a cybernetic shift in perspective as August (2021) has demonstrated for the theoretical schools of Luhmann and Foucault. Certain constructivist lines of analysis have themselves borrowed their theoretical and methodological toolbox from just that cosmology, the selectivities and limitations of which I intend to draw out here. In the following, this shall be demonstrated with reference to two recent examples of theory-building on (post-)digital society that can be easily associated with the theoretical schools of Luhmann and Foucault.

The first example refers to Armin Nassehi's book on patterns (2019). Nassehi starts from the thesis that modern society has essentially always been digital and that, with new technology, it has merely found a way to render its latent pattern visible and recombinable in manifest structures of socio-digital chains of operation. "We do not see digitization but rather key domains of society already observing digitally. Digitality is one of the crucial self-references of society" (ibid., p. 29).[2] The digital and digitization, thus one might interpret this reasoning, stand—and have always stood—in a functional relation to society. In this cosmos, digitality solves a problem, takes its functional place, and would not exist otherwise. For "[were] it not

2 All quotes from Nassehi's work have been translated from German.

an appropriate fit for this society, it would have never emerged or would have long since disappeared again" (ibid., p. 8). "The problem to which digital technology makes reference," Nassehi writes (ibid., p. 36), "lies in the complexity of society itself." Its contribution to solving that problem is, similar to that of sociology, to detect patterns in this inconceivably vast societal complexity and reorganize them at the level of digital media. It accomplishes this by first duplicating these patterns in the form of data and, by way of this form, portending to informationally process the whole world in its entire heterogeneity in a uniform, self-selective operational nexus: "If one wants to somehow conceptualize the digital, then it is ultimately nothing other than the *duplication of the world in the form of data*, including the technical possibility of relating the data to each other," that is to say, to make "the incommensurable at least relationable" (ibid., p. 33f.).

In this way, Nassehi, however, not only vividly traces the aspirations and measures involved in duplicating the world through digital data and technologies but rather duplicates this duplication once more to compose a consistent, inevitable story to which there is no alternative by couching it in a cybernetic narrative to which digital technology then lends empirical evidence. In this respect, his book is a prime example of an epistemological dynamic of closure of a postdigital constellation of order in a society in which the couplings of sociality and digitality are advancing and expanding. Nassehi's theory of the digital society allows us to study how scientific interpretations can contribute to such a politics of closure. The "systems theorist" finds analogies–oh, what a surprise!–between his cybernetic world of the social and the cybernetic world of the digital that enable him to posit a functional relationship between the two and then interpret the digital as being just that mirror which makes it possible for even the last old-European sceptic to recognize and accept the systemic nature of the functionally differentiated society (cf. ibid., p. 186 f.). The language and informational paradigm of cybernetics guide all of his interpretations from the outset. Competing theoretical languages and approaches to interpretation are mentioned at best but are at no point seriously discussed or considered as offering an alternative explanation. This pertains to Steffen Mau's (2017) diagnosis of a comprehensive measuring of the world, Shoshana Zuboff's (2019) analysis of the expansion of the power to control by means of the recursive formation of behavior through digital technology, Felix Stalder's (2016) "Kultur der Digitalität" (Culture of Digitality), and many others, all of whom Nassehi claims to "have failed to perceive the structural radicality of the digital for society" (Nassehi 2019, p. 14), as well as ultimately to science and technology studies (STS) with which he seeks to maintain some sort of truce, as STS—in the line of Dominique Cardon (2016), for instance—is at least capable of seeing "that the production of algorithms is establishing a new way of thinking" (ibid., p. 15). Only Nassehi is not really interested in reconstructing this way of thinking empirically and with an openness in all directions—as is the case in research in the vein of STS; he rather determines the interpretive framework for this analysis a priori by drawing on the cybernetic terminology of systems theory.[3]

"Like hardly any other, Heidegger understood the significance of cybernetics as a challenge to philosophy in that it reduces everything to uniform information" (ibid., p. 83). At the time when Heidegger predicted the triumphant advance of cybernetics in technology *and* science, however, he was still intent on maintaining a critical distance. Not so Nassehi: Where Heidegger still had a "critical eye" on retooling scientific theorizing along the lines of cybernetic feedback and systems thinking, Nassehi believes that we must "probably describe it in affirmative terms to fully understand it. Here, the internal intertwinement of theoretical means and object is truly carried to extremes and has certainly reached its peak in sociological systems theory" (ibid., p. 93). Accordingly, Nassehi's theory represents a self-contained cosmology in which we can no longer distinguish between those observations and diagnoses of digital society that are rooted in a contingent cybernetic worldview and those that can be traced to the historical-practical restructurations that have come with the availability of digital technology. By way of their coupling, theory and practice unfold performative power. Yet the transformation of society into a cybernetic information machine in which the uniformity of information has the effect of making the incommensurable commensurable and rendering it temporally interrelatable in recursive networks can still be "taken seriously" (ibid., p. 87) as a historical-technical development even if one scientifically reckons

3 With media duplications, the "cosmos" itself takes on a "cybernetic character," he writes in one place (ibid, p. 114). And elsewhere he maintains in apodictic fashion and contrary to all theoretical controversy: "The concept of society is controversial in sociology. What we can state with certainty is that society means the totality of all communication and action. Society is the all-encompassing system. [...] Such a system, in the environment of which there cannot be anything else that is social, must establish something resembling a comprehensive order within itself; it would collapse into itself otherwise" (ibid., p. 168). Without further ado, the author rephrases controversies in social theory as if they were pseudo-controversies with no implications for his own systems-theoretical language.

with alternative ontological conceptions and corresponding societal countermovements, that is to say, even if one does not conceive of cybernetic cosmology as absolute and as a mode of thinking to which there is no alternative.

Nassehi, however, sidelines such alternative conceptions and countermovements. One does have to give the author credit for at least marking the ontological-political gateway for this dynamic of closure. Yet he addresses this only in an excursus that remains neatly separated from his theory of digital society (ibid., pp. 188–195). There, Nassehi raises questions concerning the practical and material mediation of the digital that meets with the obdurateness of habitualized practices or the finiteness of environmental resources and energy supply. Things like the energetic substructure, rare earths, the digital information infrastructure, their materiality and the waste problems that this entails, but also their historicity and the necessity of continuous translation and mediation at the "points of intersection" (ibid., p. 34) between the digital and the "analogue" world represent a logic of practice that have ushered in problems of a very different nature for a digital society than the ones that Nassehi has in mind: "The shift toward supposedly immaterial digital value-added by no means implies the vanishing of the turnover in material goods and energy. This is not necessarily relevant to a theory of the digital but certainly for its practice—for that matter also with regard to what it means for the inclusion of working people. But that is not the issue here" (ibid., p. 192). These passages are symptomatic of the theoretical speechlessness and lack of mediation between different worldviews or cosmologies that are also characteristic of the coexistence of the discourses and strategies of digital and sustainable transformation. The counterthesis is that a theory of digital society must indeed account for, and consider in a prominent position, these different kinds of problems.

Turning to the second example, I will now directly address, take seriously as a phenomenon, and attempt to systematically illuminate the complex of problems involving materially induced disruptions, acts of partial opt-out (e.g., digital detox), and other crises of postdigital life practice. Urs Stäheli's book on the sociology of de-networking (2021) takes a comprehensive look at various problematizations of excessive networking, ranging from information overload and apophenia—the same passion for patterns that Nassehi too indulges in—through forced pauses in the wake of buffering or burnout, all the way to phenomena such as non-sellers or the social figure of the shy one, complemented by various theoretical conceptualizations from Latour's notion of dissociation to Simmel's concept of indifference. In the process, he associates de-networking, in analogy to cell biology, with Deleuze's "vacuoles of non-communication" (Stäheli 2021, p. 154 ff.),[4] which, as refuges, are partially withdrawn from the directing control of processes of communication and exchange but nevertheless remain functionally related to the cellular organism as a whole: "Vacuoles are [...] not merely holes or empty positions in a network, but rather complex infrastructures of storage and withdrawal; indeed, what we are dealing with here is a bio-logistics of temporary withdrawal with the aid of which cells create the preconditions for their own processing" (ibid., p. 157).

Here, too, theoretical affirmation of the network metaphor, which demarcates the field of criticism, remains central—less so from the standpoint of cybernetics, rather from the perspective of a relational network sociology. Yet the result is similar. In Stäheli's work, de-networking paradoxically does not refer to an outside of the network but to a part of the network that is incorporated into the network itself. Although he takes a critical look at and sheds light on the now extremely far-reaching and dispersed effects of the power of (digital) networks and their discursive duplications, this ultimately does not go beyond cybernetic self-corrections by expanding the logic of [cybernetic] connectivity via theoretically also incorporating that which remains unconnected. When it comes to opting out, Stäheli says explicitly that he is not interested in radical but only in partial opt-out: "The issue is therefore not to think of de-networking as an opt-out option but rather as a bundle of socio-technical practices, as something that operates against networking from within networking" (ibid., p. 84). In this way, the key question, which Stäheli also points out as such, thus remains unanswered, namely, the one that asks about "the mode of existence of the de-networked" (ibid., p. 383). In his perspective, this mode of existence can be defined only negatively, as the absence of the normality of networking in a world of informational networks but not in terms of a heterogeneity of ontological registers.

Stäheli and Nassehi thus both confirm the cybernetic congeniality of ideas between Foucault and Luhmann. Hinting at the power effects of epistemological orders of knowledge and discourses alone does not direct attention away from these but merely demands of them a greater degree of critical self-reflection. By contrast, greater power to unsettle such orders

4 All quotes from Stäheli's book have been translated from German.

and discourses would require a sociology that is capable of taking a broader approach and relativizing cybernetic cosmology as a whole. This is possible with the aid of anthropological theories such as the ones pursued by Philippe Descola (2013) or Eduardo Viveiros de Castro (2014). These theories typically revolve around the contrast between modern Western naturalist cosmologies and the ontological schemata and modes of relationships associated with the animistic cosmologies identified in the Amazon Basin, but not only there. Naturalism and animism stand for diametrically different socio-ecological arrangements and contrasting them helps to question the dichotomy of nature and culture in their own Western relation to nature.[5]

Yet this is not the only way to render Descola's heuristic distinctions fruitful for analysis. Although there can be no doubt that, since the onset of modernity, modern naturalism and the instrumental, productivist, or also capitalist social forms that come with it have spread all over the globe (Descola 2013, p. 173; cf. also Latour 2018, pp. 70–77). In the course of the cybernetic expansion, however, which is advancing rapidly with digitization and in which the coalescence of digitality and sociality and other socio-technical feedback loops are taking shape in practice, naturalism is being overlayed by cosmological schemata of a different kind, which Descola calls *analogism*. By contrasting animism and naturalism, Descola

5 In the cosmos of *animism*, it is possible that subjects of the most different types and forms encounter one another in symmetrical fashion (which may include not only exchange and gift[s] but indeed also predatory encounters). Here, animals and plants are part of the collective of species just as people are. The Achuar, among whom Descola conducted several years of fieldwork, attribute *a soul* to animals or also to plants and thus integrate them into their society in a very human way. To the hunter, for instance, "[t]he animals that he encounters [...] are [...] not wild beasts but beings that are almost human and that he must seduce and cajole in order to draw them out of the grasp of the spirits that protect them" (Descola 2013, p. 41). Relationships of mutual respect and recognition, but also of cannibalistic appropriation, based on taking the perspective of the other across species, form the basis of coexistence between them. By comparison, *naturalism* has great difficulty incorporating the diversity of the world within a stable framework. Since human beings, with their autonomous volition, their culture, and their pronounced self-consciousness, time and again exempt themselves from the schemata of order of the one nature, this cosmology fails to agree on an overarching principle. Within the naturalist framework, morality has no clear place and can therefore bridge neither the heterogeneity of plural cultures nor the "radical otherness" of the most diverse non-humans (Descola 2013, pp. 289–291). Modernity is consequently characterized by turbulence and restlessness. Its most important relationship schema is *production*, which comes with a strict hierarchy between humans and non-humans and a clear-cut distribution of positions between subjects and objects.

derives criteria for differentiation that he fleshes out toward a typology of ontologies that includes totemism and analogism as well (Descola 2013, p. 121): Whereas animism broadly extends the interiorities of the human (e.g., to include the soul, consciousness, or volition)–while indeed emphasizing differences in the make-up of species, that is, in the outer forms or physicality of beings in the process–modern *naturalism*, according to Descola, operates the other way around in this respect. In terms of its physicality, the naturalist ontology sees nature as based on general principles that apply to all bodies equally, whereas cultural characteristics and abilities of cultural expression are reserved for humans. However, cases that deviate from this in which both interiorities and physicalities provide a continuous connection between humans and non-humans, as in the cosmology of the Australian aborigines, correspond with the third type, which is totemism.[6] And the maximum contrast to this, one in which ruptures and differences between all existing beings pertain to both interiorities and physicalities, points to cosmologies of the analogism type.

For Descola, naturalisms' asymmetric relation to nature largely makes it "impossible to set up between all existing beings a schema of interaction with the synthesizing power and simplicity of expression of the relations that structure nonmodern collectives" (ibid., p. 397). Under these ruptured conditions, people in modernity forget their dependence on the other, their *alteri*, be it biological diversity or the alien, and tend to exploit or even destroy those others–or, conversely, to engage in hopelessly romantic attempts "to recover the lost innocence of a world in which plants, animals, and objects were fellow citizens" (ibid., p. 398). The inability of modernity to establish stable relationships between heterogeneous beings undergirds the renewed attractiveness of analogism: Its ontologies and belief systems "offer a universalist alternative that is more complete than the truncated universalism of the Moderns" (ibid., p. 300), which with the disruption of heterogeneity had emerged from analogism and the temporal dependencies

6 In the cosmological fabric of *totemism* with its collectives as a source of identity, the "coexistence between heterogeneous collectives is [...] a necessary condition of survival [...] for all those involved" (ibid., p. 297) and leads to "a remarkable case of rational cohabitation between 'ontological races' that, despite considering themselves as utterly different with regard to their essence, substance, and the places to which they are attached, nevertheless adhere to values and norms that render them complementary. Indeed, they make use of the grid of otherness on which they find themselves placed in relation to others in order to produce an organic solidarity out of taxonomic heterogeneity" (ibid.).

of which on the past, on ancestors, and on tradition were initially believed to have been overcome. This attractive alternative, however, comes in the form of a "spiritual universalism" as advocated in the "Eastern wisdoms" of Zen, Buddhism, and Daoism (ibid.).[7] What then characterizes this spiritual universalism of analogist cosmologies? And why is the worldview of cybernetics an example of this?

The language alone that Descola uses to describe analogism reminds one to a considerable degree of the rhetorical figures of cybernetic theories and the theory of autopoietic systems specifically as it makes reference to assumptions of difference, operational interlinkages of elements, proof of worth through practical effectiveness, the contingent selectivity of boundary-drawing, precedence of functionality of the whole over its parts, and many more. Thus, relations "depend less on ontological properties," which are organized into an analogical collective, "than on an imperative need to integrate them all into a single functional whole" (ibid., pp. 400–401). And he goes on to argue that "the ideology of a collective of this type is bound to be functionalism" (ibid., p. 401). Analogism does not assume robust collective identities that subsequently enter into a relation with each other along their differential distances to one another as totemism does but rather differences that separate all existing beings, which must then be woven, in an act of creative comparison, into a complex web of relations: "[T]he ordinary state of the world is one of differences infinitely multiplied, while resemblance is the hoped-for means of making that world intelligible and bearable" (ibid., p. 202). We see the respective attempts of establishing order in the "chains of being" in the ancient philosophy of Aristotle and in medieval Christianity as well as in Chinese cosmology (e.g., geomancy or feng shui), the Indian caste system, in Mexico among the Nahuas, or also in West Africa (ibid., p. 202 ff.).

However, the analogical concatenation of singular events is contingent—that is, it could always be otherwise—as this can take place according to a number of different criteria and systematics. It thus runs the risk of being permanently called into question by differences and other possible criteria of order and is therefore "constantly threatened with collapse on account of the bewildering plurality" of its elements (ibid., pp. 216–217). The taxonomy of cosmic order can hence not gradually evolve from the

7 In this context, Descola points out that the neurobiologist Francisco Varela, to whom Luhmann makes reference in his theory of autopoietic systems, was "a convinced Buddhist" (Descola 2013, p. 424).

interactions of heterogeneous and ontologically autonomous entities, as in totemism, but must rather be installed from above—as divine will—and rigorously held onto to avert uncertainties. A characteristic feature of analogism is thus a "holism" of its ontological schemata (ibid., p. 228) that borders on a forcible or "totalitarian order" because, and to the extent that, it is basically "always possible to find several possible avenues or chains of correspondences that link two entities" (ibid., p. 238). According to Descola, the Inca Empire is a typical case of such an analogical collective (ibid., p. 272). In analogism, it is necessary to offer a sacrifice to the cosmic powers of order: "Sacrifice could thus be interpreted as a means of action developed within the context of analogical ontologies in order to set up an operational continuity between intrinsically different singularities [...] a means of action that, to this end, makes use of a serial mechanism of connections and disconnections that functions either as an attractor or as a separator" (ibid., p. 231). The existential heterogeneity of the world can hence be converted into cooperation only by way of comprehensively assimilating it to an (all-)encompassing schema of classification. Whoever or whatever fails to comply with this schema is banished: "[B]eyond the limits of the home, which are usually marked out in a quite literal fashion, there lies an 'outworld' populated by outsiders, the indistinct mass of barbarians, savages, and marginal peoples, which is a constant source of threats and a potential breeding ground for co-citizens who can be domesticated" (ibid., p. 303).

It does not take much to again recognize the rigid operational boundary-drawing of binarily coded systems or the universalization of the informational principle as the cybernetic link connecting the most diverse sciences, from biology to sociology. Moreover, the schema of analogism lends plausibility to Lanier's (2010, p. 24) pointed claim that cybernetics is a universalist doctrine that tends toward totalitarianism, whose "first tenet [...] is that all of reality, including humans, is one big information system" (ibid., p. 27). By extending it and anchoring it in society via digital technologies, this analogism becomes a *digital* analogism that is rooted less in specific religious belief systems than in the belief in the all-encompassing power of the digital itself to create and maintain order and integration. To this end, cybernetic alliances are forged that promise to implement digital analogism's political project of ordering. They comprise, for example, computer science and the behavioural sciences, where the latter, with its behaviouristic tradition, has deeply committed to thinking in terms of control loops and systemic self-organization and has recently been reinvigorated through the concept of nudging from behavioural economics (Thaler and Sunstein 2008). MIT scholars such as Alex Pentland (2014) have emphasized the formative potential of using a combination of such cybernetic technologies by means of which ideas could be deliberately disseminated through social media and socio-physically anchored in society. Furthermore, in the context of AI research, neuroscientific approaches and the biology of the brain are becoming more important in combination with the behavioural sciences inasmuch as they promise to capture the connecting points and mental-material peculiarities of hybrid life forms by means of a cybernetic vocabulary. Whether this does justice to the heterogeneity of these life forms is a whole different matter (Ehrenberg 2020, pp. 184, 240).

Critics of this cybernetic expansion, such as Shoshana Zuboff (2019, pp. 416–444), have vehemently warned of the consequences of total behavioural surveillance looming in digital capitalism. In doing so, however, those critics are operating in the context of a cosmological belief system that reproduces the paradoxes of modern naturalism: The human subject, conceived as the centre of ethical action and moral responsibility, remains the normative focus (similarly also Nida-Rümelin and Weidenfeld 2018). This humanism, however, clashes with the empirically observable patterns of production and order of the digital world and thus becomes the target of cybernetic counter-criticism. Reconstructing this argument, as a perpetuation of the old controversy between sovereignty thinking and cybernetics or between a naturalistic and an analogical worldview, can make the paradoxes between both cosmologies visible and demonstrate how and where they result in futile disputes or flawed compromises. Yet the ontological heuristics can furthermore also unearth hidden potential that is more appropriate to a heterogeneously composed, hybrid life form.[8] Now, making such narrow conceptions as well as potentials visible is of great importance for assessing the opportunities and risks of AI for democracy and privacy, as the concluding section of the contribution shall illustrate.

8 The fact that neither a critique of cybernetic expansion from within nor one based on a humanistic appeal to human exceptionalism can be successful is nicely illustrated by the problematizations of Norbert Wiener (1954), one of the founding fathers of cybernetics. Wiener fails to reconcile the linguistic registers so that the cybernetic one ultimately predominates, even if it comes with a warning about unfolding a momentum of its own.

C. Heterogeneous existence and AI in the hybrid life forms of democracy and privacy

Expanding the anthropological perspective on the digital transformation pursues the goal of analysing more comprehensively the resulting postdigital constellation of society with an eye to this transformation's diverse connections and interactions between sociality and digitality and their deep impact. This implies neither denying cybernetic realities nor abandoning the humanistic values of autonomy and self-determination. What is being refuted is merely academic and political cosmologies' quest for hegemony, as, for instance, in the case of cybernetics' spiritual universalism or the frantic clinging to and invoking of subject–object dichotomies, which are constantly undermined by practice. Behavioural feedback, supported by algorithms and appropriate to the situation, can be useful in many areas of everyday life just as autonomy and self-determination as key values of democratic societies continue to be well founded and to claim validity. However, both must be grasped as hybrid, composite life forms, and we must learn to take into account the heterogeneity of their constitutive parts. In this respect, the ontologies of analogism and naturalism fall short, and remedying one through the other leads us only deeper down the path into the aporias and self-misconceptions of (post-)modernity. The latter finds good fortune neither in the techno-scientific promises of digital self-optimization by means of AI and similar forms of computational reason nor in the quest for a heroic subject who establishes the digital society according to clear-cut preferences and plans, whether focused on market-liberal distribution or centred on the state. It is precisely such modes of control, either conceived as an abstract-anonymous system of rule or as personalized sovereignty, that nevertheless make their imprint on our conception of and the debates within digital society. And the more the cybernetic chains of operation gain relevance to the whole edifice—via extending their digital reach and testing them in practice, from optimized flows of traffic, through predictive policing and smart energy grids, to an ecological circular economy—the louder the call for channelling this expansion into responsible paths. Yet the democratic power to exert control has strongly diminished and must to some extent be content with moral appeals and legal amendments addressed at authoritative regimes or those in the private sector who work the levers of corporate control.

Such contradictory dynamics of the postdigital constellation pervade private life as well as democratic opinion and will formation (Lamla et al.

2022). The call for an individual capable of self-determination becomes ever louder in practice and is normatively presupposed the more the individual is gauged via data traces and probabilistically underpinned predictions of behavior. But to develop these abilities, this individual is dependent on the socio-technical infrastructures of self-exploration and mutual recognition via social media that it is supposed to rein in sovereignly (Lamla and Ochs 2019). A way out of this can only be found both at the individual and collective level when this hybridity of life forms is taken seriously and considered in a broader perspective. To this end, theories of plural modes of existence (Latour 2013) as well as the misconceived cosmologies of totemism and animism provide good analytical tools. Totemism, for instance, shows ways toward peaceful coexistence and organic solidarity among heterogeneous groups that have always already been constituted as hybrid—that is, whose identity is rooted in arrangements that are shaped by specific technical infrastructures, semantics, and objects. The conception of such a cosmos consisting of plural and heterogeneous social worlds relativizes the role, but also the burden of responsibility, of the individual person and can at the same time more realistically work toward negotiating value systems in an associative democracy insofar as the collectives in such a social arrangement can resort to methods of collective representation and the demonstration of mutual dependencies and interdependencies. However, such a democracy cannot be conceived as a uniform cybernetic informational space as such a conception would prematurely reduce its constitutive heterogeneity again. An intelligent assembly of heterogeneous collectives cannot rely on digital analogism's inside–outside differentiation, which labels as barbaric all that fails to conform to its informational logic, but must assume elements and also consider those life forms that find their postdigital identity by distancing themselves from the predominant conventions and cybernetic constraints of connectivity.

Such a plurality of social worlds, involving diverse conventions and socio-material practices, is also important to enable and provide a foundation for the development of critical competences that is constitutive for individual self-determination (cf. Lamla 2021). For, from a pragmatic theory perspective, critical competences surely do not develop from the private self-sufficiency of an atomistic mind but rather require encounters with competing conventions and justifications in the social practice of life (Boltanski and Thévenot 2006, pp. 235–236). It is not until situations emerge in which well-established routines of action and justification no longer work and different languages and registers of evaluation vie for dominion instead that critical competences are pragmatically called for and are formed in order to mediate between them in ways that are self-determined and appropriate to the situation. Experiencing crises of this kind is essential for cultivating civil coexistence in the postdigital age, and such experiences should be enabled, and not inhibited, by the digital architecture of a democratic public sphere. Yet the structural logic of cybernetic technologies and AI applications fail to ensure this because they are geared toward the formation, support, and shielding of (everyday) routines.[9] AI and machine learning do not possess the abilities necessary for abductive and autonomous learning. Those abilities emerge only in hybrid constellations of life where heterogeneous experiences encounter one another and call for hypothetical mediation through new knowledge. AI can indeed contribute to this by (unintentionally?) unsettling the taken-for-granted, but it cannot in itself serve as a model for learning since experiencing a crisis and the autonomy of everyday life that can result from this experience only arises where algorithmic routines of problem-solving no longer work. Intelligence emerges where—in modification of Jean Piaget's (1953) theory of development—opportunities exist, in addition to repetitive assimilation to algorithmic schemata of the digital, for the practical accommodation of such schemata in everyday life, that is, opportunities for the redefinition and re-evaluation of such schemata in an expanded realm of association that holds cognitive potentials for the solution of structurally new problems. It is thus not AI that is intelligent but rather what creative thinking and action in heterogeneously constituted practices do with and make out of it.

---

9 Nassehi's (2019, p. 198) concept of technology confirms this: "Technology in this sense is [...] a schema, one that is even more restricted: a fixed schema. The thrust of such an understanding is clear: Technology is separated from utensils and tools and instead associated with practices and chains of action. Such a broad notion of technology then conceives of human actions also as technology to the extent that they occur in a schematic fashion. In this sense, most of our everyday actions are indeed trapped in a kind of prereflexive repetitiousness, whereas intelligent phases, to put it somewhat pointedly, appear only as *lucida intervalla*—at least that is the consequence of this notion of technology." Problematic here is not the notion of technology itself but the last sentence because it assimilates a priori the conduct of everyday life to a cybernetic understanding of technology. This analogism, however, obscures the possibility that it might only be the historical expansion of—especially digital—technology that leads to such a one-sided routinization of everyday action and ideologically obstructs and distorts everyday action of a heterogeneous and intelligent kind that is capable of coming to terms with crises (Oevermann 1995).

This is where we see the importance of additional sources of unsettling and disrupting the given that originates from the ontological heterogeneity of hybrid life forms. Life forms enable access to an existential form of critique that extends beyond the critical interplay of plural conventions and orders of justification (Boltanski 2011, p. 107). They do so less at the level of the different collective forms that various social worlds or group identities take but rather via their heterogeneous compositions themselves. If we look at hybrid life forms from the angle of how they practically interweave different "modes of existence" (Latour 2013), we see, analytically, different and very heterogeneous realms of experience that can more or less come into their own, each in terms of its own existential and "felicity conditions," as Latour puts it, borrowing from speech act theory (ibid., p. 18). Interestingly enough, he calls the villain among the modes of existence in modernity the "double click" (ibid., p. 93), thus identifying a mode that is tightly intertwined with the role of digitality in society. This mode is problematic because it spans—yet again totalizing and analogizing—across all other modes of existence and suggests that they can be simply translated and (readily) made available digitally. Double click denotes a modern schema that neutralizes ontological heterogeneity. By contrast, an anthropological perspective on modernity exposes the peculiarities of different modes of existence, for instance, of the physical-material reproduction of beings, of scientific lecturing, the political assembly of collectives, the psychic metamorphosis of identities, the courting and bonding of passion, and so on. The objective of such a perspective is precisely not to confirm the systems-theoretical schema of functional differentiation, which is then set a priori as a rigid system of reference for comparison, but rather to develop, by means of an exploratory, successive understanding of the case and by comparing cases, a more accurate understanding of the diversity and heterogeneity of modernity, which can be critically directed against the rigid forms of differentiation underlying its institutionalization, in particular against institutional efforts to expand individual modes of existence, which are indeed typical of modernity.

A strength of animism is that it provides schemata for interpretation, experience, and action for the ontological heterogeneity of the world and for the realities of people's lives, schemata that help develop and cultivate symmetrical transitions, connections, and modes of relations between different modes of existence. They combine reciprocal recognition with sensitivity toward otherness. This involves, for example, experiencing and recognizing animals in their animal mode of existence by adopting a reciprocal stance in approaching them. Attributing to them a soul and the status of a human-like subject is not at all to equate all that exists according to this criterion but rather involves a methodical sensitivity that is necessary for opening up to other modes of existence in encounters with them, to understand them and, as a result, to learn from such encounters, for instance, to learn how and where the animal mode of existence, the wild, also pervades one's own life (for an impressive account of this, see Martin 2021). In postdigital society, differences in ontological schemata and cosmologies are important, for example, when it comes to the question of how such a society intends and is able to adapt to ecological self-endangerment: Should this adaptation be by means of more technology and even more intelligent algorithms that analogize all acts of life and integrate them into a global circular economy or by learning, both privately and democratically, to appreciate the interdependence of heterogeneous beings and entities that co-constitute life in society, an interdependence whose relations must be reconfigured in the face of the crisis of modernity?

This is not about a simple either/or but rather raises questions concerning relations of dominance or primacy. In this respect, digital analogism—or the double click—structurally has difficulty being content in itself and imposing rules that could act as a stop mechanism upon its own mode of existence. Such an awareness of limits also remains problematic when the legitimacy of such bounds are derived, with humanistic arrogance, from the principles of abstract reason or seemingly universal morality. Instead, the experience of ontological uncertainty with regard to one's own, hybrid existence could be used as a source of critique and to mobilize new solutions for furnishing one's habitat. Yet this would require that this source of experience be granted space in postdigital society and definitely also a lead role in sounding out ontological heterogeneity. In this case, AI and digital technology would remain means among others, which, in view of their power to change the qualities of action and experience, would have to be equipped with institutional correctives. This means that balancing the benefits of connectivity against the losses in terms of resonance (Rosa 2019) would have to be assessed not only in the currency of the recursive stabilization of behavior or the recursive synchronization of cadence but rather in that of a hybrid life practice that, in learning new forms, principles, techniques, and schemata, becomes (and remains) aware of its crisis-prone, heterogeneous existence. This would require institutionally establishing a relation between AI and practice that moves the obdurate materiality and heterogeneity of postdigital life forms—for example, their manifestations of physical exhaustion or the finite nature of their resources–to the centre of attention, not least in sociology. Were we to conceive of a weak AI in terms of an AI that is subordinate to the private exploration and collective re-assembly of the ontological heterogeneity of hybrid life forms and not one that, by positing a cybernetic cosmology, already precedes or is superordinate to them, much would be gained.

References

August, Vincent (2021): *Technologisches Regieren. Der Aufstieg des Netzwerk-Denkens in der Krise der Moderne. Foucault, Luhmann und die Kybernetik.* Bielefeld: transcript.

Beck, Ulrich (1997): *The Reinvention of Politics. Rethinking Modernity in the Global Social Order.* Cambridge: Polity Press.

Boltanski, Luc (2011): *On Critique. A Sociology of Emancipation.* Cambridge: Polity Press.

Boltanski, Luc and Thévenot, Laurent (2007): *On Justification. Economics of Worth.* Princeton, Oxford: Princeton University Press.

Cardon, Dominique (2016): Deconstructing the Algorithm: Four Types of Digital Information Calculations. In Seyfert, Robert and Roberge, Jonathan (eds.): *Algorithmic Cultures. Essays on Meaning, Performance and New Technologies.* London: Routledge, pp. 95–110.

Descola, Philippe (2013): *Beyond Nature and Culture.* Chicago: The University of Chicago Press.

Ehrenberg, Alain (2020): *The Mechanics of Passions. Brain, Behavior, and Society.* Montreal: McGill-Queens University Press.

Engemann, Christoph (2018): Rekursionen über Körper. Machine Learning-Trainingsdatensätze als Arbeit am Index. In Engemann, Christoph and Sudmann, Andreas (eds.): *Machine Learning. Medien, Infrastrukturen und Technologien der Künstlichen Intelligenz.* Bielefeld: transcript, pp. 247–268.

Floridi, Luciano (2014): *The 4th Revolution. How the Infosphere Is Reshaping Human Reality.* Oxford: Oxford University Press.

Foucault, Michel (1972): *The Archeology of Knowledge and the Discourse on Language.* New York: Pantheon.

Fourier, Charles (1971): Letter to the High Judge [1803]. In Beecher, Jonathan and Bienvenu, Richard: *The Utopian Vision of Charles Fourier. Selected Texts on Work, Love, and Passionate Attraction.* Boston: Bacon Press, pp. 83–92.

Giddens, Anthony (1984): *The Constitution of Society: Outline of the Theory of Structuration.* Cambridge: Polity Press.

Lamla, Jörn (2020): Gesellschaft als digitale Sozialmaschine? Infrastrukturentwicklung von der Plattformökonomie zur kybernetischen Kontrollgesellschaft. In Hentschel, Anja, Hornung, Gerrit, and Jandt, Silke (eds.): *Mensch – Technik – Umwelt: Verantwortung für eine sozialverträgliche Zukunft. Festschrift für Alexander Roßnagel zum 70. Geburtstag.* Baden-Baden: Nomos, pp. 477–496.

Lamla, Jörn (2021): Kritische Bewertungskompetenzen. Selbstbestimmtes Verbraucherhandeln in KI-gestützten IT-Infrastrukturen. Expertise für das Projekt "Digitales Deutschland" von JFF – Jugend, Film, Fernsehen e.V., January 31, 2021. URL: https://digid.jff.de/ki-expertisen/kritische-bewertungskompetenzen-joern-lamla/.

Lamla, Jörn, Büttner, Barbara, Ochs, Carsten, Pittroff, Fabian, and Uhlmann, Markus (2022): Privatheit und Digitalität. Zur soziotechnischen Transformation des selbstbestimmten Lebens. In Roßnagel, Alexander and Friedewald, Michael (eds.): *Die Zukunft von Privatheit und Selbstbestimmung. Analysen und Empfehlungen zum Schutz der Grundrechte in der digitalen Welt.* Wiesbaden: Springer Vieweg, pp. 125–158.

Lamla, Jörn and Ochs, Carsten (2019): Selbstbestimmungspraktiken in der Datenökonomie: Gesellschaftlicher Widerspruch oder 'privates' Paradox? In Blättel-Mink, Birgit and Kenning, Peter (eds.): *Paradoxien des Verbraucherverhaltens.* Wiesbaden: Springer Gabler, pp. 25–39.

Lanier, Jaron (2010): *You Are Not a Gadget: A Manifesto.* New York: Knopf.

Latour, Bruno (2013): *An Inquiry into Modes of Existence. An Anthropology of the Moderns.* Cambridge, Massachusetts: Harvard University Press.

Latour, Bruno (2018): *Down to Earth. Politics in the New Climatic Regime.* Cambridge: Polity Press.

Mannheim, Karl (1991): *Ideology and Utopia.* London: Routledge.

Martin, Nastassja (2021): *An das Wilde glauben.* Berlin: Matthes und Seitz.

Mau, Steffen (2017): *Das metrische Wir. Über die Quantifizierung des Sozialen.* Berlin: Suhrkamp.

Nassehi, Armin (2019): *Muster. Theorie der digitalen Gesellschaft.* Munich: C.H. Beck.

Nida-Rümelin, Julian and Weidenfeld, Nathalie (2018): *Digitaler Humanismus. Eine Ethik für das Zeitalter der Künstlichen Intelligenz.* Munich: Piper.

Oevermann, Ulrich (1995): Ein Modell der Struktur von Religiosität. Zugleich ein Strukturmodell von Lebenspraxis und von sozialer Zeit. In Wohlrab-Sahr, Monika (ed.): Bio*graphie und Religion. Zwischen Ritual und Selbstsuche.* Frankfurt/Main, New York: Campus Verlag, pp. 27–102.

Pentland, Alex (2014): *Social Physics. How Good Ideas Spread: The Lessons from a New Science.* Brunswick, London: Scribe.

Piaget, Jean (1953): The Origin of Intelligence in the Child. Jean Piaget: Selected Works Volume 3. Milton Park, UK, New York, NY: Routledge.

Reimer, Ricarda T.D./Flückinger, Silvan (2021): Wachsame Maschinen. Freiräume und Notwendigkeit der Verantwortungsübernahme bei der Entwicklung sozialer Roboter und deren Integration in Bildungsinstitutionen. In Stapf, Ingrid et al. (eds.): *Aufwachsen in überwachten Umgebungen. Interdisziplinäre Positionen zu Privatheit und Datenschutz in Kindheit und Jugend.* Baden-Baden: Nomos, pp. 125–140.

Rosa, Hartmut (2019): *Resonance. A Sociology of Our Relationship to the World.* Cambridge, Medford: Polity Press.

Saint-Simon, Henri (1975): *Selected writings on science, industry, and social organisation.* London/New York: Routledge.

Stäheli, Urs (2021): *Soziologie der Entnetzung*. Berlin: Suhrkamp.

Stalder, Felix (2016): *Kultur der Digitalität*. Berlin: Suhrkamp.

Thaler, Richard and Sunstein, Cass R. (2008): *Nudge: Improving Decisions About Health, Wealth, and Happiness*. New Haven. Yale University Press.

Turing, Alan M. (1950): Computing Machinery and Intelligence. *Mind*, 59, pp. 433–460.

Viveiros de Castro, Eduardo (2014): *Cannibal Metaphysics*. Minneapolis: Univocal Publishing.

Wiener, Norbert (1954): *The Human Use of Human Beings. Cybernetics and Society*. Boston: Houghton-Mifflin.

Zuboff, Shoshana (2019): *The Age of Surveillance Capitalism: The Fight for a Human Future at the New Frontier of Power*. New York: Public Affairs.

Artificial Intelligence, Smart Orders, and the Problem of Legal and Moral Responsibility

Klaus Günther

The more precise the possible predictions of individual behavior and the more effective the possible behavior modifications through AI become, the more obvious it is to use them for the prevention of deviant behavior. The goal of using technical means to encourage the addressees of the law to behave in accordance with the law or to make unlawful behavior completely impossible without the threat or application of legal sanctions seems to have so much persuasive power that the question of what consequences this would have for the essential characteristics of normative orders, especially the law, is neglected. Above all, we must ask what would then become of a central prerequisite of law: The concept of a person who can be held responsible for their deviant behavior. Would this concept, which is based on the ability to decide individually for or against following the law, be rendered superfluous by smart orders that make deviant behavior impossible? And what consequences would this have for the related ability to question the law itself and its legitimacy?

A. How is it possible to limit instrumental power of AI?

It is not only since the accelerating development of artificial intelligence and its diverse applications that there has been growing concern about the power it can wield and the dangerous consequences for the freedom of the individual and society as a whole. This danger arises from the fact that the "data collected by the operators of such technologies during individual use is increasingly detached from its purpose of collection and transformed into independent information capital."[1] This information capital can be used to generate both economic and state power.

1 Spiros Simitis, in: Simitis, Bundesdatenschutzgesetz Kommentar (BDSG), Einleitung: Geschichte – Ziele – Prinzipien, 14. Aufl. Baden-Baden 2014. Rn. 111.

At the heart of this is a phenomenon characterized by Soshana Zuboff as "instrumental power".[2] It is made up of two components that constitute the opportunity, corresponding to Weber's classic definition of power, to impose one's will on third parties, even against their resistance.[3] This opportunity goes hand in hand with the increasing ability to predict future behavior on the basis of precise observations and to use this predictive knowledge to modify the future behavior of third parties in the pursuit of one's own interests and intentions. This is made possible by the fact that users are incentivized to produce and use as much data as possible, which is collected by the providers and analysed according to aspects determined by them at an increasing distance from the original purpose of collection. The more frequently and comprehensively this happens and the more precise and intensive the technical possibilities of data analysis become, the more effective (and efficient) the possibilities of predicting the future thoughts, feelings, intentions and actions of users on the basis of so-called profiles become. The more precise the predictive knowledge becomes, the greater the opportunities to influence or modify future behavior. Instrumental power is therefore made up of the potential for predicting and modifying behavior that comes with the use of digital media. Unlike the totalitarian power responsible for the human catastrophes of the 20th century, it does not aim to ideologically penetrate body and soul in order to motivate them to behave as desired from within, but rather to modify behavior externally through data-supported observation and prediction knowledge. The more accurate the personality profile distilled from this becomes, the more detailed the external incentives can be specified to which the users will react in the predicted way (so-called micro-targeting).

Instrumental power is driven by a "utopia of certainty" of human behavior, which should become as predictable and controllable as the functional processes of a machine.[4] The main aim is to anticipate possible deviations or errors that could impair the smooth functioning of the machine in accordance with the specified program in order to prevent them from occurring. If this utopia is transferred to human behavior, namely social interactions and communications, it can be applied above all to the practice

2 The concept of instrumental power has been introduced and explained by Shoshana Zuboff, *Das Zeitalter des Überwachungskapitalismus* (2018) 412.

3 Max Weber, Wirtschaft und Gesellschaft, 5. A., Tübingen 1921/1976, S. 29.

4 Zuboff, Überwachungskapitalismus, S. 461-480. See also: Klaus Günther, Die Zukunft der Freiheit in smarten Ordnungen, in: WestEnd – Neue Zeitschrift für Sozialforschung, 17/2 (2020), S. 165-175.

of following norms and rules by their addressees. If norms and rules are there to guide their addressees in their behavior so that they do what the norm requires or refrain from doing what it prohibits, then the avoidance of deviations is part of their meaning. However, since experience teaches us that deviations always occur in practice and that the mutual expectation of following the rules is repeatedly disappointed as a result, instrumental power could be used to perfect rule-following in such a way that the mutual expectation at least approximately reaches the level of certainty. The utopia of certainty would merge with the claim to compliance with normative orders in such a way that it would become the utopia of the certainty of norm compliance. Instrumental power would have to start at the source of deviant behavior in the norm addressee - at her/his subjectivity in relation to the norm's claim to be followed. Norms are addressed to people who must first decide to comply with the norm or at least have decided to do so at some point, even if they may currently do so out of habit or quasi-automatically in many cases.

If instrumentary power is aimed at drying up this source of constant uncertainty in rule-following, any attempt to tame instrumental power normatively, e.g. through legal regulation, could lead to a dilemma: To the extent that legal systems move towards using instrumental power to ensure general rule-following, legal regulation to limit instrumental power would in turn be dependent on this kind of power or, by shutting down the source of uncertainty in norm-following behavior, it would have lost its specific addressee, the legal person with its subjectivity. As I will show below, the reason for this is the freedom to engage in deviant behavior, which is a necessary precondition for normative orders in general and for legal orders in particular.

B. The internal connection between norm, responsibility and deviant behavior

Lon Fuller's 1964 monograph on the "Morality of Law" contains the following remark: "To embark on the enterprise of subjecting human conduct to the governance of rules involves of necessity a commitment to the view that man is, or can become, a responsible agent, capable of understanding and following rules, and answerable for his defaults. Every departure from the principles of law's inner morality is an affront to man's dignity as a responsible agent."[5]

For Fuller, there is an internal, necessary connection ("involves of necessity the commitment") between rules and the conception ("view") of addressees of these rules as responsible persons. No rule without responsible addressees. Fuller only says in a subordinate clause what exactly this means: "capable of understanding and following rules, and answerable for his defaults." While the first part refers to the cognitive and motivational abilities required for rule compliance (ability to understand and follow rules), the second part refers to a specific position or status associated with the concept of a responsible person: To be able and supposed to give a response in case of non-compliance or violation of the rule. Fuller refers here to the literal sense of the term ver-answering (Latin respondeo). Anyone who does not follow a rule is able and obliged to respond. It is therefore the specific situation of breaking the rule that makes the necessary connection between rule and responsibility evident. However, there are two further aspects to this description:

(1) When it comes to answering, a communicative relationship is presupposed, i.e. in addition to the answering speaker, there is another speaker/listener to whom the answer is addressed. It is an answer to the other person's critical question as to why the person acting did not follow the rule although he should have done so. Following a rule is therefore not only an intersubjective practice because, as Wittgenstein has shown, no one can follow a rule only once and for themselves alone, i.e. because intersubjectivity is part of the meaning of "rule".[6] Furthermore, because there is a practice of reacting to the non-observance of a rule, in which critical questions are asked and answered. Fuller's opponent, H.L.A. Hart, described this practice in a similar way: Whether someone follows a rule can only be inferred from an internal point of view, which consists of a critical reflective attitude that manifests itself in an intersubjective practice of criticizing rule violations.

"What is necessary is that there should be a critical reflective attitude to certain patterns of behavior as a common standard, and that this should display itself in criticism (including self-criticism), demands for conformity, and in acknowledgements that such criticism and demands are justified, all

5 Fuller, The Morality of Law, New Haven 1964/69, 162.

6 Ludwig Wittgenstein, Philosophische Untersuchungen, Frankfurt/Main 1975, p. 127ff. (Nr. 199ff.).

of which find their characteristic expression in the normative terminology of 'ought', 'must', and 'should', 'right' and 'wrong'."[7]

(2) The second element contained in Fuller's "answerability" is only indirectly apparent. If responsibility refers to the case of non-compliance with the rule, this presupposes that a rule cannot actually be followed. This sounds trivial prima facie - but it is not. The fact that a rule should be followed is part of its meaning. It would be nonsensical to establish a rule without the requirement that it be followed. But rules and norms are not of such a nature that they would guarantee and ensure their own compliance. A rule always includes the possibility of its violation. A rule wants to be obeyed (which makes it susceptible to the utopia of the certainty of norm compliance), but only in a way that includes the possibility of non-compliance. To put it in paradoxical terms: Following a rule presupposes the possibility of not following it. This is presumably an unavoidable presupposition of the practice of following rules.

Of course, a distinction must be made with regard to the possible reasons for non-compliance. One reason may be the incorrect application of the rule. In this case, the addressee wants to follow the rule, but makes mistakes because he either does not understand its meaning correctly (cognitive error) or because he does not manage to control his behavior in such a way that he follows the rule despite understanding it correctly (motivational error). However, if he is cognitively and motivationally capable of following the rule, but does not actually follow it, then he finds himself in a position where he has to answer to third parties. It is only because this possibility - or freedom - exists that we can also be responsible for following the rule. If we were to follow a rule automatically, the concept of a responsible person would be superfluous - any more than a machine is responsible for functioning in accordance with the technical rules of its mechanical construction. The utopia of norm-following certainty would therefore, if realized, transform norm-following subjects into machines.

7 H.L.A. Hart, The Concept of Law, Oxford 1961, p. 55f.

C. The freedom to engage in deviant behavior

It therefore seems sensible to speak of norms instead of rules in general - which is presumably also the meaning that corresponds to the use of the word by Lon Fuller (and also H.L.A. Hart). It would then apply to every social practice that is constituted and regulated by norms that it presupposes the concept of a responsible person and thus includes the possibility that the addressees may or may not follow their norms. This applies to every kind of norm, including the most elementary of all norms, which is inherent in a promise. Anyone who promises something to another person creates a norm (or, in a specific case, updates the current norm that promises should be kept) for which they are responsible. He thereby commits himself to the future behavior of another person. However, he is only responsible for keeping the promise because he has the option of not keeping the promise. It is therefore solely up to him whether he will do what he has promised or not (apart from extreme changes in circumstances that make it impossible to keep the promise - clausula rebus sic stantibus). The ability to commit oneself to one's own behavior towards others in the future is anything but natural, and it includes the freedom to behave differently. According to Nietzsche, the greatest and at the same time paradoxical task for man is therefore: "To breed an animal that is allowed to promise."[8]

Following Lon Fuller's quote, people who embark on the project of regulating their coexistence through norms are therefore taking a certain risk if following a norm also means not being able to follow the norm. The risk lies in the norm addressee as a responsible person. Instead of creating mechanisms that ensure automatic and perfect compliance with norms (as with a machine), a practice is established that H.L.A. Hart has described as a critical reflective attitude towards norms. It is the practice of criticizing deviant behavior, possibly even the practice of criticism at all.

I. Techniques of risk minimization

However, communities with a norm-guided social practice do not completely refrain from minimizing the risk of deviant behavior in other ways. Which additional measures are taken depends, among other things, on the

8 Friedrich Nietzsche, Zur Genealogie der Moral, Dritte Abhandlung, in: Werke, hrsgg. v. Karl Schlechta, Band 2, Darmstadt 1994, S. 239 (Herv. F.N.).

type of norm in question. Essential are processes of socialization, education and cultivation - what Michel Foucault called "subjectivation" - which not only contribute to the development of those cognitive and motivational skills and dispositions to follow basic social norms, but also to a person learning what it means to be a responsible person. This begins with children learning to promise and to trust in a promise made to them - but then also experiencing that not every promise made to them is kept. Of course, they also learn that there is a social practice of criticizing the breaking of a promise and how to participate in this practice. It is possible that the experience of being able to violate norms and being criticized by others for doing so is part of the process of learning what it means to follow norms as a responsible person - as can be seen in adolescents in the adolescent phase, for example.[9] In addition, there are various social conditions that must be fulfilled, at least to a certain extent, in order to become a responsible person and to be criticized as such for one's own actions. To the extent that compliance with norms becomes unreasonable because the addressees are hardly in a position to do so given the social conditions, the criticism of an addressee for violating these norms becomes unfair and the practice of critical reflective attitude among responsible persons becomes pointless.[10]

I am concentrating here only on one particular type, the legal norm. Not the only, but a central way of making norm compliance more likely is to link the legal norm with the threat of coercion or even sanctions in the event of norm violation. Some authors, such as the proponents of the coercion thesis, even consider this coupling to be a necessary part of the concept of law.[11] Irrespective of this, however, it is easy to see that the addition of a threat of coercion (and, in the case of de facto deviation, execution) does not change the fact that the addressee of a legal norm is subject to the presupposition that he has the option of not complying with the norm. If legal norms are coupled with a threat of coercion, this only means (provided that it is credible and the addressee is aware of the threat)

9 See, e.g., Gertrud Nunner-Winkler´s research results, in: Rainer Döbert/Gertrud Nunner-Winkler, Adoleszenzkrise und Identitätsbildung, Frankfurt/Main 1975; Nummer-Winkler, Prozesse moralischen Lernens und Entlernens, in: Zeitschrift für Pädagogik 55 (2009), S. 528-548 (534ff.).

10 Klaus Günther, Zwischen Ermächtigung und Disziplinierung. Verantwortung im gegenwärtigen Kapitalismus, in: Axel Honneth (Hg.), Befreiung aus der Mündigkeit. Paradoxien des gegenwärtigen Kapitalismus, Frankfurt/M. u. New York 2002, 117 – 140.

11 See, recently: Himma, Coercion and the Nature of Law, Oxford 2020.

that the violation of the norm appears less preferable to the addressee than compliance due to his individual preferences. According to Robert Nozick's analysis, it merely provides an additional reason for deciding in favour of compliance and against non-compliance; according to Joseph Raz, it even provides only a subsidiary and partial auxiliary reason.[12] However, this does not eliminate either the possibility or the freedom of the addressee to decide against compliance with the norm and to accept the sanction with its disadvantages. The threat of coercion does not eliminate the responsibility of the norm addressee; on the contrary, it is even the justifying reason for imposing the sanction on him in the event of a violation of the norm. The alternatives would be a system of brutal terror or a system of manipulation and control that penetrates into the smallest capillaries of the psyche, of complete conditioning.[13] Here, responsibility would lie, if at all, with a centre that manages the lives and psyches of the norm addressees in order to ensure compliance with the norm. In contrast, compliance with legal norms by responsible actors involves a kind of decentralized ontology of individual subjects who each comply with norms on their own - or not.[14] With regard to the alternative between a conventional criminal law with a criminal sanction for deviant behavior and a prevention that makes this impossible from the outset through technical precautions, Bernhard Haffke has clearly marked the consequences that endanger freedom - at the same time as a warning against a superficial understanding of the ultima ratio principle in criminal law, which approves of any alternative regulation that does not require a criminal sanction. "While psychological prevention, albeit by means of reward and punishment, still chooses the path - the rocky but decent path - via the subject, in technical prevention the subject is no longer considered from the outset: Deviant behavior has become impossible."[15] With the responsible subject, its basis, the freedom to decide

12 Robert Nozick, Coercion, in: Morgenbesser/Suppes/White, M. (eds.): Philosophy, Science, and Method: Essays in Honor of Ernest Nagel, New York NY 1969, 440–472; Joseph Raz, Practical Reason and Norms, London 1975, 162f.

13 Like the *ludovico technique* in Antony Burgess (1962)/Stanley Kubricks (1971) dystopical Novel/Film „A Clockwork Orange", together wirh the warning of a priest(*sic!*) to the protagonist, before he participates voluntarily in the conditioning experiment: "If a man cannot choose he ceases to be man.".

14 Günter Jakobs, Das Schuldprinzip, Rheinisch-Westfälische Akademie der Wissenschaften, Vorträge G 319, 1993, p. 34, and the parable on p. 34 f.

15 Bernhard Haffke, Die Legitimation des staatlichen Strafrechts zwischen Effizienz, Freiheitsverbürgung und

for or against compliance with the norm, also disappears: "Classical liberal criminal law deliberately chooses the path via the offender as a moral personality, as a responsible subject and, by proceeding in this way, respects his freedom to deviate from the norm."[16]

II. Compliance with norms - certainty or trust?

Every norm-guided social practice, and in particular every legal system, is therefore dependent on the existence of institutions, procedures and practices for criticizing deviant behavior, coercion and other sanctions, as well as on mutual trust that the responsible person will behave in accordance with the norm. Every legal system is based not only on this mutual trust, but also on the fact that in the event of deviant behavior, the institutionalized procedures for criticizing deviant behavior (e.g. court proceedings) are activated and the previously threatened sanctions are also imposed (legal trust).

Despite all the measures mentioned to ensure average compliance with norms, the risk of deviant behavior remains, albeit certainly to a lesser extent than without them. Trust, too, is only necessary because we have reasons to rely on others, but no certainty. According to Georg Simmel's well-known formulation, trust is "a hypothesis of future behavior that is certain enough to base practical action on, (...) as a hypothesis a middle state between knowing and not knowing about people."[17] With the help of new digital technologies, especially AI, there now seems to be a possibility of eliminating this risk or at least minimizing it to such an extent that the probability of choosing this behavioural alternative is significantly reduced. This is the promise or vision of smart orders. They are designed to minimize or completely eliminate deviations from their norms through intelligent design and with the help of algorithmic operations.[18] The trust in the ability and willingness of norm addressees to comply with the norm, which is risky due to the ever-present possibility of deviation, could thus be transformed into a certainty of compliance with the norm.

Prävention, in: Bernd Schünemann, Hans Achenbach u.a. (Hrsg.), Festschrift für Claus Roxin zum 70. Geb., Berlin/New York 2001, Sp 955 – 975, p. 967.

16 Haffee, p. 967.

17 Georg Simmel, Soziologie, Berlin 1908/1983, 263 (trans. K.G.).

18 Günther, Von normativen zu smarten Ordnungen?, in: Forst/Günther (Hrsg.), Normative Ordnungen, Berlin 2021, S. 523-552; ders., Die Zukunft der Freiheit in smarten Ordnungen, in: WestEnd – Neue Zeitschrift für Sozialforschung, 17/2 (2020), 165-175.

The risk that a promise will not be kept can be eliminated in a smart contract, for example, by automating the execution of performance and consideration in a blockchain. The risk of criminal offences can be minimized through situation- and person-related predictive policing and algorithm-based prevention of future criminals. Projects such as anticipatory governance and smart cities are motivated by the prospect of defusing social conflicts preventively ("prevention rather than cure") and organizing the "confluence" of urban interactions without conflict. The extreme case is the social credit model practiced in some regions of China.[19] With the help of such technologies, whose effectiveness can be greatly enhanced by AI, a society can come even closer to the supposed ideal of perfect compliance with norms, without it even being a question of "the view that man is, or can become, a responsible agent, capable of understanding and following rules, and answerable for his defaults."

D. AI as a new technology of self-commitment?

Of course, attempts have always been made to develop technologies that make compliance with norms more likely - coercion and its threat are perhaps the most primitive form. However, this also includes the technologies of self-coercion (or self-discipline). At the latest since economics abandoned the rationally calculating *homo oeconomicus* as the standard model, rational strategies for dealing with imperfectly rational behavior have become the focus of attention, such as the liberal-paternalistic model of nudging.[20] One possible strategy is self-commitment. The example of Ulysses has become famous: he has his companions tie him to the mast of his ship so that he can pass the island of the sirens and listen to their beguiling song without surrendering to their power, which tempts him to commit suicide. Jon Elster used this example in his early studies on imperfect rationality to show that the knowledge of one's own imperfections and weaknesses does not have to lead to fatalism, but can instead be the reason for choosing a strategy of self-binding:

19 For further elaboration on tnese examples see: Klaus Günther, Von normativen zu smarten Ordnungen?

20 Richard H. Thaler u. Cass Sunstein, *Nudge. Improving Decisions About Health, Wealth and Happiness*, New Haven: Yale UP, 2008.

"Ulysses was not fully rational, for a rational creature would not have to resort to this device; nor was he simply the passive and irrational vehicle for his changing wants and desires, for he was capable of achieving by indirect means the same end as a rational person could have realized in a direct manner."[21]

Anyone who, like Ulysses, foresees at time t1 that he will make a wrong, i.e. at least self-interestedly irrational, choice at time t2 and wants to avoid this, is behaving rationally if he takes precautions at time t1 that prevent him from behaving irrationally at time t2. This is generally more rational than relying on having sufficient psychological resilience in the decisive situation against the strong tendency to make the wrong choice. The foreseeable deficit in rationality in t2 is compensated for by the rationality in t1, so that the person behaves just as rationally as if they had acted completely rationally in t2.

It is obvious to conceive of smart orders as a means by which behavior that deviates from the norm in t1 can be technically excluded in t2. They would then be nothing other than a technically optimized tool for *precommitting oneself*[22], which would also have the advantage that it would operate with much less coarse means than Odysseus' shackles, which cut painfully into the body and were lashed even tighter at the decisive moment in response to the command given in advance. The use of a large number of apps offered on smartphones has become a widespread everyday practice in order to encourage a healthier lifestyle with more physical exercise or a reduction in body weight, for example, as a quantified self with self-tracking and an exchange with others on corresponding platforms that serves the purpose of mutual observation and control. And why shouldn't providers, software companies, health insurance companies and medicine, which can make diagnosis and therapy more effective and efficient through personalization, collect and analyse the data produced in the process and generalize it into behavioural patterns in order to perfect technically optimized self-restraint for preventive healthcare? One of the possible interpretations is that this, too, is only a technical optimization of practices of self-observation and self-care for the sake of a virtuous good life, which date back to antiquity.[23]

21 Jon Elster, *Ulysses and the Sirens*, Cambridge UK 1979/2013, p. 36.

22 Elster, *Ulysses and the Sirens*, p. 37.

23 See, e.g.: Stefan Meißner, *Lifelogging. Selbstvermessung als Möglichkeit von Selbststeigerung, Selbsteffektivierung und Selbstbegrenzung*, Berlin 2016; against rush critism

Would this not also apply to smart orders, provided they are only produced through collective self-determination? Jon Elster did indeed oppose the simple transfer of individual to collective self-binding when he interpreted constitutions primarily as a strategy for binding future political majorities to fundamental norms and less as a self-binding of the constitution-making actors themselves.[24] However, at least a democratically established coercive law could ideally be understood as an order through which the co-legislators bind themselves in their future role as norm addressees by means of the threat and execution of coercion. In this way, they would also use a technical means, acting on the body, the psyche and the emotions, to ensure compliance with the norm even in the more frequent case that someone acts not out of insight into good normative reasons or out of respect for the law, but in order to avoid disadvantages. For example, theories of negative prevention rely on the psychological effect of the threat of punishment and penalties, which create so much fear in potential delinquents that they avoid norm-violating behavior. Although the threat of coercion does not have the effect of depriving the person concerned of all freedom to behave in a deviant manner (accepting the disadvantages), it does reduce the probability. However, there are at least three reasons to doubt the equation of smart orders with analogous techniques of self-binding.[25]

The *first* reason relates to the assumption that we are actually dealing with collective autonomy through self-binding or self-intervention. When Ulysses orders his companions to bind him, it is he himself who binds himself by influencing his own future behavior with technical means and the help of third parties. Only under this condition does he preserve his autonomy, even if he obliges his companions in t1 not to listen to his expected command in t2 to untie him now. The situation is different when companies or states apply such technologies to customers or citizens in a way that is not or only partially transparent to them and over which they have no or only limited decision-making and control. In this case, those who decide on the use of technical means to modify future behavior are different from those who are affected by it. In addition, despite all efforts to ensure transparency and information, the individual modalities, duration, mode of action and, not least, the techniques used to skim and use further

see also Kathrin Passig, Internetkolumne. Unsere Daten, unser Leben, in: *Merkur* (756) 2012, S. 420 - 427.

24 Jon Elster, *Ulysses Unbound*, Cambridge UK 2000, S. 88 - 118.

25 See Günther, Die Zukunft der Freiheit.

behavioural data will remain largely hidden from them, if this is not already covered by commercial or state secrecy. A publicly applicable legal norm is different from an algorithm. Even if it is in the best interests of those affected, i.e. if it would be rational for them to submit to the externally determined smart binding, there is still an asymmetrical relationship between the two. In this respect, it makes no difference whether we are talking about smart technologies or analogue ones. Liberal paternalism, which makes use of practices such as nudging, is not immune to this criticism either, even if the asymmetrical relationship remains largely transparent here. It is all the more likely to apply if those affected are simultaneously moving in digital filter bubbles that, with the help of patterns generated from their own behavioural data, preferably only provide them with information and impulses that dispose them to accept smart ties without question.[26]

Of course, it could be the case that those affected voluntarily and in full knowledge of all the circumstances agree to a technical influence on their practical attitudes to standards, be it contractually in relation to a company or by way of collective self-binding through democratic legislation. Would it then not be in accordance with its own will? Rousseau had conceived the social contract in a similar way under similar conditions, which contains the clause that the dissenter may be forced to be free. For Kant, too, it was clear that the mechanics of coercive law, which act solely on the body, are morally unsuspicious if they are coerced in the name of practical reason.[27] Autonomy is preserved by Kant with the republican form of self-legislation. In this respect, wouldn't smart technologies for enforcing norms only be an optimization of analogous ones? However, Rousseau and Kant also foreshadow the dualism characteristic of modern capitalist societies between the two worlds of the *citoyen* and the *bourgeois*, the virtuous republican co-legislator and the private individual driven by his selfish passions. If Kant considers the task of establishing a state to be solvable even for a nation of devils, he makes it clear that the naked self-interest of each individual is sufficient to recognize that a state order of coercive law is preferable to a state in which everyone must fear for their lives in a permanent civil war.

At the same time, however, both authors maintain that man is not lost in his diabolical, instinctive nature, which tends towards selfishness and

26 S. dazu Günther, Die Zukunft der Freiheit.

27 S. Marcus Willaschek, Recht ohne Ethik? Kant über die Gründe, das Recht nicht zu brechen, in: Volker Gehrhardt (Hrsg.), Kant im Streit der Fakultäten, Berlin/New York 2005, S. 188 – 204, S. 195.

is corrupted by passions, with its cognitive and motivational deficits, but always has general human reason at his disposal. The physical mechanics of coercive law can then only be justified in the event that rational insight alone is not sufficient to comply with a rationally justified norm - not the other way around. This is why they trust the subjects of general human reason as flesh-and-blood human beings to be co-legislators and to be able to follow the law out of rational motives. There is no other way to justify the everyday mutual trust in a general willingness to follow the law in the event that the law cannot directly compel. Without such trust, no legal system would be stable in the long term, because the law cannot be enforced always and everywhere. Ulysses knows when his passions will lead him to his doom and takes specifically tailored, temporary technical precautions, thus retaining the upper hand with his insight.[28]

Smart orders, however, and this is the *second* reason for scepticism about the suitability of AI as a tool for self-commitment to self-legislation or political autonomy, silence this often conflictual interplay between the two worlds. With their appearance, the negative side of the norm addressee's fallibility becomes absolute, as if deviant behavior were the constantly disruptive normal case that constantly endangers general security. With technology, the view of norm addressees is changing. To the extent that norm compliance with or without persons qua norm addressees can be technically (re-)produced and thus perfected, the enterprise of realizing normative orders via persons who are at the same time autonomous and fallible flesh-and-blood human beings appears risky, dysfunctional and prone to disruption in comparison to the more effective technologies. The distrust in the general willingness to follow norms may also increase in modern, globalized, pluralistic and fragmented societies, so that for this reason too, smart norm realization appears to many to be a better alternative. As in the analogue two-world concept, human nature is then considered to be in need of control and mastery, but no longer with coercion, repression and the subjectification of control functions and techniques of self-control, which in extreme cases produce an authoritarian character, but with smart technologies that are softer, more sustainable, more effective and more

28 For Max Horkheimer und Theodor W. Adorno, *Dialektik der Aufklärung*, Frankfurt a. M., 1944/1973, S. 42, Ulysses is nevertheless already "the archetype of the bourgeois individual, whose concept originates in that unified self-assertion whose pre-worldly pattern is provided by the driven individual.".

efficient. In the best-case scenario, even people with fallible behavior can be completely replaced by technologies.

Based on comprehensive personality profiles, which are already being used for commercial purposes by collecting data and analysing it with the help of AI, laws could be individually tailored for each citizen. These would no longer take the form of abstract and general norms, which would then have to be cognitively and motivationally concretised by the addressees for their respective situation, but would instead take the form of individualised behavioural directives. Casey and Niblett analysed what such norms could look like back in 2013: "Predictive technology will generate greater ex ante information that can be used by lawmakers to write highly specific, complex laws. And individuals will receive notice of these complex laws in a simple form thanks to technological advances in communication. This will be the death of rules and standards and the rise of microdirectives."[29] Such microdirectives could, for example, set individualised maximum speed limits for every car driver in every situation: "For example, a microdirective might provide a speed limit of 51.2 miles per hour for a particular driver with twelve years of experience on a rainy Tuesday at 3:27 p.m. The legislation remains constant, but the microdirective updates as quickly as conditions change."[30] Legislation would only set the political goal of determining driving speeds in road traffic in such a way as to enable safe and trouble-free mobility for everyone at the same time as everyone else. This goal would then be transformed into an individual behavioural directive for each driver with the help of AI-generated micro-directives, which could be adapted to changing conditions at any time. The problem that a general and abstract standard cannot foresee all future cases of application and that the addressees have different capabilities and capacities in different situations, e.g., do not have sufficient motivation to comply with the standard in each individual case or make mistakes when specifying the standard to their case with a specific context and complexity would be solved. As Omri Ben-Shahar and Ariel Porat who both defend such a vision of personalized law frame it: "Rather than blindfolded, let the law know everything that is relevant about people, apply the underlying legal principles to facts of each person, and thus tailor personalized legal regimes. If medicine, education, or parenting can treat, teach, or nurture better when personalized and

29 Anthony J. Casey and Anthony Niblett, The Death of Rules and Standards, in: Indiana Law Journal, 92, (2017), pp. 1407 – 1447 (1446).

30 Ibid., p. 1404.

adjusted to the subjective, why not law?"[31] This even more so if the (self-driving) cars were technically equipped in such a way that they implement the behavioural directive directly, so that a driver no longer has to act at all. What applies to road traffic can be applied mutatis mutandis to all other legally regulated areas.

Thirdly, this leads to the problem of the tendency to demoralize individual behavior, as described and critically explained by Roger Brownsword and Evgeny Morozov, among others.[32] To the extent that people become accustomed to smart orders, their willingness and ability to form a moral judgment in confrontation with their own freedom to behave differently and to actively use practical reason, which can be put into action, decreases. The automation of virtue could result in a "moral disability" in the medium term.[33] In a similar way to how the constant use of a calculator atrophies the ability to apply mathematical rules and perform more complex mathematical operations by hand, let alone calculate simpler tasks in one's head, smart systems can lead to a loss of moral deliberation by either allowing norm-following behavior to be performed automatically by the person or replacing it entirely. The "citizen does not have to weigh the reasonableness of her actions, nor does she have to search for the content of a law. She just obeys a simple directive".[34] The possibility of deviating from the norm is, as it were, the sting that constantly challenges the norm addressee to use his practical reason by having to ask himself about the reasons for his judgments and actions as well as their justification to himself and others. [35] This is not least in order to consider and weigh up the reasons that may speak for or against following this norm - or perhaps another, perhaps even contradictory norm - in the specific situation. In this way, people

31 Omri Ben-Shahar, What is Personalised Law?, Faculty of Law Blogs/University of Oxford, 27 June 2022; Omri Ben-Shahar and Ariel Porat, Personalized Law - Different Rules for Different People, Oxford 2021.

32 Roger Brownsword, Lost in Translation: Legality, Regulatory Margins, and Technological Management, in: Berkeley Technology Law Journal 26 (2011), pp. 1321-1366 (1356), Evgeny Morozev, Smarte neue Welt. Digitale Technik und die Freiheit des Menschen (engl. Orig.: To Save Everything, Click Here), München 2013, p. 326 u. 343.

33 Morovzev, p. 337f; referring to: Ian Kerr, Digital Locks and the Automation of Virtue, in: Michael Geist, ed., From "Radical Extremism" to "Balanced Copyright": Canadian Copyright and the Digital Agenda, Irwin Law, 2010, p. 247 – 303 (282).

34 Casey/Niblett (n. 29) 1402.

35 Deviant behavior is therefore often also a source of innovation - in both a bad (criminal) and a good (enabling moral learning) sense.

develop (especially during and after adolescence, *see IV above*) into morally capable of judgement and action, i.e. into responsible persons who possess the critical reflective attitude described above (IV), who are able to criticize each other for behavior that deviates from the norm and thus participate freely and actively in rule-guided intersubjective moral practice. In smart orders, on the other hand, they adopt an observational attitude towards norms and allow their behavior to be passively guided by technology.

As a result, they are not only gradually losing their capacity for moral judgment and action, but also their moral critical faculties towards their normative orders themselves, which are taking on a smart form. Their ability and need for justification is increasingly fading because the norm addressees, weaned from autonomous compliance with the norm, are neither able nor willing to take a critical stance on the claim to validity and question the democratic legitimacy or, in the case of morality, the justification in the interests of all. However, normative orders are dependent on the reasons for their validity being publicly demanded, discussed and criticized, and that their factual, currently practiced interpretations can also be criticized and changed. However, this also presupposes that the norm addressees see themselves as co-legislators and have the corresponding ability and make active use of it, i.e. that something like "active moral citizenship" exists and is actually practiced.[36]

E. The normative constitutionalization of smart orders as a way out?

Of course, there have been and still are areas of society in which the benefits to society as a whole of adhering to norms that can be ensured through technical control and technical innovations outweigh the disadvantages. This is the case, for example, wherever technologies with greater risk potential are used, such as in motorized road traffic. In view of the virulent dangers there, the deadly realization of which can be measured by the annual number of traffic fatalities, why should motor vehicles not be

36 Brownsword, Lost in Translation, p. 356. This would also be an argument against the objection raised by Luna Rösinger, Der Autonomiebegriff im Kontext künstlicher Intelligenz als Prüfstein für die Rechtsphilosophie, in: Zsf. Rechtsphilosophie (ZRph), 6-7 (2022/2023), pp. 209-226 (225), that the Impossibility Structures "under the aspect of making it impossible to break the law do not represent a new challenge for legal autonomy", but would "once again expose the old misconception of a law misunderstood as behavioral control" (trans. K.G.).

equipped with a chip that automatically reduces the speed of the vehicle without the driver's intervention if a traffic rule requires this (and perhaps even be able to switch itself off in emergency situations)?

Given the ambivalent consequences of smart regulations, the question of how a democratic constitutional state should react to efforts to implement them should therefore not be answered in the sense of an either/or. Rather, it is a question of determining the degree or extent to which smart orders should coexist with normative orders and be effectively legally bound to them. Only when smart orders begin to call the concept of a responsible person into question or make it completely dispensable would it be necessary to consider whether our lifeworld of normativity is not fundamentally changing and whether the ideal of perfect compliance with norms is not a false ideal.

This could only be achieved by ensuring that normative orders with responsible persons who participate in a practice of intersubjective criticism both in the setting of norms and in the application and observance of norms remain the medium in which the substitution of normative sub-area orders by smart orders (e.g. in motorized road traffic) as well as these themselves, i.e. their goals and purposes as well as their probable consequences, must be justified. The task would therefore be to constitutionalize smart sub-orders of society through a normative order with legally institutionalized forums and procedures for public criticism and justification. This constitution of smart orders should therefore not be designed and institutionalized as a smart order, but only and exclusively as a normative order.[37] Furthermore, as the logic of constitutionalization implies both the primacy and the reservation of the constitution in a normative hierarchical relationship to smart orders must be ensured and legally controllable.

Whether such a constitutionalization of smart orders is sufficient to prevent them from a successive and comprehensive colonization of normative orders, including their subjects, is, however, questionable. Ultimately, it is likely to depend on whether and to what extent lifeworld and institutional spaces are maintained in which citizens can cultivate and participate in intersubjective practices, in which they understand themselves as responsible persons and also want to understand themselves as such. [38] Above all,

37 See for a proposal pointing into this direction: Andreas Werkmeister, Erste Überlegungen zum Begriff der »politischen Datenwirtschaftsstraftat«, in: GA 2021, Jg. 168, 570-587.

38 S. Morozev, Smarte neue Welt, p. 337.

this includes the practice of mutual criticism. Only in this way can they acquire the ability and develop and cultivate the will to bear the risk of setting imperfect norms as well as individual deviant behavior in mutual trust in a general willingness to follow norms. The fact that this self-image is a constitutive element of their role as co-legislators in a public process of democratic legitimization has already been made clear by the census ruling of the German Federal Constitutional Court. It insisted that the unrestricted collection and processing of personal data would not only jeopardize "the individual's opportunities for development", but also the functioning of "a liberal democratic community based on the ability of its citizens to act and participate."[39]

Smart orders, on the other hand, appear attractive and can be justified by the fact that they are able to minimize this risk and offer more security against deviant behavior with an approximate certainty of compliance with the norm, assuming that there is a kind of natural consensus on the meaning and purpose of the order whose security would be guaranteed by AI. The opportunity to make road traffic safer with a smart traffic code then appears as a utopian or dystopian paradigm for a social order that could make coexistence safer overall, depending on perspective and attitude.

39 BVerfGE 65, 1, 43 (trans. K.G.); Simitis, BDSG, Rn. 30.

The challenges of regulating social media platforms: A Brazilian scenario analysis

Ingo Wolfgang Sarlet, Andressa de Bittencourt Siqueira

This paper aims to describe and analyse the challenges of platform regulation, especially in the Brazilian context, in order to find out how social media providers have evolved to play a key role in the management of online content. Based on this evolutionary approach, the regulatory schemes that have been considered in the legal literature in this regard are described, allowing to identify the most appropriate model. In sequence, the goal is to explore the recent developments in the Brazilian scenario to regulate social media platforms, in order to access the quality of the regulatory scenario in Brazil, especially in its constitutional dimension. In the Brazilian case, it is noteworthy that the three branches of power at the federal level are involved, to a greater or lesser extent, in the regulation of social networks, with special emphasis on the developments in the matter carried out by the Superior Electoral Court (TSE) and, recently, by the Supreme Federal Court (STF)..

A. Introduction

The extensive power exercised by digital platforms is now evident, especially in terms of their control over discourse, impacting how fundamental rights are exercised in online environments. Especially regarding the social media platform providers[1], it can be seen that they have come to wield greater influence over fundamental rights, mainly freedom of expression

1 Note on terminology: the terms "social media provider" and "social media platform provider" are adopted to refer to companies that manage social media platforms (a.k.a. social networks), while the terms "social media platforms", "social media" and "social networks" are used to describe the online environment enabled by such providers. We use the term "platform provider" to better describe those actors that the Brazilian Federal Statute *Marco Civil da Internet* (MCI – Civil Rights Framework of the Internet, in a free translation) entitles "application provider" (*provedor de aplicações*, in Portuguese). From this perspective, a social media provider is a species of the genus platform provider.

and information, data protection and personality rights,[2] as a result of the mass use of information and communication technologies, intensified by the exponential increase in the number of social media users.

Due to the changing role played by social media platforms in the technological society, intense debates are emerging about how to regulate these platforms, especially in Brazil. In view of the proposed scenario, the following research problem is established: how can the challenges of platform regulation be analysed in the context of constitutional law? Based on the relevant doctrine, legislation, and case law, the focus lies above all on the Brazilian scenario, without neglecting some comparative elements, given the transnational reach of platforms, developments in foreign literature on the subject as well as the common problems faced worldwide, so that the view of platform regulation, to a certain extent, needs to remain open.

Therefore, the first step is to analyse how social networks have changed from mere intermediaries to protagonists. After this examination, we move on to explore the ways in which social media platforms can be managed, through self-regulation, external regulation, or hybrid regulation, so that the most appropriate model is identified. Finally, we explore the latest developments in the Brazilian scenario to regulate those environments and their providers in order to assess the quality of the regulatory panorama in Brazil.

B. The changing role of social media platforms

The understanding of how digital platforms, considered here in a broad sense, should be regulated has changed over time, given the gradual evolution of the way these players act, especially social networks platforms. Due to this change and their broad control over fundamental rights exercised in

2 Among others, see Marion Albers and Ingo Wolfgang Sarlet (eds) 96 *Personality and Data Protection Rights on the Internet: Brazilian and German Approaches* (Springer, Ius Gentium. Comparative Perspectives on Law and Justice, 2022); Indra Spiecker gen. Döhmann, Michael Westland, Ricardo Campos (eds) 64 *Demokratie und Öffentlichkeit im 21. Jahrhundert: zur Macht des Digitalen* (Nomos, Frankfurter Studien zum Datenschutz, 2022); Gilmar F Mendes, Peter Häberle, Ingo W Sarlet, Francisco Ballaguer Callejón *et al* (eds) *Direitos fundamentais, desenvolvimento e crise do constitucionalismo multinível* (Fundação Fênix, 2020); Indra Spiecker gen. Döhmann, 'The difference between online and offline communication as a factor in the balancing of interests with freedom of speech' in Clive Walker and Russel L Weaver (eds) *Free Speech in an Internet Era* (Carolina Academic Press 2013).

online environments, platforms have come to be known as "custodians"[3] or "gatekeepers"[4] and as the "new governors" [5].

It is possible to analyse in two distinct periods the evolution of the role of social network providers, which have gone from being mere intermediaries to effective protagonists, especially in terms of choosing the design of the platform (the tools that will be available to users, e.g., comments, shares, posts), editing their own rules (e.g., Terms of Use and Community Guidelines), carrying out content moderation procedures (e.g., blocking and restoring content and banning users), as well as content curation, i.e. the distribution of different content to different users by means of algorithms, made possible by the collection of users' personal data[6].

The first moment in the evolution of social media platforms, connected to the development of the internet, is characterized by the publication of rules protecting digital platforms, in a broad sense. A landmark in this context is the Declaration of Independence of Cyberspace, published in 1996 by John Perry Barlow at the World Economic Forum in Davos, which defended the free functioning of online environments, that would not be bound by state regulations[7]. Additionally, the exponential growth of providers in the 1990s removed closer state regulation, causing these companies to self-regulate[8].

As for state initiatives, mention should be made of Section 230 of the US Communications Decency Act (CDA) of 1996, which establishes a safe harbour for platform providers that do not edit content, extending this

---

3 Tarleton Gillespie, *Custodians of the internet – Platforms, content moderation, and the hidden decisions that shape social media* (Yale University Press, 2018) 209.

4 Eduardo Celeste, 'Digital Constitutionalism: A new systematic theorization' (2019) 33 *International Review of Law, Computers and Technology* 76, 79.

5 Kate Klonick, 'The New Governors: The People, Rules, and Processes Governing Online Speech' (2018) 131 *Harvard Law Review* 1598, 1662.

6 Jörn Reinhardt, „Fake News", „Infox", Trollfabriken: Über den Umgang mit Desinformationen in den sozialen Medien. Meinungsfreiheit in Zeiten der Internetkommunikation' (2019) 97(107) *Vorgänge – Zeitschrift für Bürgerrechte und Gesellschaftspolitik* 97, 99–100; Ivar Hartmann, 'A new framework for online content moderation' (2020) 36 *Computer Law & Security Review* 4 <https://doi.org/10.1016/j.clsr.2019.105376> accessed 30 March 2022.

7 John Perry Barlow, A Declaration of the Independence of Cyberspace (1996) <https://www.eff.org/pt-br/cyberspace-independence> accessed 10 May 2022.

8 Giovanni De Gregorio, 'The rise of digital constitutionalism in the European Union' (2021) 19(1) *International Journal of Constitutional Law* 41, 47; Wolfgang Hoffmann-Riem, 'Autorregulamentação regulamentada no contexto digital' 2019 46(146) *Revista da AJURIS* 529, 540.

exemption from civil liability to those platform providers that establish self-regulatory measures to curb harmful content. In the Brazilian context, Federal Statute n. 12.965/2014, popularly known as the Marco Civil da Internet (Civil Rights Framework of the Internet, in a free translation, hereinafter MCI), although close to the CDA, is not identical to it[9]. MCI was initially designed to allow the liability of application providers, including social networks, only after non-compliance with a court decision, and, exceptionally, application providers can be held liable after the reporting of users in cases of non-consensual disclosure of intimate images[10]. Nowadays – since the STF's decision on the partial (and progressive) unconstitutionality of the Art. 19 MCI enacted in June 2025 –, the framework on liability of platform providers by content generated by their users set forth by the MCI is not applied as originally proposed (see Section D., below)[11].

In this context, it is also possible to refer to the European Directive 2000/31/EC on certain legal aspects of information society services, in particular electronic commerce, in the internal market (hereafter referred to as the E-Commerce Directive). The Directive, among other aspects, defines the impossibility of establishing a general obligation to monitor towards service providers, including social networks, with regard to content generated on their platforms by their users (art. 15 (1), and recitals 46 and 48 of the E-Commerce Directive).

9 Anderson Schreiber, 'Civil Rights Framework of the Internet: Advance or Setback? Civil Liability for Damage Derived from Content Generated by Third Party' in Marion Albers and Ingo Wolfgang Sarlet (eds) 96 *Personality and Data Protection Rights on the Internet Brazilian and German Approaches* (Springer, Ius Gentium: Comparative Perspectives on Law and Justice, 2022) 250.

10 "Art. 19. In order to ensure freedom of expression and prevent censorship, providers of Internet applications can only be civilly liable for damages resulting from content generated by third parties if, after specific court order, they do not make arrangements to, in the scope and technical limits of their service and within the indicated time, make unavailable the content identified as infringing, otherwise subject to the applicable legal provisions.
[...]
Art. 21. Providers of Internet applications who make available the content generated by third parties shall be held subsidiarily responsible for the breach of privacy resulting from the disclosure, without the participants' permission of images, videos or other materials containing nudity or sexual acts of private character when, upon receipt of notification by the participant or their legal representative, fails to diligently promote, within the technical limits of their service, the unavailability of that content" (Free translation. MCI 2014)".

11 STF, RE 1.037.396 (Theme 987) e 1.057.258 (Theme 533) (2025) Full Court, judgment on June 26th, (Justices Dias Toffoli and Luiz Fux, respectively).

However, platforms no longer resemble those on which the protective laws were based[12], either those that establish total immunity or those that create more difficult procedures for their liability. Precisely for this reason, Ana Frazão states that it is not possible to use innovation as a pretext for the regulatory vacuum of platforms, in a broad sense, including social networks, given that it is possible to have a regulation that, on the contrary, can encourage technological innovation[13], once identified areas destined for external regulation and others likely to remain within the scope of self-regulation[14].

This new paradigm shift in the protection afforded to platforms can be best observed from the second half of the 2010s when the neutrality of platforms came into question. After the scandal involving the leak and misuse of data from Facebook users, led by Cambridge Analytica, both in the context of the Brexit referendum in 2016 and the US elections in the same year, social media came to be seen not just as a leisure tool, but as a powerful instrument capable of influencing public opinion, whether platform users or not, as well as potentially violating democracies[15].

Thus, in this second stage of the evolution of social media platforms, unlike the first, we can see the adoption of various external counteractions, mainly adopted by national states (e.g., the German Net Enforcement Act – *Netzwerkdurchsetzungsgesetz*, henceforth just the German NetzDG, adopted in 2017 and in full in force between 2018 and May 2024, when partially revoked by the DSA) and by civil society organizations (e.g., the Manila Principles on Intermediary Liability) for greater control over the actions of platform providers.

An inescapable characteristic of this second moment, and a factor of particular concern in terms of the powers of social media providers, is the vast number of users, which has reached the scale of billions worldwide. In Brazil, for example, according to a report published in January 2024 by Data Reportal, there are 187.9 million social media users, representing 86.6%

12 Frank Pasquale, 'Platform neutrality: Enhancing freedom of expression in spheres of private power' (2016) 17(2) *Theoretical Inquiries in Law* 487, 488.

13 Oreste Pollicino and Giovanni De Gregorio, 'Constitutional Law in the Algorithmic Society' in Hans W Micklitz and Oreste Pollicino *et al* (eds) *Constitutional Challenges in the Algorithmic Society* (Cambridge University Press, 2022) 10.

14 Ana Frazão, 'Plataformas digitais e os desafios para a regulação jurídica', in Leonardo Parentoni *et al.* (eds) *Direito, tecnologia e inovação* (D'Plácido, 2018) 656–657.

15 Francisco Balaguer Callejón, 'Redes sociais, companhias tecnológicas e Democracia' (2020) 14(42) *Revista Brasileira de Direitos Fundamentais & Justiça* 25.

of the Brazilian population[16]. Among the most widely used social networks today, Facebook is the most popular in the world, with 3.03 billion monthly active users and 2.02 billion daily active users, according to Meta Investor Report based on data from the second quarter of 2023[17]. Thus, although there is disagreement about the extent of the power and function of social media platforms, it is indisputable that they enable communication and public debate[18].

In this regard, and once the influence of social networks on everyday life has become increasingly evident, the debate on the need to regulate these online environments is gaining ground. For example, the aforementioned German NetzDG was a pioneer in this regard, establishing a regulatory framework for social media platforms in order to curb the spread of hate speech and fake news[19], including, among other specifications, the establishment of heavy fines in the case of non-compliance[20]. As a result, similar laws have been drafted in other countries, such as the French law against hate speech (*Loi Avia*)[21], although it was declared partially unconstitutional

16 Data Reportal, Digital 2024: Brazil (2025) <https://datareportal.com/reports/digital-2024-brazil> accessed 08 March 2025.

17 Meta, Meta Reports Second Quarter – Results (2023) <https://investor.fb.com/investor-news/press-release-details/2023/Meta-Reports-Second-Quarter-2023-Results/default.aspx> accessed 1 September 2023.

18 In 2019, the German Constitutional Court, in its ruling on the so-called *III Weg* case in a preliminary injunction, recognized not only the market dominance of the social network Facebook, but also the key role the platform plays in public debate, with more than 30 million people in Germany accessing it every month at the time, according to data cited in the ruling itself (BVerfGE, 1 BvQ 42/19, 6, 19).

19 William Echikson and Olivia Knodt, 'Germany's NetzDG: A key test for combatting online hate' (2018) CEPS Research Report Thinking ahead for Europe 2018/9, i, Wolfgang Schulz, 'Regulating Intermediaries to Protect Privacy Online – the Case of the German NetzDG' (2018) HIIG Discussion Paper Series 2018-01 5 <https://www.hiig.de/wp-content/uploads/2018/07/SSRN-id3216572.pdf> accessed 29 July 2020; From a Brazilian perspective, see Ingo Wolfgang Sarlet and Gabrielle Bezerra Sales Sarlet, "Liberdade de expressão e discurso do ódio nas mídias sociais – uma análise à luz da jurisprudência da Corte Europeia de Direitos Humanos e da Lei Alemã sobre a Efetividade do Direito na Internet" in Mendes, Häberle, Sarlet, Ballaguer Callejón *et al* (eds) (n. 2) 109.

20 2017 Network Enforcement Act (*Netzwerkdurchsetzungsgesetz*, NetzDG) <https://www.gesetze-im-internet.de/netzdg/BJNR335210017.html> accessed 3 May 2022.

21 Loi n. 2020-766 du 24 juin 2020 visant à lutter contre les contenus haineux sur internet (*Loi Avia*), <https://www.legifrance.gouv.fr/dossierlegislatif/JORFDOLE000038745184> accessed 3 May 2022.

by the French Constitutional Council[22]. The Charter of Human Rights in the Digital Age was also enacted in Portugal in May 2021 and a debate on its provisions has also emerged[23].

Besides, in the European Union, the Digital Services Act (henceforth DSA) was adopted on October 19th, 2022, based on systemic-risk assessment regulation, while in the United Kingdom, the Online Safety Act (henceforth OSA), approved on October 26th, 2023, has an approach based on duties of care. Besides, in the German context, on May 16th, 2024, the *Digitale-Dienste-Gesetze* (DDG) came into force as domestic legislation to implement and complement the provisions of the DSA, which, despite its relevance, will not be here further developed. From a Brazilian perspective, the Brazilian Fake News Draft Bill (PL n. 2630/2020, henceforth also *PL das fake news*)[24], which combines the approach on systemic-risk assessment and the creation of duties of care, had one of its different versions scheduled for deliberation in the Brazilian House of Representatives (*Câmara dos Deputados*) at the beginning of May 2023, but did not proceed due to a lack of political support. At the time of writing this text, the Brazilian Fake News Draft Bill was still under legislative consideration, and its future remained uncertain. During the course of the Congress' deliberations, a number of other draft pieces of legislation underwent discussion, including PL 4691/2024, proposed in December 2024, which is connected to PL 2120/2023, proposed in April 2023. However, none of these drafts have gained force so far.

In June 2025, in Brazil, the STF has taken a further step towards a regulatory approach of social media platforms[25]. By a majority of 8 to 3 Justices, art. 19 MCI was considered partially unconstitutional. Even though art. 19 MCI was intended to rule on liability of providers due to content generated

---

22 França, Conselho Constitucional, Decisão n. 2004-496 DC, judgment on June 10th <https://www.conseil constitutionnel.fr/decision/2004/2004496DC.htm> accessed 3 May 2022.

23 Interview with José Carlos Vieira de Andrade, "Carta dos Direitos na Era Digital entra em vigor na 6.ª feira com falta de consenso sobre artigo polémico" Lusa (15 julho 2021) <https://www.publico.pt/> accessed 15 November 2023.

24 The Fake News Draft Bill, which has been under discussion in the Brazilian National Congress since 2020, was initially intended to curb the spread of fake news online. Today, the Bill's wording goes beyond the disinformation agenda, aiming to regulate, in several aspects, the social media platforms used in Brazil, see (Fake News Draft Bill, Brazilian Federal Senate (2630/2020) <https://www25.senado.leg.br/web/atividade/materias/-/materia/141944> accessed 3 May 2022.

25 STF (n. 11).

by their users, the legal thesis (*tese de repercussão geral*, in Portuguese) established by the STF goes even further. It stated a proposal on the adoption of duties of care (*deveres de cuidado*, in Portuguese) by providers if a systemic risk is identified. It also recommended the presumption of liability if a piece of content is boosted/recommended by the provider or through the use of illegal artificial distribution of content through robots, as well as the adoption of complaint/report channels, publication of internal rules and transparency reports, and called for a regulation that demands legal representation of providers in Brazil[26].

It is precisely in this context, which highlights the broad power of platform providers, characterized above all by the imbalance in relation to the user in isolation[27] and the measures adopted to develop and maintain its business model[28], that a deep analysis on the regulatory panorama arises.

C. Management and regulation of social media platforms

I. Regulatory scope and categorization

With regard to the dynamic between technology and the law, Lawrence Lessig argues that the regulation of platforms is the result of the tension and interaction of four regulatory forces: (i) the code structure of the platforms, (ii) social norms, (iii) market orientations of an economic nature, in addition to the vertical influence of (iv) legal norms, notably state norms, on the online environment[29]. For this author, although regulation by means of the platforms' code structure is the most effective in terms of determining and encouraging behaviour[30], which, depending on the way that it is applied, becomes a factor of particular concern. On the other hand, it is essential to balance these regulatory modalities, above all through the intervention of legal norms, in order to achieve regulation that protects users by balancing these forces[31].

26 For more details on the judgment, see Section D.

27 Ivar Hartmann and Ingo Wolfgang Sarlet, 'Direitos fundamentais e direito privado: a proteção da liberdade de expressão nas mídias sociais' (2019) 16(90) *Direito Público* 85, 99.

28 Balaguer Callejón (n. 15) 585.

29 Lawrence Lessig, *Code: Version 2.0* (Basic Books 2006) 233.

30 ibid 123–130.

31 ibid 233–234.

In the digital environment, given that threats to fundamental rights mainly come from private actors[32], the aim of external regulation, i.e. regulation that is not developed by the platform itself but by an external actor, such as state regulations, is to ensure that the activity carried out by the platforms complies with a series of parameters and achieves certain objectives, defined based on the balance of interests at stake: the platform itself, its users, civil society in a broad sense, as well as state interests.

From a regulatory perspective, Wolfgang Hoffmann-Riem proposes categorizing the possibilities for managing technologies, understood in a broad sense, as follows: self-regulation, state regulation, hybrid regulation, techno regulation, social self-regulation, and state-regulated self-regulation, as well as the possibility of replacing legal norms with extra-legal ethical standards[33].

In order to adapt the analysis to the reality of social network platforms, considering actors with the capacity to establish a regulatory body for the management of such environments, the range of regulatory possibilities is gathered into three main axes: (i) *self-regulation*, which includes social self-regulation, conforming self-regulation or self-conforming, as well as decentralized models; (ii) *external or vertical regulation*, in which state intervention stands out, by a single state or in partnership; as well as (iii) *hybrid regulations*, which include regulated self-regulation and multi-stakeholder regulation.

II. A brief overview of regulatory models

1. Self-regulation

Self-regulated standards, in the context of social media platforms, are considered to be measures that have the scope of the organization and internal management of a given platform (self-compliance) and those aimed at creating social standards (social self-regulation), as well as other measures that are, in some way, outsourced to other subjects, but which, because they are the initiative and guided by the interests of the providers themselves, are in-

32 De Gregorio (n. 8) 46.

33 Wolfgang Hoffmann-Riem, 'Inteligência Artificial Como Oportunidade para a Regulação Jurídica' 2019 16(90) *Revista Direito Público* 11, 31–38; See also Wolfgang Hoffmann-Riem, *Teoria geral do direito digital – Transformação digital e Desafios para o Direito* (Forense, 2021).

cluded here in the scope of self-regulation. Among these measures executed by other agents or technologies are *decentralization*, carried out voluntarily by the users themselves; *techno regulation*, applied by algorithms and the architecture of the network; and *supervision*, carried out by a body or entity set up by the social network provider itself, but independent of it, in order to monitor the decisions taken in the management of the platform.

Self-compliance refers to business decisions for the organization of platforms, which do not require vertical intervention by the state, and is close to the notion of compliance, as it consists of "guidelines for companies' own behaviour"[34]. In the context of social media platforms, examples are the guiding documents for content moderation carried out by humans.

As soon as norms are adopted not only by those who drafted them but also by individuals who did not take part in the decision-making process, such as social media users, Wolfgang Hoffmann-Riem calls this modality social self-regulation (*gesellschaftliche Selbstregulierung*)[35]. The main feature of these norms is the possibility of making them legally binding, or at least of maintaining the expectation of compliance with these norms[36]. In the context of social media platforms, examples include Codes of Conduct, Community Standards and Guidelines, as well as Terms of Service, which define the rights and obligations of platforms and users[37].

Still on the subject of self-regulation, it is worth highlighting *decentralized models* which, although situated within the scope of private governance exercised by platform providers, are characterized by the fragmentation of power among users[38]. An example of decentralization is flagging,

34 Free translation. Hoffmann-Riem, 'Inteligência artificial como oportunidade para a regulação jurídica' (n. 33) 32.

35 Ibid. See also Wolfgang Hoffmann-Riem, *Teoria geral do direito digital* (n. 33) 531.

36 Wolfgang Hoffmann-Riem, *Teoria geral do direito digital* (n. 33) 136-137.

37 Gerald Spindler, 'Löschung und Sperrung von Inhalten aufgrund von Teilnahmebedingungen sozialer Netzwerke – Eine Untersuchung der zivil- und verfassungsrechtlichen Grundlagen' (2019) 35(4) *Computer und Recht* 238, 240; Nicolas Suzor, 'A constitutional moment: How we might reimagine platform governance' 2020 (36) *Computer Law & Security Review* 1, 3 <https://doi.org/10.1016/j.clsr.2019.105381> accessed 18 August 2021.

38 Thomas E Kadri and Kate Klonick, 'Facebook v. Sullivan: Public Figures and Newsworthiness in Online Speech' (2019) 93 *Southern California Law Review* 39, 94; Christian Djeffal, "Soziale Medien und Kuratierung von Inhalten. Regulative Antworten auf eine demokratische Schlüsselfrage" in Indra Spiecker gen. Döhmann, Michael Westland, Ricardo Campos (eds) 64 *Demokratie und Öffentlichkeit im 21. Jahrhundert: zur Macht des Digitalen* (Nomos, Frankfurter Studien zum Datenschutz, 2022).

in which providers allow users to report content that they believe to be infringing[39]. For its part, *technoregulation* (*Technoregulierung*), permeated with concerns and risks, involves governance by algorithms through the use of artificial intelligence on a large scale, replacing human decision-making[40]. In fact, this perspective of platform management is intrinsically connected to the aforementioned concept of regulation by code, proposed by Lawrence Lessig, but which is of particular concern given the high potential for side effects to occur through the indiscriminate use of algorithms and artificial intelligence, such as algorithmic discrimination[41] and misidentification of infringing content[42].

Self-regulation through oversight, on the other hand, is related to the development of mechanisms to monitor the measures applied by social media providers by bodies or entities in a neutral position. Popularly known as the "Facebook Supreme Court," the Meta's Oversight Board is the pioneering and paradigmatic example to this day. Notwithstanding its precursory nature,[43] it cannot be perceived as a Constitutional Court and cannot, in a Constitutional State, occupy its functions. It is important to recognize the Board's limitations, mainly in terms of its action in a few representative cases and its difficulties in setting minimum standards of protection to be applied by Meta at a global level, especially in relation to freedom of expression[44].

---

39 Kate Crawford and Tarleton Gillespie, 'What is a flag for? Social media reporting tools and the vocabulary of complaint' (2016) 18(3) *New Media & Society* 410, 411.

40 Hoffmann-Riem, 'Inteligência artificial como oportunidade para a regulação jurídica' (n. 33) 36.

41 Laura Schertel Mendes and Marcela Mattiuzzo, 'Discriminação Algorítmica: conceito, fundamento legal e tipologia' (2019) 16(90) *Revista Direito Público* 39, 47–52; Christopher E Peterson, User-generated censorship: manipulating the maps of social media (B.A. Legal Studies, Thesis, MIT 2013) 16, 40.

42 Thiago D Oliva, Dennys M Antonialli and Alessandra Gomes, 'Fighting Hate Speech, Silencing Drag Queens? Artificial Intelligence in Content Moderation and Risks to LGBTQ Voices Online' (2021) 25(2) *Sexuality & Culture* 700, 712.

43 Evelyn Douek, 'Facebook's Oversight Board: Move fast with stable infrastructure and humility' (2019) 21 *North Carolina Journal of Law & Technology* 2 <https://scholarship.law.unc.edu/ncjolt/vol21/iss1/2> accessed 4 March 2022.

44 Ibid 74.

2. External regulation

As mentioned in section B. The changing role of social media platforms, the dynamic and disruptive nature of social networks initially pushed aside state regulation, encouraging self-regulation of such environments[45]. However, as Ana Frazão rightly points out, technological innovation cannot be used as an excuse to avoid regulation,[46] and, above all, with the consolidation of a given technology, it is becoming increasingly difficult to justify exceptions from state regulations[47].

Wolfgang Hoffmann-Riem notes that the term "regulation" (*Regulierung*) is now commonly used to refer to state interventions "in social processes which, with a specific objective, establish general guidelines for behaviour"[48]. It should be noted that external regulation, despite being easily linked to state intervention, can be drawn up and implemented by economic and political blocs, such as the Digital Services Act, as well as multilateral initiatives, such as the Christchurch Call Initiative, drawn up by the governments of France and New Zealand in 2019, and international treaties, such as the Budapest Convention on Cybercrime and its protocol on Xenophobia and Racism.

Thus, regulatory interventions arise when self-regulation triggers undesirable results, as well as from the need to protect fundamental rights and social and cultural values in the online environment[49]. It is recognized, however, that if applied widely and in isolation, this model triggers side effects in areas that require greater flexibility, creativity, and cooperation[50]. However, we do not want to say that this model is outdated, as it remains relevant and up-to-date for specific matters. Ana Frazão even points out

---

45 Hoffmann-Riem, 'Autorregulamentação regulamentada no contexto digital' (n. 8) 540.

46 Frazão (n. 14) 654.

47 Thomas Wischmeyer, 'The role and practices of online stakeholders' in Mart Susi (ed) *Human Rights, Digital Society and the Law* (Routledge Handbook, 2019) 5.

48 Free translation. Hoffmann-Riem, 'Autorregulamentação regulamentada no contexto digital' (n. 8) 532.

49 Patrícia Baptista and Clara I Keller, 'Por que, quando e como regular as novas tecnologias? Os desafios trazidos pelas inovações disruptivas' (2016) 273 *Revista de Direito Administrativo* 123, 140; Hoffmann-Riem, 'Inteligência artificial como oportunidade para a regulação jurídica' (n. 33) 36.

50 Hoffmann-Riem, 'Inteligência artificial como oportunidade para a regulação jurídica' (n. 33) 36.

that the reformulation of regulatory techniques is necessary in order to allow the rules and procedures implemented to be flexible to new situations[51].

It is therefore not surprising that regulation faces a number of setbacks in order to be sufficiently effective. The code structure of the platforms is one of the main challenges for a regulation that pretends to be solely state-driven[52], especially because the state alone does not have the technical knowledge to implement a sufficiently adequate regulation. Nevertheless, removing the state from the regulatory scheme is not a wise move.

Since the state is the paradigmatic regulator, state regulation faces difficulties in terms of the timing of its actions[53]. If the state regulates a certain segment prematurely, i.e. social networks, there is a risk that the approved regulation will quickly become outdated or will be applied without the slightest legal certainty[54]. However, if there is an excessive delay in regulation, either due to excessive caution or inability to create a set of rules applicable to reality, there is a state protection deficit – or, in more serious cases, a state protection omission. In addition, the regulatory state is challenged in terms of the scope of its intervention, running the risk of drawing up a regulatory framework that is either too comprehensive, with the aim of including as many management possibilities as possible, or too restrained, resulting in excessively limited regulation[55].

In view of this, there is a need to be aware of the separation between areas that are likely to be subject to external authorities, especially state authorities, and those that work better within the scope of self-regulation or based on hybrid models[56], which will be developed further below.

3. Hybrid models of regulation

Hybrid models have emerged as an alternative to the *a priori* uncontrolled management of self-regulation and the state's rigid regulatory capacity and, for this reason, involve two or more actors with the capacity to manage

51 Frazão (n. 14) 651.

52 Patrícia Pinheiro, *Direito digital* (5th edn, São Paulo, 2013) 50; Hoffmann-Riem, 'Autorregulamentação regulamentada no contexto digital' (n. 8) 530–531.

53 Baptista and Keller (n. 49) 145.

54 Hoffmann-Riem, 'Inteligência artificial como oportunidade para a regulação jurídica' (n. 33) 26; Baptista and Keller (n. 49) 145.

55 Baptista and Keller (n. 49) 145.

56 Hoffmann-Riem, 'Autorregulamentação regulamentada no contexto digital' (n. 8) 537; Patrícia Baptista; Baptista and Keller (n. 49) 145.

a given technological segment. With regard to the regulation of social media platforms, there are two possible classifications in terms of hybrid nature: (i) hybridity in the process of creating and drafting regulations, i.e., multistakeholder regulation; (ii) hybridity in terms of supervision and enforcement of standards, i.e., regulated self-regulation.

A terminological nuance needs to be mentioned beforehand, given that the research carried out here is based on the studies of Wolfgang Hoffmann-Riem. According to the author, hybrid regulatory models are characterized by the development of rules in which the state and private actors participate, which emerge from social self-regulation and in which the State participates in the development of the rules[57], thus approaching the notion presented here of multi-stakeholder regulation. The concept of regulated self-regulation presented by Wolfgang Hoffmann-Riem is adopted here in its entirety. According to the proposed categorization presented here, therefore, the difference lies in the fact that hybrid regulation is a genus of which multi-stakeholder regulation and regulated self-regulation are species.

The multistakeholder regulation model is also gaining ground as an alternative, especially as it involves standardization through a regulatory governance triangle[58]. In this model, each actor – states, NGOs, and private companies – is divided into zones of action, maintaining their autonomy while fostering cooperation between them[59]. There are a number of benefits to including the widest range of players in the debate on social media platforms, especially platform providers, otherwise regulation will be ineffective[60].

In this regard, Ronaldo Lemos goes further and points out that the multi-stakeholder model is not a point of arrival, but rather a starting point. Not only do we need to understand the most diverse perspectives on a given technological segment, but in order for regulation to be able

---

57 Hoffmann-Riem, 'Inteligência artificial como oportunidade para a regulação jurídica' (n. 33) 35.

58 Kenneth Abbott and Duncan Snidal, 'Strengthening international regulation through transmittal new governance: Overcoming the orchestration deficit' 2009 (42) *Vanderbilt Journal of Transnational Law* 501, 513.

59 ibid 501; Robert Gorwa, 'The platform governance triangle: conceptualizing the informal regulation of online content' (2019) 8(2) *Internet Policy Review* 1, 7ff.

60 Wischmeyer (n. 47) 14. At the same time, Thomas Wischmeyer also draws attention to the limitations of the multisectoral regulation model, since there is not enough consensus on illegal content on the Internet, especially hate speech and fake news, which could lead to any regulation coming from this model being hampered, ibid 12–13.

to achieve minimally satisfactory results, it is necessary to avoid radical positions and to compromise[61] – one of the main lessons learned from the Brazilian MCI decision-making process.

The Brazilian MCI, although is legislation enacted by the state, originated from a debate with various sectors of society, which is why it is pointed out as an example of a multistakeholder regulatory model[62]. In the Brazilian scenario, the consulting process with users, companies, civil society organizations, government sectors, and universities, in which all those interested were able to provide public comments, lasted eighteen months, so that the stakeholders collaborated in the preparation of a draft which, in the end, was submitted to the Brazilian National Congress, resulting in advanced legislation for the time, and is considered an achievement in terms of protecting rights on the Internet[63].

The second model of hybrid regulation discussed here – regulated self-regulation – emerges as a procedural model, focusing on autonomy and co-operation between agents with management capacity[64], in order to acquire technical knowledge and overcome the complexities of the digital environment[65]. For this reason, Dan Wielsch mentions that the development of digital services, including social networks, must be linked to legal norms that ensure the fundamental rights of users, especially those linked to communicative freedoms, and the autonomy of the institutions that provide the space for the exercise of these rights[66].

Based mainly on the studies of Wolfgang Hoffmann-Riem, it is understood that the model based on regulated self-regulation, in general terms, involves a hard normative core set by the state, while a margin of choice is provided to the platforms, outside the scope of this state core, in which private entities themselves can define internal rules allied to technological

61 Ronaldo Lemos, 'The Internet Bill of Rights as an Example of Multistakeholderism' in Carlos Affonso Souza, Mario Viola *et al* (eds) *Brazil's Internet Bill of Rights: A Closer Look* (2nd ed, ITS Rio, 2017) 48.

62 Ibid 42.

63 Ibid 42–43.

64 Ingo Wolfgang Sarlet, 'Liberdade de expressão e o problema da regulação do discurso do ódio nas mídias sociais' (2019) 5(3) *Revista Estudos Institucionais* 1207, 1230; Pollicino and De Gregorio (n. 13) 16.

65 Wolfgang Hoffmann-Riem, *Teoria geral do direito digital* (n. 33) 137.

66 Dan Wielsch, 'Die Ordnungen der Netzwerke. AGB – Code – Community Standards' in Martin Eifert and Tobias Gostomzyk (eds) *Netzwerkrecht – Die Zukunft des NetzDG und seine Folgen für die Netzwerkkommunikation* (Nomos, 2018) 73; Spiecker genannt Döhmann (n. 2).

development and innovation[67]. It is therefore an action by the state, based on cooperation and trust, as the guardian of individual and collective interests, to prevent reckless self-regulation, for example by creating a regulatory framework and/or state incentives for social media platforms, which are subsequently managed by their providers with relative autonomy[68].

The paradigmatic example of regulated self-regulation of social media platforms is the pioneering proposal contained in the German NetzDG, full in force between 2018 and 2024, which listed a series of duties to be fulfilled by providers of such online environments. Under the terms of the legislation, providers of social media platforms with at least two million users in Germany are obliged, among other things, to monitor and block content deemed to be infringing on the basis of the crimes set out in the German Criminal Code, which is generally removed from the platform within 24 hours of the provider becoming aware of it, or within seven days in borderline cases where the definition of illegality is difficult to assess, under penalty of a fine. Platforms providers, based on NetzDG, had also to publish transparency reports regarding content removal. In other words, NetzDG aimed to create commitments with private entities that have large market power[69] and the capacity to manage the environments at hand, based on state legislation itself (i.e. the Criminal Code), which fits in with the concept of regulated self-regulation presented here.

The NetzDG, despite the pioneering spirit and progress represented by the legislation in terms of platform regulation, is not immune to criticism from specialized literature, which highlights not only the potential for the law to violate European rules[70] but also shows concern about the privatization of decision-making power over illegal content, as well as the possibility of overblocking content in order to avoid the payment of fines[71], which,

67 Wolfgang Hoffmann-Riem, *Teoria geral do direito digital* (n. 33) 137.

68 Ibid 136–137.

69 As recognized by the German Constitutional Court in the *III Weg* case, highlighted above (see n. 18), v. BVerG, 1 BvQ 42/19, paras. 6 e 19.

70 Gerald Spindler, 'Internet Intermediary Liability Reloaded. The New German Act on Responsibility of Social Networks and its (In-) Compatibility with European Law' (2017) 8 *Journal of Intellectual Property*, Information Technology and Electronic Commerce Law 166, 175.

71 Ibid 166; Schulz (n. 19); Sandra Schmitz; Christian Berndt, 'The German Act on Improving Law Enforcement on Social Networks (NetzDG): A Blunt Sword?' (2018) <https://ssrn.com/abstract=3306964> accessed on 15 July 2020; Matthias Cornils, 'Behördliche Kontrolle sozialer Netzwerke: Netzkommunikation und das Gebot der Staatsferne' in Martin Eifert and Tobias Gostomzyk (eds) *Netzwerkrecht – Die*

despite the relevance of the criticisms, will not be explored in depth. As already stated above, the German NetzDG was partially revoked by the DSA and the domestic main legislation on the matter is the German DDG since May 2024.

In addition, it is important to emphasize that regulated self-regulation implies the protection of fundamental rights in online environments through procedure[72]. As Jörn Reinhardt rightly demonstrates, once their leading role has been recognized, social media platforms are gradually improving their community terms and standards, as well as developing structured procedures for moderating user-generated content[73], such as the aforementioned implementation of the Meta's Oversight Board. Due to the flawed nature of human interpretation and limited artificial intelligence mechanisms, there is a growing demand for decisions to be re-examined through appeals within the platform itself, giving rise to the need to implement procedural safeguards, to guarantee impartiality in decisions, as well as limited discretion on the part of the decision-maker[74].

With regard to regulated self-regulation with an emphasis on procedures, the NetzDG is also a leading example – even though Art. 3 NetzDG is no longer into force. According to the terms of the law, the social media platform provider can offer the user with a right of reply before deciding on the unlawfulness of the content (art. 3, (3)(a) of the NetzDG) in cases of non-manifest unlawfulness, as well as informing the user of its decision and consequent justification (art. 3, (2)(5)(a) of the NetzDG).

In addition to legislative provisions, in 2021, a new chapter in the evolution of regulated self-regulation of social networks was opened by the German Federal Court of Justice (*Bundesgerichtshof*, hereinafter BGH), in which compliance with specific parameters in content moderation procedures was required, namely: the obligation of social network providers to notify the user at least after the removal of content, in addition to the prior notification required in the case of partial or total blocking of

Zukunft des NetzDG und seine Folgen für die Netzwerkkommunikation (Nomos, 2018).

72 Wielsch (n. 66) 90.

73 Jörn Reinhardt, 'Algorithmizität und Sichtbarkeit – Konflikte um Bilder in den sozialen Medien' in Eva Schürmann and Levno von Plato (eds) 4 *Rechtsästhetik in rechtsphilosophischer Absicht* (Nomos, 2020) 254.

74 Nicolas Suzor, 'Digital Constitutionalism: Using the Rule of Law to Evaluate the Legitimacy of Governance by Platforms' (2018) 4(3) *Social Media + Society* <https://doi.org/10.1177/2056305118787812> accessed 8 September 2021.

user accounts[75]. These decisions are in line with what Gerald Spindler has already pointed out, regarding the need to develop judicial mechanisms to deal with disputes arising from content platforms[76].

In fact, the BGH's decisions show that regulated self-regulation of social media platforms can take place through the Judiciary, based on procedural regulation and the moderation structure of a given platform. Augusto Aguilar Calahorro highlights the indispensability of access to the courts in the digital society, especially with regard to supranational and international courts, from the perspective of multilevel constitutionalism[77], which, despite its relevance, will not be explored in depth here.

Finally, it can be seen that the current configuration of the regulatory landscape allows for multipolar regulation, in which the models briefly discussed so far are applied simultaneously[78]. There is both self-regulation by the platforms, which adopt self-managing rules, as well as making use of artificial intelligence, distributing the ability to identify infringing content among users and building supervision mechanisms, and there are also certain sectors of the platforms subject to external regulation and others subject to hybrid regulation, depending on the country or supranational structure from which any analysis is carried out.

D. Recent developments on social media regulation in Brazil

As for the Brazilian regulatory structure for social media platforms, recent developments show the need to move forward with the process of building a regulatory model that is consistent and effective, but above all constitutionally adequate. The issue here is highly controversial, complex and involves not only political and economic interests of almost incalculable magnitude, but also interests of the members of society as a whole. Sig-

---

75 As decided by the German Federal Supreme Court (*Bundesgerichtshof*) on BGH, III ZR 179/20, paras. 87–88, as well as on BGH, III ZR 192/20, para. 99.

76 Spindler (n. 70) 175. See also Amélie Heldt, 'Content Moderation by Social Media Platforms: The Importance of Judicial Review' in Edoardo Celeste, Amélie Heldt and Clara Iglesias Keller (eds) *Constitutionalizing Social Media* (Hart Publishing 2022) 264.

77 Augusto Aguilar Calahorro, 'Direitos fundamentais, desenvolvimento e crise do constitucionalismo multinível', in Mendes, Häberle, Sarlet, Ballaguer Callejón *et al* (eds) (n. 2) 708–709.

78 Lessig (n. 29) 233; Zulmar Fachin, 'Desafios da regulação do ciberespaço e a proteção dos direitos da personalidade' (2021) 25(56) *Revista Jurídica FURB* 1, 16.

nificant developments have been identified at least since the last election campaign in 2022, mostly related to the need to tackle disinformation on social media platforms[79].

For instance, in the final stage of the 2022 electoral process, the Brazilian Superior Electoral Court (*Tribunal Superior Eleitoral* – TSE) issued the Resolution n. 23.714/2022 – within the scope of its functions during election periods – with the aim of more effectively combating the so-called *fake news*, which is defined as content "that is intended to undermine the integrity of the electoral process, including the processes of voting, collecting and counting of votes", given the dynamism of digital environments and their widespread use during the electoral campaign period[80].

Among other provisions, the mentioned Resolution, whose effects ended alongside the 2022 election period, established a one-hour deadline to remove disinformation content against the integrity of the electoral process between the election's eve and the third subsequent day (Art. 2º, § 2º of the Resolution). It also provided that it was unnecessary to file isolated lawsuits to remove disinformation electoral content that has been replicated on other websites. In cases where disinformation content that undermines the integrity of the electoral process, for which a decision to remove has already been issued by the TSE Full Court and which has reappeared on social media in an identical format, it is possible for the TSE Presidency to determine, by order, the extension of a collegiate decision already issued (art. 3, *caput* of the Resolution), indicating, in the same act, the URLs, URIs or URNs with identical content that should be removed by the provider.

Not surprisingly, the constitutionality of this Resolution was analysed by the STF in the Direct Action for the Declaration of Unconstitutionality (*Açao Direta de Inconstitucionalidade* – ADI) 7261. The collective decision upheld, by a majority, that by issuing the Resolution the TSE acted legitimately within the scope of its prerogatives, reinforcing that the reaction time, in the electoral disinformation scenario, if it is short, can impose immeasurable damage to the legitimacy of the election, since it is recog-

79 Ingo Wolfgang Sarlet and Andressa de Bittencourt Siqueira, 'Direitos fundamentais e regulação de plataformas digitais no Brasil' (2023) Consultor Jurídico, *Coluna Observatório Constitucional* <https://www.conjur.com.br/2023-jun-03/observatorio-constitucional-direitos-fundamentais-regulacao-plataformas-digitais/> accessed 15 July 2023.

80 TSE, Resolução n. 23.714, de 20 de outubro de 2022 <https://www.tse.jus.br/legislacao/compilada/res/2022/resolucao-no-23-714-de-20-de-outubro-de-2022> accessed 8 September 2023.

nized the abuse of those who disseminate disinformation on their profiles, accounts and channels on the Internet. It also stated that the democratic Institutions must take action to guarantee the isonomy and legitimacy of the electoral election[81].

In the first semester of 2023, the regulatory agenda reached another level. The debate on the aforementioned Fake News Draft Bill was reignited after the attacks on democratic institutions in Brasília, which took place on January 8th, 2023, through invasions of the STF, the National Congress and the Planalto Palace (where the Office of the President of the Republic is located). Very similar to the attack that occurred against the Capitol on January 6th, 2021, in the United States, the key difference between both events is that, differently than the Capitol Attack, in which only the Legislative Branch was invaded, in the January 8th Attack in Brasília all Branches of Power were attacked.

In addition, in mid-April there was a tragic wave of violence in schools across Brazil, especially given the inertia of platform providers in removing content posted by users that aimed to promote or encourage those acts of violence. In order to remove this type of unlawful content, the Ministry of Justice and Public Security, part of the Executive Branch, issued the Decree (*Portaria*) n. 351/2023, to preventing the dissemination of blatantly unlawful content online[82]. It, among other clauses, provides for need of social media platform providers to mitigate measures for systemic risks, including the use algorithms, as well as the need for the Public National Security Department (*Secretaria Nacional de Segurança Pública* – SENASP) to create a *hash* data-base on illegal content.

As already stated above, in this scenario, the Fake News Draft Bill, that was discussed since 2020, regained its strength[83]. Differently from its original text, that was intended to curb the spread of disinformation content, by May 2023, around 40% its text was modified to broaden its scope and propose a regulation in several aspects of the social media platforms used in

81 ADI 7261 MC-Ref (2022) STF Full Court, judgment on October 26th, (Justice Fachin) [7]–[9].

82 Ministério da Justiça e Segurança Pública, Portaria do Ministro n. 351/2023, de 12 de abril de 2023 <https://www.gov.br/mj/pt-br/centrais-de-conteudo/publicacoes/categorias-de-publicacoes/portarias/portaria-do-ministro_plataformas.pdf/view> accessed 4 May 2023.

83 See n. 24.

Brazil, but it was not further discussed openly in society and due to lack of political support was not enacted[84].

Among its many provisions, besides combining the concepts of systemic-risk assessment and the creation of duties of care, approached in the DSA and in the OSA, respectively, the main discussion regarding the Fake News Draft Bill lies in the creation of an agency for the enforcement and oversight of the statute once enacted. It shall be stated that the creation of an agency for this purpose, according to the Brazilian Federal Constitution, shall be made only by the President of the Republic and not by the Congress, that, in turn, can set forth how this agency is organized (art. 61, §1º, n. II, letters "a" and "e", Brazilian Federal Constitution)[85].

Therefore, it is worth mentioning the proposal of the Special Commission on Digital Law of the Federal Council of the Brazilian Bar Association (CFOAB). The Commission suggests the creation of a Brazilian Digital Platform Regulation System, structured and organized on a tripartite basis, through the creation of a Digital Policy Council (CPD), a deliberative body made up of people appointed by the Legislative, Executive and Judiciary branches at federal level, as well as those appointed by the Brazilian National Telecommunications Agency (ANATEL), Administrative Council for Economic Defense (CADE), Brazilian Data Protection Authority (ANPD) and the CFOAB. In addition to the CPD, the System would also include the Brazilian Internet Steering Committee (CGI.br), as the body responsible for carrying out studies and issuing recommendations, as well as Self-Regulation Entities, in charge of analysing practical cases involving content moderation on platforms.

---

84 PL das Fake News: 44% do seu texto foi alterado desde sua primeira versão em 2022 in (2023) Mobile Time <https://www.mobiletime.com.br/noticias/26/04/2023/pl-das-fake-news-44-do-seu-texto-foi-alterado-desde-sua-primeira-versao-em-2022/> accessed 23 October 2023.

85 "Art. 61
(...)
§ 1º The President of the Republic shall have exclusive power to initiate the following laws:
(...)
II - laws that deal with:
a) creation of public offices, positions or jobs in the direct administration and autarchies, or an increase in their remuneration;
(...)
e) creation and abolition of Ministries and agencies of public administration, observing the provisions of art. 84, VI" (Free translation. Brazilian Federal Constitution 1988)".

As for progress in the Judiciary, mention should be made regarding the decisions enacted by the higher courts, STF the Brazilian Superior Court of Justice (*Superior Tribunal de Justiça* – STJ).

In 2021, STJ has issued a decision in a Special Appeal (*Recurso Especial* – REsp) that upheld the liability of a social media provider to be established based on a report of a user within the platform, not applying Art. 19 MCI[86]. Concerning the reasoning, STJ stated that a platform provider that, after being notified, refuses to delete an offensive publication involving a minor, should be held liable, based on the principle of full protection of children and adolescents and from the perspective of their social vulnerability[87].

Finally, in June 2025, as already anticipated above on Section B., STF ruled Art. 19 MCI as partially unconstitutional. Between April 2014 and May 2023 (moment in which Art. 19 MCI was full into force), as a general rule, the liability of platform providers, including social media, was established only after non-compliance with a court decision (Art. 19 MCI). Exceptionally, platform providers could be held liable after the reporting of users in cases of non-consensual disclosure of intimate images (Art. 21 MCI)[88].

In general, the constitutional interpretation adopted by the STF points out to the application of the "notice and take down" approach to the liability of platform providers – beforehand only applied under the Brazilian legislation for content related to nonconsensual distribution of intimate images (NCDII) on Art. 21 MCI. Providers must demonstrate that acted diligently and in a reasonable timeframe against unlawful and unauthorized content. Art. 19 MCI continues in force if the content is related to crimes against honour (slander, defamation, and libel), i.e., the liability of platforms will continue to require a court order as already stated by the legal

86 The Brazilian Supreme Federal Court (STF) exercises both the function of abstract constitutionality control and the concrete constitutionality control of norms as the final instance, as it was originally based on the model of the US Supreme Court and has shown a growing tendency towards the European model of constitutional jurisdiction, especially since 1988 (with the current federal constitution). The Brazilian Superior Court of Justice (Superior Tribunal de Justiça – STJ) is the highest instance of ordinary jurisdiction for controlling the uniformity and authority of federal laws and can exercise the concrete control of constitutionality of norms, subject to the STF's review. In principle, STJ can be equated with the German Federal Court of Justice (BGH).

87 STJ, REsp n. 1.783.269 (2021) 4th Panel, judgment on December 14th, (Justice Ferreira) [16].

88 See n. 10.

provision before the STF's decision, but the shared content can still be removed by platform internal rules, or by user notification.

The thesis of general repercussion (*Tese de repercussão geral*) is remarkable, as it is quite extensive compared to what Art. 19 MCI aimed to address[89]. Among its 14 paragraphs (21, if sub-paragraphs are also taken separately into account), the following additional aspects deserve particular attention, in addition to those already highlighted:

(i) the presumption of liability if a piece of content is boosted/recommended by the provider or through the use of illegal artificial distribution of content through robots;
(ii) the adoption of duties of care (*deveres de cuidado*, in Portuguese) by providers if a systemic risk is identified, as well as the adoption "additional duties", such as the implementation of complaint/report channels, publication of internal rules and transparency reports, including the obligation to point out a legal representative in Brazil;
(iii) email services (e.g., Gmail), instant messaging services (e.g., What sApp) and closed meetings platforms (e.g., Zoom) are considered as "neutral providers", i.e., STF considers that that those providers do not interfere with content, as long as it concerns interpersonal communications[90].

The thesis of general repercussion set forth by the STF is applied to cases after June 26th, 2025. Besides, STF called upon the Brazilian National Congress "to elaborate a legislation that is able to remedy the shortcomings of the current regulatory scenario with regard to the protection of fundamental rights"[91].

By taking the lead in regulating the matter, STF made clear that judicial intervention (though exceptional!) was necessary due to the congressional inertia. The expectation, now, is that the Brazilian National Congress

89 STF, Informação à Sociedade, RE 1.037.396 (Tema 987) e 1.057.258 (Tema 533) - Responsabilidade de plataformas digitais por conteúdo de terceiros, 27 de junho de 2025 <https://www.stf.jus.br/arquivo/cms/noticiaNoticiaStf/anexo/Informac807a771oa768SociedadeArt19MCI_vRev.pdf> accessed 28 June 2025.

90 At the time of finalizing this text, the full Justices' opinions had not yet been made publicly available. Nevertheless, based on the trial report (n. 89) and the general repercussion thesis, which have already been published, it is possible to infer that, despite the thesis's broad normative reach, *instant messaging groups* continue to occupy a regulatory gray area. This persisting regulatory gap underscores the need for targeted legislative action by the Brazilian National Congress on the matter.

91 Free translation, see (11), item 13 of the thesis of general repercussion.

will respond accordingly, taking up the task of enacting comprehensive and democratically debated legislation to ensure a more consistent and legitimate framework for the protection of fundamental rights in the digital environment.

E. Final remarks

From an evolutionary perspective, it can be seen that the regulation of social media platforms is still far from a consensus, especially due to the complexity of the matter and the substantial change in the way digital platforms operate. In fact, the models for management and regulation – self-regulation, external regulation, and hybrid regulation – apply simultaneously in the context of social networks, contributing to the multiplicity of proposals for changing the regulatory landscape currently shaped.

Numerous regulatory models have emerged to reconcile the protection of users compatible with the promotion of innovation. These models illustrate the tensions that exist in this context, namely between users, platforms, states, civil society organizations, and supranational bodies, such as the European Union. In addition to the debate on Internet governance, the discussion on the regulation of social media platforms also includes doubts about the legitimacy of the actions adopted by providers and the resulting impact on fundamental rights.

It is clear that the dynamic nature of the Internet makes it particularly conducive to self-regulation, which, however, as we have seen, cannot rule out the possibility of external or hybrid regulation without creating deficits in the protection of rights online. Although there are various proposals for regulating online environments, it is argued that the most appropriate position is the one based on cooperation and interaction between entities with the capacity to manage digital environments, i.e., regulated self-regulation of social media platforms.

Regarding the Brazilian scenario, despite recent developments in the regulatory framework, we are still far from a regulated self-regulation of social media platforms. Recently the debate has reached a new level as the discussion has been guided by a clearly emotional and even passionate dimension, involving the persistence of polarization in society. Social pressure put on the National Congress, but also on the Executive Branch and the Judiciary, has been intense. What is certain is that the regulatory debate has already gone beyond the definition of the civil liability of platform providers, and is now discussing matters regarding transparency, oversight agency, mitigation of systemic risks and the creation of duties of care.

The recent declaration of partial (and progressive) unconstitutionality of Article 19 MCI by the STF reveals the elevation of the debate on the responsibility of digital platforms to a new level of regulatory density and constitutional relevance, in contrast to the persistent omission of the Brazilian National Congress to comprehensively regulate the matter. As stated beforehand, the thesis of general repercussion established in the judgment goes beyond the limits of civil liability for third-party content, traditionally attributed to providers in Brazil through Art. 19 MCI, and inaugurates a broader understanding, which incorporates duties of care, assumptions of liability, and normative parameters applicable, not only liability of providers due to content generated by their users, but also liability due to the platforms' own actions and omissions.

The STF ruling, thus, has an evident regulatory vocation, which seeks to fulfil, albeit provisionally, the existing legislative void as Art. 19 MCI no longer no curb the challenges related to liability of the providers in isolation in the digital realm. The breadth of the thesis highlights not only the centrality of the issue in the current stage of digital constitutionalism, but also the urgency of legislative action that consolidates, with democratic legitimacy, the parameters of platform regulation in Brazil.

Regardless of what is yet to come, it is clear that situations of social upheaval tend to speed up discussions in Brazil, and this has been no different when it comes to regulating digital platforms. Although this phenomenon drives the search for solutions, it also tends to lead to a problematic reduction of complexity, a deficit in democratic-deliberative legitimacy, contradictions and regulatory gaps, as well as the undermining the multi-stakeholder nature of the debate, among other worrying aspects.

Risk Machine? Risk Human? Can AI Help? A study from the perspective of the philosophy of science

Gerd Doeben-Henisch

In a turbulent development of empirical science, democracy, sustainability, digitalization, and now also artificial intelligence, ever larger spheres of action have opened up. At the same time, risks are becoming overwhelmingly visible: Will global problems overwhelm us? Are we humans the problem? Can AI help here, or is ultimately the development of AI itself a new problem? The following sketch of the current situation tries to work out that the various forms of risks cannot be divided from each other. They are all interconnected. It will be crucial to shape this profound interconnection.

A. A Simple Timeline

For the sketch presented here, some historical data are provided in advance, suggesting a connection that seems important for understanding the current challenges. Looking back from the year 2024 in our calendar, there have been cells on our planet for about 3.8 billion years that indicate the beginning of biological life. However, traces of the life form to which we humans belong, Homo sapiens, only appear from about 300,000 years ago. This is a point in time that occurs after 99.99% of the preceding time. Evolutionary biology can tell us a lot about what happened in the time before Homo sapiens. Here, it only counts that we have been actors on this planet only since this relatively short time. And it is only about 6,000 years since we humans invented and used writing systems to improve our communication. This happened after about 98% of the time since the appearance of Homo sapiens. University forms of education can be observed for about 920 years, i.e., after 99.7% of the time. We have known modern printing for about 570 years (after 99.8% of the time). Modern empirical sciences began about 425 years ago (after 99.85%). Modern formal logic and mathematics have been found at least since about 125 years ago (after 99.95%). Modern democracies since about 100 years ago (after 99.96%). The concept of the universal Turing machine has existed for 87 years (after 99.97%), soon followed by the first ideas of system engineering (after 99.97%) and about 75 years ago with the first ideas for artificial intelligence (after 99.97%), albeit largely only among specialists. The first comprehensive idea of a sustainable society – here the Brundtland Report – was created 37 years ago. The Internet, as we know it as the World-Wide Web (WWW), has existed for 30 years (after 99.987%), and a generative artificial intelligence that has made it into the everyday lives of many people, including those who are not computer scientists, has existed for 19 months (after 99.999%).

Innovative Event	*Label*	*Time BC*
Homo sapiens	1	300.000
Writing	2	6.000
University	3	920
Printing Press	4	570
Empirical Science	5	425
Mathematics and Formal Logic	6	125
Democracies	7	100
Turing Machine	8	87
Systems Engineering	9	84
AI	10	75
Sustainability	11	37
World Wide Web	12	30
Generative AI	13	1

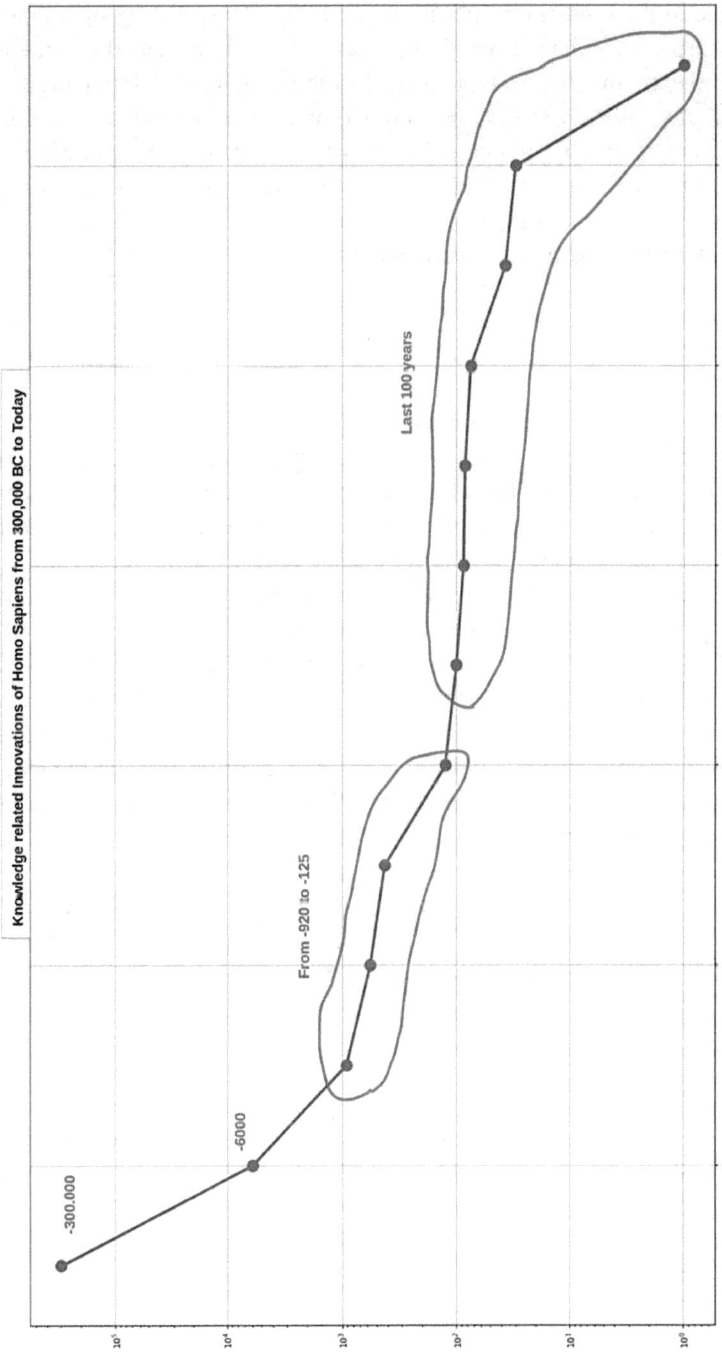
Knowledge related Innovations of Homo Sapiens from 300,000 BC to Today
-300.000
-6000
From -920 to -125
Last 100 years

These data in themselves may not mean anything. However, the sometimes enormous spans of time between individual events can indicate the tremendous complexity that had to be managed in the ongoing development. It is striking that significant achievements of Homo sapiens have all occurred in the last 2% of its sojourn on planet Earth, with a particular concentration in the last 0.3%. Mathematically, this can also be seen as a form of 'increasing event density,' also as a kind of 'acceleration': more and more in less time and simultaneously with an increase in complexity.

B. Cluster Effects

Upon closer examination, it also becomes apparent that these events are not independent of each other. The increasingly complex scientific and cultural achievements of humans over time are not possible without intensive and efficient coordination of many individual brains with each other. Without communication, this would be impossible. This requires suitable languages and sign systems, as well as highly networked work methods that rely on shared knowledge (books, journals, libraries, databases, internet, ...). Information-rich and verifiable linguistic communication is a minimum (standardizations, empiricism and prognosis, mathematics, ...). The increasing liberation from time and place (internet, databases, mobile networks, distributed data collection, ...) is added, as well as the management of ever larger amounts of data and the automation of routine tasks (algorithms, computers).

This short list already shows that the many new techniques and technologies did not arise 'just like that.' They were triggered by corresponding demand, and they were possible because the 'collective thinking of humans' was capable of ever greater achievements and continues to be so.

C. Irritations

When considering how many paths biological life on Earth had to take over 3.8 billion years to keep life on this planet 'in the game,' it should not be surprising that there can also be challenges in the current phase of life on the planet that can somewhat disrupt the 'usual course of business of the last centuries or even millennia.' The mere occurrence of such events perceived as 'disturbances' does not necessarily mean that the project of life on the planet is fundamentally in question (there have been many events in the past that, even from today's perspective, appear so enormously threatening that the present may seem harmless by comparison).

For simplification, the current challenges for the following discussion will be grouped as follows:

1. Changes in the Earth system that threaten the existing habitats and habits of humans as well as large parts of the entire ecosystem.
2. Changes in the everyday structures of human societies, which can have various reasons, here those that have nothing to do with digitalization.
3. Changes in the everyday structures of human societies that are related to digitalization.

In the following, the changes in everyday life in the sense of point (3) will be considered, i.e., those related to digitalization.

D. Irritations in the Context of Digitalization

While the new methods of system engineering in conjunction with digitalization, modern empirical science capable of prediction, and increasingly intelligent programs have proven to be enormously powerful and continue to prove so daily, there are constellations in societies that call this fundamental capability into question. Here are some examples:

- The focus of the development and deployment of this new socially relevant technology cluster is predominantly in the hands of private companies, whose interests are not the same as those of the overall society. Important further developments may thus be blocked.
- Large parts of the users of the new technologies largely lack a sufficient understanding of the effects of the system on themselves as individuals and on entire user groups.
- For democracies, a functioning common public sphere is vital. For years, we have been experiencing a fragmentation of one potential public sphere into many 'quasi-private' public spheres (in some cases up to 90% of a country's population) due to the comprehensive availability of the internet, which not only prevents the formation of a sufficiently common opinion but also accompanies this fragmentation with streams of opinions that promote the formation of enemy images among each other and 'false truths.'

- The successful deployment of digital technologies pays off economically. This reinforces further development, where 'intelligent programs' have a sales value that gives them significant importance in the thinking and feeling of people. In direct comparison with the collective power of humans, these programs are rather simple, but the interest in the collective intelligence of humans is thereby factually weakened. This is not without danger.

In the following, points (1) - (3) will not be discussed further, although they may be of high societal relevance. Instead, further thought will be given to point (4), namely the relationship between 'Collective Human Intelligence' and 'Artificial Intelligence'.

E. Paradox: The Disappearance of Genius

A paradox: In earlier times, when it was individual people who produced outstanding achievements (painters, architects, war heroes, captains, musicians, composers, ...), these individuals enjoyed high and highest esteem, and people were even willing to see in them a 'genius' at work, a 'divine spark,' the 'world spirit,' and similar concepts. However, as the actions spread across more and more people, large workshops, networks, complex working groups with many thousands of experts with different focuses, the 'human genius' became less and less tangible. When thousands of scientists, engineers, and various workers create great structures, bridges, rockets, airplanes, ships, one still sees the product, may still be impressed, but the collective human achievement behind it becomes strangely invisible, disappears. An ordinary individual is usually no longer capable of even remotely grasping the entire collective effort behind it. How could they? When 10,000 or more people research and work together in highly complex ways for years, who can understand this process? To whom is it attributable, and who bears the responsibility? Schools often still operate in the realm of old work and knowledge models that no longer exist, and even a university is far from these fantastic achievements of modern engineering; and where do modern media stand? Newspapers, television, podcasts... one can search for a long time and find virtually nothing about the reality of modern collective intelligence. Are we humans making ourselves invisible?

F. Intelligence in Humans and Machines

I. Measuring Intelligence

In the context of modern psychology, there has been the concept of intelligence as the 'Intelligence Quotient' (IQ) since at least the beginning of the 20th century. This does not mean that one knows what 'intelligence' is, but one knows how to measure certain behavioural performances of people in such a way that the measurement result can be labelled 'Intelligence Quotient' (IQ).

This concept of intelligence was based on the assumption that a list of typical tasks that a group of people of the same age in a certain region can usually solve provides an indication of which behaviours should be called 'intelligent' (what other reference point should one have chosen?). In the evaluation, one obtains the number of correctly solved tasks for each person. Assuming a 'normal distribution (Gaussian distribution)' of the values, one can set the mean value as 100 (IQ of 100), and arrange the weaker or stronger values 'left and right.' For the chosen tasks and the chosen group, one can then assign an IQ value from the distribution to each person. If one disregards all the nuances and conditions, then the IQ value here functions as an index related to a set of selected tasks and the correlating observable behavior of the acting agents. Of course, this implies nothing about the 'internal structure' of an actor that may be available in the actor and responsible for whether and how an actor behaves.[1]

Considering the range of possible human behavior in relation to the many action situations that are possible in everyday life, the typical collections of tasks already seem somewhat overly simplistic, especially when one knows how great the individual variability of characteristics is and that in real life it is not only about the individual behavioural characteristics in isolation, but also and increasingly about the ability to solve difficult tasks 'in the collective with others.' This requires many abilities that are hardly of significance for an individual. These considerations are not meant to deny that individual tests can nevertheless provide indications of a person's

1 In the history of IQ measurement, there have been collections of tasks that have challenged a wide variety of abilities, and there have been attempts to correlate the behavioral data with 'hypothetical structures inside the actor.' However, none of these approaches have been entirely convincing to date. So far, no integrating model has been presented that can uniformly process all these different sets of tasks.

performance potential, but these indications should be critically placed in larger contexts.

II. Cognition and Intelligence

At the end of the 19th century, modern psychology dealt with many cognitive performances of humans independently of intelligence tests. These included topics such as 'perception,' 'memory,' 'language learning,' 'language understanding,' and much more. These research works were based on targeted experiments, which then formed the starting point to develop hypotheses about functional structures 'in the actor.' All the hypotheses together can then function as a 'functional model' designed to derive 'predictions of behavior' from it.

If the 'models of cognition' were suitable for processing tasks from intelligence tests, such models could also be correlated with an IQ value. In this way, cognitive models of humans could then be indirectly evaluated using IQ tests.

III. Intelligence in Psychology and AI

Although Alan M. Turing had openly contemplated the possibilities of machine intelligence as early as 1948 and discussions about intelligence and 'intelligent machines' in computer science became a constant companion, the way computer science deals with intelligence and the way psychology does it have never really converged. Computer science has always had a strongly pragmatic approach and examined the capabilities of algorithms in specific task scenarios. Generalization has been and remains difficult with this approach.

IV. Human and AI

From these preliminary remarks, it becomes clear that a unified discussion about intelligence in humans and machines is currently still difficult. Unified task scenarios would be a first step. In addition, increasing the diversity of scenarios. This would at least make it possible to provide a rough estimate of the strengths and weaknesses of the two types of actors (human and machine).

Currently, the discussion about the relationship between machine and human intelligence is very unsatisfactory, especially since the possibly most important aspect of human intelligence, the so-called 'Collective Human Intelligence,' is still rather 'unexplored'.

V. Collective Human Intelligence and AI

Research on collective human intelligence is overall not very advanced yet[2], but there are already new works on the topic of 'Hybrid Collective Intelligence,' which investigates the interplay between collective human intelligence and machine intelligence.[3]

Here, as an example of collective human intelligence, a modern application scenario is taken, which is prototypical for collective intelligence: a development process in the style of system engineering. In this, the role of collective human intelligence can be made visible, including how it can generate machine intelligence. In this context, further open points can be clarified.

VI. Human in System Engineering

As already noted in the introduction, the tasks of the modern age require not just the efforts of individual masters and their assistants but huge teams, often with many thousands of experts, possibly distributed across many locations. Without efficient communication underpinned by corresponding documents, a valid result is out of the question. In addition, numerous abilities are necessary beyond mere cognition for human collaboration to

2 For example, see the MIT project 'Handbook of Collective Intelligence,' edited by Thomas W. Malone and Michael S. Bernstein, URL: https://cci.mit.edu/cichapterlinks/ or 'Understanding Collective Intelligence: Investigating the Role of Collective Memory, Attention, and Reasoning Processes' by Anita Williams Woolley and Pranav Gupta, URL: https://kilthub.cmu.edu/articles/journal_contribution/Understanding_Collective_Intelligence_Investigating_the_Role_of_Collective_Memory_Attention_and_Reasoning_Processes/24049830/1.

3 For example, see 'Collective Intelligence in Human-AI Teams: A Bayesian Theory of Mind Approach' by Samuel West and Christoph Riedl, Proceedings of the 37th AAAI Conference on Artificial Intelligence (2023), August 24, 2022, URL: https://www.networkscienceinstitute.org/publications/collective-intelligence-in-human-ai-teams-a-bayesian-theory-of-mind-approach.

function over the long term and even under stress. An orderly creation process must be organized, in which all human actors work together communicatively coordinated from an initial idea to a real product or a real service. One type of such joint creation processes is called 'System Engineering,' and the whole process is the 'System Engineering Process (SEP).'[4]

So, simplifying, there is the group of human experts EXP_{HS}, who both create the important documents DX and then use these documents as guidelines for the implementation of an order. Specifically, simplifying, the documents are:

1. Problem statement $D_{problem}$: Description of which problem is to be solved.
2. Requirements D_{requ}: Translation of the problem statement into concrete requirements.
3. Technical Design Document D_{design}: Translation of the requirements into concrete technical design decisions.

Important at this point is that all documents consist of the character strings (STR) of a particular language L (STRL). These character strings have an associated meaning space MEAN(STRL), which itself is not present as a document but exists exclusively in the form of 'internal states (IS)' within an acting agent. This highlights a special characteristic of the human actors in this process. They have the ability to link the character strings of a language L with internal knowledge states IS_{know} so that all participants in the language can activate these internal knowledge states through the character strings, and vice versa for internal knowledge states, they have the corresponding means of expression.

This duality of character strings STRL of a language L on one hand and internal meaning structures IS_{know} on the other, linked via a meaning assignment $MEAN_L$: $STR_L <---> I_{Sknow}$, enables great flexibility in constructing different meaning structures and their encoding through meaning assignments using character strings.

However, this flexibility has its price: all users of a language L must not only coordinate their interindividual knowledge contents I_{Sknow} with the

4 A formalized example of a System Engineering Process can be found here (i) Erasmus, L. D. and Doeben-Henisch, G. 2011. A Theory of the System Engineering Process. In the 10th AFRICON Conference: Sustainable Energy & Communications Development for Africa, Livingston, Zambia, and here (ii) L. D. Erasmus and G. Doeben-Henisch, A Theory of the System Engineering Management Processes in ISEM 2011 International Conference, Sept. 2011.

perceived properties of the real external world, but also the interindividual coordination of their linguistic meaning assignments to the respective character strings. This requires a continual reassessment of these assignment and coordination processes. There is no fixed point in this process!

This structure implies 'by design' a 'false normality,' as the human actor only briefly possesses sensory perception of the real external world, interpreted through prior knowledge. The 'current' then partially transitions after a brief 'moment' into the mode of the 'memorable.' 'Presence' then exists primarily in the mode of a 'memorable present.' This can—as is known—be distorted or even false. Whoever does not continually work against this distortion lives, by doing nothing, in a 'distorted world' where much is not as it is 'in the real world out there.'

The various documents $D_{problem}$, D_{requ}, and D_{design} thus do not necessarily describe the 'world as it is,' but the 'world as seen by the authors of the texts.' This is, of course, true in a very explicit way for all 'future situations.' The consequences can be varied. Since a design document D_{design} can only approximate the object M_{tst} to be realized or the service to be realized in the mode of the meaning knowledge of the authors, it may be that properties come into play in the real implementation of the linguistic concepts from the design document that are due to changed meaning spaces of the involved authors or implementers. Even if a verification of the test object M_{tst} with the design document D_{design} appears formally correct (as verification), the verification may still lead astray, as the real-world reference of the design documents may lead to conflicts due to incorrect assumptions about the world.[55] Such a 'fundamental error' can remain undetected in the context of verification, but if one begins to evaluate a test system M_{tst} with real application situations, it can happen that the assumptions about

5 This problem has long been known in the context of research on Safety-Critical Systems (SCS). For example, see Nancy G. Leveson, who has identified this problem as a fundamental issue in numerous articles and books, most recently in 2020 with N.G. Leveson. 'Are you sure your software will not kill anyone?' Communications of the ACM, 63:25 – 28, [https://doi.org/10.1145/3376127], and in 2023 with Nancy G. Leveson and John P. Thomas, 'Inside Risks Certification of Safety-Critical Systems. Seeking new approaches toward ensuring the safety of software-intensive systems.' COMMUNICATIONS OF THE ACM, OCTOBER 2023, VOL. 66, NO. 10, pp.22-26, [https://dx.doi.org/10.1145/3615860]. Also see Gerd Doeben-Henisch, 'Review of Nancy Leveson (2020), Are you sure your software will not kill anyone?' URL: [https://www.uffmm.org/2023/10/21/review-of-nancy-leveson-2020-are-you-sure-your-software-will-not-kill-anyone/] and text: [https://www.uffmm.org/wp-content/uploads/2019/06/review-leveson-2020-acm-yourSWwillNotKill.pdf].

the application situation lead to concrete conflicts when confronted with real application situations. This is the only way to discover implicit false assumptions about the real application situation.

With all this, it becomes clear that a design process with final verification and evaluation can ultimately be understood as a 'dialogue' between the previous expectations of the world and the way the real world 'actually shows' itself.

In summary, one can say: the human in the 'mode of his collective intelligence' uses the maximum of his current knowledge, which can be partially wrong due to the nature of human cognition, to generate possible new products or behaviours in a possible imagined (predicted) future. To avoid falling victim to the existing—albeit unconscious—knowledge errors, collective intelligence tries to make these visible and eliminates them during the development process through the most informative tests possible. However, this can only ever work to a limited extent, as the entire collective knowledge lags behind the surrounding dynamic complexity at any given time. Therefore, the collective knowledge must be repeatedly not only 'partially corrected' but also fundamentally adjusted.

VII. Can AI Help?

At this point, the question will be addressed whether the new forms of Artificial Intelligence (AI) can help human Collective Intelligence in any way, or whether AI could perhaps completely replace the role of collective human intelligence eventually?

Starting with the fundamental question of a possible complete replacement, this question is quickly answered, as so far neither the concept of 'collective human intelligence (CHI)' has been defined in a way that allows for verifiable comprehensive tests[6], nor does a similar definition exist for the term 'artificial intelligence (AI).' In the case of AI, there are collections of various performance tests, but it is not clear how these can be 'generalized.' Even less clear is how a connection to 'collective human intelligence' can be established as long as this term is not really defined.

6 For example, see the draft by Thomas W. Malone and Michael S. Bernstein in 'Chapter 1. Introduction' for the planned book by Thomas W. Malone & Michael S. Bernstein (Eds.), 'Collective Intelligence Handbook,' MIT Press, in press. URL: [https://docs.google.com/document/d/1CRVN8uxa_g8i3oLRfVxhsltWNZ_ZMwoI-pl5IosG9VU/edit?pli=1].

Therefore, the following will only address whether the current AI—and its possible extrapolated extensions—could help collective human intelligence in any way.

Based on the previous discussion, there are so far only two possible starting points for a discussion: Firstly, the connection of the term 'intelligence' via the 'intelligence quotient' with observable performance in the face of tasks to be solved, and secondly, certain formats in which people collectively solve tasks to which the property of 'intelligence' is assigned—rather intuitively. One such collective format is the previously mentioned 'System Engineering Process (SEP).'

Since known intelligence tests always only consider individual persons, they are methodologically of little help for the discussion of the phenomenon 'collective human intelligence.' In addition, there are so far no systematic comparisons between humans and intelligent machines for measuring individual performances.[7] Therefore, an attempt will be made here, at least for the example of a System Engineering Process, to clarify whether there are areas in which intelligent machines could support or even replace humans, or not.

G. World Models: Open or closed

I. Language: With and without meaning

In the context of a System Engineering Process, collective human intelligence (CHI) starts with a problem statement $D_{problem}$, which uses the currently available knowledge about the 'application situation' and the 'available solutions' to work out a 'concretization,' initially 'mentally' (D_{requ}, D_{design}), but then also 'materialized' with a verifiable real test version M_{tst}. This test version is then tested in a variety of 'application situations' ANW_{tst} to see if all the anticipated behavioural properties from the requirements and design document (D_{requ}, D_{design}) can be positively fulfilled.

The entirety of the agreed-upon documents ($D_{problem}$, D_{requ}, D_{design}) represents the current 'world model (WM)' of the CHI.

7 Of course, one can cite examples where individual humans have competed against computers in defined games (checkers, chess, Go, and many more), and now almost exclusively lose against computers. These examples are certainly informative, but they do not replace a real comparison with a variety of tasks.

As previously made clear, such a world model is fundamentally incomplete and highly likely to be partially inaccurate. It is a world model that is 'closed on paper,' but in the face of confrontation with the real world through real tests, it must be classified as partially changeable. From this perspective, the world model is 'partially open.' An experienced CHI 'knows this' and therefore organizes appropriate tests for verification.

The minimal elements of a world model are (i) a defined initial situation (S), (ii) a set of possible change rules (R), (iii) an agreed procedure on how to change an initial situation—or any situation—using change rules (|--), and (iv) at least one goal (G) that can serve as a benchmark to assess whether—and if so, to what extent—a current situation already corresponds to the agreed goal.

In the case of a CHI, there is also the ability (v) to 'decide' whether a currently reached linguistically defined state S 'in the light of the active meaning functions of all participants' is 'true' or not in the real situation. This would not be a purely formal verification as can be performed within a SEP, but an empirical verification that is only possible by explicit reference to the surrounding empirical world.

It is also known that a CHI is capable, in the event of conflicts between the current world model and the real world experienced in testing, of modifying its world model to the extent that the conflict no longer occurs. In the worst case, the world model would have to be 'discarded.'

Modifying a world model is not trivial. Many change rules have effects both 'in breadth' (side effects) and over many successive time points. Identifying the decisive misalignment is not easy to achieve. Additionally, complex meaning functions are interposed between the character strings of the documents and the possible reality, which can differ among the individual members of a CHI without these differences being directly visible. If the specific elements of a misalignment are discovered, the challenge arises of finding alternative change rules, possibly also a change of goal. For these creative tasks, there is often/mostly no 'rational assurance' through existing knowledge, as it often involves 'truly new' situations that no one really knows yet.

At this point, considering those intelligent algorithms that now routinely defeat the world's best players in defined game contexts, one might wonder whether this type of algorithm—let's call it a 'closed world model (CWM) algorithm'—would be suitable for making a constructive contribution in the context of a System Engineering Process (SEP).

If the world model of a CHI were fully formulated, it would be conceivable that a CWM algorithm could master this task.

Here, however, an immediate fundamental 'obstacle' becomes visible: Unlike the closed world models of a game, the rules of the world model of a CHI are predominantly 'not formalized,' as the rules are written in 'normal language,' which is not applicable without an explicit meaning function. This may initially be interpreted as a 'weakness,' but real practice shows that this 'weakness' is precisely the strength that makes a powerful CHI possible.[8]

A CWM algorithm could therefore only be applied if it were capable of not only processing 'meaning-free' character strings with 'hard-wired meaning objects'[9] but also of appropriately interpreting freely interpretable character strings with one of the many available meaning functions in the context of natural languages. Due to the radical 'meaninglessness' of computer languages, there is so far no indication of how this problem could be satisfactorily solved.[10]

II. Reality Check: True or false

As the example with the System Engineering Process makes clear, it is fundamentally important that the active world model of a Collective Human Intelligence (CHI) is repeatedly and extensively verified and validated

8 This was the attitude of those logicians and mathematicians who, from the end of the 19th century, advanced modern formal logic and the formalization of mathematics. They 'liberated' logic from any 'meaning,' except for some 'abstract truth values.' This enabled very elegant formal calculi, but when applying these to the 'real world,' all character strings of the formal logic languages had to be interpreted back to the real world in an extremely laborious and error-prone manner. All modern computers suffer from this fundamental 'withdrawal of meaning.' This is so far 'irreparable.'

9 The 'hard-wired meaning objects' in the case of game applications are those character strings to which fixed objects from the game are uniquely assigned within the scope of a game. A game rule refers to such objects and describes defined changes that can then be directly translated into a change on the game board.

10 Of course, computer languages are not 'completely devoid of meaning,' since they can be interpreted by the respective machine in such a way that character strings of the programming language can lead to state changes within the machine. However, there is so far 'no natural connection' between the state changes within the machine and possible meaning assignments of character strings of everyday language in the real world 'outside the machine.' This would have to be specially established in each individual case. So far, there is no known approach that could solve this problem (see also note (9)).

through tests with the 'real world.' This is possible because all human actors within a CHI have the ability not only to correlate language strings with learned meaning functions and acquired knowledge (also known as 'decoding,' 'interpreting,' or 'understanding'), but also to relate this knowledge activated through interpretation to current sensory perceptions of the real external world. Within this non-trivial process, a 'judgment' may be made that the 'activated knowledge' sufficiently matches the 'perceivable aspects' of the 'real world' or not. This 'empirical control' plays a fundamental role in assessing the current world model and for possible changes to this model. Without this, all world models would be nearly worthless.

Modern algorithms, such as the type of a 'generative AI' exemplified by chatGPT4 or similar programs, exhibit behaviours that can easily give the impression that they 'understand' the 'meaning of character strings of everyday language' as a human actor would. Indeed, this performance is extraordinary because the algorithms of the 'generative AI' type actually do not possess a meaning function that is comparable to that of a human actor.

This capability is based on two fundamental functions of a generative AI: (i) These AIs are 'fed' millions—or more—documents created by human actors, from which they independently 'extract' individual character strings with their various 'contexts with other character strings' and frequencies. This already allows for determining which character strings are commonly used with others. In a further step (ii), typical dialogue situations are identified with the help of human actors, and it is trained how character strings within such dialogue formats can be organized so that they correspond to conventional formats. This also happens without any explicit meaning function. The fact that such AI can generate long dialogues and extensive texts in a way that at first glance seems as if they were generated by a human actor is impressive and the result of excellent engineering work.

Due to a lack of a meaning function, which goes along with an absence of human-like world knowledge based on sensory input, further modified by various cognitively relevant brain processes, a generative AI can only move within the predefined paths of available texts. A current empirical reference is thus excluded unless there were an empirical segment of the world whose properties are translated into character strings of everyday language in real-time, in a way that this translation meets the requirements of a human meaning function. If there were such 'Real-time Empirical State Descriptions (RESD)' for a specific 'area,' then a generative AI could at least partially match its character strings with these RESD character strings.

Where in our world would there then be such RESD character string generators? Where would such RESD character string generators get their meaning function from? Would it ultimately be human actors themselves who translate a current situation into character strings using their own meaning function, which they then communicate to a generative AI?

When asked: 'Would you be able to judge, that a statement, which I would communicate to you, is 'true' or 'false'?' @chatGPT4 responds, 'I can help evaluate the accuracy of a statement based on known facts and information. Please share the statement, and I'll do my best to assess its truthfulness.' Yes, the current world model of a generative AI marks the space of possible utterances, which are either 'fit' or 'do not fit' relative to it. This includes the case that a generative AI has adopted documents that are 'inherently wrong.' When this fact is addressed in a dialogue with a generative AI, one gets many good suggestions on how to check the usability of documents or detect errors, but one does not get a clear statement from the AI that it itself cannot directly verify the empirical validity of a statement.

For the task of direct empirical verification, a generative AI falls short, but it still appears that a generative AI can be helpful for initial orientations.

III. Cooperation: Models of the other

As became clear from the description of a CHI using the example of a System Engineering Process, all human actors in such a process are required to have the ability to continuously and comprehensively communicate and cooperate with other actors in this process to enable a CHI.

This is a highly complex matter, the description of which is omitted here. Part of the task is that each human actor must not only have internalized parts of the common world model but also have minimal knowledge about all behavioural and communication structures. In particular, they need 'minimal models of the other' in their minds, enabling them to form useful 'expectations about the behavior' of the others.

H. Postscript

After these considerations, it should be clear that the various risks cannot simply be attributed to a single actor. In collective intelligence—whether purely human or hybrid—every individual actor is part of a larger entity that acts and decides as a whole. Uncertainties and possible partial maladaptations are essential to the process of collective intelligence moving in a dynamic world. Here, truth can only ever be taken as a 'temporary state' that must be repeatedly achieved anew together. The price of success is called 'life,' and the price of failure may be 'extinction.' This fundamental fact has not changed after about 3.8 billion years of life on this planet.

Being and Becoming in the Algorithmic Age

Bernard E. Harcourt

To change the world: the prerequisite, most often, is to change our experience of the world, to experience the world differently, to be shaken to our foundations, to have one's sense of self shattered. That is a process of both being and becoming. In order to turn that process in our favour, in this age of artificial intelligence, it will be crucial to transform data and algorithms into bits of justice.

The greatest fears about our new expository society and its doppelgänger logics in the age of artificial intelligence - but also perhaps their greatest promise - revolve around the ways in which algorithmic predictions shape who we are, what we desire, how we understand ourselves. The new algorithmic age forms our conceptions of selves by aggregating our past behaviours, predicting our future desires, and then recommending and suggesting what we will want - melding those very desires and our future selves as our smart devices grow artificially. The digital age works on us from the inside. As Antonio Negri notes, "The digital machine does not apply its devices of government from the outside but from the inside, it does not separate to command but on the contrary it implicates individuals, it projects its light, it exerts a power: the digital machine applies itself through the relationship between who commands and who obeys."[1]

The problem, then, is that our subjectivities are being shaped by forces that don't have "our best interests" at heart. We are being shaped by commercial ventures that merely want to make a profit and by political projects that simply seek power—or combinations of the two, in the guise of a Donald Trump or an Elon Musk. One need not believe in the notion of an "authentic" self or a "pure" or "unadulterated" subjectivity to fear being pushed or prodded and buffeted in different directions—away from those selves that, one might say, would have been more "organic." The concept of

1 Antonio Negri, "Lire Harcourt *Exposed*," trans. Judith Revel, December 14, 2016, p. 2, available at https://blogs.law.columbia.edu/revolution1313/files/2022/05/Toni-Negri-Lire-Exposed-Decembre-2016-FR.pdf.

"organic" is of course overly simplistic. If we experience shifting desire—if we are always in a process of becoming—is any one particular direction or desire more organic than the other? What does it mean or what would it mean to be left to our own devices? No, there are of course no "authentic" selves.

Yet we all have the intuition of what a *more* authentic self might mean. I, at least, have that intuition. I am a bit of a recluse. I like to think through things myself. I would prefer to be shaped by my own happenstance rather than being subject to other people's financial and other interests. It is the difference between spending a day writing and thinking, or spending a day following social media and responding to incoming emails.

Again, this is not to suggest that there is an authentic self, nor a self that is independent of the influence of others. We are creatures of our upbringing and nurturing. We learn to desire things as children, from our parents or siblings, our family and friends. We develop a way of being that is comfortable, surrounded by others, ensconced in their lives too. I am still surrounded by my parents' furniture and dishes and rugs and paintings and many of their books; and often, what I acquire resembles what they left me. I am not so naïve as to think or believe that I have an authentic self or an essence of my own.

Yet I genuinely fear forms of subjectivation that are influenced by algorithmic predictions intended to generate consumption through advertisements and recommendations. I fear that the solicitations—or worse, all of the hidden messaging from artificial intelligence—will bend me into another self.

Before getting carried away or too anxious, though, let me come back to where I started. I said: "but also perhaps their greatest promise." Let us take seriously Negri's challenge that we must not merely look at the dangers, but at the potentialities of new technologies.[2] What would it mean to do so?

The place to start would be to recognize the extent to which experiences shape our subjectivity and change it. Experiences are foundational to our sense of self. Michel Foucault, you will recall, often spoke of desiring experiences that would "de-subjectivate" and allow him to become other than he was. He often spoke of a desire to change himself. A desire to experience

2 Antonio Negri, "Lire Harcourt *Exposed*," trans. Judith Revel, December 14, 2016, https://blogs.law.columbia.edu/revolution1313/files/2022/05/Toni-Negri-Lire-Exposed-Decembre-2016-FR.pdf.

new things that make us new subjects. I feel a kindred spirit to that notion of de-subjectivation, though, I recognize, others may want to be the same or to find and anchor their true selves.

For Foucault, the goal of historicizing ways of experiencing the world was precisely to challenge our own experience of the present, our experience of reality. In interviews, he asserted this as his goal, for himself and for his readers. "I aim at having an experience myself—by passing through a determinate historical content—an experience of what we are today, of what is not only our past but also our present," he told Duccio Trombadori in 1978. "And I invite others to share the experience," he added.[3] Foucault spoke of creating "an experience of our modernity that might permit us to emerge from it transformed." This meant that, "at the conclusion of the book we can establish new relationships with what was at issue; for instance, madness, its constitution, its history in the modern world."[4]

Phenomenological approaches, he contended, tend to end up seeking ontological truths about being—in the case of Martin Heidegger, an ontological foundation of human caring (his term was "*Sorge*" or care), for Ludwig Binswanger and his *Daseinsanalyse*, an ontology of love.[5] But for Foucault, drawing on the work of Friedrich Nietzsche, Maurice Blanchot, Georges Bataille, the historical analysis of experience led rather to "the task of 'tearing' the subject from itself in such a way that it is no longer the subject as such, or that it is completely 'other' than itself so that it may arrive at its annihilation, its dissociation." Foucault goes on:

> It is this de-subjectifying undertaking, the idea of a "limit-experience" that tears the subject from itself, which is the fundamental lesson that I've learned from these authors. And no matter how boring and erudite my resulting books have been, this lesson has always allowed me to conceive them as direct experiences to "tear" me from myself, to prevent me from always being the same.[6]

In this, we are inevitably situated between being and becoming. That is certainly the case in our expository society in the algorithmic age.

3 Michel Foucault, *Remarks on Marx: Conversations with Duccio Trombadori*, trans. R. James Goldstein and James Cascaito (New York: Semiotext(e), 1991), 32-34.

4 Foucault, *Remarks on Marx*, 32-34.

5 Michel Foucault, *Binswanger et l'analyse existentielle*, ed. Elisabetta Basso (Paris: Éditions de l'EHESS-Gallimard-Seuil, 2021), p. 133.

6 Foucault, *Remarks on Marx*, 31-32.

Nietzsche championed "becoming" in the nineteenth century. He championed every aspect of the aesthetic of becoming, of the discovery of truth, of the fabrication of truth, of the creation of new selves, of the invention of the self.

In certain passages, Nietzsche is adamant that there is only becoming and that the constant effort to impose the quality of being on becoming is precisely the recurring human struggle—it is the ultimate expression of the will to power. Women and men exercise power when they transform someone's act into their human nature, for instance when they turn a deviant act into someone's status as a "felon," a "convict," or a "dangerous individual": when they impose on something someone did, the character of an essence.

It should not come as a surprise that Heidegger, who championed being, would seek to tame Nietzsche's thought after his publication of *Being and Time* in 1927. Heidegger turns to Nietzsche in about 1936, and throughout his lectures and manuscripts from 1936-1946, Heidegger struggles to force the round peg of Nietzsche's writings on becoming (as well as on the will to power and the eternal return) into the square hole of *Being and Time.*

Being and Time was unquestionably transformative when it was published, and, for many readers, including Jean-Paul Sartre and Foucault, liberating: whereas before, philosophical discourse was trapped not only in religious dogma (and proofs of God's existence), but also in a disembodied repulsion for our materiality—with the body-mind divide, *cogito,* and such a fundamental distrust for everything body-related. Heidegger felt like a breath of fresh air and an embrace of our human experience, in 1927 at least—of our angst, of our fears, of our anguished concerns, of our bodily existence, of being *here* in the world, of our real experiences in relation to time and our own mortality. Heidegger changed the course of philosophical discourse in the twentieth century.

But Heidegger's writings were still tied to a metaphysical discourse that remained rigid in its embrace of the very concept of being. Nietzsche is the one who challenged that most a century before—in part because he was not a metaphysician but rather a philologist, in part because of his temperament and intellect. Regardless, his writings fundamentally challenged the notion that there is permanence, being, a doer.

It is precisely the tension between Heidegger's being and Nietzsche's becoming that is at the heart of Heidegger's constant effort to both recognize his distance from Nietzsche, but simultaneously to attempt to close the gap. As Tracy Colony remarks, this reflects the "enigmatic composite of proximity and distance that formed the interpretive horizon for Heidegger's inaugural confrontation with Nietzsche."[7] Heidegger resolved this enigma, I would argue, by means of the notion of eternal return. To be somewhat reductionist, I would contend that, for Heidegger, becoming becomes being by means of the eternal return. For Heidegger, the tension between being and becoming is resolved by converting becoming into being through the recurrence of becoming. Heidegger says as much when, referring to the most emblematic passage in Nietzsche on becoming ("To *stamp* Becoming with the character of Being—that is the *supreme will to power*"), Heidegger writes: "We ask: Why is this the *supreme* will to power? The answer is, because will to power in its *most* profound essence is nothing other than the permanentizing of Becoming into presence."[8]

"*The permanentizing of Becoming into presence*": that is what Heidegger believed that Nietzsche's concept of eternal recurrence could achieve. Throughout his lectures, Heidegger rehearses this central argument: for Nietzsche, the two central concepts were will to power and eternal return, and those two must be understood together, in order to grasp "in a unified way the doctrines of the eternal return of the same and will to power," and understand how they lead back to the idea of being.[9] "Both thoughts —will to power and eternal recurrence of the same—say *the same* and think the *same* fundamental characteristic of beings as a whole," Heidegger wrote.[10]

Nietzsche, more loyal to becoming, had anticipated Heidegger's later move, and warned against it, precisely in that emblematic passage that Heidegger returned to, again and again, from the unpublished fragments (included in the infamous compilation, *The Will to Power* § 617). Following the first sentence, "To *stamp* Becoming with the character of Being—that is the *supreme will to power*," Nietzsche adds, a paragraph later:

---

7 Tracy Colony, "The Death of God and the Life of Being: Heidegger's Confrontation with Nietzsche," pp. 197-217, in *Interpreting Heidegger: Critical Essays*, ed. Daniel Dahlstrom (Cambridge University Press, 2011), at p. 198.

8 Martin Heidegger, *Nietzsche: Volumes 3 and 4*, trans. David Farrell Krell (New York: HarperOne, 1987 and 1982 [1961]), "Vol. III: The Will to Power as Knowledge and as Metaphysics," p. 156; see also *id.*, p. 213.

9 Martin Heidegger, *Nietzsche: Volumes 1 and 2*, trans. David Farrell Krell (New York: HarperOne, 1979 and 1984 [1961]), "Vol. I: The Will to Power as Art," p. 17.

10 Heidegger, *Nietzsche: Volumes 3 and 4*, p. 10; *see also*, *id.*, p. 166 and 180-181; *id.*, "Volume IV: Nihilism," p. 7-8 and Heidegger, *Nietzsche: Volumes 1 and 2*, "Vol. II: The Eternal Recurrence of the Same," p. 198-199.

> That *everything recurs* is the closest *approximation of a world of Becoming to one of Being: -peak of the meditation.*[11]

It is almost as if Nietzsche were writing to Heidegger: at best an approximation. Certainly not an equation. For Nietzsche, it seems, we are left in a world of becoming.

We might say that de-subjectivation is a form of becoming. A form of becoming that alters our being, even if it is only a momentary being. Transformation, then, implies moments of being and of becoming—they are constant becoming and being, constantly becoming other.

In this struggle between becoming and being, there emerges something of critical import: an unexpected graft of the ethical reading of the eternal return (as Gilles Deleuze understood the concept) onto the permanence of being, under the guise of an aesthetic model of creation. The ethical reading of the concept of the eternal return is the idea that the threat of one's actions recurring over and over imposes on us a moral imperative to act ethically—since we will relive our actions in eternity. It is that conjoining of the eternal recurrence of ethical choice, heightened by the gravity of being, and understood as artistic production, that I would call an "aesthetics of being."

It can be placed in fruitful discussion with other critical concepts from the twentieth century, for instance, André Breton's aesthetics of the *frisson*, or Foucault's aesthetics of existence. It is not Heidegger's concept, but it emerges from his herculean struggle—and ultimate failure—in the face of Nietzsche.

The aesthetics of being is how we craft our changing selves, how we negotiate the relation between becoming and being—going back and forth to appreciate and transform our subjectivity, to de-subjectivate ourselves at time, to resubjectivate ourselves at another time, to change ourselves in order to change the world.

In the end, I would not attribute this aesthetics of being to Heidegger, but to Nietzsche—which is all the better, since Heidegger's fascist politics were so utterly intolerable. Or perhaps, to be more modest, I would characterize it as an effort *toward* an aesthetics of being and becoming. It emerges from a confrontation. It serves to heighten the gravity of our constant ethical

11 Quoted in Heidegger, *Nietzsche: Volumes 1 and 2*, Vol. I, p. 19; *see* Friedrich Nietzsche, *The Will to Power*, trans. Walter Kaufmann and R. J. Hollingdale (New York: Vintage Books, 1967), §617, p. 330.

choices and to model them on aesthetic creation. Later, Jean-Paul Sartre pushed the concept of being toward existence in the 1950s, embracing a notion of existence that was closer to becoming: a constant becoming through one's actions *en situation.* Later still, Foucault pushed it further toward the notion of de-subjectivation. In the digital age, it may be time to push it even further toward an aesthetics of being and becoming.

We live in a world that is a competition for attention and desire. Meta wants us to spend more time on Instagram and to encourage our friends to join, and Elon Musk on X. Authors want us to spend more time reading their books—and sharing their experiences. We are surrounded by attention merchants, as Tim Wu tells us.[12] The time could not be more pressing to imagine an ethics directed toward that aesthetics of being and becoming.

I have come to appreciate the relationship between being and becoming, especially today, in light of our debates over identity politics. The fact is, identities can be motivating forces that push people to action, without being static, without being pure being. There are many times in life in which our identities have real, tangible consequences. We may be treated by others in certain ways because of our identities. Women may be treated in certain ways because they appear to be women. A person may be treated differently because they appear to be Black or of Latin descent. Those are moments of political mobilization. They produce social movements like Black Lives Matter and MeToo. They represent forms of being with consequences—as the Combahee River Collective wrote, when it coined the term "identity politics."[13]

The Combahee River Collective not only coined the term "identity politics," it introduced the expression "interlocking" systems of oppression and developed a paradigm for how to think and act at the intersection of multiple political struggles.[14] The Collective exposed the way in which people are treated because of their appearances and how that can be galvanizing. It

12 Tim Wu, The Attention Merchants: The Epic Scramble to Get Inside Our Heads (New York: Knopf, 2016).

13 Combahee River Collective, "Combahee River Collective Statement," p. 15–27, in How We Get Free: Black Feminism and the Combahee River Collective, ed. Keeanga-Yamahtta Taylor (Chicago: Haymarket Books, 2017 [1977]).

14 "Combahee River Collective Statement," p. 19, 15; see also Keeanga-Yamahtta Taylor, "Until Black Women Are Free, None of Us Will Be Free," New Yorker, July 20. https://www.newyorker.com/news/our-columnists/until-black-women-are-free-none-of-us-will-be-free.

can politicize. Identities are not always associated with biological traits, but they are forms of being that we cannot always easily escape. In the political struggles around what we call "identity politics," we are constantly navigating between identities and the transformation of identities—between being and becoming. We can, at times, take on new identities. Some are more malleable than others. But at the same time, we resist forms of subjectivation by negotiating the space between being and becoming.

In order to achieve social change, a prerequisite is that people's experience of reality, of present reality, change. In order for people to get agitated and to act, they have to have experiences that shape how they encounter and understand their world. That will necessarily take place at the intersection of being and becoming. When asked to describe what "revolution" means to him, Toni Negri responds that it means "to constantly live and construct moments of novelty and rupture."[15] "A revolution isn't made, Toni says, "it makes you."[16]

How then do we allow ourselves to be transformed without fear that we are being manipulated by artificial intelligence and other people's interests? How do we live in the algorithmic age without being its pawn?

The only way forward will be to push the algorithms toward justice. We need to create experiences of justice and feed the databases and cloud storage with stories and achievements of justice. If we just fear technology and withdraw from the digital age, then we will have ceded the ground. Algorithms, big data, artificial intelligence are here to stay. They are the space of the future. We need to shape them now. To create genuine experiences of justice. Truth is, we will never return to the analogue world.

We do not have a choice, in the end. We must find ways to deploy the digital experience in such a way as to inspire political activism and engagement. How? Through the very same seductions, temptations, desires, and experiences that move us, transform us, de-subjectivate us. By finding ways to draw in users and readers into the arc of justice. To create experiences that will shape the way that people experience the world and lead them to fight or continue fighting for justice—in the face of all odds.

15 Roberto Ciccarelli, "Antonio Negri: 'The central banks are today's Winter Palace'," *il manifesto*, November 7, 2017, https://global.ilmanifesto.it/antonio-negri-the-central-banks-are-todays-winter-palace/.

16 Ciccarelli, "Antonio Negri: 'The central banks are today's Winter Palace'," https://global.ilmanifesto.it/antonio-negri-the-central-banks-are-todays-winter-palace/.

At the same time, we must fundamentally transform the political economy of the digital realm. Why is it that someone like Elon Musk, the richest man in the world, owns X? It is because he understands that these are the spaces of influence and subjectivation. It is not for nothing that Twitter was worth $44 billion when he bought it.

The social media platforms make their money from digital advertising. Meta, X and others most of their revenue selling personal data and advertisements—in the billions of dollars. In 2021, Twitter generated $4.5 billion through its advertising services, mostly by selling promoted products, such as Promoted Ads, Twitter Amplify, and Follower Ads to advertisers.[17] This advertising revenue represented about 90% of Twitter's income. The other 10% was from the sale of data—more technically, data licenses that allow partner enterprises to collect, mine, and analyse historical and real-time data on Twitter's platform.[18]

In order to generate this revenue, Meta, X, and other social media and technology companies need to have a large and growing user bases. In other words, we are the ones generating their revenue. Their algorithms are trained on us. So in the long-run, we need to lay claim to those resource—our own data—in order to transform the political economy of the digital realm. But in the meantime, we all—the targets of their algorithms—need to feed their servers with experiences of justice. We need to overwhelm their data with the lived experience and the struggle for justice.

In sum, we must tweak the algorithms for justice: we must inspire others by making justice more appealing than injustice and deploy these new technologies to promote equality. We must push the frontier and develop new ways of thinking beyond the actuarial, the statistical, the merely algorithmic, toward algorithmic justice. It is an ethical imperative, one that aims, ultimately, toward an aesthetics of being and becoming.

17 Nathan Reiff, "How Twitter Makes Money," April 28, 2022, https://www.investopedia.com/ask/answers/120114/how-does-twitter-twtr-make-money.asp.

18 Reiff, "How Twitter Makes Money."

List of Contributors

Prof. Dr. Michael Bäuerle, LL.M.
Professor of Public Law, Faculty of Law, Hessian University of Applied Sciences for Public Management and Security, Wiesbaden, Germany

Prof. Dr. Anna Beckers,
Professor of Private Law and Social Theory, Faculty of Law, Maastricht University, Maastricht, Netherlands

Prof. Dr. Martin Belov
Professor of Constitutional Law, Faculty of Law, University of Sofia "St. Kliment Ohridski", Sofia, Bulgaria

Prof. Dr.-Ing. habil. Jürgen Beyerer
Professor of Computer Science, Faculty of Computer Science, Karlsruhe Institute of Technology (KIT), Karlsruhe, Germany; Head of Institute, Fraunhofer IOSB, Karlsruhe, Germany

Andressa de Bittencourt Sequeira
Ph.D. candidate in the Graduate Program in Law, Faculty of Law, Pontifical Catholic University of Rio Grande do Sul, Porto Alegre, Brazil

Prof. Kiel Brennan-Marquez
Professor of Law, Center on Community Safety, Policing and Inequality, University of Connecticut, Mansfield, United States of America

Dr. Stefan Brink
Former State Commissioner for Data Protection and Freedom of Information (LfDI), Baden-Württemberg, Stuttgart, Germany; Head of the scientific institute for the digitalization of the working world (wida), Berlin, Germany

Prof. Dr. Beatrice Brunhöber
Professor of Criminal Law, Criminal Procedure Law, Legal Philosophy and Comparative Law, Faculty of Law, Goethe-University Frankfurt am Main, Frankfurt am Main, Germany

Prof. Dr. Christoph Burchard, LL.M. (NYU)
Professor for Criminal Law and Criminal Procedure, International and European Criminal Law, Comparative Law and Legal Theory, Faculty of Law, Goethe-University Frankfurt am Main, Frankfurt am Main, Germany

Prof. Dr. Hadar Dancig-Rosenberg
Professor of Criminal Law and Procedure, Faculty of Law, Bar-Ilan University, Ramat Gan, Israel

Prof. Dr. Gerd Doeben-Henisch
Professor Emeritus of Computer Science, Department of Computer Science and Engineering, Frankfurt University of Applied Sciences, Frankfurt am Main, Germany

Prof. Dr. Klaus Günther
Professor of Legal Theory, Criminal Law and Criminal Procedure, Faculty of Law, Goethe University Frankfurt am Main, Frankfurt am Main, Germany

Dr. des. Johannes Haaf
Research Associate, Chair of Legal and Constitutional Theory, Faculty of Arts, Humanities and Social Science, Technische Universität Dresden, Dresden, Germany

Prof. Bernard E. Harcourt, Ph.D.
Corliss Lamont Professor of Law and Civil Liberties, Columbia University, New York, United States of America; Chaired Professor, École des hautes études en sciences sociales, Paris, France

Dr. Clarissa Henning
Personal advisor to the State Commissioner for Data Protection and Freedom of Information (LfDI) Baden-Württemberg, Stuttgart, Germany

PD Dr. Bernhard Jakl, M.A.
Adjunct Professor of Civil Law, Philosophy of Law and Medical Law, Faculty of Law, University of Münster, Münster, Germany; Judge, Landgericht (Regional Court) Frankfurt am Main, Germany

Mathieu Kiriakos
Independent scholar, Cornell Law School, Cornell University, New York, United States of America

Prof. Dr. Jörn Lamla
Professor of Sociological Theory and Director at the Research Center for Information System Design (ITeG), University of Kassel, Kassel, Germany

Prof. Dr. Katja Langenbucher
Professor of Civil Law, Commercial Law and Banking Law, Faculty of Law, Goethe University Frankfurt am Main, Frankfurt am Main, Germany

Prof. Dr. Sabine Müller-Mall
Professor of Legal and Constitutional Theory, Faculty of Arts, Humanities and Social Science, Technische Universität Dresden, Dresden, Germany

Prof. Frank Pasquale
Professor of Law, Cornell Law School and Cornell Tech, Cornell University, New York, United States of America

Prof. mr. dr. Sofia Ranchordas
Professor of Administrative Law, Faculty of Law, Tilburg Law School, Netherlands; Professor of Public Law, Innovation and Sustainability, Faculty of Law, Libera Università Internazionale degli Studi Sociali (Luiss), Rome, Italy

Prof. Dr. Ingo Wolfgang Sarlet
Professor of Constitutional Law, Faculty of Law, Pontifical Catholic University of Rio Grande do Sul, Porto Alegre, Brazil

Prof. Burkhard Schäfer
Professor of Computational Legal Theory, Faculty of Law, University of Edinburgh, Edinburgh, Scotland

Prof. Jonathan Simon, Ph.D.
Lance Robbins Professor of Criminal Justice Law, UC Berkeley School of Law, University of California, Berkeley, United States of America

Prof. Dr. Tobias Singelnstein
Professor of Criminology and Criminal Law, Faculty of Law, Goethe University Frankfurt am Main, Frankfurt am Main, Germany

Prof. Dr. Indra Spiecker genannt Döhmann, LL.M. (Georgetown Univ.)
Professor of Public Law, Law of Digitalization, Environmental Law and Legal Theory, Faculty of Law, University of Cologne, Germany

Prof. em. Dr. Gunther Teubner
Professor Emeritus of Private Law and Legal Sociology, Faculty of Law, Goethe University Frankfurt am Main, Frankfurt am Main, Germany

Dr. Tim Zander
Senior Research Assistant, Vision and Fusion Laboratory IES, Karlsruhe Institute of Technology (KIT), Karlsruhe, Germany

Prof. Lucia Zedner, DPhil.
Senior Research Fellow in Law, All Souls College and Professor of Criminal Justice, Faculty of Law, University of Oxford, Oxford, England